PELICA

# REVOLUTIONARY GUERRILLA WARFARE

Geoffrey Fairbairn was educated at Melbourne University and Trinity College, Cambridge. During the Second World War he served in a R.A.N. Beach Commando in the South West Pacific. He now lectures in history at the Australian National University, Canberra. He is a council member of the Institute for the Study of Conflict (London) and has studied the guerrilla environment in Malaya (during 'The Emergency'), North East Thailand, Burma, Vietnam, Israel and Belfast. Since 1951 he has been making study tours of South East Asia. He has previously published *Revolutionary Guerrilla Warfare and Communist Strategy* (1968) and many articles on aspects of the subject, and is currently producing a *Handbook of Revolutionary Warfare*.

GEOFFREY FAIRBAIRN

# REVOLUTIONARY GUERRILLA WARFARE

*The Countryside Version*

PENGUIN BOOKS

Penguin Books Ltd, Harmondsworth, Middlesex, England
Penguin Books Inc., 7110 Ambassador Road, Baltimore, Maryland 21207, U.S.A.
Penguin Books Australia Ltd, Ringwood, Victoria, Australia

—

First published 1974

—



—

Made and printed in Great Britain by
Richard Clay (The Chaucer Press), Ltd,
Bungay, Suffolk
Set in Linotype Plantin

—

For Anne
and
in memory of
Mamma

# CONTENTS

Acknowledgements 9
Introduction 11
1. The Modern Historical Background 39
2. Leninism 65
3. China 85
4. Malaya and South East Asia 125
5. The First Indo-China War 175
6. The Second Indo-China War 210
7. Cuba and All That 263
8. Aspects of the Problem 284
Afterword 358
Appendix 1: A Note on T. E. Lawrence 369
Appendix 2: The Guerrilla and International Law 373
Appendix 3: The Palestinians 375
Index 395

Many regard subversion as being principally a form of redress used by the down-trodden peoples of the world against their oppressors, and feel, therefore, that there is something immoral about preparing to suppress it. Undoubtedly subversion is sometimes used in this way, and on those occasions those supporting the government find themselves fighting for a bad cause. On the other hand subversion can also be used by evil men to advance their own interests in which case those fighting it have right on their side. More often, as in other forms of conflict, there is some right and some wrong on both sides, and there are high-minded and base people amongst the supporters of both parties . . . if any man, soldier or civilian, is convinced that his country is wrong he should cease to support it and take the consequences.

BRIGADIER FRANK KITSON,
*Low Intensity Operations*, Faber & Faber, 1971, pp. 8–9.

# ACKNOWLEDGEMENTS

ACKNOWLEDGING the help of various kinds which one has received from individuals is always a somewhat invidious undertaking: some of those mentioned resent the possible implication that they approve of what the author has written, when they do not; some of those not mentioned feel that the author has been ungrateful in omitting their names.

I should therefore like to make it clear that only one person mentioned below has seen the typescript, and he is a man I have never met; those whose names have been omitted should know that the omissions have been made only in order to avoid possible embarrassment or, in some cases, possible danger in future.

Invidiousness aside, since I have had the pleasure of talking with a very large number of people concerned with insurgencies over nearly a quarter of a century, and in places ranging from Belfast to Saigon, from Israel to Thailand, it obviously would be impossible to thank all those people who have tried to make me understand the nature of guerrilla warfare, especially of the revolutionary kind.

But I must thank the following here: Lt Colonel John Coates M.B.E.; Brigadier F. P. Serong D.S.O.(Rt); Sir Robert Thompson D.S.O.; the late Freddy Spencer Chapman D.S.O.; the late Colonel John Vann; Dennis J. Duncanson; Brian Crozier; Howard Simpson; Robert Moss; Keith Hyland; Robert O'Neill; Leonard Cotton; Richard Clutterbuck; General Saiyud Kherdpol in Thailand; Generals Truong, Hon and Phu in South Vietnam; Tran Kim Phuong; 'Minh'; 'Quang'; Lt Colonel Peter Gration; Major Peter White M.C.; Dennis Warner; Professor Harkabi and Dr Wallach in Israel; and (for the trenchant expression of their deeply opposed views) Milton E. Osborne, John Girling and Alex. Carey. In the USA I owe much to George Tanham and Stephen Hosmer.

I also owe much to many students but in particular to Kevin

Hindle, Kim Jackson, Valda Krastins, Andy Selth, Ashton Robinson, Nicholas Warner, Bill Stefaniak, Andrew Griffiths, and the late Tony Camillieri.

In terms of human experience I have of course learnt most from people of no obvious importance or public recognition: middle-rank Vietnamese; young US Marines out in the scrub; men on leave in bars in Belfast, Nakhorn Rajasimha, Nongkhai, Kutkai, Vung Tau, Vientiane, Bangkok, Saigon ...; young Australians at Hao Long; planters in Johore; various members of the Australian Advisory and Training Team (AATTV), a unit which in a decade became one of the most highly decorated in the history of British warfare; but above all to certain Vietnamese officers who never wanted to be soldiers and yet fought on, patiently and without hatred.

One of them, a man who never wanted to be anything other than a teacher but who was mobilized in Hanoi in 1951, epitomizes for me the quiet nobility that is so often to be found even in the most terrible of human situations; and reminds me frequently that there must be many like him, mobilized by the 'other side' as many years ago. It is an ugly curiosity of our time that truly rancid acrimony is usually to be found, not amongst the combatants, except for those who have found a vocation in agitational-propaganda, but amongst cosseted Western intellectuals who risk nothing.

The first casualty of modern warfare doubtless is the truth. The second is, indubitably, any sense of generosity towards the enemy. The third is a loss of that deeper understanding of the human condition, which was stated, perhaps two millennia ago, in the *Bhagavad-Gita*: 'A man has the right to act, but not to expect the fruits of his actions.'

For having learnt this truth, albeit extremely imperfectly, I owe as much to obscure, though certainly not inscrutable, Asians as I do to a man of eminence, an old friend and teacher, Charles Manning Clark. He alone probably will understand the depth of my thanks expressed in that fashion.

To Miss Patricia Romans who typed most of the study at a very difficult time for her, I am very grateful.

# INTRODUCTION

'But where can we draw water',
Said Pearse to Connolly,
'When all the wells are parched away?
O plain as plain can be
There's nothing but our own red blood
Can make a right Rose Tree.'

W. B. YEATS

Yesterday at the Methodist Ladies College [opponents of private schools] disguised themselves as parents – dark suits for the men, well-cut, modest dresses for women – and just walked in . . . present were about 1,000 parents and the camouflaged guerrillas from the Defence of Government Schools organization . . . In the middle of the assembly a DOGS lady with a banner stood and was immediately assailed by a dignified woman in bright pink. After a brief feminine struggle they were separated by a teacher . . . Parents had a second cup of tea. The DOGS people dispersed.

*Sunday Australian*, 30 April 1972

DURING the last few years the word guerrilla has come to be applied to all manner of activities not usually associated with warfare. For example, the Manifesto of the New Left spoke of the 'new politics' as 'pressure-point politics', 'guerrilla politics', 'like jazz',[1] and a trade-union leader: 'Lightning strikes and guerrilla tactics at job level have their place, but when the crunch comes it is the ability of the union to "stop everything" that can force a strike victory at a higher level.'[2]

A Penguin blurb refers to: '. . . the problems of liberation – of physical and cultural "guerrilla warfare" to free man from mystification, from the blind destruction of his environment, and

1. Lewis Feuer, *Conflict of Generations*, Basic Books, New York, 1969, p. 459.

2. *Australian Left Review*, August–September, 1970, pp. 5–6.

from the inhumanity which he projects onto his opponents . . .'[3] This was intended to describe a symposium of (mostly) scholars at the Roundhouse in Chalk Farm, England.

Doubtless the privileged young man who wrote the following would classify himself as a guerrilla:

> What has happened to our generation is that we never got what we wanted. We've only been led to believe we have. Many of us know now what we want. Or at least we know what we don't want. We don't want the war or any part of the whole civilization. It might be necessary to go back two hundred years and start again.
>
> We have an irreconcilable tension in our existence, all the way from breakfast to bedtime. Blowing up a bad thing (i.e. a building, a draft board, an institution) will relieve much of that tension. So that the preceding sentence doesn't become evidence for any of the rampant psychological reductionism theories about radicals, it should be pointed out that the psychological problems most of us have are directly capitalism's fault . . . With all the words and images we have around us, it may be that action is the only way to open fresh areas of consciousness. In any case, it will take a very concrete destruction of the material foundations of the regime we are fighting before we get rid of them. Only then will we be able to plant trees all over our woes, and begin again.[4]

Even clergymen are on occasion given to such language. For example the Anglican chaplain of the University of New South Wales was reported to have said that 'Christians were pessimistic about human nature and the ability of total revolution to produce a Utopian society. Christians should engage in guerrilla tactics of confrontation and protest against social and political injustice with the establishment.'[5] The misuse of the term is becoming so gross as to make it reasonable to suppose that in the near future pack rape will be described as guerrilla sex.

A good part of the use of 'guerrilla' language, however, reflects the romanticism of youth, which is certainly no new thing.

3. David Cooper (ed.), *The Dialectics of Liberation*, Penguin Books, 1968.

4. Supplement to the *Harvard Crimson*, cited in *Encounter*, April 1970, p. 30.

5. *Canberra Times*, 23 January 1972.

The guerrilla hero of yesteryear, T. E. Lawrence, felt impelled to write:

> We were fond together, because of the sweep of the open places, the taste of wide winds, the sunlight, and the hopes in which we worked. The morning freshness of the world-to-be intoxicated us. We were wrought up with ideas inexpressible and vaporous but to be fought for. We lived many lives [in the First World War Arab guerrilla campaign], never sparing ourselves: yet when we achieved and the new world dawned, the old men came out again and took our victory to re-make the world in the likeness of the former world they knew. Youth could win, but had not learned to keep: and was pitiably weak against age. We stammered that we had worked for a new heaven and a new earth, and they thanked us kindly and made their peace ... All men dream: but not equally.[6]

However, whereas T. E. Lawrence was a hero to others as a romantic symbol of Anglo-Saxon imperial derring-do, rather than as a theoretician of guerrilla 'liberation' warfare (which he very much was – see Appendix 1), in recent years guerrilla leaders have become the particular heroes of alienated youth and of certain famous ideologists of revolt. For example, the Nobel Prizewinner M. Jean-Paul Sartre has declared that the Argentinian guerrilla leader and theoretician of liberation warfare, Ernesto Guevara, was 'the most complete man of his age'.[7]

A good deal of the recent adulation of the Guevaras, Ho Chi Minhs, Eduardo Mondlanes and suchlike in the West doubtless springs from a bad conscience about the white man's pacification (as it used to be called) of the non-European world rather than a penchant for a guerrilla mode of behaviour in the West.[8]

But this is not wholly true. By late 1970 newspapers in the

6. *Seven Pillars of Wisdom*, Cape, 1946, pp. 22–3.

7. Andrew Sinclair, *Guevara*, Fontana Books, 1970, p. 47. It may be noted that Guevara, in a letter to his parents, described himself more modestly as 'this little soldier-of-fortune of the twentieth century' (*Reminiscences of the Cuban Revolutionary War*, Allen & Unwin, 1968, pp. 286–7).

8. The term 'non-European world' is inadequately descriptive of Latin America, of course, but it avoids having to choose between 'developing', 'undeveloped', 'under-developed' and the most recent (New Left) 'under-developing' world.

USA were reporting the appearance of what seemed to be a kind of guerrilla war at home. For example, *The New York Times Weekly Review* of 9 September:

> Now, America's cities seem to be on the edge of guerrilla war.
>
> In the first eight months of this year, at least sixteen policemen have been slain in what officials describe as unprovoked attacks, primarily snipings and bombings.

This is certainly so far a small matter in terms of human lives compared with another guerrilla war across the Pacific which between January 1961 and March 1970 had cost over three quarters of a million *military* lives.[9] Nevertheless, the methods are similar: the hidden attack and the 'booby-trapping' of buildings by un-uniformed men and women – and the strategy of indirect approach implicit in this mode of politico-military behaviour; also the militarizing of political rhetoric in a fashion barely conceivable in the West a decade ago.[10]

Moreover, the theorists of urban guerrilla warfare in the West explicitly link their struggle with that of the guerrilla liberation movements in the Third World. On occasion this identification with a world-wide movement can take grotesque forms. Ted Gold, of the American Weatherman urban terrorist group, who was blown up by an explosive cache on 11th Street, New York, saw in the wake of the defeat of American power abroad 'an agency of the people of the world' appearing from Africa and Asia to run the USA, and welcomed the prospect even if it meant 'fascism'.[11]

But this guilt-ridden formulation is not confined to such people. The distinguished writer on Latin America, Mr John

9. The following figures taken from the United States Department of Defense Statistical Summary were cited by the Australian Minister of Defence in May 1970: total US deaths from action by hostile forces were 40,947; Republic of Vietnam combat deaths were 103,507; enemy combat deaths were estimated at 610,308 (*Current Notes*, Canberra, 10 September 1970).

10. See not only the examples cited below, but also Chapter 2.

11. *Current*, May 1970, New York, p. 15. It was estimated that in the USA in 1971 there was a bombing every 30 minutes.

Gerassi, while not advocating guerrilla warfare in the West, has written in this manner:

> The whites . . . are lost. They do not starve, they do not suffer. The dignity they lack is interpreted as personal – the one-dimensionality of their souls. I am pointing out here that the cause of their mental torment is fundamentally the same [as that of people in the Third World]: the brutal but intelligent, totalitarian but liberal, constraining but law-respecting capitalist structure which thrives off the physical anguish of the rest of the world. Thus, we white, Anglo-Saxon, alienated, self-conscious, middle-class tools of the structure must rebel too.[12]

Such utterances are not being cited in order to draw attention to what may prove to be a crisis within the liberal-capitalist West – the potentialities of urban guerrilla warfare and the possibility of future links between Western and Third World revolutionary guerrilla movements cannot be a significant part of this study[13] – but rather in order to suggest at the beginning that a study of guerrilla warfare in the modern world cannot be divorced from the much wider struggle that for many decades has been waged against the universal Western pacification[14] or, if it is preferred, Western international hegemony.

The author accepts the diagnosis of Mr I. R. Sinai:

> . . . the great issue before the democratic peoples is not the political unification of the globe; the fateful question is not whether Western democracy or Russian or Chinese communism are going to establish a future planetary order. The basic issue of world affairs, the axis around which revolves the tumult and menace of the cold war between communism and the West is, rather, whether Western civiliza-

12. David Cooper, op. cit., p. 94.

13. Two studies by Robert Moss are available: *Urban Guerrilla Warfare* (with an appendix, 'Minimanual of the Urban Guerrilla', by Carlos Marighella), Adelphi Papers No. 79, International Institute for Strategic Studies, London, 1971; and *Urban Guerrillas*, Temple Smith, London, 1972. See also Richard Clutterbuck, *Protest and the Urban Guerrilla*, Cassell, London, 1973.

14. Cf. Herbert Lüthy: '. . . for the non-European world the age of colonial empires was by and large an age of peace and security such as Asia and Africa had scarcely known before' (*Encounter*, November 1967).

tion itself can and will survive, or more correctly, whether it has the resolute will to survive, in a world increasingly dominated by anti-Western forces and tendencies.[15]

It is the argument of this short study that *revolutionary* guerrilla warfare has evolved out of Marx–Leninist modes of political behaviour and organizational principles, on the one hand, and out of the exigencies of anti-Western revolt in predominantly agrarian societies, on the other. This is not of course to say that all the revolutionary guerrilla campaigns of recent times have been ideologically Marx–Leninist, though most of them have been; but it is to say that nearly all of those which have nationalist pretensions have been or are profoundly anti-Western. The dimensions of their anti-Westernism has become obvious in recent years as campaigns in politically independent countries have proliferated, such campaigns being directed not only against a presumed economic 'neo-colonialism'[16] but against the modes of thought and behaviour, as well as against the institutions, transmitted from the West and willingly adopted by the political nationalist movements of the slightly more distant past.

There are a few guerrilla campaigns still being waged against European political rule: in Rhodesia, South Africa, and Portuguese Africa.[17] The organizations concerned do not appear to be purely Marx–Leninist but it is probable that Western European attitudes will make them so eventually. As an African leader who provides sanctuaries for guerrillas operating in Rhodesia, Mr Kenneth Kaunda, has remarked, 'The only people who will teach young Africans to handle dangerous weapons are in the

15. *The Challenge of Modernisation*, Chatto & Windus, 1964, pp. 241–2.

16. Cf. Lüthy, op. cit.: 'Often it seems that the entire non-European world has been seized by the Cargo Cult. The wealth and living standards of the West are not the work of human hands, nor created by labour, but a right which we have arrogantly denied to non-European nations; and now they are claiming this right. The West owes it to them, and if the West does not carry out its parental obligations or tries to deduce from them a right of tutelage, it is threatened with the most radical form of rupture of all links, Communism.'

17. The campaigns in Rhodesia and parts of Portuguese Africa reached serious dimensions by early 1973.

eastern camp, how can we expect that they will learn to use the weapons without learning the ideology as well?'[18]

The chief accused at a South African trial under the so-called Terrorism Act, Benjamin Ramotse, is alleged to have received guerrilla training in the USSR, Egypt and Tanzania,[19] to cite but one example. Though the ideological and organizational make-up of the anti-Portuguese, anti-South African, and anti-Rhodesian guerrilla movements remains slightly confused, it is to be reasonably expected that the 'demonstration-effect' of Viet-nam will further incline African guerrilla organizations towards the Marxist–Leninist mode of ordering such affairs.

As the Prime Minister of Singapore has put it,

> Only China, still in the evangelistic phase, is interested in African liberation movements. When China appears likely to develop political and economic influence as a result of its active role in urging and helping insurgency, then the competition will start. Then pressure will be exerted in earnest on the white regimes in South Africa.[20]

Apart from white Africa, revolutionary guerrilla struggles, however disguised as struggles against 'neo-colonialism', are basically now internal wars, though often aided and armed from abroad.[21] The chief armourers and aiders remain the Soviet bloc and the Communist Peoples' Republic.[22] But though this is in

18 .*Newsweek*, 23 December 1968.

19. *Canberra Times*, 5 August 1970.

20. *Canberra Times*, 11 September 1969. Though Mr Lee has been conspicuous amongst those Asian leaders urging on the Americans in South Vietnam, on 31 July 1970 he spoke as follows: 'The day black Africans in Southern Africa are disciplined and determined enough to create their "Black-cong", then all the automatic fire-arms, armoured personnel carriers, tanks and strike aircraft, equipped with rockets, anti-personnel bombs, and defoliating agents – all these and more, will not be able to prevent the black Africans from regaining their human dignity which apartheid has deprived them of' (*The Mirror*, Singapore, 10 August 1970).

21. By the same token, it is of interest to notice that the Western-trained leadership of the Biafra secessionist struggle never opted for guerrilla warfare.

22. Cuba has supplied arms to guerrilla movements in Latin America; the Angolan revolutionary movement for some time received Western arms through the Congolese defence ministry (*The Economist*, 10 May 1969); the

part the result of 'exported rivalries' between the USSR and the CPR, whereas the CPR continues to assert its belief in the efficacy of revolutionary guerrilla warfare throughout the Third World,[23] 'the Soviet stance is that of attempting a foreign policy that is all things to all men. In Latin America, and, within limits, the Middle East as well the Russians give priority to co-existence so that they can stay on tolerably good terms with the United States. In Eastern Asia they give priority to revolutionary expansionism so that they can keep the left wing of the Communist movement happy. They rationalize this by saying that they support a policy of expansion only in countries that are "ripe" for revolution. They do not say what the tests of ripeness are, or who the judges of it should be.'[24]

This is not in the least to suggest that guerrilla struggles can be conjured up by infusions of arms and aid from distant supporters; it is simply to underline the point that it is deemed by the two greatest Communist governments to be in their interest to assist such struggles over a large area of the globe.

For example, despite its acute internal problems, political as well as economic, the People's Republic of China has been busy in Africa:

---

oil Sheikhdoms have supplied money for the non-Marxist Arab guerrillas, and so on. But the arms are normally Russian or Chinese versions of Russian arms. With the August 1970 cease-fire in the Middle East, Chinese arms shipments to the guerrillas, via the Iraki port of Basra, became the only easy source of supply. Up till then the Chinese appear to have concentrated on supplying the Marxist–Leninist Palestinian guerrilla groups as well as the Popular Front for the Liberation of the Arab Gulf. (*The Australian*, 22 August 1970.)

23. Since these words were written there has occurred the Sino-American *rapprochement*. But this *rapprochement* did not involve a Chinese disavowal of their belief in the efficacy of revolutionary warfare; and if anything it exacerbated the 'exported rivalries' referred to above. See particularly W. A. C. Adie, *The Communist Powers in Africa*, Conflict Studies No. 10, December–January 1970–71, Institute for the Study of Conflict, London, and his 'Exported Rivalries' in *Current Affairs Bulletin*, Vol. 48, No. 6, 1971, Sydney, on these exported rivalries. See also his *China, Israel and the Arabs*, Conflict Studies No. 12, May 1971.

24. *The Economist*, 6 January 1968.

Portuguese plans for establishing an industrial complex around the huge Cabora Bassa dam in Mozambique, which could supply hydro-electricity to neighbouring African States, might have tended to orientate them away from any militant anti-white grouping; but the [Chinese-engineered] Tanzam railway will automatically orientate Zambia towards Tanzania, headquarters of the liberation movements and Peking's best friend in East Africa.

In Peking's scenario, the 'masses' will no longer see any reason for restraining guerrilla activities; these will bring down Israeli-type retaliation raids on Zambia and perhaps other countries which will then face the same sort of problem as Jordan and Lebanon, for example, face now.

China will also have trained and armed stateless guerrilla forces large enough to defy the African regular armies (if necessary), as in Lebanon. China's friendly and popular technicians, doctors, etc., will have disseminated the thought of Mao, so that any African politician or military leader who should appear hesitant to fight the whites would lose popular support.[25]

It may be said that though no guerrilla campaign in recent years has ultimately prevailed without large-scale infusions of outside aid and arms, the strategy of modern revolutionary warfare is to escalate the momentum of the struggle by way of symbiosis: 'getting possession of part of the security forces' weapons and supplies, making part of the Government's manpower – military and civilian – to work for the revolution . . .'[26] The greater the resources used by the incumbent government, the greater the resources available to the guerrillas. But in fact, in both Indo-China wars, for example, outside aid had been of crucial significance for the insurgents.

This aspect of the international component in contemporary

25. W. A. C. Adie in the *Canberra Times*, 28 February 1970.

26. Dennis J. Duncanson, *Government and Revolution in Vietnam*, Oxford University Press, 1968, pp. 295–6. Cf. '. . . while substantial exogeny is neither necessary nor sufficient for successful [Rebellion], an ambiguous history seems to suggest that [Rebellion] has never been suppressed *unless* external help has previously been terminated. [Rebellion] *may* win without external support; [Authority] is unlikely to win if [the Rebellion] continues to receive it' (Nathan Leites and Charles Wolf, Jr, *Rebellion and Authority*, Markham, Chicago, 1970, p. 24).

guerrilla wars may serve to point up another aspect: international concern is naturally related to the effect that the outcome of specific guerrilla wars may have on the international order. For example, the civil war in Tchad, which has had some of the attributes of modern revolutionary guerrilla warfare – roving bands, primitively armed so far as military weapons are concerned, yet employing a now well-known radical rhetoric and calling themselves FROLINA (Tchad National Liberation Front) – made few headlines outside France. This was because a victory for the guerrillas in this very poor country of $3\frac{1}{2}$ million people could only threaten the anti-Communist regimes in the former French Cameroon, Niger and Central African Republic.[27] The French government did reinforce but also planned a phased withdrawal for 1970. As *The Economist* of 3 August 1969 remarked, 'it is not clear what France hopes to gain from a country whose per capita income is only £23 a year, and which seems to have no economic attractions for the outsider at all'.

Again, the capture of the Indonesian Embassy in the Hague in September 1970 – a guerrilla act in its unexpected, if only very temporary, seizure of the initiative, and in its (rather half-hearted) essay in terrorism – only momentarily caught the headlines. This was because the operatives were Ambonese refugees, representatives of an exiled group of Indonesians, some 30,000 strong, who live in camps scattered throughout Holland.[28] Their aim was to persuade Indonesia's President Suharto, who was about to pay a state visit to Holland, to negotiate the future of Ambon, whose self-styled President-in-exile lives in Holland. The Indonesian regime now being regarded by the West as a friendly one in South East Asia, the guerrillas had no hope of support from the Western Establishment; and not being able to propagate their cause as 'progressive' or 'revolutionary', they could not obtain that instant recognition of purity of motive accorded by the Western liberal-left to far more squalid movements, the colour of whose cockades have been made more readily obvious to the jaundiced eye.

27. *Newsweek*, 15 September 1969.
28. *The Australian*, 2 September 1970.

By the same token, the seizure of the Cambodian Embassy in Prague by a Cambodian diplomat and a group of dissident students on behalf of the Communist-backed National Liberation Front of the deposed Prince Norodom was foredoomed,[29] since the Prince was a prisoner of Peking and hence this particular NLF was unacceptable to the Russian masters of Prague.[30]

An awareness of a potential international component in urban guerrilla violence is sometimes to be found in the apparently most unlikely governing circles, as the distinguished Australian journalist, Mr Maximilien Walsh, found when visiting Japan:

> Japan is the last place in Asia where you would imagine that there could be a war of national liberation.
>
> It is highly urbanized, successfully industrialized, with rising standards of living that will, within the foreseeable future, put it on an equal footing with European countries.
>
> . . . it comes as something of a shock to find that the military stance of Japan is conditioned to a large extent by the belief that the greatest threat it faces is an internal rebellion.
>
> It is not that the nation is seething with discontent, but rather that a hard-nosed assessment by its defence people of the hypothetical threats it could face has come up with the conclusion that overt external aggression is much less likely than internal revolt.
>
> The possibility of external aggression by Russia or China is not ruled out, but the belief is that should either of these two nations move against Japan it would be by the way of encouraging, inciting and financing internal disorder.
>
> Consequently much of the Japanese defence effort is directed towards equipment and training more suited for the terrifying prospect of guerrilla warfare in the streets than striking a strong defensive posture against some outside attack.[31]

29. *Canberra Times*, 12 August 1970.

30. Since this was written, the hijacking of aircraft and the seizure of embassies and other buildings, sometimes resulting in the murder of hostages, as at the Olympic games and in Khartoum in March 1973, by Arab terrorists, has begun to threaten the international community itself.

31. *Sun–Herald*, Sydney, 5 July 1970. Another distinguished Australian journalist, an analyst of international repute, Mr Denis Warner, reported in the Melbourne *Herald* of 8 December 1972, that Japanese defence planners were still much preoccupied with the threat of internal violence.

Then there is what can be designated a guerrilla struggle in an old cockpit of strife: Northern Ireland. Like Tchad *vis-à-vis* France, what happens in Ulster has little interest for the world outside Ireland and Westminster. But – because of historical memories – eruptions of urban political violence there quickly engendered the presence of 8,000 British troops[32] (not to speak of articles reminding the English that 'It was the Irish Republican Army who, in the context of modern society, were the first to use indiscriminate terrorism as a major political weapon').[33]

Aside from direct arming and aiding of guerrilla campaigns (or arming and aiding the countering of such campaigns), perhaps the most striking international component in recent times lies in the field of international propaganda. The role of the press in Castro's guerrilla struggle in Cuba is well known, as are the spectacular attempts of the Palestinian guerrilla groups to seize the world headlines for their cause. Another example of this technique was the exploding of bombs outside the Portuguese Embassy and the Rhodesian Information Office in Washington, a demonstration that was accompanied by a letter to an American news service explaining that the explosions were the work of the Revolutionary Action Party, an African organization, which declared itself to be at war with both countries.[34]

A similar attempt to gain international prestige through the use of bombing embassies was reported of the Indian Maoist revolutionaries known as Naxalites. The Calcutta police claimed to have smashed a plot to blow up the American and Russian consulates.[35]

Another kind of guerrilla war with an international component in the struggle is that being waged in Burma's northern borderlands. This area is populated by minority peoples, Shans and Kachins, which overlap the Sino-Burmese border. The Shan

32. *Canberra Times*, 2 September 1970. By 1973 there were 16,000 troops.

33. Douglas Brown in *The Australian*, 26 August 1970.

34. *Canberra Times*, 31 August 1970.

35. *Canberra Times*, 22 July 1970.

and Kachin guerrillas rose for internal reasons (the Kachins as far back as 1949): opposition to Rangoon policies which they see as manifestations of 'Burman chauvinism'. The Burmese government of General Ne Win has taken great pains, at very considerable economic cost, to remain outside the South East Asian Cold War. Nevertheless, he had to disclose the fact of border battles with Chinese troops, doubtless acting in support of the insurgents, at the end of 1969.[36] The Chinese activity there was probably also related to its activities in neighbouring western Laos and possibly in relation to gaining access to the frontier regions of Thailand in order to increase pressure on an American ally.[37]

Meo tribesmen in north Thailand, disturbed by the Thai government's modernizing programme (itself largely an attempt to forestall Communist subversion), have, some of them, been trained in North Vietnam, taught to use Chinese-made AK–47 automatic rifles and instructed in guerrilla tactics of the modern kind. One was reported to have been found with a Thai-language edition of Mao Tse-tung's Thoughts. The Communist propaganda line here is to promise a Meo autonomous region which will still pursue the traditional occupation of growing opium and ravaging the forests, activities discouraged by the Thai government.[38]

A considerable increase in insurgent training camps in Yunnan province of China was reported early in 1970; and a possible division of responsibility between China and North Vietnam – the former controlling subversion in Thailand, Burma, Malaysia and Singapore, the latter in Laos, Cambodia and South Vietnam.[39] But Thailand is also afflicted by a revolutionary guer-

36. General Ne Win's speech disclosing these border battles was reported in *The Australian*, 8 November 1969, as having been delivered the previous day.

37. Stanley Karnow in *The Australian*, 4 November 1969. Since the Nixon–Kissinger initiative of 1972 towards opening up a new era of inter-State relations in place of the 'Cold War', such assistance may be decreased. But even if it is, a revolutionary guerrilla war, once got under way, acquires a momentum of its own.

38. *Newsweek*, 20 January 1969.

39. Jack Foisse, in *The Australian*, 30 April 1970.

rilla campaign in its arid, comparatively poor north-east and in its southern provinces neighbouring Malaya, where there is a minority problem based on religious differences (Islam in a predominately Therevada Buddhist country). As is so often the case in border areas, the line between politically motivated guerrilla activity and mere banditry is often for some time a tenuous one.[40]

However, the Thai-Malayan border area contains the base and training camp of the Malayan Communist guerrilla force which survived the long Malayan 'Emergency' between 1948 and 1960. The murder of an ex-Communist, Mrs Chen Kon Yin, believed to be a police informer, in northern Malaya in July 1969, resulted in the kind of incident that in such a context naturally gave rise to fears that the Malayan guerrilla war was being reactivated:

> Within hours of the funeral ... a patrol of young and inexperienced soldiers looking for Kon Yin's killers walked into an ambush. Four men died – and their bodies were booby-trapped to kill more the next day. Other booby traps injured more men a couple of days later. The final toll was six dead and eight injured.
>
> Small beer in a disturbed region, perhaps ... Yet the incident made the headlines and attracted comment throughout Malaysia on three counts.
>
> First, it confirmed predictions that the May riots (in the capital, Kuala Lumpur) gave the border Communists an unparalleled chance to bid for support among the Chinese who still feel themselves victims of Malay attack. The ambush was only the second Communist incursion into Malaysia in ten years ... It was impossible not to associate the ambush with Malaysia's embarrassment since May.
>
> Second, it was seen as significant that the Communists hit a patrol of the Royal Malay Regiment rather than the Police Field Force operating in the same district. This was because the Royal Malay Regiment had discriminated brutally against the Chinese in the

40. For example the *Canberra Times*, 22 September 1969: 'Press reports said yesterday that several hundred Moslem bandits in the Narathiwat province on the Malaysian border were terrorizing the local population. The bandits had extorted money from rubber plantation owners and workers and merchants, reports added. Local police believed a group of ten well-educated Moslems was directing the extortion activities ... because the extortion notices were well written in Thai, Malay and English. The police were looking for a young Malaysian Harvard University graduate.'

Malay riots while the police emerged comparatively well. To many Chinese, no matter what their politics, the ambush came as good news.

Third, the incident was staged in an area well away from the Communist stronghold in [the base area] where the military watch against the border guerrillas is most acute.[41]

This is a nice example of a disguised international component – racialism – at work; not to speak of a number of facets of guerrilla warfare – terrorism, ambush, clandestine mobility and the 'exploitation of contradictions' (between races and between units in the incumbent government's armed forces).

In social-democratic Singapore, where the old colonial device of preventive detention is employed (as in some form or other it has been employed in almost all South and South-East Asian states), there was an outbreak of bombings accompanied by propaganda scrawling in August 1970 on a new scale. Isolated bomb outrages had occurred every few months but this well-organized demonstration of what Communists call 'armed propaganda' was sufficiently well considered, occurring as it did at the approach of the National Day celebrations, to cause unusual concern.[42] Whether this can properly be called guerrilla warfare is a matter of argument, but it is worth mentioning since terrorism has become a major facet of that urban revolutionary struggle

41. *Canberra Times*, 14 August 1969. Like Thailand, Malaysia has more than one insurgency area. It was reported from Kuching, East Malaysia (Borneo) in September 1970: '. . . the focus is shifting to East Malaysia where some senior policemen say that the level of violence is surpassing the terrorist acts committed during the 1963–5 confrontation with Indonesia. Indonesia and Malaysia today co-operate in the unending jungle hunt for terrorists, estimated at about 600 hard-core guerrillas operating on both sides of the 600-mile border. But the present danger looms larger than confrontation in Sarawak's jungles. No British troops patrol with the Malaysians today, as they did against the Indonesians. Furthermore, there are no longer external circumstances that could force a communist retreat' (*The Australian*, 19 September 1970). This may look like a struggle without any international component, but this is not so. The report goes on to say: 'Police officials estimate communist supporters in the thousands among the Chinese. They say the guerrillas are led by Peking-trained Bong Kee Chok.'

42. Neil Jillett in the *Canberra Times*, 2 August 1970 and 7 August 1970.

which prompted *The Economist* to dub 1969 as the Year of the Guerrilla.

It is perhaps desirable at this point to touch briefly upon two other countries in this region, Indonesia and the Philippines, not so much for the intrinsic importance of their struggles at this time but rather in order to draw attention to certain other facets of the problem. In Indonesia the Communist Party, after the failure of a rising in 1949, opted for the path of 'legal struggle' until it attempted a *coup* in 1965. This was followed by a terrible massacre of Communists (and probably very many non-Communists for reasons of local or private vengeance), since when the Party has been firmly ideologically committed to the Maoist protracted, armed mode of struggle. Though this form of struggle does not appear to have developed very far, except perhaps in Borneo, an awareness of the possibility on the part of the government seems to have orientated Indonesian army organization and activities along police-action-cum-civic-action lines.[43] This is an example both of what the French revolutionary warfare theoretician Régis Debray has called the 'revolutionizing of the counter-revolution' and of the enormous enhancing of the army's political role in Third World countries as a result of the politico-military behaviour of revolutionary guerrillas.

The Philippines at the present time are chiefly of interest in that it demonstrates how – particularly in Luzon – largely defeated revolutionary guerrillas can yet come to persist in a symbiotic relationship with society-at-large. A Philippines Senate report of 1969 revealed a reign of terror based on poverty, corruption, oppression and dubiously legal killings. The report de-

43. *The Bulletin*, Sydney, 22 March 1969. Of course, the army's role is also very important in Indonesia in quelling regionalist, potentially separatist activities. For example, 4,000 Indonesian troops are deployed in West Irian (New Guinea). It may also be noticed that the Administration of Australian Papua–New Guinea introduced a contentious Public Order Bill in September 1970 in order to meet a situation of what may be called not unfairly non-violent political guerrilla warfare directed in part by a sophisticated young leader, Mr John Kaputin, educated in Australia and the East–West Center of Hawaii. (*Canberra Times*, 13 August 1970 and 1 September 1970). This is cited simply in order to show another international component: education.

clared that in the region around the American Clark air base, fifty miles from Manila, the capital, the Communist guerrillas known as Huks had infiltrated so deeply that most of the police were either Huks or had been recommended for the job by Huk leaders. The Senate's investigators agreed that most people in the region were too afraid to talk and that there had been a breakdown of law and order.[44] And yet President Marcos announced late in 1970, without adducing any very convincing proof, that the Huk threat had been beaten.[45] It is reasonable to suppose, clear contrary evidence lacking, that in fact the symbiotic relationship persists, and this despite the fact that the Philippines counter-insurgency under the late President Magsaysay has so often been held up as a model of its kind.[46]

Late in 1969 the U S Congress became startlingly 'aware' that in Laos the Central Intelligence Agency had been building up a considerable guerrilla army from amongst Meo tribesmen under their own general, Vang Pao. U S 'advisers' had been with General Vang Pao at least since 1961, but the extent of the force created by CIA arms, equipment and funds had not been generally realized. Estimations of the size of the force varied between 15,000 and 40,000, one estimate suggesting that some half of the (estimated) quarter of a million Meos in Laos were involved with the 'Armée Clandestine', as it was romantically named:[47]

The opium-growing tribesmen, alienated always from the Lao of the plains, subject to bullying from the Pathet Lao (the Vietnamese-

44. *The Australian*, 14 May 1969.

45. *Canberra Times*, 12 September 1970.

46. See for example Napoleon D. Valeriano and Charles T. R. Bohannan, *Counter-Guerrilla Operations: The Philippines Experience*, Praeger, 1962. Readers of *The Ugly American*, a best-seller by William J. Lederer and Eugene Burdick (Gollancz, 1959), will recall Colonel Edwin B. Hillandale (really U S Air Force General Lansdale), the Ragtime Kid, who won this counter-guerrilla war on p. 114, according to the authors. It makes hilarious re-reading in 1973.

Late in 1971, *habeas corpus* was temporarily suspended on the ground that a renewed, partly urban Communist struggle was in the offing. But this measure may have been taken for other political reasons. By 1973 the Philippines were under martial law.

47. Michael Molloy in *Far Eastern Economic Review*, 20 November 1969.

controlled liberation movement) and from the North Vietnamese, suddenly found themselves recipients of manna from heaven:

> ... rice, salt, shoes, clothing, coffee, sugar, detergent, wrist watches, transistor radios, umbrellas and jeeps fell from the skies upon the Meo who flocked to Vang Pao's leadership. It was easy to keep the opium trade going through CIA planes which returned to Thailand and Vientiane. Vang Pao's followers enjoyed visits to the comparatively urban wonders of the Laotian capital. The half-educated former sergeant was himself treated to two journeys to the United States, where he savoured the delights of Disneyland.
>
> Van Pao's private kingdom was a godsend to Americans absorbed in trying to influence the intractable political situation in Laos. Every crisis seemed to call for armed force, and Vang Pao's was the only force the Americans could count on when fighting was called for. The Meo became more necessary when Lyndon Johnson started bombing North Vietnam. Their isolated outposts provided radio beacons for American bombers and helicopter pads for air rescue teams. Meo guerrillas slipped into North Vietnam itself to monitor enemy activities and help save American pilots.[48]

There is nothing new about Western powers using tribals or hill peoples from peripheral areas; and this is guerrilla warfare of a kind. But not of the modern kind: it involves no coming to grips with the social question or working towards some permanent, dictatorial solution.[49] The same kind of activity was undertaken by the French in North Vietnam; thousands of tribesmen flocked to the *maquis* (eventually some 20,000 strong), but after what their leader exquisitely called 'the regrettable Dien Bien Phu incident' they were abandoned to a terrible retribution at the hands of the Vietminh.[50] Dependent upon air supply, and mentally conditioned by the largesse of their patrons,

48. ibid.

49. Cf. Manfred Halpern in Richard A. Falk (ed.), *The Vietnam War and International Law*, Princeton University Press, 1968, p. 51: 'Lacking a theory that would help us understand the transformation of societies, we have tended to play for lucky breaks in history, though the breaks have not always come or do not always linger. Or else we have tended to be hard-headedly manipulative, but without a sense of theory or ideology. We are the inventors of a new kind of revolution – the hit-and-run revolution.'

50. Roger Trinquier, *Modern Warfare*, Pall Mall Press, 1964, p. xiv.

such guerrillas are peripheral to the revolutionary guerrilla warfare with which this study is chiefly concerned.

But the existence of these tribal or hill belts – in South Vietnam, northern Burma, north Thailand, and north-east India (not to speak perhaps of the Indians of Latin America) – is of considerable significance at the present time, since it is not only the Americans who seek to use tribals for their own ends. In mid-1970 it was reported that the Naxalites, one of whom declared he believed in the 'principle of MMG' (man, money and gun),[51] were receiving arms from the Chinese through 'hostile' Nagas as well as being in communication with Peking through East Pakistan and Nepal.[52]

A British observer of the Nagas in 1841 had the perception to understand that they were natural guerrilla fighters:

> On approaching the enemy's territories, they collect their troops and advance with great caution. Even in their hottest and most active wars, they proceed wholly by stratagem and ambuscade. They place not their glory in attacking their enemies with open force. To surprise and destroy is their greatest merit of a commander, and the highest pride of his followers ... Such a mode of warfare may be supposed to flow from a feeble and dastardly spirit, incapable of any generous or manly exertion. But when it is considered that many of these tribes, on occasions which call for extraordinary efforts, not only defend themselves with obstinate resolution, but attack their enemies with the most daring courage, and that they possess fortitude of mind superior to the sense of danger or the fear of death, we must ascribe their habitual caution to some other cause than constitutional timidity. The number of men in each tribe is so small, the danger of rearing new members amidst the hardships and dangers of savage life so great, that the life of a citizen is extremely precious, and the preservation of it becomes a capital object in their policy.[53]

51. *The Statesman*, Calcutta, 6 June 1970.

52. ibid., 27 June 1970. For a study of the Naxalites, see C. R. Irani, *Bengal: The Communist Challenge*, Lalvani Publishing House, Bombay, 1968.

53. Elwin Verrier (ed.), *India's North-East Frontier in the Nineteenth Century*, Oxford University Press, 1959, pp. 61–3. It may be observed, however, that these guerrilla fighters out of biological necessity very seldom used the bow and arrow: they needed one hand to carry their shield. The

However, the activities that, as we have seen, prompted *The Economist* to declare 1969 the Year of the Guerrilla were a far cry from the politico-military exploitation of Asian peasant unrest, let alone the involvement of tribals. The reference was to urban guerrilla terrorism in Latin America, a region nearly all of which had very long ago thrown off the political domination of European colonial powers. Moreover, despite innumerable *coups*, Latin America had known no real social revolutions between the Mexican of 1910 and the Bolivian of 1952.

That the emphasis here should be on urban guerrilla warfare is not in the least surprising:

> Many years before the First World War, when industrialization was very much a thing of the future, Rio de Janeiro, Buenos Aires, Mexico, and Santiago already occupied a preponderant position in their respective countries and contained an impressively high proportion of the national population. In most Latin American countries 50 per cent or more of the total population lived in three or four major cities, while in Uruguay or Chile almost one-third of the population lived in one city. Even today the degree of urban concentration in centres of 100,000 or more inhabitants is greater in Latin America than in Europe or the Soviet Union.[54]

This fact was obscured by the agrarian myth woven about the Castro revolution, which will be examined later. The apparent failure of Castro-style guerrilla warfare campaigns in the countryside of Brazil, Venezuela, Guatemala, Nicaragua, Peru and most spectacularly (since Ernesto Guevara was leader) in Bolivia paved the way for an attempt at urban guerrilla warfare.[55] The Soviet policy of concentrating support on urban-orientated Communist parties also indirectly assisted this trend towards city operations (though Moscow has not advocated urban terror-

---

production of appropriate weapons has been a major development of modern guerrilla warfare.

54. Claudio Veliz (ed.), *Obstacles to Change in Latin America*, Oxford University Press, 1965, p. 3.

55. The list is indicative, not comprehensive. There was also for example, the Colombian guerrilla popularly associated with the revolutionary priest, Fr Camilo Torres.

ism), since this resulted in the cities being chief recruiting grounds for activists.[56]

Nevertheless when Mr Nelson Rockefeller's report on Latin America for President Nixon was made public it became clear that he still saw the threat in Castroite-Cuban terms:

At the moment there is only one Castro among the twenty-six nations of the hemisphere – there can be more in the future. A Castro on the mainland, supported militarily and economically by the Communist world, would present the gravest threat to the security of the western hemisphere and pose an extremely difficult problem for the United States.[57]

On the surface, such an expectation seems eminently reasonable, since life in the countryside in many Latin American countries is appalling. To take an extreme example:

The principal product of the Brazilian north-east is despair. Its principal export is people. Twice the size of France, the north-east is the largest area of hard-core poverty and backwardness in the Americas. The yearly income of its 27 million people is estimated at £50 a head. Eighty per cent live outside the cash economy. Half are illiterate. Nearly as many live on the brink of starvation. There are schools enough for one child in five. Infant mortality is between 300 and 600 per 1,000 births: witness the rows of tiny wooden coffins outside the carpenters' shops.[58]

But of course the clue lies in the reference to the export of population. It is the same with Guatemala City where terrorists murdered the German Ambassador, Count Carl von Spreti, in April 1970. Most Guatemalan peasants are landless, illiterate and terribly poor. But the result has been this:

56. The bitterness with which 'Maoists' in the Latin American countryside view Soviet policy is reflected thus: 'The whole of reaction, including the Soviet revisionists who have given financial and material aid to the reactionary ruling clique of Colombia, have thrown themselves against the liberation struggle. Of late, the Soviet revisionists have also given them mobile motor-vehicles to be used against the People's Liberation Army forces' (*World Revolution*, New York, Vol. 2, No. 2, May–July 1969).

57. *Canberra Times*, 10 November 1969.

58. *Economist*, 6 June 1968.

The sudden growth of the capital (now with a population of over 500,000) has created the conditions in which urban terrorism can flourish. The revolutionary groups that have operated since 1960 originally concentrated on the countryside. They still control large sectors ... But after suffering some major military reverses in 1967, the Rebel Armed Forces (FAR) made it their chief aim to disrupt the life of the capital. The police have never been able to control the city slums, where bands of terrorists can operate with impunity. They have proved that nobody, from the Foreign Minister and the Archbishop to foreign ambassadors and the local beauty queen, is secure in Guatemala City.[59]

It is no accident that the chief theorist of urban guerrilla warfare, Carlos Marighella (killed in an ambush in 1969), should have been a veteran Moscow-line Communist who later turned towards Peking. The Brazilian's *Manual of Urban Guerrilla Activity* is Muscovite in its concern with the city, Maoist in its dedication to armed struggle. Marighella's declared objective was to paralyse Brazil's state system, through attacks on Rio de Janeiro, São Paulo and Belo Horizonte. The attacks took the forms of murder and kidnapping of foreign officials; the burning down of television and radio stations; and the bombings of newspaper offices and government and military buildings. In addition to these activities (which may not all have been the work of the one organization), there was a train robbery, a number of bank robberies and of course the procuring of the release of political prisoners through the seizure of hostages (the kidnapping of the Japanese consul, for example).

The result was predictable, and doubtless purposefully sought: the death penalty was introduced and even the armed services were reported to have got involved in torturing political suspects. It was not long before the investigating team of the London *Sunday Times* were syndicating on a world-wide scale their findings that 'There was no shortage of recruits, either among middle-class students appalled by the trend of Government policy, or among the poor in the *favelas* of Rio and São Paulo, which are among the worst slums in the world';[60] and

59. *Canberra Times*, 30 April 1970.

60. *Sydney Morning Herald*, 30 May 1970.

that a confrontation was developing between the government and important sections of the Catholic Church, including the great Dom Helder Camara, Archbishop of Recife.

It was very easy for decent people all over the world to conclude that what was happening simply erupted out of the intolerable conditions of life in Brazil. But the fact that guerrilla violence was not quite as simply explained as that became clear in August 1970, when the hitherto apparently amiable urban guerrillas of Uruguay, the so-called Tupamaros, began to display the same form as the Brazilian urban guerrillas: the murder of a hostage, the American Dan Mitrione, a counter-insurgent police expert.

Uruguay, along with Chile, had been regarded even by Sr Fidel Castro as a country where armed struggle might not be necessary. Certainly there was ground in recent times for economic discontent; and ground for political discontent in the dictatorial behaviour of the President. But in general there was not in Uruguay the kind of political and social conditions which could justify, in (for example) Ernesto Guevara's terms, a resort to armed struggle.

But it was no time after Mitrione had been murdered that it was being argued world-wide, this time by a radical authority on the Latin American revolutionary milieu, Mr Richard Gott, that '... this year things have taken a more serious turn. A lot of Tupamaros have been captured and humane Uruguay has been horrified by the stories of torture in prison, stories that are familiar enough in the Brazilian context but unusual for Uruguay.'[61]

Later that month it was announced that a US House of Representatives subcommittee was to investigate charges that US advisers 'have taught torture methods to Latin American police forces'. Part of the background to this was the charge by the International Commission of Jurists that Brazilian police received torture training from US experts in the Panama Canal Zone.[62]

61. *The Australian*, 24 August 1970.
62. *Canberra Times*, 28 August 1970.

The author cannot presume to judge this issue, but apart from the point that even Sr Castro saw Uruguay and Chile as democratic societies it may be noticed that the apparently very thoroughgoing (and anti-government) analysis of Brazilian counter-revolutionary politics made by the *Sunday Times* team included this observation:

> It is true that torture is not altogether new in Brazil. The country's history is marked by the torture of Indians and of Negro slaves ... during World War II, under the dictator Vargas, the notorious Rio police chief Felinto Muller made torture a part of police routine in dealing with Communists.

It is therefore rather difficult to understand why members of the Brazilian security services had to receive instructions in this trade from American advisers in the Canal Zone. Any apparent labouring of this point here is simply in order to draw attention to another international component in modern guerrilla warfare, and perhaps the most powerful of all on a certain level: propaganda.

What also ought to be underlined at this stage is what appears to be an increasingly successful attempt by guerrilla theorists to narrow down the options to the point where armed struggle is made to seem the *only* proper way forward for those determined radically to alter a society and destroy the *status quo*. It may be that the success of the Moscow Communists in Chile will slow down this process.[63] But of course it is a process that has developed as much in India and South East Asia as in Latin America, not to speak of the Palestinians. Indeed the US President, rightly or wrongly, felt sufficiently impressed by the pro-

63. Mr Richard Gott commented on Sr Allende's election: 'Only Argentine at present lies hand and foot in the American camp. Given its own internal instability and revolutionary potential, it is improbable that its generals will make a move to crush "red" Chile. Assassination would seem a more likely solution. The assassination of Gaitan in Colombia in 1948 postponed a social and economic revolution there for twenty years.' The assumption of power by the military *junta* late in 1973, with its attendant savage repression of 'progressive' forces, shows the danger of making such predictions. More importantly, the outcome will surely discredit the Moscow political 'Front' approach in favour of guerrilla violence elsewhere in Latin America.

liferation of guerrilla rhetoric and behaviour at home to think it politically meaningful to proclaim that 'Those who bombed universities, ambushed policemen, hijacked aircraft and held their passengers hostage shared not only a contempt for human life but also a contempt for those elemental decencies on which a free society rested ... we cannot stand successfully for the rule of law abroad unless we respect the rule of law at home.'[64]

Put another way, there seems to be developing on a world scale a kind of moral confrontation of a post-colonial kind between the modern liberal capitalist West (and those non-European countries imbued, in varying degrees, with the same hopes for the future) and those who see themselves as representing a different kind of future and possessed of politico-military techniques for the violent subversion of institutions and modes of behaviour which they have come to despise – or which they affect to believe are intrinsically oppressive.

What is shared by these enemies of Western democracy is not an ideology in any precise sense; nor a strict adherence to the same kind of tactics; nor (often) international links of a direct political kind; but rather a mode of behaviour which these days is increasingly coming to be described as guerrilla.[65]

It is the purpose of this study to try to show how this situation has come about through exploring the development of guerrilla warfare in parts of the modern world. After all, as the great French sociologist M. Raymond Aron has pointed out, 'In our time, the war of partisans has changed the map of the world more than the classical or atomic destructive machines ... Partisan warfare has given the *coup de grâce* to European overseas empires.'[66] Whether guerrilla warfare, adapted to a different kind of 'terrain', can bring down liberal capitalism is quite another matter.

It is clear that so far modern revolutionary warfare, despite

64. Speech at Kansas State University, *Canberra Times*, 12 September 1970.

65. See Martin Oppenheimer, *Urban Guerrilla*, Penguin Books, 1969.

66. Leon Bramson and George W. Goethals (eds.), *War: Studies from Psychology, Sociology, Anthropology*, Basic Books, New York, 1964, p. 382.

the meretricious language of some segments of the New Left in the Western world, has been of true political significance only in the poor countries of the world. There it has been, and it is likely to remain, of very great political significance indeed in the foreseeable future. In a speech of 6 June 1966, Mr Robert McNamara drew attention to the very high and increasing incidence of revolutionary violence:

> In the past eight years alone there have been no less than 164 internationally significant outbreaks of violence – each of them specifically designed as a serious challenge to the authority, or the very existence of the governments in question. 82 different governments have been directly involved. What is striking is that only 15 of ... 164 significant resorts to violence have been military conflicts between two States. And not a single one ... has been a formally declared war ... The planet is becoming a more dangerous place to live on – not merely because of a potential nuclear holocaust – but also because of the large number of *de facto* conflicts and because the trend of such conflicts is growing rather than diminishing.
>
> At the beginning of 1958, there were 23 prolonged insurgencies going on about the world. As of 1 February 1966, there were 40. Further, the total number of outbreaks of violence has increased each year: in 1958 there were 34 – in 1965 there were 58. But what is most significant of all is that there is a direct and constant relationship between the incidence of violence and the economic status of the countries afflicted.
>
> ... Among the 38 very poor nations – those with a per capita income of under $100 a year – no less than 32 have suffered significant conflicts.[67]

Mr McNamara went on to show that amongst the less poor, but still comparatively very poor, nations the incidence of political violence was very high indeed. Since the economic gap between developed and poor nations was undoubtedly widening, he rightly argued that a very large part of the world was 'pregnant with violence' – and would be even if there were no 'threat of Communist subversion'. However, clearly the matter is not quite so simple as the establishment of a general relationship

67. *The Bulletin*, Sydney, 6 June 1966.

between poverty and violence might suggest. If it were so simple, then widespread and persistent violence should have been expected in, say, East Pakistan long before it occurred in, say, the Mekong delta of Vietnam.

Professor S. P. Huntington has argued that violence and instability are 'in large part the product of rapid social change and the rapid mobilization of new groups into politics coupled with the slow development of institutions'.[68] Clearly there is truth in this too, though the present writing will be more concerned with a different kind of 'mobilization', since it is concerned very much more with the nature of revolutionary warfare than its social setting. However, the figures of political violence which Professor Huntington supplies from the US Defense Department are of considerable interest in the guerrilla context:

*Military Conflicts, 1958–65*

| | 1958 | 1959 | 1960 | 1961 | 1962 | 1963 | 1964 | 1965 |
|---|---|---|---|---|---|---|---|---|
| Prolonged, irregular or guerrilla insurgency | 28 | 31 | 30 | 31 | 34 | 41 | 43 | 42 |
| Brief revolts, coups, uprisings | 4 | 4 | 11 | 6 | 9 | 15 | 9 | 10 |
| Overt, militarily conventional wars | 2 | 1 | 1 | 6 | 4 | 3 | 4 | 5 |
| Total | 34 | 36 | 42 | 43 | 47 | 59 | 56 | 57 |

*Source:* US Department of Defense

A more recent analysis and survey of what may loosely be described as guerrilla situations of a revolutionary kind (or support therefore) lists 'Groups advocating, or engaged in, armed action': Cuba, Argentina, Bolivia, Brazil, Chile, Colombia, Guatemala, Peru, Uruguay and Venezuela, in Latin America; Tanzania, Congo-Brazzaville, Congo-Kinshasa, Guinea, Algeria and Egypt (more marginally, recently), Ethiopia, Angola and Mozambique (Portuguese territories), Cameroun, Tchad, Rhodesia, South Africa, in Africa; the (Palestinian) Arab ex-

68. S. P. Huntington, *Political Order in Changing Societies*, Yale University Press, 1969, p. 4.

tremists and the Popular Front for the Liberation of the Occupied Arab Gulf (PFLOAG) in the Middle East; the Naxalites in Bengal, Kerala and Andhra, particularly, in India – plus possible Naga and Mizo tribal allies; and various insurgencies in Burma, including minority peoples, Thailand, Vietnam, Laos, Cambodia, Indonesia, Malaysia and the Philippines in South East Asia.[69] Since then there has occurred the abortive revolutionary guerrilla struggle in Sri Lanka (Ceylon) and a guerrilla component in the struggle for Bangla Desh.

A recent survey lists over eighty organizations engaged in some kind of irregular violence of a roughly guerrilla nature, urban and rural, in nearly fifty countries. Of course the growth in numbers of such movements in itself proves nothing about the efficacy of this kind of politico-military behaviour. It does, however, suggest that an increasingly large number of extremists throughout the world are either persuaded of the efficacy of guerrilla struggle, in a loose sense of that term, or have been forced to adopt that form of struggle.

It is perhaps worthwhile, in the light of this proliferation of a mode of politico-behaviour that was not long ago regarded as barbaric, to study some examples of it and to examine some of its facets. That is all that the present writer is concerned to do.

69. Brian Crozier, *The Study of Conflict*, Conflict Studies No. 7, October 1970, Institute for the Study of Conflict, London. Ethiopia and the Sudan should be added to the list.

# CHAPTER 1
# THE MODERN HISTORICAL BACKGROUND

**Guerrilla** 1809. 1. An irregular war carried on by small bodies of men acting independently. 2. One engaged in such warfare. 3. attr. (or adj.) esp. in g. war (= sense I) 1811.

*Shorter English Dictionary*

A People's War in civilized Europe is a phenomenon of the nineteenth century . . . [its opponents] either considering it in a political sense as a revolutionary means, a state of anarchy declared lawful, which is as dangerous as a foreign enemy to social order at home; or on military grounds conceiving that the result is not commensurate with the expenditure of the nation's strength.

CLAUSEWITZ: *On War*

THOUGH the struggle against Napoleon's occupation army in Spain was 'national not liberal, a super Vendée, peasant, a combination of modern national fanaticism with the fanaticism of the Wars of Religion',[1] it revealed many of the features of guerrilla warfare essential for an understanding of the subject in general. What was missing was any real revolutionary content; and that for the obvious reason that the army of occupation represented the 'progressive' forces of the day.[2]

This particular struggle arose out of the fact that the Spanish regular army, after an early victory against nondescript French troops in July 1808, was defeated again and again. The result was a struggle carried on by some 30,000 guerrillas, 'ranging from small bands to Mina's organized group of 8,000 men who were scarcely distinguishable from regular troops'.[3]

1. Theodore Ropp, *War in the Modern World*, Collier Books, New York, 1962, p. 126.

2. But see Raymond Carr, *Spain: 1808–1939*, Oxford University Press, 1966, p. 109: 'It had undertones of social war.'

3. ibid., p. 108.

Like many other guerrilla wars, this struggle had a very important international component, Wellington's army; nevertheless, as a great historian of war has remarked, '... the Spanish guerrillas, as much so as Wellington's small army, pinned down scores of thousands of [Napoleon's] troops ...'[4]. What the guerrillas were chiefly concerned to do was to exploit a rugged terrain in order to attack communications and reoccupy areas evacuated by the French. This was done by the now classic guerrilla ploy of attacking only when they could do so with overwhelming superiority of numbers and quickly disbanding well before there was any danger of their being annihilated.

This kind of warfare revealed itself as being peculiarly savage, prompting an observer, Jomini, to remark that he preferred 'the good old times when the French and English Guards courteously invited each other to fire first ... to the frightful epoch when priests, women, and children throughout Spain plotted the murder of isolated soldiers'.[5] Jomini saw quite clearly that this was a war against communications of a peculiar kind. Though the occupation army of some 275,000 men by 1812 included 40,000 Spaniards, and though the commitment or not of members of

4. J. F. C. Fuller, *The Conduct of Modern War: 1789–1961*, Eyre & Spottiswoode, 1961, p. 58.

5. Quoted in Ropp, op. cit. It should also be noticed that reprisals were terrible too and often only exacerbated the hatred for the foreign invader. This fatal relationship between terrorism and counter-terrorism will be explored, but it may be noticed here that war against the population, even when guerrilla activity was only sporadic and marginal, was Sherman's policy in Georgia during the American civil war: 'If the people raise a howl against my barbarity and cruelty, I will answer that war is war ... If they want peace they and their relatives must stop the war.' The decline in civilized restraints upon war-making cannot be attributed primarily to the growth of guerrilla warfare in recent years. Consider Cyril Falls, *A Hundred Years of War*, Duckworth, 1953, pp. 350–51: 'Disregard of neutrality, unrestricted submarine warfare, sinking of merchant shipping without the prospect of providing for the safety of the crew, even the widespread looting of the allied forces of occupation in Germany – all these are instances of retrogression in the conduct of war ... whereas the British Army of the Rhine after the First World War hardly took a button from the Germans, after the Second, wine, works of art, cameras by tens of thousands, and watches by hundreds of thousands were taken.'

the Spanish élite depended on political beliefs, assessment of the likely outcome and geographical location,[6] the French in Spain found (as they were to find in Vietnam nearly a century and a half later) that this kind of 'people's war' imposed an impossible task, in so far as they strove not only to keep open communications between the easily held city centres but also to pacify the countryside. The guerrilla bands were, to employ a phrase from the First Indo-China War, '*partout et nulle part*', everywhere and nowhere.

As Mr Raymond Carr has put it:

> It was this continuous resistance, feeble though it often was, which broke Napoleon's doctrine of maximum concentration ... 'If I concentrate 20,000 men,' wrote Bessières, worn out in the north by 1811, 'all my communications are lost and the insurgents make great progress. We occupy too much territory ...' Spain would have been cowed without Wellington's field force: Wellington could not have operated with a small army without the diversionary effects of Spanish resistance. It was the Spaniards who proved Wellington's own maxim: 'the more ground the French hold, the weaker they will be at any point'.[7]

The important features common to many large-scale guerrilla wars that were revealed by this struggle are, apart from the mode of harrying communications, several in number. First, the terrain was appropriately rugged; secondly, a measure of popular support conferred upon the guerrillas (along with their tactics) superior Intelligence and hence superior mobility; thirdly, they were receiving crucial foreign support and aid; and lastly, they had at their disposal not only a favourable terrain but plenty of space.

But since the nature of popular support is one of the most hotly disputed aspects of contemporary guerrilla warfare it is desirable to notice that despite the fact of a readily identifiable foreign occupation army and propaganda very modern in its stridency,[8] the scattered guerrilla bands were comparatively small

6. Carr, op. cit., p. 111. 7. ibid., p. 108.

8. This struggle also evoked from Goya's pen and brush the most terrible of all portrayals of war.

in total numbers and saw it as their task 'to impose a patriot terror, bullying the population into resistance'.[9] This also is a common feature of what today are often called, all too facilely, 'peoples' wars'.

The greatest military thinker of this time, Carl von Clausewitz, saw in what he himself called 'people's war' something very important:

... we must observe that a People's War in general is to be regarded as a consequence of the outburst which the military element in our day has made through its old formal limits; as an explosion and strengthening of the whole fermentation-process which we call War. The requisition system, the immense increase in the size of Armies by means of that system, and the general liability to military service, the employment of militia, are all things which lie in the same direction ... and the *levée en masse,* or arming of the people, now lies in the same direction ... In the generality of cases, the people who make judicious use of this means, will gain a proportionate superiority over those who despise its use.[10]

Of course, Clausewitz is here considering what the late General Fuller called the 're-tribalizing' of warfare in general. But as a defensive strategy this involved using the people at large in a guerrilla capacity. For example, when Prussia, allied with Russia, declared war on Napoleonic France in 1813, it was laid down that every man not in the regular army was to support the army by attacking the enemy's rear and communications; to cut off supplies, kill stragglers, destroy food stocks, bridges and boats in the enemy's line of advance, and then retreat to the terrain appropriate to guerrillas.[11]

Clausewitz saw guerrilla warfare as playing a role auxiliary to regular armies, chiefly because he was concerned primarily with the problems of war between monolithic nation-states in a symmetrical system of international relations. (As will be shown, it was Lenin's belief that 'The main seams of power struggle

9. Carr, op. cit., p. 108.

10. *On War,* Intro. and Notes by Col. F. N. Maude, Routledge & Kegan Paul, 1949, pp. 341–2.

11. Fuller, op. cit., p. 58.

are not along national boundaries but along chasms separating the interests of social class'[12] that gave a new dimension to guerrilla warfare.) But he also believed that 'Without the support of a few regular troops as an encouragement, the inhabitants generally want an impulse, and the confidence to take up arms.' (Substituting élitist professional revolutionaries for regular soldiers, the Debray–Castroite theory of guerrilla warfare also holds this infusion of professional revolutionaries to be necessary to activate the peasantry against the incumbent government.)

What Clausewitz had to say that is of assistance in understanding the general nature of guerrilla warfare may be briefly noticed. First, he believed there were certain indispensable conditions for it. The war had to be carried on in the heart of the country and it had to be a war that could not be decided by 'a single catastrophe'. He believed that 'the national character' had to be favourable to such warfare and that the terrain had to be appropriate: 'of a broken and difficult nature, either from being mountainous, or by reasons of woods and marshes, or from the peculiar mode of cultivation in use'.[13] Though he believed that density of settlement was not crucial, nor the living standards of the population, he did remark that 'a poor population accustomed to hard work and privations usually shows itself more vigorous and better suited for War'.

In regard to tactics, he made certain points that are useful for understanding the nature of this kind of warfare. (The danger of repetitiveness is being risked here in order to make it plain that most of the essentials of guerrilla warfare were grasped long before the great works were published in the present century; but also in order to try to bring out these essentials in a historical atmosphere uncluttered by political prejudices and propaganda.)

Clausewitz believed that a guerrilla war 'should be like a kind of nebulous vapoury essence, never condense into a solid body',

12. Anatol Rapoport (ed.), *Clausewitz on War*, Penguin Books, 1968, p. 32. This edition of Clausewitz, though it includes an important introduction by the editor, does not include the original Book VI on People's War.

13. *On War*, op. cit., p. 345.

as T. E. Lawrence was to repeat in Arabia; but he also believed, as Chairman Mao insisted later, that it was necessary to build, with the aid of regular units, larger forces in order to venture 'upon enterprises on a larger scale'. This is a foreshadowing of the Maoist doctrine that guerrilla warfare when used on a very large scale must not only have a cumulative effect but gradually transform itself into mobile warfare. But like all who have understood guerrilla warfare in modern times, from El Empecinado (who boasted that he had never lost a man in action) to Che Guevara, Clausewitz recognized that courage and confidence must first be engendered through presenting the guerrillas with successful attacks on weak bodies of the enemy.[14]

He also recognized something that has been of great importance in contemporary revolutionary guerrilla warfare: the necessity to build outwards from base areas untroubled by the enemy main forces:

> They should rise in the provinces situated at one of the sides of the theatre of War, and in which the assailant does not appear in force, in order to withdraw these provinces entirely from his influence. Where no enemy is to be found, there is no want of courage to oppose him, and at the example thus given, the mass of the neighbouring population gradually takes fire. Thus the fire spreads as it does in heather, and reaching at last that part of the surface of the soil on which the aggressor is based, it seizes his lines of communications and preys upon the vital thread by which his existence is supported.[15]

Lastly, for present purposes, Clausewitz, discussing sudden attacks on enemy garrisons, wrote of such operations as serving to create 'a feeling of uneasiness and dread' and as increasing 'the moral impression of the whole', adumbrating thereby the very important psychological warfare component of guerrilla activities. In this context, he also touched upon one of the most unnerving aspects of guerrilla warfare so far as small (or even medium-sized) counter-guerrilla units are concerned: the ambush after an apparently disorganized dispersal.[16]

However, despite the potentialities Clausewitz perceived in

14. ibid., p. 345. 15. ibid., pp. 344–5. 16. ibid., p. 345.

what he called 'people's war', including its guerrilla aspect, the thrust of European politics in the nineteenth century was not favourable to the development of guerrilla warfare. For the most part the leadership of the upthrusting nationalities was composed of urban-orientated and civic-minded groups; the new social revolutionaries were even more urban-orientated even if less civic-minded. As the rising in the Vendée during the French Revolution had intimated, peasantry could make formidable guerrilla fighters even without a foreign army of occupation on the scene.[17] But it was not until the twentieth century that a new kind of political organization, the Bolshevik Party, discovered how to mobilize the peasantry for disguised political ends of a revolutionary kind.

In the meantime, with some temporary exceptions, as in 1848 and 1870,[18] it proved possible for the modern European nation-states to subsume, at least in times of major crisis, the hopes and energies of the people-at-large within the confines of their own nationalist guidelines. And for all the liberal protests and attempts at reformulation, the guidelines were those laid down by Clausewitz: the State was a 'real' entity of a sovereign nature, which ineluctably sought to enhance its power at the cost of other States. War was simply a continuation of this political contest of State wills carried on by other means.[19]

17. See Charles Tilly, *The Vendée*, Edward Arnold, 1964. Its pacification was also notable, involving 'an ingenious mode of reducing the country without laying it waste, by depriving it of its arms and taking part of its produce . . . [A line] was composed of very strong detachments connected by patrols so as to leave no free space by which an enemy who was at all numerous could pass. [To disarm the people] the posts were directed to seize the cattle which usually grazed together, and the corn stored away in the barns; they were also to secure the principal inhabitants; they were not to restore the cattle or the corn, nor release the persons taken as hostages, till the peasants should have voluntarily delivered up their arms' (Thiers, *Consulate and Empire*, quoted in C. A. Dixon and Otto Heilbrunn, *Communist Guerrilla Warfare*, Allen & Unwin, 1954, p. 156).

18. The conflict of 1870 in France saw the first sustained guerrilla attack on the communications so vital for modern armies. See F. O. Miksche, *Secret Forces*, Faber & Faber, 1950, p. 26.

19. See Rapoport, op. cit.

War was a business of industrial and technological power, transformed into the immense firepower of great armies seeking to concentrate upon the enemy's weak points, these armies in turn being supported by populations increasingly subjected to that most odious of modern 'intellectual traditions', propaganda. And yet from the point of view of Marx's collaborator and patron, Frederick Engels, war had ceased, in a special sense, to be people's war: 'It seems that only the Barbarians have recognized and made use of the right to fight individually and that the civilized nations conform to a certain etiquette which precludes them from continuing the struggle after the official capitulation.'[20]

But this was also the age in which some European nations were pacifying a very large part of the 'Barbarian' lands; and it was in these distant regions, as they were for the most part, that the Europeans devised appropriate means of pacification. How this was done is of relevance to an understanding of guerrilla warfare as it has developed in more recent decades.

The word pacification was in common use amongst the British in India in the eighteenth century, when it meant something much more constructive than it usually means today. For example, a very senior servant of the East India Company, Sir John Shore, commented in 1793 on a peace settlement imposed upon a Muslim chieftain by the Governor-General, Lord Cornwallis, in the following terms:

> His losses by the war may have moderated the violence, without changing the Principles of his Character, but the defalcation of his Territories, and the deprivation of his property, will impose silence upon his resentment, and restraint upon his ambitions.
>
> In considering the terms of pacification and the various and clashing interests which were to be consulted in the adjustment, I see the strongest reasons to applaud the wisdom and moderation that dictated it.[21]

20. Quoted in Miksche, op. cit., p. 23.

21. Holden Furber (ed.), *The Private Record of an Indian Governor-Generalship*, Harvard University Press, 1933, p. 145. It was about Lord Cornwallis's earlier failure to pacify America that Ropp wrote in extenuation,

Though it is probably true to say that the Europeans began to install themselves in Asia by proving their superiority in military violence and weapons of war, this would not in the least be an adequate explanation of the persistence of their rule. They also brought to bear upon the scene two particular skills that were lacking: vastly superior modes of organization and equally superior skills in what today in revolutionary guerrilla circles would be called 'the exploitation of contradictions'.

On the one hand, particularly in India, Europeans (French as well as English) quickly demonstrated, as soon as they became politically involved, their capacity to make out of native mercenaries military forces altogether superior to the traditional armies in terms of discipline and tactics. The orderly employment of firepower and the staying-power of an organization that took its strength from its intrinsic solidity, and not only from the qualities of individual commanders, proved capable of putting to rout even the most bravely led horde.

On the other hand, the Europeans learnt how, not only to play off one local ruler against the other, but how to create a new class, civil as well as military, whose future would be bound up with the fortunes of the foreign overlords and opposed to a restoration of the old order by traditional leaders.

This is not to say that there were not some formidable revolts against the European overlords. But it is to say that such revolts were foredoomed to failure unless the 'natives' could alter the military rules imposed by the conquerors and also change their political organization in such a way as to forge an effective command system.

The central point being made here is that *both* things had to happen. This is best demonstrated by briefly considering the Indian Rising of 1857, known until fairly recent years as the Indian Mutiny. The East India Company's Bengal army, which was in effect the north Indian army, the other two being the Bombay and Madras armies, began to mutiny in May 1857 at a station near Delhi. The causes of the army mutiny were

---

'The problems of partisan warfare are the most difficult of all problems' (*War in the Modern World*, op. cit., p. 94).

various. It was a mercenary army which, despite some localized mutinies from time to time, functioned well enough until the sub-continental conquest was completed and it entered on a period of comparative martial unemployment.

It was a privileged and rather spoilt army, composed most significantly of high-caste Hindus whose religious susceptibilities had been upset by recently introduced conditions of employment in polluting places outside Hindustan; and by rumours that an insouciant ordinance department's decision to grease cartridge wrappers with animal fat (pigs' fat being offensive to the predominantly Muslim cavalry, cows' fat to the caste Hindu infantry) had not been rescinded; and this for a rumouredly most sinister reason – in order to try to convert the Bengal army to Christianity by rendering its members out-caste in the eyes of the communities to which they belonged and regularly returned on leave and upon retirement.

The mutineers immediately marched to Delhi, seat of the last of the Mughal Emperors, set up a Hindu–Muslim military directorate and tried to fan a 'prairie fire' that would race across the sub-continent to burn out the *ferenghi* (European) overlords.

Though the mutineers had a good deal in their favour politically – rulers disaffected by the application of an inheritance law threatening the dissolution of their families, landlords whose traditional authority was being whittled away by British law and administrative practice, peasants disabled by land revenue assessment and a transformation (under British law) of the power of the moneylender, not to mention the generalized fear of conversion and that sudden eruption of a sense of anarchic freedom which accompanies the breakdown of law-and-order – the Rising came to nothing. It was for the most part put down within a year; partly through the use of exemplary terrorism,[22]

22. For example, General Neill, who saw that '. . . the rising was becoming something more than a military mutiny and . . . had not the tenderness to deter him from striking root and branch the people who were rising on the ruins of the Native Army' (Sir John Kaye, quoted in S. B. Chaudhuri, *Civil Rebellion in the Indian Mutiny*, World Press, Calcutta, 1957, p. 265). Hatred engendered by stories of atrocities against British women and children helped justify the counter-terror.

partly because recruits (especially in the Muslim-hating Sikh areas of the Punjab) to the anti-Delhi cause were easily come by, partly because the new class in the cities perceived that their future lay with the new British order, and partly because the British at this period were not a people to be unnerved by an explosion of violence and hence all too prepared to use their naval supremacy to reinforce to the necessary extent.

But what is germane to this study is, first, the military methods adopted, and secondly, the matter of political organization. It was clearly recognized at the time by the Governor-General and others that this had not been a mere military mutiny; it had been in northern and parts of central India an insurrection.[23] But this fact has been very often obscured, first by English writers who wished (sometimes perhaps unconsciously) above all to be able to assert the essential righteousness of the British 'civilizing mission' in general; later by Indian writers concerned to show the 'unprogressive', 'non-patriotic' nature of this struggle, in contrast to the modern nationalist movement in India associated with Mahatma Gandhi's non-violent methods.[24]

On the military plane, the rebels fatally disabled themselves by getting immobilized in or around cities – Delhi, Lucknow and Kanpur in particular.[25] It was not that this leadership was

23. S. Gopal, *British Policy in India, 1858–1905*, Cambridge University Press, 1965, p. 1.

24. The largest claims for 1857 are naturally made by the Communists and by 'right-wing' terrorists. See for example P. C. Joshi (ed.), *Rebellion 1857*, People's Publishing House, Bombay, 1957, and V. D. Savarkar, *The Indian War of Independence*, Phoenix, Bombay, 1947.

25. One rebel leader, Tantia Topi, showed skill in mobile warfare in Central India; and insurgents adopted guerrilla tactics after the fall of Bareilly and Lucknow. A General Order put out there showed considerable insight into guerrilla tactics: 'Do not attempt to meet the regular columns of the infidels because they are superior to you in discipline, *bandobast* [system or mode of regulation], and have big guns but watch their movements, guard all the ghats on the rivers, intercept their communications, stop their supplies, cut their *daks* [communications] and posts, keep constantly hanging about their camps, give them no rest' (Joshi, op. cit., p. 194). But this was exceptional. Engels sagely predicted that, '. . . the fate of the insurrection is dependent upon its being able to expand . . . if the movement remain

unaware of the propaganda aspect of the struggle – the proclamations put out were well designed to appeal to the various levels of Indian society;[26] it was the inability of the leadership either to spread the areas of disaffection by armed, guerrilla destruction of British communications and administration, or to fashion a political organization in which the various Indian interests could be subsumed, which spelt disaster for the Indians who rose in arms.

The military error, doubtless inevitable in the military circumstances of the East India Company army (in which the Indian officers were elderly by the time they reached the top of their hierarchy, a hierarchy subordinate to the British), was an attempt to *imitate*, most imperfectly, what they believed was British military policy.

The political error was something of the same order: a belief that slogans and appeals directed towards re-establishing the pre-British society, if couched in apparently rational phrases, would suffice to bring about the expulsion of the *kafir* (if one were a Muslim), the *mleccha* (if one were a Hindu). But whereas the leaders in Delhi were capable on occasion of using a quasi-modern rhetoric of 'popular front' resistance to a foreign *raj* they were quite unable to fashion a political organization appropriate to the propaganda ploy. A revolutionary approach was required for that.

A recent and most distinguished historian of the Indian nationalist movement has commented:

> The armed challenge proved that the Indians could not turn the British out by force: not because the foreigners were the stronger, but because they were more united. As long as any internal crisis in

---

confined . . . then, no doubt, the next winter will suffice to disperse the bands, and to turn them into dacoits [bandits], which will soon be more hateful to the inhabitants than even the pale-faced invaders' (21 July 1958: K. Marx and F. Engels, *The First Indian War of Independence*, Moscow, n.d.).

26. For example, the Azimgarh Proclamation in Embree, T. Ainslie (ed.), *1857 in India*, D. C. Heath, Boston, 1963, pp. 1–3. See also N. A. Chaudhury (ed.), 'Documents Collected by Captain Briggs from . . . the Delhi Palace the Day it was Captured', *Journal of the Research Society of Pakistan*, Panjab University, Vol. II, Part II, April 1965.

the future was capable of a military solution, then they would be able to solve it. For some decades after 1857 this seemed to be the only type of internal crisis likely to threaten them; consequently the Raj sheltered behind a panoply of force which could evoke terror and inspire respect.[27]

But it must be added that what the British learnt from 1857 was not only the necessity to keep in view a panoply of force (the Indian component of which was thenceforth to be organized on a strictly 'divide and rule' principle);[28] but also to see to it that Indians were disarmed. The chief storm centre of 1857 was the recently annexed, former Muslim kingdom of Oudh, which had not been at all properly disarmed.

This aspect of imperial rule in South Asia has been for the most part inadequately understood. The term 'pacification' in the case of rulers over which the British exercised paramountcy involved disarming to a degree that was found compatible with fairly easily asserted British-Indian control[29]. In British India, that is, the area directly administered, the policy was to keep the population-at-large effectively disarmed. (Complaints against this policy, held to be humiliating by the Western-style politicians of the Indian National Congress, founded in 1885, were to be a regular component in nationalistic rhetoric throughout the British period.)[30] The point about this popular disarmament will become clear when European policy in Asia during the Second World War is considered.

The result of this policy was an imperial preoccupation with

27. Anil Seal, *The Emergence of Indian Nationalism*, Cambridge University Press, 1969, p. 2.

28. See Hugh Tinker in Embree, op. cit., pp. 97–8.

29. From early days such control was essentially civilian. See for example Sidney J. Owen (ed.), *A Selection from the Despatches, Memoranda, and Other Papers relating to India of Field-Marshal The Duke of Wellington, K.G.*, Oxford, 1880, especially the 'tranquillizing' of Wynaad in 1802, pp. 147–9.

30. N. C. Chaudhuri, *The Autobiography of an Unknown Indian*, Bombay, 1964 edition, pp. 244–5, evokes the wonderment of Indian boys at the sight of a revolver early in the twentieth century. Manmathnath Gupta, *They Lived Dangerously*, New Delhi, 1969, p. 95, writes that his revolutionary group in the 1920s had too little ammunition to be able to practise revolver shooting.

what came to be called 'small wars', wars that were nearly always confined to frontier areas whose inhabitants could sometimes receive modern weaponry across the borderlines drawn by imperial mapping pens. It was in these wars that the fashioning of what today would be called counter-insurgent principles was begun.

Of course, some of the lessons of pacification had been learnt during the conquest itself. Amongst those who had to be put down in India was the bandit host known as Pindaris, who displayed two features to be found in modern guerrilla campaigns – mobility and dispersal:

> In the rapidity of their movement, their endurance of fatigue, their attachment to their horses, their want of discipline, and their predatory mode of warfare, the Pindarries strikingly resemble the least civilized of the Cossacks. Their number is stated to amount to between thirty and forty thousand . . .
>
> Each person carries merely a few days' provision for himself, and provender for his horse, and thus they travel for weeks at the rate of thirty or forty miles a day, over roads and countries impassable for a regular force . . . As their object is not fighting, but plunder, they have seldom been known to resist the attack of even an inferior enemy; and, if they are overtaken, they disperse, and reassemble at some appointed rendezvous.[31]

It was against such irregulars that the British slowly built up a great knowledge of this kind of warfare and modes of countering it. Such knowledge was political as well as military, since the British were concerned to view pacification as a matter of permanently consolidating power. This involved not only bringing home to the natives the fact of that permanency (often a matter of bluff in peripheral areas) but also a concern with proper military behaviour towards civilians that has still been inadequately inculcated in some Asian armies fighting guerrilla insurgents. This is nicely exemplified in an appeal put out by a British officer, Herbert Edwardes, in 1848:

31. *Selections from the Indian Journals, Vol. I, The Calcutta Journal,* Calcutta, 1963, pp. 50–2.

Last spring half of you ran away to the mountains; some because they were afraid of being barbarously treated by the Sikhs and some to escape paying revenue. You saw that I did not allow plundering and that the soldiers stood guard over your corn and therefore you need not run away out of fear. And it is no use your running away to avoid payment. Above all keep in mind that the Army which is now coming to the Bunnoo is coming to stay.[32]

It was the pacification of the Punjab in north-west India that evoked from an eccentric British Commander-in-Chief, Sir Charles Napier, some astonishing insights that foreshadow the principles laid down by T. E. Lawrence. For example:

There can be but two kinds of war in the Punjab. A war made by regular invading armies or an insurrectionary war. In the first case the forts can do us no harm; nothing better than that the enemy should disseminate his army to hold these petty forts. The principle of regular war is to concentrate. The nature of insurrectionary war is the reverse; the people suddenly congregate and falling on some weak part destroy it and disperse; and the troops sent hurriedly to support the part attacked find the mischief done, and with nothing to show how or by whom. Now what leader in such a war would shut himself up in one of these forts? His game is freedom, is enterprise. He who would occupy a fort would be a fool! They are of no importance, and may be safely left to themselves. If ever available in war, it would be as a temporary refuge for a detachment of our police until after relief came.[33]

Nevertheless, there was in evidence in Napier's day, in the case of war against the tribes beyond the pacified area, the kind of military behaviour that has so often been complained about in very recent years: attacks against the population. Napier's anger about this kind of punitive action has a very modern ring:

It is with surprise and regret that I have seen . . . that villages have been destroyed . . . I desire to know why a proceeding at variance

32. *Lahore Political Diaries,* Vol. V, p. 136, Punjab Government Records. The author is indebted to Mr Andrew Griffiths for reference to these records.

33. Sir Charles James Napier, *Defects, Civil and Military, of the Indian Government*, London, 1853, p. 397.

with humanity and contrary to the usages of civilized warfare came to be adopted. I disapprove of such cruelties, so unmilitary and so injurious to the discipline and honour of the Army. Should the troops be again called to act, you will be pleased to issue orders that war is to be made on men; not upon defenceless *women and children*, by destroying their habitations and leaving them to perish without shelter. . .[34]

Punitive expeditions never could be a substitute for administrative pacification. Pacification involved, as it still does involve, protection for the majority of people who out of habit resolved to accept the new administration. The permanency of the new rulers had to be clearly demonstrated. It was this that was crucial in gaining what is today, often misleadingly, called 'popular support'. This was ultimately a matter of gradually thickening the administration, particularly in the form of police authority as distinct from military force.

But first had to come the subjugation of the active enemies of the new government. The dilemma inherent in this phase of pacification was neatly described by Sir Charles Crosthwaite in respect of Upper Burma in 1886:

There were few districts in which the guerrilla leaders were not active. Their vengeance on every Burman who attempted to assist the British was swift and unmerciful. As it was impossible at first and for some time to afford adequate protection, villages which aided and sheltered the enemy were treated with consideration. The despatch of flying columns moving through a part of the country and returning quickly to headquarters was discouraged. There was a tendency in the beginning of the business to follow this practice, which was mischievous. If the people were friendly and helped the troops, they were certain to suffer when the column retired. If they were hostile, a hasty visit had little effect on them. They looked on the retirement as a retreat and became more hostile than before.[35]

34. Quoted in Arthur Swinson, *North-West Frontier*, Hutchinson, 1967, p. 102. A century later George Orwell was to write about this kind of activity: 'Defenceless villages are bombarded from the air, the inhabitants driven into the countryside, the cattle machine-gunned, the huts set on fire with incendiary bullets: this is called *pacification*.' The reference was to India's North-West Frontier. (All italics in quotations are as in the original.)

35. *The Pacification of Burma*, London, 1912, p. 9.

It required four years of patient work 'before the country was pacified and the peasant who wished to lead a life of honest industry could accomplish his desire'. The measures adopted to bring this situation about included the periodical fining of persistently unhelpful villages, the removal of the relatives and sympathizers of the guerrilla chiefs, 'by holding certain points fairly close together throughout the district ... and by having constant parties of troops and police always on the move'.

British methods of pacification were brought to bear against white men in South Africa at the beginning of the twentieth century. The Boer guerrilla campaigns arose out of a failure to press home orthodox military advantages while the opportunity offered. The struggle between part of the white British Empire (as in a sense it became) and the Boer Republic of the Transvaal and Orange Free State was in some respects similar to the present war in Vietnam: Great Britain's waging of the war was regarded by much of Europe as odious in itself and execrable in its methods; and it created a severe division of opinion between Conservatives and many Liberals at home. Though outside help to the Boers did not eventuate, the hope of intervention by European powers was a factor in Boer calculations.[36]

The struggle revealed a number of features very relevant to an understanding of guerrilla warfare, some of them foreshadowing contemporary guerrilla warfare. Looking at the struggle for convenience sake, through the mind of one commander who was to become world famous in other spheres of activity, Jan Christian Smuts, some very modern features are immediately evident. Though he was not in the event able to implement his ideas, Smuts understood the importance of what is today known, in the jargon of Communist revolutionary warfare, as 'exploiting contradictions'. He considered sowing disaffection in the Indian Empire; he believed that attacks on the mines along

36. Namely, the three powers which had intervened against Japan in 1895: Russia, France and Germany. A. J. Grant and Harold Temperley, *Europe in the Nineteenth and Twentieth Centuries*, Longmans, 1945, p. 419; W. K. Hancock and J. van der Poel (eds.), *Selections from the Smuts Papers*, Vol. I, Cambridge University Press, 1966, p. 399.

the Witwatersrand might show the British financial interests that war was not worthwhile for them and so induce them to bring their influence to bear to halt the political imperialists; and he sought to bring off a diversionary movement into Cape Colony 'to bring about a constitutional revolution in the Cape Colony, so that Colonial Afrikaners who take up arms can acquire the status of legal combatants instead of rebels ... [and] force the enemy to throw 30,000 to 50,000 men on to the Cape railway lines to protect them and to raise a very large number of columns to fight us, and even that will not help them'.[37]

The Boer mounted riflemen relied primarily upon their superior mobility:

> Owing to their greater mobile efficiency, their superior scouting, and smaller numbers, the Boers could always give their enemies long odds in the matter of covering mere distance. While the heavy English columns of mounted infantry on their clumsy horses and accompanied by their long convoys and artillery, including guns of heavy calibre, would, like a wounded snake, wind their slow length along, the agile Boer commandos were easily maintaining their start by short, rapid strides followed by rests which the enemy could not afford. The result was that after a so-called chase of some weeks the Boers and their horses would be comparatively fresh and fit for work while the English mounted infantry would be tired and used up and their animals either dead or fit only for the remount camps.[38]

Out of this superior mobility there was developed by General de la Rey what was called '*vlucht volmoed*' or 'flight in full courage'. De la Rey 'masked his essentially offensive plan in continual retreats until at last his unwary enemy was lulled into a false sense of security and would think he was no longer worth much care or watchfulness; and then he would pull his forces together at a suitable opportunity and like a tiger make a terrific spring at his enemy'.[39]

However, though Smuts could point out that the select few

37. *Smuts Papers*, op. cit., pp. 372 and 502.

38. ibid., p. 659.

39. ibid., p. 609. Two horses per man were used wherever possible (Deneys Reitz, *Commando*, Faber & Faber, 1929, p. 156).

Boers did not 'quail before the absolute destruction of their property and the sufferings of their women and children', it was on occasion necessary 'to winkle out the burghers' through the threat of punishment and the creation of military courts. The point is being made in order to underline the fact that guerrilla fighting, even when undertaken for the clearest of causes – the future of a race in this case – is never simply a matter of spontaneity for most of those engaged. Smuts and other commanders had to mobilize and re-mobilize their forces.[40]

This was a particularly difficult task in view of the British policy of farm-burning (in a sense this was a war of the countryside against the modern industrial city) and of incarcerating the wives and children of combatants in concentration camps where a high proportion of them died. As Smuts noticed in June 1901:

> The two republics are a desert where food for the troops is more and more scarce. The families who are not captured, are refugees in the bushes and the mountains; several families have in the end been murdered by the Swazis and the Zulus; almost all the Native tribes in the North are excited and commit atrocities. A certain number of our burghers are fighting against us with our enemies . . . Is it to be wondered that a certain portion of the burghers are discouraged and depressed? A certain portion persevere in the most marvellous manner but it is to be feared that if there are no better hopes soon, a significant number will, out of discouragement, surrender to the enemy.[41]

The British method of waging what is today called psywar (psychological warfare) was that mixture of threats and promises designed to 'exploit contradictions' between the zealous and the average which has become a notable feature of contemporary guerrilla and counter-guerrilla warfare. On the one hand, the countryside was strewn with proclamations offering security of

40. For example, *Smuts Papers*, op. cit., p. 351: 'My plan is to establish a military court immediately, to call the above-named districts out on commando. . . '. Reitz, op. cit., pp. 160–61: 'The Boers had their full share of laggards . . . a full share, too, of steadfast yeomen.'

41. *Smuts Papers*, op. cit., pp. 396–7.

property and a safe return home in return for the swearing of an oath of neutrality. On the other hand, there were the proclamations threatening the destruction of homesteads, and a thoroughgoing destruction of livestock and fodder. As well, the Boer combatants were in effect declared outlaws and hence liable to forfeiture of property and possibly to execution on capture if they were not wearing proper uniforms.[42]

Besides the psychological warfare waged against Boer morale, the British in the course of time devised a method of 'cutting up the country into compartments by chains of blockhouses and barbed wire and then systematically swept each enclosure. A further advantage was that the sixty columns now operating did not have to tie themselves to the railway for supplies; these could be collected at any point on a blockhouse line ... [The Boers were] rendered physically incapable of carrying on the war.'[43] But it required the resources of an imperial power to put paid to a comparatively small number of mounted riflemen, using their superior mobility, superior Intelligence often,[44] ambushes, the ammunition of the enemy on many occasions,[45] and a spirit of desperation, on a terrain – the vast veldt – which was very much their own. It was, as Smuts had maintained earlier, 'the manner in which the enemy has carried on this

42. This not through choice; for example, Reitz, op. cit., p. 209: 'My own wardrobe was typical: a ragged coat and worn trousers full of holes, with no shirt or underwear of any kind. On my naked feet were dilapidated rawhide sandals, patched and repatched during eight months of wear, and I had only one frayed blanket to sleep under at night.' Regarding capture, see footnote 48 below. Executions were very few. On the question of uniforms, see Appendix 2.

43. Falls, op. cit., p. 248.

44. Through superior scouting chiefly, but also through use of a 'vibrator' that permitted tapping of British messages. See *Smuts Papers*, op. cit. p. 620.

45. Reitz, op. cit., pp. 187–8: 'The English soldiers were notoriously careless with their ammunition. If a round or two dropped from their bandoliers they would never trouble to dismount, as they knew they could get more, and at their halting-places one could almost always find cartridges lying spilt in the grass ... I doubt if the British ever realized to what an extent the Boers were dependent upon this source of replenishment.'

war and still carries it on' that 'has reduced us to a condition of exhaustion which will ultimately make the continuance of the war a physical impossibility'.

But it should also be noticed, since it differentiates even the most zealous Boer fighter from the ideological totalitarians who wage contemporary guerrilla warfare, that Smuts believed it was impermissible to sacrifice the Afrikaners for 'a mere idea, which cannot be realized'.[46] The British had separated the guerrillas from the population base and were prepared at this stage in their imperial history patiently to counter what would nowadays be called a 'protracted war' through attacking resources[47] and encircling the commandos. Help never came from outside; independence for the republics became an impossible goal; there was exile for some in the event of defeat but no prospect of reprisals of the contemporary kind after an armistice. Surrender was to be conditional and honourable; despite the concentration camps, peace was to be made between men who had fought cleanly in the field.[48] It had not been a modern totalitarian 'people's war' that the Boers had waged. So an ending of the struggle was quite possible and was made in mid-1902, the guerrilla phase of the war having commenced in July 1900.[49]

46. *Smuts Papers*, op. cit., p. 531.

47. ibid., p. 467: 'All living animals – horses, cattle, sheep, pigs, fowls, even dogs – have been killed, and generally in a manner too shocking to relate.'

48. Reitz, op. cit., p. 136: 'Amid all the cruelty of farm-burning and the hunting down of the civilian population, there was one redeeming feature, in that the English soldiers, both officers and men, were unfailingly humane. This was so well known that there was never any hesitation in abandoning a wounded man . . .'

49. Apart from the suffering and the apparent hopelessness of the guerrilla cause, Boer leaders had become afraid of a 'Kaffir' rising, owing to the depredations of the commandos, and were also afraid that the British, though they had refrained from using blacks in the armed struggle, might unilaterally offer a franchise subversive of the Boer racial position. The author owes this insight to Mr Ashton Robinson.

As regards numbers involved: the Boers disposed of 85,000 men in their commandos at the beginning, though they did not all immediately take to the field. The British did not have more than 10,000 at the beginning of 1899 (Falls, op. cit., p. 146). Reitz, op. cit., p. 44, argues: 'Had the Boers made for

The British experiences in this and other imperial wars were brilliantly explored by a soldier, C. E. Calwell, in his *Small Wars*.[50] Calwell was concerned to emphasize that what he called small wars had no particular connection with the scale of operations but simply denoted the operations of regular armies against irregular, 'or comparatively speaking, irregular, forces', forces which not only often used new methods that needed to be studied but which were marked by a reluctance to meet the regulars 'in the open field'.

> The art of war, as generally understood, must be modified to suit the circumstances of each particular case. The conduct of small wars is in fact in certain respects an art by itself . . . It is difficult to conceive methods of conduct more dissimilar than those employed respectively by the Transkei Kaffirs, by the Zulus, and by the Boers, opponents with whom British troops successively came in conflict within a period of three years and in one single quarter of the African continent.

Though he did not believe it was an invariable rule, Calwell maintained that in such wars a usual condition was for the regular army to be at a disadvantage in regard to Intelligence, a disadvantage that has persisted right up to the Communist 'Tet' Offensive in South Vietnam early in 1968.

It is perhaps of interest today to notice that one of his ex-

---

the coast, instead of tying up their horsemen around towns that were of no value to them, the outcome of the war might have been different, but they sacrificed their one great advantage of superior mobility, and allowed splendid guerrilla fighters to stagnate and demoralize in the monotony of siege warfare, at a time when our only salvation lay in pushing to the sea.' In this respect, there was a repetition of the mistake made by the Indian insurgents in 1857. The total British strength engaged was about 450,000 troops, including nearly 80,000 drawn from the white colonies, most of them from South Africa itself. The total Boer forces probably were not more than 50,000 (W. H. Chamberlain, *To Ride and Shoot*, Military Historical Society of Australia, 1967, p. 17). Smuts estimated that the two Republics surrendered with 18,000 men in June 1902 (*Smuts Papers*, op. cit., p. 626). The area of Natal, Transvaal and the Orange Free State combined was 194,000 square miles; Cape Colony, in which the diversionary attempt was made, was 279,000 square miles.

50. *Small Wars, Their Principles and Practice*, HMSO, 1906.

amples, which with slight alterations could have referred to the Chinese guerrillas fighting the Japanese occupation army or the Vietminh fighting the French, came from Cuba at the end of the nineteenth century:

The Spanish troops were obstructed by the intense hostility of the inhabitants. They could get no good information of the rebel movements, while the rebels were never in doubt about theirs. An insurgent was distinguished from a peaceful cultivator only by his badge which could be speedily removed and by his rifle which was easily hidden. Hence the Government forces, whether in garrison or operating in the country, were closely surrounded by an impalpable circle of fierce enemies who murdered stragglers, intercepted messages, burned stores, and maintained a continual observation.[51]

Mountains and densely wooded country, a very bad climate – malaria, smallpox and yellow fever then taking a toll which they no longer do – and poor road communications also favoured the rebels. But Calwell argued that these factors 'are obstacles to success rather than the causes of failure...'. It was his belief that failure was due to a defensive strategy, trying to defend lines of communication that were too long with a series of blockhouses, but above all through displaying a defensive stance that lacked the exercise of initiative.

Calwell insisted that a strategic offensive was essential in such wars: 'The regular army must force its way into the enemy's country and seek him out. It must be ready to fight him wherever he may be found. It must play to win and not for safety.'[52] On the other hand he recognized the dilemma that plagues the commanders of regular armies to this day:

... guerrilla warfare is a form of operations above all things to be avoided. The whole spirit of the art of conducting small wars is to strive for the attainment of decisive methods, the very essence of partisan warfare from the point of view of the enemy being to avoid

51. ibid., p. 130, See also Albert Merglen, *Surprise Warfare*, Allen & Unwin, 1968, Chapter I.

52. As will be shown, in a revolutionary war the approach of hit-or-miss is misconceived. See also F. E. Kitson, *Low Intensity Operations*, Faber & Faber, 1971, especially pp. 102 ff.

definite engagements . . . the French experiences in Algeria and the British in Afghanistan, show that these irregular, protracted, indefinite operations offer often far greater difficulties to the regular armies than the attainment of the original military objective . . . The regular army has to cope not with determinate but with indeterminate forces. The crushing of a population in arms and the stamping out of widespread disaffection by military methods, is a harassing form of warfare even in a civilized country with a settled social system; in remote regions peopled by half-civilized races or wholly savage tribes, such campaigns are most difficult to bring to a satisfactory conclusion, and are always most trying to the troops.[53]

In nearly all cases at this time the European will prevailed. In most cases the protracted pacification campaigns were financed out of the empires themselves and were fought to a large extent by 'native' forces; the metropolitan seats of empire normally did not have to count large losses either in money or blood.[54] (Which is not to say that such campaigns were necessarily always mounted in order to enrich the imperial powers.)

It was pointed out earlier in this chapter that pacification meant very much more than what the term has come to connote in recent years. Men like Lyautey in North Africa liked to emphasize factories; men like Servière and Gallieni in the Tonking delta saw themselves as winning popular support as much through social and economic as military measures; and there were intense debates between representatives of the European overlord class as to what should be preserved, what had to be destroyed, in the subjugated societies.[55]

Nevertheless it is probably fair to say that the various European 'civilizing missions' were seen by colonial servants ultimately in terms of pacification rather than development: pacification in the sense of imposing a quite new kind (and intensity)

53. ibid., pp. 124, 37, 26.

54. One of the most persistently voiced complaints of Indian nationalists from the 1880s up to the Second World War was about the financing and employment of Indian troops abroad.

55. See for example, Milton E. Osborne, *The French Presence in Cochinchina and Cambodia: Rule and Response 1859–1905*, Cornell University Press, 1969.

of order, law and peace.[56] At any rate it was in this field that they were much more successful. The attitude of mind is perhaps best illuminated in the words of a late-nineteenth-century British imperialist:

> Now the essential parts of European civilization are peace, order, the supremacy of law, the prevention of crime, the redress of wrong, the enforcement of contracts, the development and concentration of the military forces of the state, the construction of public works, the collection and expenditure of the revenue required for these objects in such a way as to promote to the utmost the public interest, interfering as little as possible with the comfort or wealth of the inhabitants, and the improvement of the people.[57]

A 'cold' administration resting on a great concentration of force and the prestige of a belligerent civilization enabled the European overlords to fashion and hold intact – until they exhausted themselves in Europe and had their prestige terribly damaged by the Japanese armed forces in the Second World War – political societies of a kind (and sometimes of an extent) which only this foreign and superimposed rulership could retain in being. The chance for revolutionary nationalism was provided by the promiscuous distribution of arms to Asian resistance movements, which attempted, with varying degrees of success, to occupy the administrative vacuum left by the retreating Japanese.

The case of the largest nationalist movement in imperial Asia was of course different because of the methods adopted and the success of British–Indian arms in defending the sub-continent. But the effect of the 'Quit India' movement of 1942, which involved a good deal of guerrilla violence and required more than fifty-four battalions to put down, was of considerable significance.

56. Manmathnath Gupta reported of the inadvertent firing of a revolver, 'Fortunately none had noticed it. Our British rulers had so disarmed the country that people were not even familiar with the sound of a gun' (*They Lived Dangerously*, op. cit., p. 95).

57. James Fitzjames Stephen, 1883, quoted in C. H. Philips, *Select Documents on the History of India and Pakistan*, Vol. IV, p. 57.

However, what was required for comparatively quick success in anti-imperial struggle – passive resistance in India had been tried from time to time for nearly half a century – was something more than a 'ramshackle coalition' whose momentum could not be sustained in lack of coercion. What was required was an armed Leninist party controlling a 'national united front', which would wage a carefully phased form of revolutionary struggle not only in the imperial territory but also by proxy in the 'imperialist' homeland as well.

## CHAPTER 2

# LENINISM

> The centralization of the most secret functions in an organization of revolutionaries will not diminish, but rather increase the extent and quality of the activity of a large number of other organizations which are intended for a broad public and are therefore as loose and non-secret as possible, such as workers' trade unions, workers' self-education circles ... socialist and also democratic circles among *all* other sections of the population, etc., etc.
>
> LENIN

> What other organization except a universal militia with women participating on an equal footing with men can effect these measures? . . . Such a militia would draw the youngsters into political life, training them not only by word, but by deed and work.
>
> LENIN

FOR Lenin, organization was of primary importance. 'In its struggle for power the proletariat has no other weapon but its organization ... International capital will not be able to withstand this army.'[1] The use of the word army is of significance in understanding the kind of organization that Lenin fashioned in the early years of the twentieth century. Its command system was modelled on military counterparts: 'Unless ... an organizing and leading staff exists the victory of the proletariat and the maintenance of its power is impossible. Hence the enormous importance of Party Organization, of unity of view and singleness of will, the strictest Party discipline, and the expulsion from its ranks of all opportunist and alien elements.'

The organization was to be drawn from all social strata; and it had to be composed 'first and foremost of people whose profession is that of revolutionists ... As this is the common

1. Lenin, *On Organization*, quoted in W. R. Kintner, *The Front is Everywhere*, University of Oklahoma Press, 1955, p. 59.

feature of the members of such an organization, *all distinctions between workers and intellectuals*, and certainly distinctions of trade and profession, must be *utterly obliterated*. Such an organization must of necessity be not too extensive and as secret as possible.'[2] As Professor S. P. Huntington has observed, 'The distinctive characteristic of Communist party members . . . is that they are classless. Their devotion is to the party, not to any social group. The prominent role accorded intellectuals simply derives from the fact that intellectuals are less attached than most other members of society to any particular group.'[3]

But not only was the command system within which the professional revolutionaries operated to be of a quasi-military kind, the revolutionaries were to regard themselves as engaged in actual warfare against incumbent governments and State systems. Reversing the famous dictum of Clausewitz (whom he studied most carefully), Lenin insisted that politics was warfare continued by other means; but whereas Clausewitz argued that 'war is a normal phase in relations among States', Lenin insisted that warfare was a normal phase within States, between classes.[4] But it was the task of the organization of revolutionaries to lead the proletariat in this class war; indeed to bring to the proletariat a consciousness of the existence of this war.

Given this belief, there were clearly no limits imposed upon the political behaviour of the organizations chosen by history to liberate men from an unjust and anyway disintegrating social system. In a special sense, Lenin had created what has come to be recognized as an organizational weapon.

> The bolshevik type of party is an effective organizational weapon because it has solved many of the problems associated with transforming a voluntary association into a managerial structure. This is the key to whatever mystery there may be about the organizational

2. V. I. Lenin, *Selected Works*, Foreign Languages Publishing House, Moscow, 1950, p. 323.

3. S. P. Huntington, *Political Order in Changing Societies*, Yale University Press, 1968, p. 337.

4. Rapoport, op. cit., p. 32, '. . . in the Clausewitzian image, the state is an autonomous entity; *it* has interests. In the Leninist image, the classes have interests, and the ruling class *uses* 'it' [the state] to promote its own.'

power of communism. Put simply, the process ... is one which changes *members* into *agents*, transforms those who merely consent into those (at an extreme, soldiers) who do work as well as conform. 'The thing we need,' said Lenin, 'is a militant organization of agents.'[5]

What was next required was the expansion of this organization of cadres engaged in warfare against society. As Lenin's great disciple, Chairman Mao, put it many years later:

> The organization of our Party must be expanded throughout the country; it must purposefully train tens of thousands of cadres ... These cadres ... must understand Marx–Leninism, they must have political insight and ability to work, they must be full of self-sacrifice, capable of solving problems independently; and they must remain firm in the midst of difficulties and work loyally for the nation, the class, and the Party ... Our revolution depends on the cadres, just as Stalin has said, 'Cadres decide everything'.

The essence of the Leninist approach has seldom been better summarized than by a former political commissar of the Malayan guerrilla army who surrendered to the British authorities during the insurgency (1948–60):

> Communism is really very simple. All the theory and talk about it only serve to confuse what Communism really is. Communism starts with a very simple idea: equality for all people, no capitalists, no poor people. Then the Communists claim that all of history is moving in this direction, and that in time all countries will be Communist. This serves to frighten the enemies and make them waste time arguing about why this will not happen. The Communists know that actually they will win only if they work hard. Thus all the rest of Communism is tactics and strategy. The tactics of Communism are very simple too. First of all it is important to develop organizations. Only by having organizations can you have tactics and strategy, and to use organizations you have to have discipline. Discipline is

5. 'P. Selznick, *The Organizational Weapon*, Rand, New York, 1952, p. 21. 'We shall speak of organizations as organizational weapons when they are used by a power-seeking élite *in a manner unrestrained by the constitutional order of the arena within which the contest takes place*. In this usage, "weapon" is not meant to denote *any* political tool, but one torn from its normal context and unacceptable to the community as a legitimate mode of action' (p. 5).

all-important ... The group or party which has discipline is bound to obtain power. This is as true in politics as in armies.[6]

However, it was necessary for Lenin to devise a means of enlisting the masses in the struggle. This was to be done in two ways: first, by the penetration of existing associations or through the creation of associations for purposes ostensibly having aims unconnected with the ultimate aims of their Communist creators. Secondly, by disguising the ultimate Communist aim of total power for the small revolutionary party behind the 'simple idea' of providing equality and ending poverty, the masses could be involved in political activities of the required kind.[7]

In regard to the former stratagem, Lenin maintained that his kind of organization, 'A small, compact core of the most reliable, experienced and hardened workers', could move large numbers of people gathered together in free associations or in 'front' organizations, provided two rules were observed. First, the Communist Party must retain its separateness from these associations; secondly, the question of violence must be resolved if the Party were to avoid the tendency to hesitate before, and argue about, the employment of force when the moment for its use arose.

It is desirable to consider the first rule precisely as Lenin stated it himself:

The centralization of the most secret functions in an organization of revolutionaries will not diminish, but rather increase the extent and quality of the activity of a large number of other organizations which are intended for a broad public and therefore are as loose and non-secret as possible, such as workers' trade unions, workers' self-education circles and circles for reading illegal literature, social-

6. Quoted in Lucian W. Pye, *Guerrilla Communism in Malaya*, Princeton University Press, 1956, pp. 299–300.

7. Professor Gabriel Almond estimates in his *The Appeals of Communism*, Princeton University Press, 1954, p. 19, that in Lenin's *What is to be Done?* 'only six out of a total 801 references to the traits and actions of militants and the revolutionary party deal with the ultimate constructive aims of the movement'. In *Left-Wing Communism*, less than 4 per cent of a total of 764 references relate to ultimate aims.

ist and also democratic circles among *all* other sections of the population, etc., etc. We must have such circles, trade unions and organizations everywhere in *as large a number as possible* and with the widest variety of functions; but it would be absurd and dangerous to *confuse* them with the organization of *revolutionaries,* to obliterate the border line between them, to dim still more the ... already incredibly hazy appreciation of the fact that in order to 'serve' the masses we must have people who will devote themselves exclusively to [Communist] activities, and that such people must *train* themselves patiently and steadfastly to be professional revolutionaries.[8]

The issue of violence was resolved in his tract, *Two Tactics of Social-Democracy in Democratic Revolution.* Lenin was replying to critics who seemed to him to be accusing his group of revolutionaries of being in danger of 'throwing overboard propaganda and agitation, the economic struggle, and criticism of bourgeois democracy, of becoming inordinately absorbed in military preparations, armed attacks, the seizure of power, etc.'[9] He saw the situation otherwise: in terms of a 'real danger to the movement, which may degenerate, and in some places is degenerating, from one that is revolutionary in deeds into one that is revolutionary in words'.

Lenin insisted that 'An army [that word again] cannot be energetically and successfully mustered and led unless we "dare" to win.' And he intended to lead his quasi-military revolutionary party to 'complete, absolute and decisive victory' by the 'shortest route', while accepting quite frankly that the bourgeoisie would recoil and the reaction would be harsh along that route. Nevertheless, 'The workers will not be frightened ... The workers are not looking forward to striking bargains, are not asking for sops; they are striving to crush the reactionary forces without mercy, i.e. to set up the *revolutionary democratic dictatorship of the proletariat and the peasantry.*'[10]

It must be stressed that the violent stance was not being built into Communism by Lenin simply because of the conditions of

8. *What is to be Done?* (1902), quoted in Robert V. Daniels (ed.), *A Documentary History of Communism,* Vol. I, Vintage Books, 1960, p. 17.

9. *Selected Works,* Vol. I, op. cit., p. 110.

10. ibid., p. 120.

Russian autocracy in the early years of the twentieth century but rather because he understood that only in this manner – through a violent insurrection involving the smashing of the existing State power – could Communist parties gain the decisive kind of victory necessary for the exercise of total political power. It was also a perfectly natural stance for men who saw politics as a form of warfare to take up. As Colonel W. R. Kintner has remarked, 'The military structure of Communism is not accidental; it is accounted for in the development of the Communist movement. The men whom the Communists themselves honour as trail blazers of revolution have been, almost without exception, men familiar with war and military organization ... all have been students of military organization and tactics.'[11]

It is quite true that Lenin insisted, most clearly in his *Left-Wing Communism* of 1920, that certain conditions were necessary before a revolutionary situation existed. The conditions were these: all classes hostile to the revolution had to be confused and weakened through internal struggle, and the ruling classes unable to continue to rule in the old way; the vacillating and feeble elements, 'petty bourgeois democrats' had to have exposed themselves as inadequate to the task of bringing about real change; the proletariat had to be in a mood of favouring the support of 'the most determined, unreservedly bold revolutionary action'; the armed forces of the incumbent regime had to be in an advanced state of 'revolt and disintegration'.[12]

Nevertheless, this was not how Lenin viewed actual revolutionary events, however hopeless they may have been from the

11. *The Front is Everywhere*, op. cit., p. 16. An admirer of Lenin's, Lozovsky, wrote: 'In the whole of Lenin's activities the following passes like a red thread: Initiative, determination, ruthlessness, the pursuit of the enemy until he is destroyed, quick action and the concentration of the proletarian forces at the weakest spot of the enemy's front' (quoted in Kintner, op. cit., p. 36).

12. There are other versions of the 'necessary conditions', with slightly different emphases, e.g. his letter on 'Insurrection as an Art', William J. Pomeroy (ed.), *Guerrilla Warfare and Marxism*, International Publishers, New York, 1968, p. 110. See also: Robert C. North, *Moscow and the Chinese Communists*, Stanford University Press, 1952, p. 25, and Alfred G. Meyer, *Leninism*, Praeger, New York, 1957, pp. 176–81.

very beginning. This comes out very clearly in what he had to say about the Irish Rising of Easter 1916 at a time when it seemed to have been an exercise in heroic fatuity:

> The misfortune of the Irish is that they rose prematurely, when the European revolt of the proletariat had not yet *matured.* Capitalism is not so harmoniously built that the various springs of rebellion can immediately merge of their own accord, without reverses and defeats. On the other hand, the very fact that revolts break out at different times, in different places, and are of different kinds, guarantees wide scope and depth to the general movement; only in premature, sporadic, and therefore unsuccessful, revolutionary movements do the masses gain experience, acquire knowledge, gather strength, and get to know their real leaders, the socialist proletarians, and in this way prepare for the general onslaught, in the same way as separate strikes, demonstrations, local and national, mutinies in the army, outbreaks amongst the peasantry, etc. prepared the way for the general onslaught in 1905.[13]

If further proof were required that Lenin in practice was no scientific judge of objective revolutionary conditions necessary for revolutionary action, it may be found in the fact that he altered his tactics five times between the two revolutions of 1917 as a result of reappraisals of a confusedly shifting situation[14]; and that he thought Western Europe and China had reached, or were about to reach, the critical point at the beginning of the 1920s.[15] The point is being emphasized because, as will be shown, the spurious argument that revolutionary wars erupt spontaneously out of conditions grown socially and economically intolerable – and can only erupt out of such conditions – is a very

13. October 1916. *The National-Liberation Movement in the East*, Foreign Languages Publishing House, Moscow, 1957, p. 179.

14. Lloyd Churchward, *Australian Left Review*, April–May 1970, p. 44. Lest those changes in tactics be regarded simply as fresh insights into changing historical reality: 'Napoleon wrote: "*On s'engage et puis . . . on voit.*" Rendered freely this means: "First engage in a serious battle and then see what happens." Well, we did first engage in a serious battle in October 1917, and then saw such details of development . . . as the Brest Peace, the New Economic Policy, and so forth' (quoted in Georg Lukács, *Lenin*, NLB, London, 1972, p. 81).

15. North, op. cit., p. 25.

important propaganda weapon in the hands of sympathizers with revolutionary warfare.

In understanding the central significance of Leninism for revolutionary guerrilla warfare, two other points must be made. First, the Leninist view of the class struggle has enabled the cadres of the Communist parties to view all who stood in their way rather as resistance movements view enemy occupation armies: as an enemy against whom all methods are permissible. Lenin made this very explicit. When discussing the problem of revolutionary ethics, he stated, 'We say that our morality is entirely subordinated to the interest of the class struggle of the proletariat. Our morality is derived from the interests of the class struggle of the proletariat ... Morality is that which serves to destroy the old exploiting society and to unite all the toilers around the proletariat, which is creating a new Communist society.'[16] Conditioned by such a belief, possessed of an acceptance of the legitimacy of violence, and holding a militarized view of politics, a Communist cadre is peculiarly well prepared for actual guerrilla warfare of the shooting kind.

It is true that the military have played a large role in the politics of much of modern Asia, but it has been observed that even there 'what is significant is that the Communists obtain from their theories an apparently rational explanation of the role of violence and the justification for its use. While in non-Communists the use of military force often evokes apologetic and even shamefaced attitudes, the Communists are not troubled by such inhibitions; they feel that there is glory and respectability in the use of "armed struggle".'[17]

The last point that must be made here about Leninism as an 'idea-organization'[18] peculiarly appropriate to the waging of

16. *Collected Works*, Vol. XVII, pp. 321–3, quoted in David Shub, *Lenin*' Mentor, New York, 1948, Appendix.

17. Pye, op. cit., p. 28.

18. 'Communist parties may split up and fractionate, yet Communism continues to diffuse through "idea-organizations", not primarily through the spread of ideas *for* organizations ... In many nations where the Communists have a small minority, they nevertheless have the only tightly organized and effective party' (Raymond D. Gastil, in *Can We Win in Vietnam?*, Pall Mall Press, 1968, p. 66).

revolutionary guerrilla warfare is the way in which Lenin saw revolutionary class warfare: as *irregular* warfare, using all means to hand, not being tied to one set method, exploiting what may be called the social 'terrain', in particular any dissensions between 'enemy' elements in society and, on the international scale, dissensions between nations.

Once again it is desirable to understand what Lenin was saying in the language in which this was formulated:

> Let us begin from the beginning. What are the basic questions every Marxist must ask when he analyses the problem of the types of struggle? First of all . . . Marxism does not tie the movement to any particular combat method. It recognizes the possibility that struggle may assume the most variegated forms. For that matter, Marxism does not 'invent' those forms of struggle. It merely organizes the tactics of strife and renders them suitable for general use. It also renders the revolutionary classes conscious of the form of the clashes which emerge spontaneously from the activities of the movement. Marxism rejects all abstract thinking and doctrinaire prescriptions about types of struggle. It calls for a careful study of the *mass struggle* which actually is taking place. As the movement develops, as the consciousness of the masses grows, and as the economic and political crises are becoming more intense, every new and different methods of defence and attack will be used in the conflict. Hence Marxism will never reject any particular combat method, let alone reject it forever . . . In this field, if we may say so, Marxism is *learning* from the practice of the masses.[19]

It was in organizing 'the tactics of strife' that the Bolshevik cadre party was to show its mettle. Trained to master all forms of warfare,[20] organized in military fashion, employing the organization as a weapon, disguising its ultimate aims, mobilizing the masses through penetration of existing associations or creating new ones, exploiting contradictions amongst its enemies, quite at home with violence, the Leninists set about their task of acquiring total power.

19. (1906). *Orbis*, 1958.

20. 'Everyone will agree that an army which does not train itself to wield all arms, all the means and weapons of warfare that the enemy possesses or may possess, behaves in an unwise and even in a criminal fashion' (*Left-Wing Communism*, op. cit.).

Though Lenin's party was aware of the importance of the colonial regions for the realization of their dream of world-wide revolution, the emphasis until 1920 was very definitely placed on Europe and on urban insurrection. For example, Lenin referred to the Irish Rising as being 'a hundred times more significant politically than a blow of the same force struck in Asia or Africa ...' It was failure in Europe outside Russia that turned Lenin's eyes purposefully towards the East.

However, before examining this move, it may be useful to consider another group of a very loose kind which also believed it had an answer to the question of how to overthrow its imperial overlords. By considering briefly those nationalists in India who came collectively to be designated Extremists it is possible further to point up the peculiar strength of the Leninist organizational weapon. Two of the best known of them, Bal Gangadhar Tilak and Aurobindo Ghose, considered early in the twentieth century the possibility of starting guerrilla warfare against the British Raj but rejected this mode of armed struggle as impractical in an effectively disarmed population, and for other reasons not strictly germane to this study.[21] At the same time, though both were held by the British to have had ambiguous relations with the small terrorist groups who believed the assassination of officials would rid India of the foreign overlord, their chief relevance to this study lies in their development of what they called 'passive resistance', which Aurobindo defined thus:

> The first principle of passive resistance, which the new school have placed in the forefront of their programme, is to make the administration under present conditions impossible by an organized refusal to do anything which shall help either British commerce or British officialdom in the administration of it – unless and until the conditions are changed in the manner and to the extent de-

21. In view of the fame of Mahatma Gandhi, it is of interest to notice that Aurobindo thought passive resistance was 'our most natural and suitable weapon'. But he also believed the boycott campaign might enable India to avoid 'the Russian tragedy' of 1905. See Haridas Mukherjee and Uma Mukherjee, *'Bande Mataram' and Indian Nationalism (1906–1908)*, Firma K. L. Mukhopadhyay, Calcutta, 1957.

manded by the people. This attitude is summed up in one word, Boycott.[22]

Such an approach may not seem to be relevant to a study of guerrilla warfare. Nevertheless it very much is relevant, since Aurobindo and the Extremist leaders were foreshadowing a vital component of contemporary revolutionary warfare: they were trying to establish what has come to be called 'parallel hierarchies' or parallel government. The boycott being advocated was not simply an economic boycott of British goods, though that was regarded as an important aspect of the campaign because the Extremists saw the British Raj as primarily an instrument of economic exploitation. It was also to be a boycott of the government Western-orientated educational system, the judicial system and the administration itself. Aurobindo argued that 'We must always remember ... that alien despotism in this country depends helplessly on the co-operation of our own people. Let that co-operation be withdrawn and bureaucratic absolutism tumbles in like a pack of cards.'[23]

The attempt was being made to polarize the political situation by withdrawing very large numbers of the population from the political society created by the British overlords and to establish parallel educational, judicial and economic modes of ordering affairs, or, as Tilak once picturesquely described the process, to take India outside the Penal Code. Large numbers of people were to be 'mobilized' against the Raj in two ways: through an appeal to certain cult strands in Hinduism and through the political exploitation of specific grievances. It was to be a phased, protracted form of political warfare. For example, though Aurobindo argued, like a modern Western 'protestor', that 'to break an unjust coercive law is not only justifiable but, under given circumstances, a duty', he insisted that a refusal to pay taxes must not be adopted since this would be in the nature of an ultimatum to the government and the movement was not strong enough for that kind of confrontation.

Aurobindo also believed, like a modern revolutionary warfare

22. ibid., pp. 23–4.

23. ibid., p. 43.

practitioner, that government repression of the campaign would itself significantly contribute to the strength of the nationalists: '... there will soon be only two parties in the country, the people with their persecuted leaders [*versus*] the bureaucrats with their thirty thousand civil servants and seventy thousand soldiers and we almost forgot the handful of signatories to the loyalist manifesto'.[24]

However, though Aurobindo thought he descried one important sign of success – the inability of officialdom to collect evidence against those brought up for trial for boycott offences – the British were able to beat this campaign. Some of the reasons were peculiar to Indian society and the political options of the day: the extraordinary lack of homogeneity in a Hindu caste society existing side by side with a very large Muslim minority and the British capacity to devise political reforms designed to enhance the standing of the constitutionalist Moderates.

The Indian Government was also able to introduce measures of repression, forbidding 'seditious meetings', providing speedy trial without jury, and curbing the press through threat of confiscation of printing-presses; and despite what Aurobindo thought he descried, the immeasurable majority of Indians believed in the permanency of the Raj and so, even if there was difficulty in getting witnesses in some cases, the sources of secret intelligence never dried up. This was of central importance to this kind of government when faced by fairly widespread political subversion, just as it is of central importance in Vietnam today; and this not simply as a test of administrative efficacy but as a gauge of the confidence the people at large have in the permanency of the regime.[25]

24. ibid., p. 44.

25. It was not until after the Second World War that the British Intelligence apparatus found its sources drying up because 'the impending demise of the British raj made everyone uncertain who would be his next master' (H. V. Hodson, *The Great Divide*, Hutchinson, 1969, p. 185). The bulk of such Intelligence is of course gathered by a properly functioning police force disposing of a good Special Branch.

On the other hand, the activities of revolutionary terrorists in preventing people giving evidence in time led to the introduction of those forms of

It must be emphasized that the Extremists' passive resistance campaign in the latter half of the first decade of the twentieth century is being touched upon here only in order to bring out certain facets relevant to an understanding of modern revolutionary warfare. The Extremists did see the necessity to 'change the rules' of what today would be called liberation struggle; they did understand the necessity of mobilizing large numbers through appeals intelligible to them, though their chief successes in this regard seem to have been with the young;[26] and they did express that great resentment against the West that was to be so important in the revolt of Asia.

But though Aurobindo understood the necessity of organizing the national will 'in a strong central authority ... a popular Gevernment in fact though not in name', such an organization was never fashioned and the Extremist movement soon began to subside with the sentencing to transportation of Tilak and others, and the turning away to the contemplative life by Aurobindo himself. Even when the All-India National Congress itself was taken over by activists, albeit under Gandhi's very special kind of leadership, the organizational problem never really was solved in terms of 'liberation struggle': the British and their allies and the nationalists were both described with some justice as 'ramshackle coalitions'.[27]

---

detention and internment which have recently been introduced in Northern Ireland. It is less often noticed that the Indian Government in recent years has felt impelled to bring these imperial devices to bear against the new brand of (Maoist) revolutionary terrorists, the Naxalites.

26. This is brought out beautifully in N. C. Chaudhuri, *The Autobiography of an Unknown Indian*, Macmillan, London, 1951. The author relates how at that time, as a very young boy, he 'judged all political action by the criterion of insurrection' whereas his mother, having carefully packed away the family's western clothing, performed her only boycott gesture by breaking an English-made jug. The zeal of youth was so great as to enable them to reject presents of sweets made with foreign sugar (*Source Material for a History of the Freedom Movement in India*, Bombay Government Records, Vol. II, 1958, pp. 616–17).

27. Anil Seal, *The Emergence of Indian Nationalism*, op. cit., Ch. I, p. 250. But Seal also remarks importantly: 'It seems bizarre that the largest exemplar of struggle against colonial rule should have been fought with such limited

Nevertheless the ideas of the Indian Extremists in the early twentieth century are of significance in foreshadowing some of the techniques of contemporary revolutionary warfare; and also as an example of a variegated revolt against the West that was beginning to develop in much of Asia at that time. Though they were very modern in some of their political techniques, their ideological attempt to draw upon certain combative aspects of cult Hinduism were scarcely more successful in the event than the attempt of the so-called Boxers in China at the turn of the century to advance 'the I-ho magic boxing so as to protect our country, expel the foreign bandits and kill Christian converts ...'[28]

And yet they were adumbrating modes of resistance predicated upon a belief in the corrupting and humiliating effect of Western capitalist dominance and also predicated upon a belief in the necessity of combative self-reliance of a kind appropriate to local conditions. At the same time they were beginning to assert a belief in Asian unity against the West and they were concerned to demonstrate the role of force in relations between 'the East' and the West. Even before the victory of Japan over Russia in 1905 displayed in most dramatic fashion the viability of the most modern military technology in the hands of an Asian power, Tilak had written in the following manner:

> To win big battles a well-trained army is needed, but for guerrilla warfare only a gun is needed. There is no need for a trained army. This is proved by the Afridis and the Boers. Our readers will understand why the Afridis [on the north-west frontier of India] say that

---

liability. But there is a certain justice about this. If imperialism and nationalism have striven so tepidly against each other [in India], part of the reason is that the aims for which they have worked have had so much in common' (p. 351).

28. Quoted in Ssu-yu Teng and John K. Fairbank, *China's Response to the West: A Documentary Survey 1839–1923*, Atheneum, New York, 1965, p. 190. This uprising, made in the name of superstitious beliefs and aided by conservative Chinese officials, directed against everything Western, from Christian missions to foreign legations, did involve considerable cutting of railway and telegraph lines but by way of destructive protest rather than as part of what could usefully be called a guerrilla warfare campaign.

the British Empire in India is the reward given by Allah sitting in the barrel of a gun. Unless we understand the true nature of where the power of the British lies, and where they have hidden the small bottle of nectar which they possess, our readers will not understand the secret of the success which the Boers achieved with the help of guerrilla warfare.[29]

It is only now, nearly seventy years after Tilak wrote those words, that Maoist Communists (known as Naxalites) are beginning to mount peasant-based guerrilla warfare campaigns on a fairly wide scale in India. Apart from the unique problems posed by the caste stratification of the Indian social 'terrain', there was at that time a lack of arms and organization (and an absence, except on the part of the terrorists, of serious attempts to subvert the armed services); an inability or perhaps an unwillingness to mobilize the poor peasantry[30]; and a decision not to opt for guerrilla tactics, for good reasons – not the least of which was an awareness of the thoroughness of the British pacification of the sub-continent.

It required the mutiny of a significant part of an army in conditions of administrative breakdown in a country that was never pacified by the West before there could be mounted a Communist guerrilla campaign of truly great importance. But this campaign in China was organized by a Communist party forced by circumstances to rely upon a peasant rather than a

29. Quoted in Stanley A. Wolpert, *Tilak and Gokhale: Revolution and Reform in the Making of Modern India*, University of California Press, 1962, p. 150. If Tilak may take credit for adumbrating the now famous slogan 'Power grows out of the barrel of a gun', Aurobindo in 1907 must take credit for Mao's almost equally famous simile of the 'prairie fire'. See Haridas Mukherjee and Uma Mukherjee, *Sri Aurobindo and the New Thought in Indian Politics*, Firma K. L. Mukhopadhyay, Calcutta, 1964, pp. 201–3.

30. Even in the case of Mahatma Gandhi's much larger passive resistance movement, as most of his political adherents understood it to be, it was intended to bring the peasantry into play only at the end of a carefully phased campaign and only in the sense of refusing to pay land-tax, an act of civil disobedience not of revolution. This was not only because Gandhi disavowed the class-war (or war of any kind) and was afraid of mass peasant participation quickly devolving into violence, but in order to preserve the *unity* of the passive resistance movement which it had no means at its disposal of *enforcing*.

proletarian base; it was also mounted in a country that had a history unique in the scope and incidence of peasant revolts.

In order to understand the origins of this greatest of all guerrilla wars it is necessary first to examine Lenin's plans for the East in the wake of revolutionary failure in Europe outside Russia. But it should be noticed that even towards the end of the first decade of the twentieth century Lenin thought he had descried a chain of events in Asia that had been started by the Russian revolt of 1905.

> In Eastern Europe and in Asia the period of bourgeois-democratic revolutions began only in 1905. The revolutions in Russia, Persia, Turkey and China, the wars in the Balkans – such is the chain of world events of *our* period in our 'Orient'. And only the blind can fail to see in this chain of events the awakening of a *whole series* of bourgeois-democratic national movements, striving to create nationally independent and nationally uniform states.[31]

Lenin was concerned to emphasize the 'Asian' qualities of Russia and the vast masses of mankind living in Asia again and again from that time onwards.

Asia was also seen as an area of exploitation whose natural resources, according to his version of imperialism, were vital for the development of the capitalist West (as well as providing the means whereby the Western capitalists could neutralize the revolutionary zeal of their workers). As early as 1908 Lenin had argued that,

> In India ... the proletariat has already developed to conscious political mass struggle [referring to demonstrations against Tilak's gaol sentence] and, that being the case, the Russian-style British regime in India is doomed! By this colonial plunder of Asian countries, the Europeans have succeeded in steeling one of them, Japan, for momentous military victories which ensured her independent national development. There should be no doubt that the age-old British system of plunder in India, and the present struggle of these 'progressive' Europeans against Persian and Indian democracy, will *steel* millions upon hundreds of millions of proletarians throughout Asia, for a just struggle against their oppressors, that will be just as

31. (1908). *National Liberation Movement in the East*, op. cit., p. 60.

victorious as that of the Japanese. The class-conscious European worker already has comrades in Asia, and their number will grow with every passing day and hour ... these old Chinese revolts are bound to develop into a conscious democratic movement.[32]

By 1920 comrades in Asia were regarded as urgently necessary in what was to be a strategy of indirect approach against the capitalist West, and Chinese comrades appeared to be in the most promising condition for the task at this time. The question debated at the Second Congress of the Communist International in July 1920 was the nature of revolutionary strategy in Asia. Was it to be support for the 'bourgeois-democratic' nationalists or a mobilizing of the vast peasant masses by Communist parties?

The Indian M. N. Roy argued that the masses were not interested in nationalism: 'These tens of millions of people [particularly landless peasants] have no interest whatsoever in bourgeois-nationalist slogans; only one slogan – "land to the tillers" – can interest them.'[33] The point Roy was concerned to make was that though elements existed in India for the creation of a powerful Communist party, the revolutionary movement was quite a different thing from the 'national-liberation' [nationalist] movement.

The result of the debate was a kind of compromise between this view and the view favouring all-out support for the bourgeois-nationalist movement: '... the Communist International must enter into *temporary arrangements, even alliances*, with the bourgeois democrats in the colonies and backward countries, but should not merge with them and should maintain at all costs

32. ibid., p. 15. Lukács was surely right in arguing that 'Lenin's theory of imperialism, unlike Rosa Luxemburg's, is less a theory of its necessary [*sic*] economic generation and limitations than the theory of the concrete class forces which, unleashed by imperialism, are at work within it: *the theory of the concrete world situation created by imperialism*' (Lukács, op. cit., p. 43). Put otherwise, a call to political action rather than an economic analysis; politically 'necessary' propaganda occasioned by the Bolshevik failure amongst Western Social Democrats.

33. Hélène Carrère D'Encausse and Stuart R. Schram, *Marxism and Asia*, Allen Lane The Penguin Press, 1969, p. 151.

the independence of the proletarian movement even in its most embryonic form.'[34] The form of such alliances was to be determined by the degree of development attained by Communist parties among the proletariat or among what was termed the 'revolutionary liberation movement'.

This was not simply a debate about tactics in a given situation; involved in it from the beginning was the attitude of Communist parties to the peasantry as such. Though Lenin believed that the final outcome of the world struggle was determined in advance 'by the fact that Russia, India, China, etc., account for the overwhelming population of the globe' and though this overwhelming majority was composed overwhelmingly of 'peasants' of one kind and another, Lenin's party was profoundly suspicious of the ultimate aims of peasants in a revolutionary situation. They were not, in the Bolshevik view, basically revolutionary, since their attachment to, or desire for, land even on a small scale deprived them of that 'rootless' quality the proletarian was presumed to have and which was deemed necessary for true revolutionary endeavours, that is, the complete destruction of the old order of society.

Thus by as early as 1905 Lenin had taken great pains to formulate a clear strategy towards the peasantry:

> We must help the peasant uprising in every way, up to and including confiscation of the land, *but certainly not including all sorts of petty-bourgeois schemes*. We support the peasant movement to the extent that it is revolutionary-democratic. We are making ready (doing so now, at once) to fight it when, and to the extent that, it becomes reactionary and anti-proletarian. The essence of Marxism lies in that double task . . .
>
> At first we support the peasantry *en masse* against the landlords, support it to the hilt and with all means, including confiscation, and then (it would be better to say, at the same time) we support the proletariat against the peasantry *en masse* . . . Without falling into adventurism or going against our conscience in matters of science, without striving for cheap popularity we can and do assert *only one thing*: we shall bend every effort to help the entire peasantry to achieve the democratic revolution, *in order thereby to make it easier*

34. ibid., p. 154.

*for us*, the party of the proletariat, to pass on as quickly as possible to the new and higher task – the socialist revolution.[35]

The art of mobilizing the peasantry for Communist parties was thus to involve the perpetration of a vast confidence trick on the peasantry: before the Communist victory, 'land to the tiller' was to be the recruiting slogan; after victory the peasantry was to be politically emasculated by the collectivization of agriculture and its subordination to the more rootless, and hence more revolutionary, urban proletariat whose consciousness the Communist Party claimed to represent in vanguard form.

Another point Lenin made in that article should be noticed since it was tactically important in getting the Chinese Communist guerrilla movement under way. Lenin argued that

> Wherever possible we shall strive to set up *our* committees, committees of the *Social-Democratic Labour* [Communist] *Party*. They will consist of peasants, paupers, intellectuals, prostitutes (a worker recently asked us in a letter why not carry on agitation among the prostitutes), soldiers, teachers, workers ... We are in favour of a peasant uprising. We are absolutely opposed to the mixing and merging of heterogeneous parties. We hold that for the purpose of insurrection Social-Democracy should give all impetus to *all* revolutionary democracy, should help it *all* to organize, should *march shoulder to shoulder* with it, but without merging with it.[36]

Since a nationalist movement was very much in evidence, and was embodied in the Kuomintang party, the Communist task in China at the beginning of the twenties was seen as that of infiltrating, influencing and ultimately controlling this movement. Guerrilla warfare in China was to arise out of the failure of this tactic. As Lenin had said, the movement was not bound to 'any one particular form of struggle'.

What was so important were the vast numbers of human beings living in the East. Shortly before he was finally incapacitated by a paralytic stroke, he wrote:

35. V. I. Lenin, *Alliance of the Working Class and the Peasantry*, Progress Publishers, Moscow, 1965, pp. 111–12.

36. ibid., pp. 112–13.

> I think . . . that the outcome of the struggle as a whole can be forecast only because in the long run capitalism itself is educating and training the vast majority of the population of the world for the struggle.
>
> In the last analysis, the outcome of the struggle will be determined by the fact that Russia, India, China, etc., account for the overwhelming majority of the population of the globe. And it is this majority that, during the past few years, has been drawn into the struggle for emancipation with extraordinary rapidity, so that in this respect there cannot be the slightest doubt what the final outcome of the world struggle will be. In this sense, the complete victory of socialism is fully and absolutely assured.[37]

Forty years later the Communist Party of China, arguing from its own experience of twenty years' guerrilla struggle, was to express its agreement with Lenin's thesis while insisting that in the undeveloped world the Communist parties *were* tied to one form of struggle: revolutionary guerrilla warfare or people's war.

37. (March 1923), ibid., p. 377.

# CHAPTER 3

# CHINA

> Day and night the anti-Communist elements dream of our party having the same numerous branches and sects as theirs ... they do not understand that our party is united, is based on belief in Communism and class consciousness and revolutionary training . . . It differs entirely from the Kuomintang, which allows sects and branches to exist and is not unified at all.
>
> CHOU EN-LAI, 1943

> Apart from armed struggle, apart from guerrilla warfare, it is impossible to understand our political line and, consequently, to understand our Party-building ... Without armed struggle, without guerrilla warfare, there would not have been such a Communist Party as exists today. Comrades throughout the Party must never forget this experience gained at the cost of blood.
>
> MAO TSE-TUNG, 1939

THOUGH China had a history of peasant revolts that was unique in terms of scope, intensity and frequency, nothing was further from the mind of the Moscow-controlled Comintern in the early 1920s than an attempt to engender guerrilla warfare.[1] The young bourgeois nationalist movement of Sun Yat-sen, the cities, and the urban proletariat were the Comintern hopes for the future. If the background factors are considered, this view becomes quite intelligible.

Before the end of the first half of the nineteenth century 'the irresistible power of the new manufacturing interests of Britain' had begun a series of imposed and unequal treaties which had opened up China to the industrialized West. 'Against those who came equipped with steam-power and Adam Smith the discipline of Confucius was of little avail.'[2] One facet of this steam-power

1. See James P. Harrison, *The Chinese Communists and Chinese Peasant Rebellions*, Gollancz, 1970.

2. Michael Greenberg, *British Trade and the Opening of China 1800–42*, Cambridge University Press, 1951, p. 215.

was the gunboat, which became one of the symbols as well as instruments of overwhelming Western power and the humiliating international relations it imposed. As late as 1925 British warships were sent nine hundred miles up the Yangtze River to punish by gunfire an open city whose inhabitants had boycotted British goods and demonstrated against the British presence.[3]

The xenophobia evoked by the behaviour of those who had turned China into a 'semi-colony' appears to have been much more intense and widespread in China than anywhere else in those great areas of the globe subjugated or otherwise subdued by the West in the nineteenth century. This was probably as much the result of the nature of the humiliating relationship as of the peculiar pride of one of the world's greatest people. As an English historian once remarked, 'It was nihilist exploitation by "old China hands" and not direct rule by "Indian Civilians" which evoked a Soviet substitute.'[4]

Certainly the Kuomintang nationalist movement was centrally informed by a nationalism directed against the local effects of this 'semi-colonial' status. Thus the Moscow government, by tearing up the Tsarist-imposed unequal treaties with China, was in a position quickly to establish a special relationship with the Kuomintang of the kind hammered out in the Comintern discussions about the appropriate policy for the 'peoples of the East'.[5]

Sun Yat-sen wanted an army with modern equipment which could reunify a country dominated for the most part by warlords exploiting the administrative breakdown that had followed the collapse of Imperial China in 1911. The Moscow government and the Comintern wanted a bourgeois nationalist movement which they could influence against the Western capitalists

3. F. L. K. Hsu, *Americans and Chinese*, Cresset Press, 1955, p. 394.

4. Michal Vyvyan, *The Twentieth Century*, February 1951, p. 134. But see also John K. Fairbank, in John K. Fairbank (ed.), *Chinese Thought and Institutions*, University of Chicago Press, 1957, pp. 204–31.

5. Though, even then, the Chinese Eastern Railway was to be discussed at a later date. See Conrad Brandt, Benjamin Schwartz and John K. Fairbank, *A Documentary History of Chinese Communism*, Allen & Unwin, 1952, p. 70.

and perhaps, in the course of time, infiltrate and refashion according to revolutionary requirements.

Sun was strong on Han nationalism and the necessity for a period of élitist tutelage designed to create the conditions for democracy, but he was vague about aims in the field of social reform. He was committed to a military solution to the problem of China's weakness, but he had not created the kind of organization necessary for the task. Michael Borodin, a Russian agent, was set the task of reorganizing the Kuomintang politically; a Russian general undertook the military task.[6]

The Kuomintang was solemnly declared by the Comintern to be an organization representing all nationalist classes and it persuaded the small Chinese Communist Party to accept, though not without demur, this thesis. Chinese Communists were to enter the Kuomintang as individuals. The accord between the Moscow government and the Comintern, on the one hand, and the Kuomintang on the other, was predicated quite explicitly on the understanding that 'it is not possible to carry out either Communism or even the Soviet system in China'.[7]

This understanding did not prevent the Chinese Communists attempting to enlist students (who in 1919 had come to the fore in the politics of protest against Japanese aggrandizement during the First World War) or in fomenting strikes, for example on the Peking–Hankow railway early in 1923, the ruthless suppression of which helped validate the Comintern thesis of working through the Kuomintang. Such strikes, combined with boycott of foreign goods, resulting in the shooting of Chinese by foreign arms, was a feature of Communist activity in 1925 in Shanghai, Hongkong and Canton, though it was undertaken sometimes against Comintern advice.

But what was crucial at this time was the political conduct of the Kuomintang armed forces, and in particular the attitude of

6. 'Americans too often forget that, from that day to this, the Kuomintang and the Chinese Communist Party have both been proponents of "democratic centralism" in the Leninist pattern' (ibid., p. 18). That it was not quite so simple as that will be shown.

7. ibid., p. 70.

Chiang Kai-shek, who had been trained in the Soviet Union and had commanded the Whampoa Military Academy of which the political commissar was Chou En-lai. For a number of very different reasons, among them faction struggles within the Kuomintang and the conduct of Soviet advisers towards him, Chiang Kai-shek began to feel impelled to curb the Communists and then to put paid to them. This he believed he had done in 1927, in Shanghai in particular.[8]

The catastrophe for the Chinese Communist Party that issued out of this period, sometimes known as that of the First United Front (1923–7), is germane to this study for three reasons. First, because it exemplifies Lenin's dictum that the Party is not confined to one form of struggle (though the proletariat is the vanguard of that struggle). Secondly, because it shows again a case of guerrilla warfare being adopted as a result of the *failure* of other tactics. The latter point is of great significance in view of Chairman Mao's latter-day insistence that revolutionary guerrilla warfare is *the* form of revolutionary struggle for what is nowadays called the Third World. He did not realize this at the time. Thirdly, since the catastrophe arose directly out of Russian Communist theses on tactics, which in turn arose partly out of the struggle for leadership between Stalin and Trotsky, it could be (though it certainly was not for many years) attributed to foreigners, however theoretically comradely.

The desperate cleaving to the United Front line during this period, and its results for the Chinese Communist Party, were doubtless caricatured – but not all that much – by the translator of Trotsky's account in his introduction:

> The Chinese Communist Party was driven into the bourgeois Kuo Min Tang with the Stalinist whip, and there it was compelled to swear allegiance to the petty bourgeois philosophy of Sun Yat Senism. The policy of the class struggle was liquidated in the interests of the 'united national front'. Strikes were prohibited or else

8. See Franklin W. Houn, *A Short History of Chinese Communism*, Prentice-Hall, Englewood Cliffs, N.J., 1967, pp. 25–32. See also Sir John Pratt, *War and Politics in China*, Cape, 1943, pp. 260–61, on the evidence of Communist machinations used by Chiang Kai-shek for his moves in 1927.

settled by 'arbitration commissions' in the best class collaborationist style ... So as not to irritate the bourgeoisie, Stalin sent telegrams to restrain the peasants from taking the land ... the Chinese Communists were prohibited from forming Soviets ... Even though the caliber of the man was known – he had already attempted a reactionary *coup d'état* in 1926 – a veritable cult was built up for Chiang Kai-Shek by the International Communist Press ... on the eve of Chiang Kai-shek's march into Shanghai to establish the counter-revolutionary regime and to massacre the militant workers, the French Communist Party and its central organ, *L'Humanité*, sent him a solemn message of greetings, hailing the establishment of the Shanghai ... Commune.[9]

Chiang Kai-shek appeared at this time not only to have fatally maimed the Communists but to be about to destroy warlordism and re-unify China along Kuomintang lines. The lines were perhaps chiefly lines of communications, roads and postal system rather than railways, which had been built already as part of the Western capitalist opening up of China. But as well as this there was an important currency reform; and the sort of accommodation with capitalist entrepreneurship that in other circumstances might have benefited China. Land reform was not brought about, partly because some of the Kuomintang experts believed that the population : land ratio was so disadvantageous as to make reform in terms of re-distribution a silly idea: it would not make sense further to subdivide rural holdings. Irrigation projects, designed to enhance productivity, were undertaken.

As Mr McAleavy has remarked,

in spite of everything, during those years of the early and middle 1930s, down to 1937, much was accomplished by the National Government. It was in effective control only of the Lower Yangtze

9. Max Shachtman, Introduction to Leon Trotsky, *Problems of the Chinese Revolution*, Paragon Book Gallery, New York, 1962, p. 11. In view of what was to come, it is of interest to notice that in 1928 Trotsky wrote, '... the imaginary hundred thousand members who figured on paper in the Chinese Communist Party only represent a gross self-deception. This would constitute one-sixth of the total membership of the [Communist Parties] of all the capitalist countries' (ibid., p. 231).

Valley, but although today Nationalist China has become a synonym for corruption and ineptitude, to foreign observers at the time it was a truism that the provinces ruled by Nanking [the seat of Kuomintang government] were the heart of an emerging, modern state which was attracting the loyalty of more and more Chinese.[10]

But to return to the year 1927: in that year the former assistant librarian at Peking University, Mao Tse-tung, a foundation member of the Chinese Communist Party, was sent to his home province, Hunan, to take charge of what has become known as the Autumn Harvest Insurrection. Now it has been said of Mao that his 'chief claim to greatness does not lie in his originality or in his capacity for minute analysis. It lies rather in the directness of his observation and thinking and the pertinence of his conclusions to the realities confronting him.'[11] What Mao saw in Hunan, while 'learning from the masses' according to Lenin's injunction, was the poor peasantry as the revolutionary vanguard class of the Chinese revolution.

In his now famous report on the peasant movement in Hunan of February 1927 Mao predicted that,

> Within a short time, hundreds of millions of peasants will rise in Central, South, and North China, with the fury of a hurricane; no power, however strong, can restrain them. They will break all the shackles that bind them and rush towards the road of liberation. *All imperialists, warlords, corrupt officials, and bad gentry will meet their doom at the hands of the peasants.* All revolutionary parties and comrades will be judged by them. *Are we to get in in front of them and lead them or criticize them behind their backs or fight them from the opposite camp?*[12]

However, despite the heady language about peasant spontaneity, the peasant's perfect eye for what was good and bad in rural society, the lack of a 'dinner-party' quality in peasant revolution, and the necessity for every village to be put in a

10. Henry McAleavy, *The Modern History of China*, Weidenfeld & Nicolson, 1967, p. 267.

11. P. C. Kuo, quoted in Guy Wint, *Communist China's Crusade*, Praeger, New York, 1965, p. 31.

12. Brandt, Schwartz and Fairbank, op. cit., p. 80.

'state of terror for a brief time', the task of the Communist Party was really much less simple than merely taking over an apparent tidal wave of spontaneous peasant unrest. The Autumn Harvest rising was not in fact the beginning of a chain-reaction against wretchedness and oppression. What Mao had really done was to point to a new area of political exploitation at the very time the Kuomintang was making the Communist Party's position in the cities intolerable. When this situation became abundantly clear, the Chinese Communist Party came to accept Mao's thesis.

After an abortive attempt to capture the provincial capital, Mao and his followers retreated to the Chingkangshan mountain region, where they were joined by Chu Te's mutinous military detachment that had failed in an attempt to establish power in Nanchang. The Red Army in embryo now existed, though in a situation of precarious isolation. It was built up initially from deserters, peasant militiamen, prisoners-of-war, workers and peasants from the border areas. But it was remarked in 1928 that 'Few of the peasants in the border areas are willing to serve as soldiers. Since the land has been divided up, they have all gone to till it. Now the soldiers of peasant or working-class origin in the Fourth Army in the border area constitute an extreme minority. Thus the position is still serious.'[13]

The bulk of the force at this time was composed of what were called '*éléments déclassés*', men from the mercenary armies, good enough as fighters but badly in need of political indoctrination. They received very little pay indeed: 'The common saying of the soldiers, "Overthrow the capitalists, and eat pumpkin every day", expresses their misery ...'[14] As a result of this situation there came into being in the Chinese Red Army what appears to have been an emphasis on indoctrination unique in its intensity. But it would be a mistake to see this simply in terms of propaganda and manipulation of men's minds. Mao's words on what he called 'democracy in the army' at this time repay attention:

13. Quoted in Stuart R. Schram, *The Political Thought of Mao Tse-tung*, Praeger, New York, 1963, p. 196.

14. ibid., p. 197.

Apart from the role played by the Party, the reason why the Red Army can sustain itself without collapse in spite of such a poor standard of material life and such incessant engagements is its practice of democracy. The officers do not beat the men; officers and men receive equal treatment; soldiers enjoy freedom of speech; cumbersome formalities and ceremonies are done away with; and the account books are open to the inspection of all. The soldiers handle the messing arrangements and, out of the daily five cents for oil, salt, firewood and vegetables, can even save a little sum for pocket money (called 'Mess savings') . . . for each person every day. All these measures are very satisfactory to the soldiers. The newly captured soldiers in particular feel that our army and the Kuomintang army are worlds apart. They feel that, though in material life they are worse off . . ., spiritually they are liberated. The fact that the same soldier who was not brave in the enemy army yesterday becomes very brave in the Red Army today shows precisely the impact of democracy. The Red Army is like a furnace in which all captured soldiers are melted down and transformed the moment they come over.[15]

Nevertheless political indoctrination was regarded by Mao as being of central importance. Noting that the Party had failed to get a hold on the soldiers of the Kuomintang army during the first united front period because there was only one Party branch to a regiment, in 1928 he had the Party organized on a company basis and one Party member to every four men.[16] Far from being preoccupied with a guerrilla struggle carried on by small units, Mao was concerned to build up a regular Red Army, its battalions having a machine-gun and a trench-mortar company along with the rifle companies. Though he was aware even at this time of the importance of securing base areas and making use of the 'strategic advantages of the mountains', he was also emphasizing the fact that 'In our experience, the dispersion of forces has almost always led to defeat . . .'[17]

15. *Selected Works*, Lawrence & Wishart, 1955, Vol. I, pp. 82–3.

16. ibid., p. 83.

17. ibid., p. 85. Since the view that what was primarily in train at this time was a spontaneous peasant revolt is still quite widely held, it is perhaps desirable to quote Mao on the role of the Red Army yet further: '. . . the existence of a regular Red Army of adequate strength is a necessary condition for the

Certainly, this army was to be an instrument of revolution, the chief instrument in fact, since the tidal wave of spontaneous peasant revolution which he thought he had descried early in 1927 was by 1928 'subsiding in the country as a whole'; 'Wherever the Red Army goes, it finds the masses cold and reserved; only after propaganda and agitation do they slowly rouse themselves.'[18] What was involved in the future of the Communist Party was not at all a persistent spontaneous upsurge of the poor peasantry but a complex struggle for influence over a peasant society, which differed from area to area, and whose loyalties fluctuated according to the surge and ebb of a military struggle between the Red and Kuomintang armies. When the 'tide of counter-revolution' was rising, Mao frankly admitted, then the intermediate class in the countryside clung to the 'landed gentry' and the poor peasant vanguard became an isolated force. Indeed at the end of 1928 Mao was writing: 'We have an acute sense of loneliness and are every moment longing for the end of such a lonely life. To turn the revolution into a seething, surging tide all over the country, it is necessary to launch a political and economic struggle for democracy involving also the urban petty bourgeoisie.'[19]

Hence the crucial role of the Red Army:

> To regard the task of the Red Army as similar to that of the White Army – merely fighting [is an error] . . . the Chinese Red Army is an armed force for carrying out the political tasks of the revolution . . . besides fighting to destroy the enemy's military strength, it should also shoulder such important tasks as agitating the masses, organizing them, arming them, and helping them to set up political power, and even establishing organizations of the Communist Party. When the Red Army fights, it fights not merely for the sake of fighting . . .

---

existence of the Red political power . . . Unless we have regular armed forces of adequate strength, even though we have won the mass support of the workers and peasants, we certainly cannot create an independent regime, let alone an independent regime that lasts long and develops daily' (written in 1928, cited in Stuart R. Schram, *Mao Tse-tung: Basic Tactics*, Praeger, New York, 1966, p. 6).

18. *Selected Works*, Vol. I, op. cit., p. 99.

19. ibid., p. 99.

apart from such [political] objectives, fighting loses its meaning and the Red Army the reason for its existence.[20]

By the beginning of 1931 the Red Army numbered more than three hundred thousand men, only about a tenth of them belonging to Chu Te's army group, and the Party was administering a total area with perhaps fifty million inhabitants.[21] At the end of 1930 Chiang Kai-shek launched the first of a number of offensives designed to annihilate the Kiangsi Soviet, as the main Communist area officially became known on 7 November 1931. A good deal has sometimes been made of the failures of most of these Kuomintang 'encircle and exterminate' campaigns and of the losses sometimes sustained, for instance the destruction of three Kuomintang divisions and the loss of 10,000 rifles during the June 1932–March 1933 campaign. But the third campaign (July–September 1931), which was very threatening, was halted by the news of Japanese aggression in Manchuria; and by the time the last, and by far the largest, campaign was launched in October 1933 an answer to the Kiangsi Soviet and Communist mobile and guerrilla warfare had been fashioned by Chiang Kai-shek's German military advisers: the shrinking ring of blockhouses and barbed wire, allied with a stringent blockade, above all of salt, reminiscent of Kitchener's campaign against the Boers.

Though it has been argued that the all-out attempt to defend the Kiangsi Soviet was a move contrary to Mao's now famous dictum – 'The enemy advances, we retreat; the enemy halts, we harass; the enemy tires, we attack; the enemy retreats, we pursue' – two things are clear about this period: first, the masses were not in fact adequately mobilized despite the land reforms (of a much more moderate kind in the Kiangsi Soviet than in the earlier Hunan political operation) and secondly, Mao was wrong

20. ibid., p. 106. Written at the end of 1929.

21. McAleavy, op. cit., p. 284. Mao estimated that the maximum population controlled by the Soviet Central Government in 1934 was nine millions (Edgar Snow, *Red Star over China*, Grove Press, New York, 1961, p. 73 (first published 1938)). The higher figure refers also to areas where Red partisans were thought to be in control.

about the intensity of 'contradictions' he thought he saw developing critically in 1930 between sections of the upper strata in the non-Communist areas and between them and the masses.[22] He had hammered out of experience in this period a theory the essentials of which were the central role of the army, the importance of rural bases, and the necessity for protracted struggle; but by the middle of 1934 it was recognized that the Communist position in Kiangsi had become untenable and the Long March, an epic of human endurance, not a contribution to the history of guerrilla warfare, was the only alternative to destruction. What was to save the armed Communist Party of China was not its quality as an agrarian reform organization or its role as the harbinger of a new world but its efficacy as an organizational weapon and fighting machine in the conditions created by the invasion of China by the Japanese Army.

For some time before the heroic march to North Shensi was undertaken, the Communist Party had been calling for an end to the civil war and a united front of the Party and the Kuomintang against the Japanese threat. This call was reiterated after the Red Army, reduced to 20–30,000 men, had established itself in its new base area in the vicinity of Chinese regular armies a main part of which was composed of expelled Manchurians. Chiang Kai-shek persisted in pursuing what Professor C. P. Fitzgerald has called 'the will-o'-the-wisp of internal pacification'. But so long as the Communists persisted in trying to defend base areas, it seemed, after the experience of the last campaign in Kiangsi, a sensible policy. There were three chief reasons for Chiang Kai-shek's policy. First, he did not wish to provoke the Japanese army at a time when his German army advisers insisted that his own armies were not prepared for such a contest. Secondly, he believed that in the long run the Communists were to be the main threat to his regime. Thirdly, he

22. For Mao's examination of 'contradictions', both on the Chinese and international scenes, see his article, 'A Single Spark Can Start a Prairie Fire' (*Selected Works*, Vol. I, op. cit., especially pp. 118–21), written in 1930. On the failure of mobilization, see his exhortation of 1934 (*Selected Works*, Vol. I, pp. 147 ff.).

foresaw a Pacific contest in which the Americans would bring their enormous power to bear against Japan.

It must be remembered that Chiang had learnt about Communism at first hand, as chief of the nationalist Military Mission to Moscow and at the Whampoa Military Academy. As an American observer sympathetic to the Kuomintang once put it, Chiang 'learned everything that the Communists had to teach about irregular fighting, subversive propaganda, revolutionary situations, mass agitation ... The old war-lord armies were helpless in the face of [Chiang's] agents, agitators, poster crews, student strikes, press propaganda and indoctrinated troops.'[23]

Mao saw the nature of the struggle in terms some of which were very similar to Chiang's: 'a life-and-death struggle between revolution and counter-revolution ... the struggle for national salvation by the Chinese people against the partition schemes of the Japanese and other imperialists; and, finally, the struggle between the imperialists who are actively preparing for a Pacific war and an attack on the Soviet Union, and the toiling masses of China and the East ...'.[24] Mao's understanding of international potentialities was at this time inferior to Chiang's and as late as 1937 he underestimated the Japanese capacity to sustain major warfare very seriously indeed.[25]

However, the Chinese Communist Party clearly needed a respite from the Kuomintang 'extermination' campaigns, another of which was being planned in 1936. At the end of that year Generalissimo Chiang Kai-shek was held prisoner by the exiled Manchurian General, Chang Hsueh-liang, was visited by Chou En-lai in circumstances that remain slightly vague, and agreed to the terms imposed during this so-called 'Sian Incident'. The terms were amnesty for rebels, an armistice and peace pact with the Communists, a united front against the Japanese and Chiang's recognition as supreme commander and head of the Chinese government. The Communists abolished their claim to

23. Paul M. A. Linebarger, *Psychological Warfare*, Combat Forces Press, Washington, 1954, p. 75.

24. Brandt, Schwartz and Fairbank, op. cit., p. 227.

25. ibid., p. 250.

have a separate government, called the Red Army the Eighth Route Army, and suspended land confiscation and redistribution.

As a distinguished scholar of modern China, unsympathetic to the Kuomintang, has remarked, 'The Communists henceforth had a fascination for the Chinese educated class; could it really be that here was a party ready to sacrifice its own interests for the good of China? That may not be in fact, as will be shown, what the Communists were doing, but the appearance was very valuable to them and won them wide support.'[26] Undoubtedly quite large numbers of educated Chinese went to the Communist base at Yenan and were valuable later as cadres, but what was much more to the point so far as popular support is concerned was the nature of the Japanese invasion itself in the year 1937. As Professor C. P. Fitgerald has put it:

> The Japanese made all the mistakes which the most fervent Chinese patriot could have hoped for. They advanced far into the interior, only holding key cities and lines of communication. They sought to destroy the Chinese field armies, those of the Kuomintang, but neglected to search out and scotch the beginnings of guerrilla resistance. They continued to cherish the hope that the capture of this or that city would bring the capitulation of the Chinese Government. They permitted their troops to treat the population with great brutality and disgraced their army by the ferocious sack of Nanking, the wanton attacks on universities and other cultural institutions, and the slaughter of prisoners ... They could not have adopted policies more calculated to rouse the Chinese people to enduring opposition.[27]

On the other hand, as the writer of one of the most persuasive explanations of the following period in north China has put it, 'Possessing a valuable cadre of battle-tested and militarily competent veterans, as well as commitment to war as a mode of social change, the Communist Party was not only willing but eager to lead the Chinese *maquis*.'[28] Or as a very sympathetic

26. C. P. Fitzgerald, *Revolution in China*, Cresset Press, 1952, p. 76.
27. ibid., pp. 78–9.
28. Chalmers A. Johnson, *Peasant Nationalism and Communist Power*, Stanford University Press, 1962, p. 156.

observer of the Eighth Route Army said, '... the administrative bureaucracy collapsed. In the cities it was replaced by Japanese and puppets, but a kind of political vacuum existed in the hinterland towns and villages, the interstices between enemy garrisons. Into that temporary vacuum moved the former Red Army of China – with arms, with teachers, and with faith in the people's strength.'[29]

The conduct of a hated foreign occupation army created the conditions for mobilization of the peasantry; the Communist Party provided the kind of leadership, organization and agitational propaganda skills designed to exploit those conditions. Whereas the flower of the Kuomintang armies, having borne the brunt of the initial offensive and suffered appalling casualties, were withdrawn in order to keep in being the Kuomintang regime, reliance being placed on the vast spaces of China and an eventual American involvement, the Communists, secure in their base area, set about penetrating the enemy-occupied territories. They too intended to use the great spaces of China, but in order to mount a protracted 'people's war'; in doing this they managed to represent themselves over vast areas of northern China as *the* protagonist of Chinese nationalism and doubtless also as *the* government of China.[30]

Before attempting to examine what happened when this policy was implemented, it is desirable to consider further the lessons Mao had learned from the earlier struggle in Kiangsi, since it was on this experience that the fighting of the anti-Japanese War was in some important respects to be based. But it must always be remembered that Mao, though he believed there were laws of war, knew that it was essential always to examine the specific features of China's revolutionary war. He believed that

29. Snow, op. cit., p. 501.

30. Cf. Guy Wint, op. cit., pp. 43–4: '[The Communists] represented communism, not the Kuomintang, as the best custodian of the national interests. They spread the impression that the Kuomintang was fighting a phoney war against Japan, while the communists fought in hard earnest. Although in fact the communists fought very little, and when they did so, often fought not the Japanese but the Kuomintang, they used the war to build up communism as true nationalism.' The Japanese sources used by Chalmers Johnson say otherwise about Communist fighting.

the Red Army in Kiangsi had eventually been defeated because of its 'fear of losing territory'.[31] In Japanese-occupied north China there was no territory to be lost in that sense.

He also believed that in circumstances of strategic defensive, victory was basically dependent upon one thing: concentration of forces. What was necessary was not a war of attrition, particularly because of the Red Army's dependence in large part on captured weapons and because of the overall ratio of forces, but a war of annihilation. This was to be carried out through a highly mobile tactical concentration of forces in the ratio (according to the slogan) of 'ten against one'. In order to do this two organizational extremes had to be avoided: on the one hand, 'guerrillaism', the scattering of the armed forces in small bands, prevented the necessary concentration taking place; on the other hand, the slogan of his early opponents, 'every single gun must go to the Red Army', was also held to be incorrect, since this would prevent the development of people's war. '... an armed people and small-scale guerrilla war, on the one hand, and the Red Army as the main force, on the other, constituted the two arms of the same man. A Red Army as the main force without an armed people and small-scale guerrilla warfare would be a one-armed warrior ... the condition of people in the soviet area is a people under arms. This is also the main reason of the enemy's fear.'[32]

It was out of this concept of revolutionary warfare that there developed the famous slogan, attributed at various times to Mao, Chu Te and P'eng Te-huai, 'the people are water, the Eighth Route Army are fish; without water the fish will die'. The greatest attention had been given over a long period of time to the problem of how to get the people on-side. This had a negative and a positive aspect. First, there were laid down rules for the behaviour of the Red soldier towards the population:

1. Replace all doors when you leave the house;
2. Return and roll up the straw matting on which you sleep;

31. *Strategic Problems of China's Revolutionary War*, People's Publishing House, Bombay, 1951, p. 64.

32. ibid., p. 65.

3. Be courteous and polite to the people and help them when you can;
4. Return all borrowed articles;
5. Replace all damaged articles;
6. Be honest in all transactions with the peasants;
7. Pay for all articles purchased;
8. Be sanitary, and especially establish latrines at a safe distance from people's houses.[33]

The cadres of the Communist Party were required to be much more positively solicitous of the people's needs. As Mao put it in 1934:

As the revolutionary war is a war of the masses, we can carry out the war only by mobilizing the masses and relying on them . . . all problems facing the masses in their actual life should claim our attention . . . we [must] take a deep interest in the living conditions of the masses, from their land and labour to their fuel, rice, cooking oil and salt. The masses of women want to learn ploughing and hoeing? Whom can we get to teach them? Children want to go to school. Has any primary school been set up? The wooden bridge over there is too narrow and people may fall off. Should not repairs be made? Many people have boils or other complaints. What measures can we take? All such problems concerning the living conditions of the masses should be placed on our agenda. Discussions should be held, decisions reached, actions taken and results checked.[34]

This was undoubtedly the right attitude of mind towards the popular 'water', but what was chiefly required in north China from 1937 onwards was what a Communist general called 'organizing the hatred of the people towards the enemy into effective armed resistance'.[35] It was here that Japanese conduct was altogether crucial. A *Times* correspondent reported in November 1943 as follows:

The Japanese really lost their opportunity in 1937, when they could have obtained at least popular tolerance by enforcing behaviour towards the civilian population. It might almost be said that they

33. Snow, op. cit., p. 176.
34. *Selected Works*, Vol. I, op. cit., pp. 147, 149.
35. Quoted in Stuart Gelder, *The Chinese Communists*, Gollancz, 1944, p. 73.

could have conquered North China by shooting a few hundred of their own officers . . .

In the central Hopei campaign, shortly after my village was occupied, all the people were compelled to attend a meeting at which speeches were made saying that the Japanese are only fighting the Communists and wish to help the people. However, at the end of such a meeting the Japanese usually took several hundred people and tortured them to find out where the Chinese supplies or Government workers were hidden.

There were also continual demands for money and supplies. Many villages reported that the first few weeks of Japanese occupation had cost them four or five times as much as a year's taxes under Chinese control.[36]

The singling out by the Japanese of the Communists as their chief enemies was in itself of great propaganda benefit to the Party. But this could only be exploited by their presence in the dislocated and leaderless rural society. The alliance between the Communists and the peasants was doubtless forged without great difficulty in the context of Japanese oppression and outrage. But the Japanese did not persist in relying only upon this kind of pacification; they established in March 1940 a puppet regime in Nanking, headed by a very notable and powerful defector from the Kuomintang, Wang Ching-wei. Their regime was also called Kuomintang, the Communists again reaping the propaganda benefits.[37]

The major cities and towns secured, there then commenced a competition in government in the countryside between the adherents to the puppet regime and the Communist-organized peasantry. The Peace Preservation Committees were assailed by the guerrilla self-defence units, the latter being 'motivated' by propaganda couched solely in terms of nationalist outrage, in no way politically revolutionary. The revolution was to come later and the armed, militarized and politicized society created out of the nationalist mobilization was to be the instrument, under the

36. Quoted in O. M. Green, *The Story of China's Revolution*, Hutchinson, 1945.

37. McAleavy (op. cit., p. 305) describes Wang's defection 'as having inflicted a mortal wound upon Nationalist China . . .'

Communist Party, of that revolution ... so far as China as a whole was concerned.

What was crucial for the Communist Party during the war years so far as the long-term future was concerned were two things: the building up of a very powerful Red Army and the insertion into as wide a rural area as possible of a parallel administration. The first aim required the retention of the Yenan base area; the second aim required both the politico-military mobilizing of the masses and the destruction of the puppet administration. This is set out very clearly in an extract from a Communist Party training manual:

> The enemy has adopted a policy of living off the land in the areas that he has occupied and, by means of traitor and puppet organizations, of utilizing our manpower, financial strength, and resources to satisfy his military means. Therefore, by mobilizing the broad masses and strengthening our internal unity, we must break this link with the enemy, and blockade him. By exterminating spies and traitors and by destroying all puppet organizations, we must isolate the enemy politically and blockade him economically and militarily. The result will be that the enemy cannot exploit a single tree or blade of grass that belongs to us.[38]

Despite its rather grandiose tone, that passage states just about as well as it can be stated what revolutionary guerrilla warfare – and its countering – is really about: breaking 'the link' between the target administration and the people at large. Now though Mr Chalmers Johnson rightly warns against elevating organization, 'the party structure, communes, the cult of Mao, brainwashing, and so forth', to the level of a 'sociological secret weapon',[39] the author has earlier attempted to show that Leninist parties are peculiarly well equipped to mobilize large numbers of people for disguised purposes in situations of acute social dislocation and administrative breakdown.

It was not, of course, simply a matter of organization; the organizers, the cadres, upon whom everything depended according to Mao, were possessed by a pseudo-religious faith that in

38. Quoted in Chalmers Johnson, op cit., p. 86.
39. ibid., p. 12.

Communism lay the resolution of mankind's problems, a belief that universal peace would crown their warlike endeavours. It would be the height of foolishness to doubt the testimony of that great American enthusiast, Mr Edgar Snow, when he wrote of the cadres that, 'However badly they have erred at times, however tragic have been their excesses ... it has been their sincere and sharply felt propagandist aim to shake, to arouse, the millions of rural China to their responsibilities in society, to awaken them to a belief in human rights ... and to coerce them to fight ... for a life of justice, equality, freedom and human dignity.' It has been a feature of the totalitarian movements of the twentieth century to be able to enlist many very noble (and romantic) young as propagandists, of a self-sacrificing kind. So it was in China at this time: the Central Committee of the Party survived; 'those beardless young', as Mr Snow called them, mostly died.[40]

There was also, of course, as Mr Snow pointed out, the international component: 'This idea of having behind them such a great ally – even though it has been less and less validated by any demonstrations of positive support from the Soviet Union – is of primary importance to the morale of the Chinese Reds. It has imparted to their struggle the universality of a religious cause, and they deeply cherish it.'[41] This belief in a doctrine was not to be quite separated from a confidence in the source of that doctrine for many years to come.

40. M. Jean Chesneaux points out in footnote 1, p. 562, of his *Le Mouvement ouvrier chinois de 1919 à 1927*, La Haye, Paris, 1962, that the accounts of foreign observers Agnes Smedley and Edgar Snow provide evidence of the very important cadre role played in the countryside by urban militant Communist workers who had escaped the Chiang Kai-shek repression of 1927 in the cities. This again emphasizes the present writer's point that Leninists are peculiarly well suited to conditions of guerrilla warfare, through not being *tied* to one form of struggle.

41. Snow, op. cit., p. 406. Cf. Agnes Smedley, *Battle Hymn of China*, Gollancz, 1944, p. 319: '... I soon found that I was once more with a group of men to whom knowledge was as important as guns. The [guerrilla newspaper] called a conference to which almost everyone came. They sent me a list of subjects I was expected to discuss ... They included: (1) the present European war, (2) Soviet–Finnish hostilities, (3) Chinese–American relations, (4) the present military situation in China ...'

Yet, despite all this, and despite the fact that the Japanese occupation policy had, so to speak, prepared the peasantry for whatever intelligible mode of leadership proved to be available, it really was importantly a matter of organization that enabled the Chinese Communist Party to use the situation in north China for its own purposes. Amongst other things, the Party's mode of organization through apparently nationalist-orientated 'fronts' in rural areas, and the ability to sustain the appropriate kind of propaganda, enabled it to enlist the military skills of very many non-Communist units cut off by the Japanese advance from their main forces. It certainly was not the case that all of the guerrilla bands were themselves engendered by the Communist Party.

But the organizing capacity of the Party went far beyond that. After all, it had formed its first Red Army not only from mutineers, 'uprooted elements', deserters and the like, but also from bandits. It was the capacity of this peculiar kind of organization to subsume within its ranks all manner of activist groups that made it so formidable. Though it did use mere bandits outside its own areas of control, while permitting them to go on being mere bandits, the general policy was to make very great efforts to transmute the dubiously motivated into politically reliable soldiers through absorbing them into the Red forces.

The mode of organization was typical of the Leninist 'front' policy elsewhere; that is, the creation of associations for the various natural groupings – women, teachers, traders, peasants, youth. Within these associations political indoctrination was carried out, in all probability mostly through teaching literacy. The people were thereby exposed to Party propaganda in the very process of learning; having attained literacy they were then continuously exposed to the only available reading matter – the Party wall newspapers. The formally literate person is far more easily guided along a Party line than the illiterate.[42]

42. He is also, of course, particularly perhaps in the liberal-capitalist West today, more likely to lose all sense of civilization. See for example Ananda Coomaraswamy, *The Bugbear of Literacy*, Dobson, 1947. The point is not irrelevant in 1973, which has seen the murder of diplomats in Khartoum

This mass approach to organization and propaganda did not really bespeak a belief in the peasant as a revolutionarily reliable person. He was regarded by the Chinese Communist Party, as by every other Leninist party, as conservative and all too easily satisfied by minor alterations in society. When the Red forces entered an area the cadres carefully sought out 'the handicraft workers, middle-school students, small businessmen, and "self-respecting" bureaucrats and landlords who sense the existence of a "national crisis" '.[43] The support of such people provided the approach to the peasantry.

Except in conditions of intensive Japanese pacification drives, it was very much easier for the 'traitor extermination' squads to kill or cow members of the rural puppet administration than the reverse, for the simple reason that the puppet officials were public figures whereas the others were clandestine. By the same token it was vastly easier to discredit puppet officials since they were the government; the guerrillas could plausibly argue that they could do little constructive for the people, outside the guerrilla base areas, until the National Salvation struggle was successfully concluded.

In the base areas (or 'liberated areas') the Party's emphasis was placed on maximizing social unity to the highest degree possible. Government was based on what was called the 'One-Third' system, which amounted to the Party taking a third, sympathizers a third, and 'others' a third of representation and of government posts. The 'New Democratic' programme being implemented was based on a denial of class conflict and Party members were required to co-operate closely 'with all anti-Japanese democratic elements irrespective of class, political affiliation and religion. Similarly, in their military work Kungchantung [Communist Party] members should collaborate with all anti-Japanese democratic elements, in and out of the liberated areas, in building a powerful people's army . . .'.[44]

---

referred to in terms of 'execution' by some Australian, and probably other, newspapers .

43. Chalmers Johnson, op. cit., pp. 87–8.

44. Mao, quoted in Gelder, op. cit., p. 58.

Political control was, of course, easily retained through the 'One-Third' system, but the agrarian policy of this time was designed to reassure all agriculturalists above the tenant level while succouring the latter by reducing rents. This disguising of ultimate aims by the Party in order to use the anti-Japanese nationalist struggle for purposes of mass mobilization resulted in a wave of misapprehension about the nature of the Chinese Communist Party in the Western world. The situation was described correctly enough by an enthusiastic observer:

> The Chinese Communists have not eliminated private property – even the property of the landlord. They encourage private industry by exempting all such enterprise from taxation (landlords and peasant proprietors pay taxes). Although they are theoretically opposed to landlordism, they do not eliminate it. They contend that national liberation from Japan comes first, and that to attempt to destroy any class by force or decree is to push it into the arms of the enemy.[45]

However, it was regarded quite otherwise by prominent experts on China writing in the West. For example, O. M. Green of the London *Observer* wrote,

> All the extremist doctrines have been dropped from Chinese Communism. Nationalization of the land has gone in favour of something very much like Joe Chamberlain's 'three acres and a cow', and even landlordism is permitted if it does not mean exploitation of tenants. There is no universal State-ownership of industries; some are State-owned, others are not. Minerals are owned and developed by the State, but this is merely the ancient Chinese principle that, while the surface of the ground and its fruits can be privately exploited, everything under the surface belongs to the State.[46]

A former diplomat in China, Sir John Pratt, wrote:

> It is not a problem of communism at all, for communism has faded out in Russia and never really existed in China . . . The Communists in Shensi have declared that the aims of the Communist Party can be realized within the framework of [the doctrines of Sun Yat-sen] . . .

45. Israel Epstein, quoted in Gelder, op. cit., p. 61.
46. *The Story of China's Revolution*, op. cit., p. 153.

The difference between the Communists and Kuomintang are not greater than those between a radical left and a conservative right.[47]

Sir John Pratt thought there *was* a serious difference between the Communists and the Kuomintang in regard to agrarian and social reform. But '. . . no vital question of principle is involved'. Anyway, he declared flatly, 'The Confucian tradition is still the greatest living force in China.' Another former diplomat in China pointed out that '. . . the Chinese as a race are individualists and hard-headed materialists, with an agricultural society founded on village, clan, and family; and lack in their national character that strain of emotion and imagination which breeds religious or Communistic fervour.'[48] That this impression was not altogether accidentally gathered by such Western experts is proved by Mao's remark to a Western reporter, Harrison Forman: 'To begin with, we are not striving for the social and political communism of Soviet Russia. Rather, we prefer to think of what we are doing as something that Lincoln fought for in your civil war; the liberation of slaves shackled by feudalism.'[49]

It is not being suggested that the Communists owed their victory in China to the effect of this propaganda in the West. Though it doubtless had some background influence on the Allied stance towards the Chinese Communists, and may have had some influence on the situation immediately post-war (see below), the military victory of the Chinese Communists must be attributed primarily to their politico-military organization of the Red Army and of the people in north China (and later Manchuria) – and to the deteriorating morale of the Kuomintang regime. Nevertheless it was thought important to underline the international component in this revolutionary war, in its two forms: the value to morale of the belief in being but part of a great 'liberation movement' extending far beyond the confines

47. *War and Politics in China*, op. cit., pp. 256–66.

48. Sir Erich Teichman, quoted in Green, op. cit.

49. Quoted in F. L. K. Hsu, op. cit., pp. 389–90. Ho Chi Minh was to use the same kind of approach to American officers towards the end of the Second World War, except that George Washington was the subject of the analogy.

of China, and the more or less successful attempt to misrepresent the nature of Communist aims to the capitalist West as well as to the Chinese society itself.[50]

It is necessary to consider at this point the Red Army as it developed during the Second World War. This development was quite as important as the political mobilization of the peasantry and its organization into 'front' associations. Indeed the two were inseparable: the Red Army bore within itself the capacity for meaningful armed propaganda, on the one hand; the mobilization of the peasantry against the Japanese alone permitted the Red Army to wage its chosen form of guerrilla and mobile warfare, on the other hand.[51]

Though statistics are very rough-and-ready, it seems probable that the Red Army had grown to about 180,000 by 1938; by 1941–2 the Eighth Route Army itself was about 400,000; by 1945, the Red Army in north China must have been something of the order of 800,000. Looked at from a purely military point of view, the Red Army's task was the old traditional guerrilla task of harrying communications; as early as 1939 Japanese army reports were adverting to its increased efficacy in this regard.[52] By 1940, according to a Communist general, the situation was not so simple for the Red Army:

New tactics were adopted by the enemy who, from experience in fighting against the guerrillas, had acquired much knowledge of their tactics. The plan was started of building more lines of communications, cutting up guerrilla bases into small sections, and then des-

50. The misrepresentation may chiefly have been for local consumption. Cf. Fitzgerald, op. cit., pp. 76–7: 'The Communists were respectable; members of a united front, patriots; perhaps only "agrarian reformers", a harmless name, which they cunningly allowed to be given currency.'

51. See Chalmers Johnson, op. cit., pp. 80–81, where he points out that Communist spokesmen told the Yenan press party of July 1944 that 'no guerrilla army can fight successfully, or even last long, without the support of the people of the areas in which they campaign . . . indoctrination is primarily aimed at training the troops to act in such a manner that they will gain this total support.' This is not really quite the same thing (as it is so often supposed to be) as believing that the Red Army *represented* a spontaneous peasant upsurge.

52. Chalmers Johnson, op. cit., p. 56.

troying them one by one – the so-called 'forming a cage around'. The number of Japanese posts and defence works along the lines also increased tremendously. 1940 witnessed North China in the turmoil of fighting for and against the lines of communication.[53]

In other words, the Japanese adopted the tactics of the Kuomintang Fifth 'Extermination' drive against the Kiangsi Soviet (or Kitchener's tactics against the Boers, for that matter). In August 1940 the Eighth Route Army launched its only great offensive against the Japanese; more than a hundred regiments (some 400,000 men) engaged in a series of battles, lasting three months, directed against not only communications (particularly railways) and against an important coal mine but also against Japanese strongposts and blockhouses that were advancing into Red Army (guerrilla) territory. According to the Red Army General, this counter-offensive was undertaken in order to prevent the Japanese crossing the Yangtze River; according to Chalmers Johnson it was undertaken because of the deteriorating international situation. Almost certainly it was undertaken in order to avoid a repetition of the Fifth Kuomintang offensive against the Kiangsi Soviet, possibly with the full knowledge that the consequence of such a series of operations could only be such as to make the peasantry believe that their sole chance of survival lay in accepting Communist leadership.

The consequences were a 'three-all' pacification drive – 'kill all, burn all, destroy all' – by the Japanese forces in an attempt to cut the link between the guerrillas and the peasant population. But in its frightfulness the Japanese campaign only served to remind the peasantry (as was the case in Yugoslavia and the Ukraine) that its only chance of survival lay in acquiescence to the demands of the one national organization on the scene.

The organization on the scene at this time, the desperate courage of which had been all too clearly made manifest, was the Red Army, itself politicized by its commissars, moved by a great hope about the future of mankind, and possessed of an organizational mode appropriate to such a situation. It is necessary to consider at this point Mao Tse-tung's most famous pronouncement:

53. General Yeh, quoted in Gelder, op. cit., p. 76.

'Political power grows out of the barrel of a gun.' The implications of this statement are important in a way that is not always, even now, quite understood. Chairman Mao was a man who believed at that time – and doubtless still believes – that 'Conscious activity is a distinctive characteristic of man, especially of man at war.' But he was also, despite his peculiar experiences in Hunan in the late twenties when the Comintern was misunderstanding the situation, a thoroughgoing Leninist:

> Every Communist must understand this truth: Political power grows out of the barrel of a gun. Our principle is that the Party commands the gun; the gun shall never be allowed to control the Party. But it is also true that with the gun at our disposal we can really build up the Party organizations; the Eighth Route Army has built up a powerful Party organization in North China. We can also rear cadres and create schools, culture and mass movements. Everything in Yenan has been built up by means of the gun. Anything can grow out of the barrel of the gun.[54]

One of the things that grew out of the 'barrel of the gun' during the Second World War was grain. While making full allowance for the extreme enthusiasm of Mr Israel Epstein, his testimony should be considered for its relevance to the growth of support to the Communists at this time during the Second World War. What Mr Epstein had to say was this: by engaging every man, woman and child in a systematic fashion, harvesting – cutting, threshing, storing the crop and building hayricks – could be cut down from six weeks to between ten days and a fortnight. During this period the area was defended by Red Army regular forces. 'Defend the harvests' was the chief slogan; and if there were no enemy attack the Red Army took part in the harvesting operation. This policy 'denies grain to the Japanese army, disrupts the fiscal basis of the puppet government, which rests on the grain-tax in kind, and creates the only possible basis for the people's resistance'.

Mr Epstein goes on to make the point that

> Guerrilla warfare means first of all that the armed forces fight the enemy, and the people take the consequences. The people may

54. Schram, op. cit., pp. 209–10.

be willing to do this out of abstract patriotism, or because the army is considerate and treats them well for a season or two. They cannot, with the best will in the world, bear more unless they are helped to live and produce in the zone of warfare their food supply and to protect themselves from reprisals, to live better, more fully and more freely by fighting than they could by submission. The present conditions in the various Communist-led bases bear testimony that this has been done.[55]

While the Red Army was pursuing this policy to the very best of its abilities, the Kuomintang, which was necessarily concerned to keep in being the semblance of the Chinese government, while waiting for an American victory, began to wither on the vine. In order to meet the Japanese invasion, the Kuomintang

> resorted to a series of special measures – the expansion of the new Life movement devoted to a regeneration of Confucian teachings, the formation of a rigidly disciplined . . . Youth Corps, the granting of extraordinary powers to Chiang, the arbitrary designation (rather than election) of a portion of the National Congress membership, the reintroduction of party cells . . . and the further development of party purging facilities . . . all of them features which impressed Westerners as essentially nondemocratic and potentially authoritarian in spirit.[56]

There was developing a process that was later to be found in Diem's Vietnam and might well be called an attempt at a very imperfect replication of Communist organization. In a sense, as has been pointed out, the Kuomintang was from the early 1920s a replica of a Leninist party. But it was never wholly the case: a faction such as that led by Wang Ching-wei operated for a long time in a way that would not have been possible in a Communist party. The Kuomintang had become long before the Second World War – it always was in a way – a *coalition* of interest groups, military, financial, political and so on. It contained within itself both reformist and reactionary elements; it experienced fissures unknown to the Chinese Communist Party; it lacked a meaningful ideology of the kind possessed by the CCP. But above all it lacked the self-correcting mechanism of the CCP.

55. Quoted in Gelder, op. cit., p. 69.
56. North, op. cit., pp. 202–3.

This point was brought out very clearly by Mr Chou En-lai in 1943:

> Is the Chinese Communist Party split internally? Day and night the anti-Communist elements dream of our party having the same numerous branches and sects as theirs ... they do not understand that our party is united, is based on belief in Communism, and class consciousness and revolutionary training. There is the voluntary discipline to consolidate it. It differs entirely from the Kuomintang, which allows sects and branches to exist and is not unified at all. Our party has made many mistakes, and it contains many who have made mistakes; but it grows and develops from the struggle, and finally rectifies the mistakes. Thus it attains unity of ideas in the party and the consolidation of party organization. Those who have made mistakes but wish to be corrected will naturally again walk along the correct party line; those who repeatedly make mistakes and refuse to be corrected will naturally be spat upon and forsaken by the party ... In these three years, while our party, united under the leadership of Comrade Mao Tse-tung, has undergone the ideological reformation movement and carried out the work of understanding and examining the cadres, it has also reached the highest degree of consolidation ... We think that while the war with Japan is becoming more and more difficult, the revolution spreading farther and farther, what will split is not the Communist Party, but something else. Examples have already occurred in history.[57]

It was not of course simply a matter of organization. It was also a question of the form and weight of government. The Kuomintang regime was placed in a very difficult financial predicament indeed by the Japanese seizure of the coastal areas of China. Before the Japanese invasion, the government had derived 'more than 40 per cent of its annual income from customs duties, about 20 per cent from the salt tax, and about another 20 per cent from the consolidated excise taxes'.[58] The impressive earlier currency reform saved the situation until 1939, but thereafter the measures became ever more desperate and they began increasingly to include resort to the printing press and inflation began to grow ominously. (This doubtless contributed

57. Quoted in Gelder, op. cit., pp. 176–7.
58. Houn, op. cit., p. 61.

to the increasing disaffection of the intellectuals just as much as their disillusionment with the growing corruption of the regime; and the business interests outside the inner clique were disaffected by the government assumption of monopoly control over necessities.)

Equally important was the fact that the land tax had become the principal source of national revenue. The contrast in this regard between the Communist and Kuomintang areas was not just a contrast between the behaviour of Communist and Kuomintang officialdom, though that was clearly very important: 'since [Kuomintang officialdom] continued to think in the manner of their predecessors, the dynastic bureaucracies, these officials redoubled their efforts to grab whatever they could whenever they could.'[59] (And what they were liable to grab in a time of inflation was land.) But it also was a fact that the overheads of Communist administration were far lower than those of Kuomintang China and therefore the burden on the people was less in Communist areas.

And yet it was not only a question of the Communists' reduction of the costs of administration. It was also a matter that must be underlined yet again of the CCP leadership's constant preoccupation with sustaining the correct relationship with the people. It is fairly obvious from the following that a correct relationship with the people on the part of the Red Army was not something that was automatically maintained. Incessant indoctrination was necessary:

> ... all party comrades should work effectively to unify the mass. Comrade Mao asked all comrades to follow the example of Comrade Chen Tsung-yao ... a regimental commander of the Eighth Route Army. He led his whole regiment in an expedition of several hundred miles to get rice, and throughout the whole expedition he did not once mount his horse, but let it carry rice, and himself carried a full load all the time, so that every member of his regiment was much moved and cheered by his spirit, and nobody asked for leave.
>
> Comrade Mao called on all party members to emulate the spirit of this comrade – to mix with the masses and overcome all bureau-

59. Hsu, op. cit., p. 391.

cracy that keeps them separate. He said that we Communists do not want to be officials. What we want is to revolutionize ... Not for a single hour or a single second do we want to be away from the masses. If we do not separate ourselves from the masses we shall surely be victorious.[60]

Towards the end of the Second World War the Communists could claim, apparently with some justice, that about half of the Japanese army in China proper (excluding Manchuria, under threat from the Soviet Union) plus 200,000 Chinese puppet troops were engaged in fighting the Red Army or in other pacification activities. More importantly, some 100 million Chinese supported, or were controlled by, the 800,000-strong Red Army and parallel government.[61]

Largely as a result of the guerrilla campaigns the Communists, though outnumbered perhaps four to one by the Kuomintang, were in a geographically favourable position in the race for control of the former Japanese-occupied areas. But the outcome was clearly going to be affected significantly by the roles taken up by the Soviet Union and the USA, the latter's role as a supplier of weapons and aid to the Kuomintang having been very important during the war. The Soviet government altogether underestimated the situation of the CCP and negotiated with the Kuomintang government. On the other hand there is

60. Quoted in Gelder, op. cit., pp. 172–3.

61. Snow, op. cit., p. 500, writes of a Japanese Army of 350,000 in China proper in 1944 opposed by what it estimated to be 500,000 to 600,000. McAleavy, op. cit., pp. 317–18, gives figures for March 1945 of 328,000 men in the 8th Route Army, 150,000 men in the New Fourth Army in central China, and 27,000 guerrillas in South China. North, op. cit., p. 223, gives a figure of 1,200,000 Japanese troops in China proper at the war's end; and (p. 235) cites a US White Paper giving figures for mid-1946 of 3,000,000 in the Kuomintang forces, something over 1,000,000 Communists 'of whom an estimated 400,000 were not regular troops'. Chalmers Johnson, op. cit., p. 11, writes of a Communist 'loyal constituency of about 100,000,000 peasants *during* the war'. Houn, op. cit., p. 60, states that the Chinese Communist Party grew from 40,000 members in 1937 to 1,210,000 in 1945. McAleavy, op. cit., p. 317 refers to an estimated 688 out of the 914 counties theoretically Japanese-controlled as being actually under Communist control in March 1945.

no doubt that the Russian occupation forces in Manchuria made it easy for the Chinese to obtain Japanese arms and arms from the Manchurian puppet forces. Indeed, as an observer has put it, 'With the generous assistance of the Soviet Army, the Chinese Reds immediately obtained the arms, gradually seized regions rich in manpower, and eventually occupied all of Manchuria, freeing Lin Piao's field army to swing the balance of military power in China proper.'[62]

At the risk of greatly over-extending his supply lines, Chiang Kai-shek (against American advice) contested Manchuria as well as making a great drive against Chinese Communist base areas in the north. Though the USA did help with the transportation of Kuomintang troops, both by sea and air, and even landed Marines to hold certain urban points in support of the Kuomintang, US policy in general in this immediately post-war period later became a matter of savage debate at home in the USA. It is quite clear that many policy-makers were extremely naïve about the real nature of the movement they were apt to describe as the 'so-called Communists'. There is no reason to doubt that some influential American voices at this time were the voices of enthusiasts for a Communist victory.

This may well have affected the movement of Kuomintang forces at certain moments, and it did result in an exceeding ill-judged attempt to mediate in the hope of bringing about a Kuomintang–Communist coalition government.[63] The united national front had long since been broken by the CCP wherever circumstances suited its breaking, but the CCP, like a good Leninist party not bound to any one particular form of struggle, gave the quite false impression of welcoming such an arrangement on the ground that it too was really only pursuing the ideals of Sun

62. Colonel Robert Rigg in Franz Schurmann and Orville Schnell, *Republican China*, Penguin Books, 1968, p. 286. The Chinese Red Armies which later swept south were composed half of Manchurians, half of North Chinese.

63. Geoffrey Hudson, *Questions of East and West*, Odhams Press, 1953, p. 153, argues that 'Time was definitely against the Nationalists; they had to win in 1946 or not at all. They were deprived by American interference of whatever chance they had of winning in 1946 . . .'

Yat-sen. Mao Tse-tung produced his *On Coalition*, a work which if read carefully should have made it plain that for the CCP the coalition manoeuvres were only yet another form of struggle towards the seizure of total power.

Nevertheless, Robert C. North is surely right in raising the question of whether anything short of massive American military involvement could have saved the Kuomintang by 1946–7, when General George Marshall was naïvely speaking of the possibility of a government of small-*l* liberals and minority groups.[64] What was happening in the country by this time was a recrudescence of guerrilla-cum-mobile warfare, with the Kuomintang forces slowly eroding their own morale by sitting in cities and pillboxes while the Red forces concentrated on mobilizing the population in their areas (crucially, in Manchuria): the countryside was surrounding the cities.

At the same time, and though Chiang Kai-shek seemed to be veering towards a more democratic rhetoric, the Kuomintang was hamstrung by its reactionaries and beset by a now appalling inflationary spiral.[65] Besides, apart from a desperate concentration on a military solution by now beyond its resources, the Kuomintang was bereft of a clear strategy for the political war.[66]

But even on the purely military plane, events began to turn against the Kuomintang, despite its apparently impressive early successes in expanding its areas of control. It is difficult to doubt General Chassin's assertion that

> man for man, Mao's troops were clearly superior to Chiang's. The Nationalist Armies, except for those composed of the veterans of the Burma campaigns, were ... undisciplined, poorly trained, com-

64. North, op. cit., p. 237.

65. '... during 1946 prices rose by 700 per cent, while gold reserves dwindled by 50 per cent' (Lionel Max Chassin, *The Communist Conquest of China*, Weidenfeld & Nicolson, 1966, p. 94).

66. This was significantly reflected in the Kuomintang's lack of a minorities policy for Manchuria etc., whereas in good Leninist style the Communists had as early as the Kiangsi Soviet constitution of 1931 promised, quite falsely of course, the right of secession to minorities, including Mongolians, Tibetans, Koreans and 'tribals'. See Brandt, Schwartz and Fairbank, op. cit., pp. 223–4.

pletely lacking in morale, and ready, from corporal on up to general, to change sides whenever circumstances beckoned. With the Communists, things were far different. Once again, the historical lesson of the wars of religion was to be repeated: the more fanatical side is always more daring, more enterprising; the majority, trusting in its superior strength, lacks nerve, and invariably garners defeat.[67]

By 1949 these differences in morale (and in politico-military organization) were being dramatically reflected in the statistics of Kuomintang losses of men and weapons. Towards the end of 1948 the Kuomintang had lost in a series of battles more than 300,000 men and 230,000 rifles, of which 100,000 were American.[68] This was not a guerrilla struggle, though Communist guerrillas were important in their old, traditional role of harrying communications; it was a large-scale war of both mobile and positional kinds. But then for Mao guerrilla warfare was different from regular warfare only in degree and form of manifestation.[69] What was important was not the routing of the enemy but the annihilation of his units; and it was this that was being achieved by the Communist armies with whose commanders the initiative now lay.

In 1949 the Red Army, which twenty years earlier had been formed out of 'declassed elements', 'soldiers, bandits, robbers, beggars and prostitutes' in Mao's classification,[70] swept everything before it and succeeded to a new Mandate of Heaven, as a traditionalist Chinese would have called it. It was undoubtedly

67. Chassin, op. cit., p. 100; cf. Falls, op. cit.: 'It has been asserted that war-weariness was one of the main causes of the government's defeat, but it was largely weariness of fighting for the Kuomintang. The best proof of this statement is that by the end of the campaign over half the Communist army consisted of deserters from the enemy . . . Allowance must be made for the Chinese passion for being on the winning side and for the habit of waiting inactive until the triumphant bandwagon passed by and then jumping on it . . . Yet the inescapable truth is that the Chinese army and people preferred Communism to the Kuomintang' (p. 386). The people were not of course being asked to choose 'Communism' as such at any time.

68. North, op. cit., p. 239. Chassin, op. cit., pp. 119–20.

69. See particularly Michael Elliott-Bateman, *Defeat in the East*, Oxford University Press, 1967, for a profound analysis of Maoism and warfare.

70. E. J. Hobsbawm, *Bandits*, Weidenfeld and Nicolson, 1969, p. 91.

an extraordinary achievement; and so far as the liberal capitalist West was concerned, a most ominous achievement. Its effect on the USA was very naturally more dramatic than upon other Western nations, not only or chiefly (as is often imagined) as a result of the very sudden growth of a rather febrile anti-Communism but rather because of the fact that, as it was stated by a great American, Dean Acheson, 'It was the product of internal Chinese forces, forces which this country tried to influence but could not.'[71] The shadow of that failure, as the American liberals were to see it, was to affect the USA's attitude to an apparently much less significant 'people's war' some years later – in South Vietnam.

What has been attempted in this chapter is in no way a history of this particular vindication of Chairman Mao's belief, now dogmatically universalized as *the* way forward for the 'progressive elements' of the Third World War, that in the Communist-led armed people lies an invincible force. All that has been attempted is to sketch such salient features of this 'people's war' as may contribute to an understanding of revolutionary warfare in general.

There is no very good reason to believe that the CCP and the Red Army would have triumphed had it not been for the Japanese invasion of China and the methods of pacification adopted in support of the consolidation of Japanese politico-military power. Even given their lack of understanding of what was politico-militarily good sense in north China, the Japanese and their puppet forces came close in 1941–2 to breaking the link between the Red Army and the peasantry. But of course failure in this regard, in conditions where few villages in Hopei and Shansi were left intact, meant that the peasantry which survived were ineluctably driven into the arms of the one resistance organization that was fully equipped, militarily, politically and psychologically, to avail itself of what was (to it) an ideal situa-

71. Quoted in Schurmann and Schnell, op. cit., p. 368. 'Nothing that this country did or could have done within the reasonable limits of its capabilities could have changed that result; nothing that was left undone by this country has contributed to it.'

tion. That organization was the armed Communist Party of China.

On the other hand, the CCP recognized (and doubtless exaggerated to some extent) the fact that its availing itself of the opportunities presented by this extreme situation was not coincidental but flowed from the very nature of its kind of 'party'. In fact Mao went very much further and argued that 'For eighteen years the development, consolidation, and Bolshevization of our Party have been undertaken in the midst of revolutionary wars *and have been inseparable from guerrilla warfare*. Without armed struggle, *without guerrilla warfare*, there would not have been such a Communist Party as exists today ...'

That Communists had long since been at home with the notion of violence has, it is hoped, been shown in the previous chapter. But Mao was going much further: he was arguing that 'armed struggle', at least in the Third World, was not only the pre-eminent form of struggle but that it created, not just assisted, the growth of a Communist party of a kind hitherto unknown. Of course this was implied rather than stated before the Sino-Soviet split. Nevertheless it was of great importance. For example, the claim of his great pupil in the leadership of revolutionary guerrilla warfare, General Vo Nguyen Giap, that 'Free Vietnam is first of all an army', implicitly questioned Lenin's insistence upon the fact that Bolshevik parties were not bound to any particular form of struggle. (The use the CCP made of the American-engineered 'truce', immediately after the Second World War, proves that it was still aware of this Leninist approach *before* victory.)

It is not being suggested that Chairman Mao wanted immediately after the war to subvert Leninism in any way in order to be able to assert Chinese leadership of the world Communist movement. There were a number of other reasons, different in kind, for the Sino-Soviet split. What is being suggested is something really very different – that Mao became conditioned, if not determined, by the peculiar experiences of his Communist Party; and when this was aligned in his mind with an increasing awareness of the grandeur of China's past, then this assertion of the universal applicability of China's 'people's war' seemed to resolve the nationalist/internationalist dilemma that has presented itself to those non-Russian Communist leaders who are indisputably impressive human beings.

It is probably true, as Professor Schram has argued, that Mao is a 'military romantic'. Such is so often the case with a certain kind of intellectual. In this age a certain kind of intellectual secretly glorifies warfare – provided the warriors do not wear the uniforms of any 'Establishment'. But this in itself is so far not very important, except propaganda-wise, in the West.

What is important about Chairman Mao is something altogether different: his intellectual-ideological fanaticism. The matter of land reform during the war had been shelved in the interests of mobilizing the masses in a nationalist (and hence socially unificatory) campaign. It would be inaccurate to argue, so far as major documents are concerned, that Mao was always dishonest about the CCP's ultimate objective. But it would be fair to say that that ultimate objective was assiduously kept from the mass of the people.

As soon as the Red Army quite clearly reigned supreme throughout China, then 'land reform' began to be implemented, and not in the least, in the long run, along the lines that the peasants had been given to understand it would be implemented. Certainly at first, as had been the case in the Soviet Union some thirty years earlier, it was a kind of redistribution of 'land to the tillers'; this is now quite clearly the invariable tactic of Communist parties which have seized power as a result of manipulating masses of people in 'front organizations'.[72]

But then came something different: the 'people's tribunals', the yelling mobs, the hysterical denunciations, and the doing to death of some million unarmed people, perhaps far more – a process of fanaticizing the masses and destroying any alternative

72. During 1950–53 700 million mou (a mou equals 1/6 of an acre) were divided between 300 million peasants: a third of an acre each, less in the more densely populated regions. This made no sense in terms of production but as McAleavy remarks (p. 339), 'The true purpose of the exercise ... lay elsewhere.'

rural leadership in order to prepare the way for what the Maoists had from the beginning been aiming at: the utter subjugation of the masses in order that the small élite Party should be able without hindrance to impose its orthodoxy upon this very great people. The heroism of the peasant armies issued in a new kind of control over the deliberately disorientated peasantry; the peasant armies had fought, under altogether phony propaganda slogans, in order to encompass their own destruction. They became an 'army of the people' in order to destroy themselves as they had wanted to be: free peasants. They had fought out of local desperation, in order to bring into being the most totalitarian society the world has ever known. That a small group of Leninist intellectuals, as the Communist Party was in the early 1920s, brought about this extraordinary reversal of the millennial hopes of the Chinese peasantry is indeed impressive in its way.

The peasants had been promised land wherever land could be promised; security of individual tenure where redistribution was impossible. That a vast confidence trick had been played on them is absolutely certain. That they acquiesced in this confidence trick is also certain – so far as the vast majority were concerned; and in part they acquiesced because of the *authority* won by the Communist Party as the result of its leadership during the anti-Japanese struggle.

Professor Schram has laid it down that the basic elements in the Chinese Communist Party's road to power were 'nationalism, guerrilla warfare, and agrarian revolution'. There will doubtless continue to be argument about the relative importance of the first and last elements, and the weight attached to each will affect judgements as to the efficacy of this kind of revolutionary warfare in other parts of the Third World. It should be remarked that though Chairman Mao and his acolytes do claim a universal efficacy for their mode of revolutionary warfare in the Third World – provided *all* its component skills are very carefully and very patiently employed in the specified right fashion – many observers have come to believe that the success of the Chinese Communists was peculiarly marked by unusually widespread support.

It is interesting to notice that a Western observer who once served with the Eighth Route Army, Lord Lindsay, felt constrained to write in the following way as late as 1955:

> Any fairly efficient totalitarian movement can obtain popular support of a kind ... To run an efficient totalitarian regime requires genuine devoted support from a small minority, perhaps 10 per cent, of the population. The real question is whether the support obtained by orthodox Communist regimes is different from the support obtained by the right-wing totalitarian regimes such as those of Hitler in Germany or Peron in Argentina ...
>
> It is very unlikely that any existing orthodox Communist regime, with the possible exception of the Chinese, would be able to survive in an environment where the masses were able to form and support organizations offering an alternative to Communist power.[73]

On the other hand, it should be noticed that no Communist Party has devoted so much time and thought as the CCP to the employment of incessant propaganda of the kind not unjustly called 'brain-washing' in order to create mental conditions in which alternative modes of thinking about politics are rendered almost literally 'unthinkable'. This perfervid concern with endless indoctrination campaigns, to the point where it could be and was said that 'he who does not understand the Party line has lost his soul', has resulted in China becoming the most totalitarian society on earth.[74]

To some extent this springs from Mao's belief that 'Without armed struggle, *without guerrilla warfare*, there would not have been such a Communist Party as exists today ...' and as a corollary, his belief that in a 'backward country' revolutionary guerrilla warfare is, 'for a long period of time, the inevitable and therefore the best form of struggle ...'. It is in this sense that by as early as 1949 'Maoism' was offering the Third World the

73. Michael Lindsay, *China and the Cold War*, Melbourne University Press, 1955, p. 108.

74. This does not, of course, mean that the old regionalism is destroyed; it remains in 1973 a most serious threat to Peking. What is being referred to is ideological totalitarianism. The finest testimony to its efficacy lies in the acceptance of the sudden *volte-face*, on a certain political level, involved in the Nixon–Chou *rapprochement* of 1972.

benefits of the CCP's experience, with the implication that this experience and the lessons Mao drew from it were more relevant to the Third World than the message emanating from Moscow. In the course of time Stuart Schram could write, 'Recent Chinese statements do not merely criticize the Soviet leaders for their "revisionism" and betrayal of Marxist principles; they virtually exclude the Soviet Union from estimates regarding the future course of events.'[75]

It has been argued by Leonard Schapiro that '... Mao is committed much less to a doctrine or an ideology than to a method or tactic – which is what Leninism really is.'[76] This is undoubtedly true of the long march to power; and it would seem true also of the manner in which the people of China have since been condemned to a state of perpetual enthusiasm. Maoism does seem to be based chiefly on a belief that contention is the way to happiness.[77]

What is certain is that the Chinese form of revolutionary warfare is offered as a model for the Third World. As Lin Piao, then Mao's designated successor, put it in September 1965,

> The October Revolution began with armed uprisings in the cities and then spread to the countryside, while the Chinese revolution won nation-wide victory through the encirclement of the cities from the rural areas ...
>
> Comrade Mao Tse-Tung's theory of people's war has been proved by the long practice of the Chinese revolution to be invincible. It has not only been valid for China, it is a great contribution to the revolutionary struggle of the oppressed nations and peoples throughout the world.[78]

The touchstone for distinguishing between fake revolutionaries and real Marxist–Leninists was to be willingness to engage in revolutionary guerrilla warfare. The touchstone of revolution-

75. *Problems of Communism*, September–October 1966, p. 6.

76. ibid., p. 22.

77. See ibid., p. 9, Arthur A. Cohen: 'If there can be said to be a Maoist philosophy of life, it is this: what matters most to a man's happiness is his activity in political and military contention.'

78. Quoted in Schram and Carrère d'Encausse, op. cit., pp. 353–5.

ary understanding was to be an appreciation of the fact that in the Third World 'the peasants constitute the main force of the national-democratic revolution against the imperialists and their running dogs'. After pointing out that in the Chinese Revolution, unlike the October 1917 Revolution in Russia, the countryside had come to 'encircle the cities', Lin Piao repeated what Lenin was saying towards the end of his life: 'In the final analysis, the whole cause of world revolution hinges on the revolutionary struggles of the Asian, African and Latin American peoples who make up the overwhelming majority of the world's population.' Numbers were to be decisive in the long run; the 'countryside of the world', led by Communist Parties according to the revolutionary warfare teachings of Mao, would, it was predicted by Lin Piao, come to encircle the 'cities of the world', North America and Western Europe . . . and the Soviet bloc?

## CHAPTER 4

# MALAYA AND SOUTH EAST ASIA

If Europe and America may be called the front . . . the non-sovereign nations and colonies with their raw materials, fuel, food, and vast stores of human material, should be regarded as the rear, the reserve of imperialism. In order to win a war one must not only triumph at the front but also revolutionize the enemy's rear, his reserves.

STALIN, 1921

Just as within a country a communist insurgency cannot be dealt with in isolation, so, in a world-wide context, it is not an isolated event but an integral part of the continuing process of communist underground aggression by means of subversion and terror. No underdeveloped or newly independent country can face this threat alone.

SIR ROBERT THOMPSON

THE swift Japanese conquest of South East Asia – the first landing in Malaya was made on 8 December 1941 and Burma was subjugated by May 1942 – gave the Communists of the region a new lease of life. They were able to join or, in some cases, form and lead local 'resistance movements'; and they became the owners of modern weapons on a scale quite inconceivable in times of colonial pacification.

Members of the Burma Communist Party were members of the broad-based Anti-Fascist People's Freedom League whose members both co-operated with the Japanese and resisted, after a fashion.[1] Some undercover Communists probably participated in the American-sponsored Free Thai resistance, but it was anyway of little account. The Malayan Communist Party, armed

1. It is interesting to notice that the AFPFL leader most assiduous in trying to win over the important Karen minority to the national resistance cause was Thakin Than Tun, who was in 1948 to lead the Communist insurgency. Most other Burman nationalist leaders were less perceptive about the minorities. See U Nu, *Burma under the Japanese*, Macmillan, 1954, pp. 98 ff.

with weapons abandoned by the British Commonwealth forces, in time got itself accepted by the (British) South East Asia Command as the armed and subsidized local resistance movement. The Indo-Chinese Communist Party founded the Vietminh front under Kuomintang auspices. The Indonesian Communist Party made one of its usual farces out of the armed struggle opportunities available.[2] The Filipino Communist resistance movement, the Hukbalahap, chiefly contented itself with removing its rivals (as did the Malayan Communist Party to some extent, the Indo-Chinese Communist Party leaving this activity till a little later for the most part).[3]

Despite the Japanese shattering of what little was left by the Second World War of Western colonial prestige – a certain vestigial local belief in the white man's racial superiority in terms of violence – colonial control, in varying degrees, was reimposed over the whole of Burma and Malaya and over parts of Indonesia and French Indo-China. The European Communist parties, eager to seek their own power through 'resistance coalitions', were ambiguous in their attitudes towards their colleagues in South East Asia; this ambiguity also reflected the Soviet government's uncertainty about Asian policy which was exemplified in their approach to the Kuomintang regime.

But by 1947 the 'Cold War' was beginning to reshape the policies of the Soviet and American governments. In fact the American 'Cold War' stance was first taken up specifically in relation to aid to Turkey and to the Greek government then beset by a Communist Front insurgency; the then President Truman has described his speech asking Congress for that aid as 'the turning point in America's foreign policy'.

It was in respect of the insurgency in Greece that the con-

2. J. H. Brimmell, *Communism in South East Asia*, Oxford University Press, 1959, pp. 223–4, cites the ill-fated Communist leader, D. N. Aidit, as writing '. . . the Party had no experience in armed struggle, which is just as necessary [as united front skills and organization] for a Party which finds itself in a revolution'. This was also proved by an abortive coup in 1949 and again in 1965.

3. Brimmell states (ibid., p. 213) that it was estimated that of the 25,000 people killed by the Huks only some 5,000 were Japanese.

tinuing debate in the West about the moral ambiguities, involved in aiding not necessarily very attractive regimes against Communist revolutionary warfare, really began. There never has been any debate, of course, about the moral ambiguities from the other point of view in Communist countries.

It is indeed arguable that the Greek EAM–ELAS Communist-led resistance movement was not in any way akin to the Communist pseudo-resistance movements of Eastern Europe; that the Communists, through their superior organizational techniques and willingness to adopt practices involving reprisals on a scale unacceptable to other resistance movements, did, like Marshal Tito's partisans in Yugoslavia, come to assume the mantle of *the* resistance movement in Greece. Flaunting an apparently democratic banner, putting forward an apparently liberal programme, the Communists did undoubtedly attract to the ranks of their Front organization a wide and brave spectrum of Greek political opinion.[4]

This raises an issue that will have to be adverted to again later: the real meaning of such an armed Front organization under Communist leadership. Is it really true that Communist parties have been forced into a posture of obduracy only by the actions of their opponents? Have they sometimes been quite genuinely willing to share power in the way power is shared within coalitions in Western democracies? Does the democratic programme of an armed Communist party acting through a coalition or front organization really mean anything, in terms of ultimate aims?

It is hoped that the examination of Leninism has dispelled any such optimistic belief. So far as the author is aware, no

4. A persuasive argument in favour of the Greek EAM–ELAS being forced into armed insurgency is presented by Todd Gitlin, in David Horowitz (ed.), *Containment and Revolution*, Anthony Blond, 1967. But it is marred by a commonly found naïveté about the significance of programmes put out by communist parties working through coalitions or united fronts. See footnote 12 below. For the other view of the Greek insurgency, see Edgar O'Ballance, *The Greek Civil War*, Faber & Faber, 1966, and J. C. Murray, in T. N. Greene (ed.), *The Guerrilla and How to Fight Him*, Praeger, New York, 1962.

Communist party that has become a nationally ruling party has ever in any meaningful sense shared power with other political parties. And it is in this context that the aid afforded by Western powers to somewhat disreputable, yet not totalitarian, regimes must surely be assessed; and also of course in the context of international relations – the most dangerous situation imaginable for the world-at-large would be one in which one 'ideological side' might seem ineluctably to be advancing against the other. A glance at world maps before and after the Second World War quickly establishes which 'side' was advancing, which retreating.

So far as South East Asia is concerned at this time (1947) the facts speak fairly clearly. After a period of international Communist confusion, the parties of this area received a world-thesis from the Cominform, the organizationally muted successor of the Comintern (which was dissolved for tactical reasons during the Second World War) to the effect that since the Marshall Plan for the rehabilitation of Europe (not originally for the rehabilitation of Western Europe only) was 'only the European part of a general plan of world expansion being carried out by the USA', there must be no collaboration with 'bourgeois nationalism', that is, with the newly independent regimes in India, Pakistan, Burma, the Philippines, in particular.

What was, quite obviously, really meant by this new 'line' was that the Marshall Plan might indeed rehabilitate liberal-capitalist Western Europe, the old Communist enemy (and it did indeed do that). Thus the attack had at this time to be directed against what Stalin in 1921 had described as the 'capitalist rear'.

Not very long after Zhdanov's article adumbrating this theme had appeared, armed revolutionary guerrilla insurrections were mounted in Burma, in Malaya and in the Philippines: Vietnam and Indonesia were excepted from Zhdanov's article, and from other articles reiterating the Zhdanov thesis, on the ground that 'A popular, anti-imperialist front has been formed in a number of colonial and dependent countries, representing a coalition of parties whose platform is the liberation struggle with the Communist Party taking the leading part (Indonesia, Vietnam).'[5]

5. Schram and Carrère d'Encausse, op. cit., p. 263.

The theoretical justification for the series of revolutionary guerrilla campaigns that began soon after the Calcutta Conference in late 1947 is of considerable relevance to the debate about the cause and nature of such campaigns. Communist propaganda had to insist that such revolutionary activities could arise only out of 'objective conditions'. The problem soon became that of explaining the coincidence between events in politically independent countries, India and Burma, and in a colonial dependency, Malaya. Clearly objective conditions were not the same: India and Burma not only had independent governments but left-liberal-cum-social-democratic governments. Though the eventual aim of self-government for Malaya had been stated in 1946, the government was colonial and authoritarian.

The difficulty was resolved by introducing in a new political context the notion of a 'semi-colony'; a semi-colony was one in which the national leadership had not been seized, and was very unlikely to be seized, by Communist parties. Where a Communist party was thought likely to seize power through participation in a nationalist coalition, as in Indonesia, then the message was that of class collaboration of the kind propounded when the Chinese Communist Party was co-operating with the Kuomintang. Class collaboration was also the theme at this time in Vietnam, where the Indo-Chinese Communist Party was seeking to represent its aims as being simply that of freeing the country of French rule in order to establish a (Western-style) democracy.

That the proceedings of the Calcutta Conference were not made public is scarcely surprising in the case of a meeting of 'parties' whose principles in regard to secrecy had been laid down by Lenin as long ago as 1902: 'The only serious organizational principle for the active workers of our movement should be the strictest secrecy, the strictest selection of members and training of professional revolutionaries. Given these qualities, something even more than "democracy" would be guaranteed to us, namely, complete, comradely, mutual confidence among revolutionaries.'

However, a Soviet delegate to the conference stated that 'the

Conference unanimously adopted a resolution supporting national liberation struggle against imperialism',[6] 'national liberation struggle' being now the designation for revolutionary guerrilla warfare or people's war. The thesis was quoted in its essentials in a Burmese government White Paper, and was adopted by the Burma Communist Party at Pyinmana in March 1948. The gist of it was that Burma's independence was a sham under cover of which the imperialists would retain a stranglehold over the economic life and the defence of the country. 'It should be clear that our [Burma Communist Party] position *vis-à-vis* the Provisional Government is, no support to it, exposure and fight against its anti-people policy ... To sum up our central slogans become the following. No support to the present Government ... National Uprising ... Set up a People's Government.'[7] The BCP then began a revolutionary guerrilla campaign which continues to this day, if not very successfully so far.

In June 1948 there began in Malaya a revolutionary guerrilla campaign the study of which will form the major part of this chapter. The reason for this decision of the Malayan Communist Party (MCP) to opt for armed struggle at this time has been disputed. Indeed the authors of a study of the left wing in South East Asia went so far as to state that those writers who believed the decision emanated from the Calcutta Conference 'disagree as to whether it was the Communists of the USSR, China, or Australia who were most influential in determining the course which the MCP should take'.[8] The distinguished Australian journalist Mr Denis Warner reported that Lance Sharkey, Secretary-General of the Australian Communist Party, and a Mr Lee Soong of Malaya reported back from Calcutta to the MCP.[9] Sharkey himself naturally argued that 'wars of national

6. Cited in Max Beloff, *Soviet Policy in the Far East 1944–1951*, Oxford University Press, 1953, p. 209.

7. *Burma and the Insurrections*, Government Printing Office, Rangoon, 1948.

8. Virginia Thompson and Richard Adloff, *The Left Wing in Southeast Asia*, William Sloane, New York, 1950, pp. 153–4.

9. *Out of the Gun*, Hutchinson, 1956, p. 81.

independence cannot be conjured up by "instructions" from anyone but arise out of existing conditions'.[10]

What is quite clear is that this revolutionary guerrilla campaign in Malaya was represented by Communists abroad as quite as much a popular, democratic and nationalist struggle as the National Liberation Front's campaign in South Vietnam was to be represented later on. For example, Sharkey argued that 'The fact that Communists are leading the rebellion does not invalidate its national independence character ... The same "Chinese Communists" led the heroic Malayan resistance to the Japanese imperialists ... they now lead the struggle of the Chinese, Indian and Malayan population ...'[11]

It was pointed out by another Communist writer that the aims of the rebellion, as stated in the MCP's programme, were simply a united Malaya, inclusive of Singapore; responsible self-government through a fully elected Central Legislature; and equal citizenship rights for all who make Malaya 'their permanent home and object of their undivided loyalty'.[12] It was also argued in Communist propaganda abroad that the war simply could not be won by the forces opposed to the MCP insurgency.[13]

It is desirable briefly to examine some of the background

10. Cited in Walter Blaschke, *Freedom for Malaya* (pamphlet), Current Book Distributors, Sydney, n.d., p. 2. A defector from the Australian Communist Party stated that Sharkey informed the National Congress of the ACP that he was in fact commissioned by the Cominform representatives at Calcutta to convey the decisions to the MCP. Anthony Short, in Wang Gungwu, *Malaysia: A Survey*, Cheshire, Melbourne, 1964, pp. 152–3, sets this kind of evidence against an Intelligence report attributing the decision to local factors. But since Malayan government Intelligence was very poor at that time (see below), this report may not carry much weight.

11. Foreword to Blaschke, op. cit.

12. An extended, though not contradictory, MCP programme (of early 1946) is given in Gene Z. Hanrahan, *The Communist Struggle in Malaya*, Institute of Pacific Relations, New York, 1954, pp. 52–3. An EAM–ELAS programme of a similar innocuousness is cited in *Containment and Revolution*, op. cit., p. 144.

13. See for example Rupert Lockwood, *Malaya Must Cost No More Australian Blood* (pamphlet), Current Book Distributors, Sydney, 1951, p. 16: 'The Malayan liberation movement cannot be suppressed any more than the Chinese liberation movement could be suppressed.'

factors before discussing the insurgency itself. Malaya was an important part of the 'capitalist rear' from the economic point of view: Malaya was the world's greatest tin producer and stood alongside Indonesia as one of the two greatest sources of natural rubber, though the future of Malayan rubber in 1947 did not look promising.[14] After the Second World War the constitutional drift was towards unification, but the special status of the Malay sultans was clearly not going to be denied easily, and the problem of fashioning a Malayan nation had not been at all adequately tackled.

A colonial government administered a racially very mixed society living in what were to some degree 'protected states'. In 1947 in the Malayan peninsula Chinese made up nearly 40 per cent of the population and there was a sizable Indian minority.[15] Some 400,000 Chinese 'squatted' on the fringes of the jungle as small farmers. More than three quarters of the population lived outside what were designated urban areas, that is, settlements of 1,000 or more. Malaya was 80 per cent jungle, rough and mountainous, rising to more than 7,000 feet. It is so dense in places (particularly near the mountain fringes) that a patrol may take four hours to cover a mile, and can 'pass within 5 yards of a man or within 50 yards of a 100-man camp without knowing it'.[16] The heavily settled areas were situated chiefly on a strip some ten to twenty miles wide along western Malaya between Thailand and Singapore. It was there that most of the country's 3 million acres of rubber plantations and 700-odd tin mines lay.[17] Clearly this was a terrain very suitable indeed for

14. P. T. Bauer, *The Rubber Industry*, Longmans, 1948, p. 344. The boom in raw materials prices during the Korean War was to be of considerable assistance to the Malayan administration during the 1948–60 insurgency.

15. The population of Malaya in mid-1950 was estimated to be 5,226,549 (*Federation of Malaya: Annual Report*, Government Press, Kuala Lumpur, 1955, p. 209).

16. Richard Clutterbuck, *The Long Long War: The Emergency in Malaya*, Cassell, 1967, p. 45. For an epic of life in the Malayan jungle during the Second World War, see F. Spencer Chapman, *The Jungle is Neutral*, Corgi Books, 1965.

17. Julian Paget, *Counter-Insurgency Campaigning*, Faber & Faber, 1967, p. 45.

guerrilla warfare: there was a very great deal of 'cover' and the target areas were very concentrated. So far as the human 'terrain' was concerned, the situation again was in one sense very favourable to guerrillas: not simply in terms of the squatters but in terms of the very large Chinese 'minority', most of whom were fairly recent immigrants, and a sizable proportion of whom were made up of a shifting population.[18]

In order to understand what the MCP made of their June 1948 decision to opt for 'armed struggle' it is necessary to consider the background to the MCP. The MCP was always overwhelmingly a Chinese organization; the groundwork for its foundation was probably laid by agents from China infiltrated in the late 1920s. It was not really very important in the 1930s, since the colonial administration's Intelligence system was then very good. Up to the Japanese invasion this situation was kept well under control through a banishment ordinance that permitted the deportation of 'agitators' and (in 1940) a trade union enactment curbing Communist activities in that sphere.

The MCP's policy cleaved fairly closely to Comintern directives, though not specifically, after the Japanese invasion of China, where such activity would damage the anti-Japanese struggle. As one expert has put it, '... true, or ideological, north was in Russia. Magnetic, or affinitive, north was in China.'[19] The MCP concentrated its activities chiefly in trade-union work and the creation of front organizations related to the anti-Japanese struggle. It seemed to pose no threat to the colonial administrations of Malaya and Singapore. Indeed this inter-World War period has been described thus:

> The British-controlled governments had presented an effective façade to the world; law and order had been maintained, economic growth encouraged, and many of the services of a modern state erected. Old Malayan hands might perhaps regard the inter-war years as a 'golden age' of mild, beneficent rule. Yet much was obviously lacking. Chinese, Indian and European communities had, with

18. For example in 1939 some 115,000 Chinese arrived in Malaya, some 106,000 returned to China (Hanrahan, op. cit., p. 4).
19. Anthony Short, in Wang Gungwu, op. cit., p. 150.

few exceptions, no loyalty to Malaya as such. Above all, there had been no genuine political advance, no preparation for the franchise – largely because of the complex communal situation. No clear political goal had been set forth for Malaya, in contrast to other parts of the British Empire. Thus, one former civil servant has described Malaya as 'a plural society with no corporate soul . . . a glorified commercial undertaking rather than a State'.[20]

The Japanese quickly smashed the façade and reduced the supposedly 'impregnable' and anyway now useless 'fortress' of Singapore in a couple of weeks.[21] Amongst those prepared to fight on after the capitulation were some British officers skilled in commando and jungle warfare tactics, Eurasian and Chinese Christians, some members of the Kuomintang, and – much the greatest in strength – the MCP. The colonial regime was very dilatory in accepting MCP offers of help against the Japanese, but eventually some were permitted to get training at the 101 Special Training School run by Major F. Spencer Chapman, who described the young MCP trainees as 'probably the best material we had ever had at the school'.[22] Such trainees were to be used according to British policy. But the 'stay-behind' policy, designed to supply Intelligence and, if overrun, to sabotage the Japanese lines of communications, received neither understanding nor support from the Malaya Command.

At the same time the MCP had started its own Anti-Japanese Mobilization Society, the declared objects of which were to unite 'all the peoples of Malaya', arm the party 'and the masses', wipe out all fifth-columnists and resist the Japanese occupation through the formation of guerrilla bands and planned terror.[23]

20. David McIntyre, in ibid., p. 144.

21. 'The naval base had been more or less useless since the moment when the Japanese had occupied airfields within easy bombing distance. It had been totally useless since the Japanese came within artillery range.' C. Northcote Parkinson, *A Short History of Malaya*, Donald Moore, Singapore, 1956, p. 36.

22. Spencer Chapman, op. cit., p. 15. 165 men graduated from 101 STS's ten-day courses and 'were subsequently to prove their metal, forming the hard core around which grew the Malayan People's Anti-Japanese Army' (Hanrahan, op. cit., p. 33).

23. Hanrahan, op. cit., p. 32.

Early in 1944 there was a meeting between a party of British officers and some MCP leaders, including 'a young and attractive Hokkien who was later to become Britain's most trusted guerrilla representative', and later still, and up to the time of writing, the political leader of the MCP revolutionary guerrillas: Chin Peng, as he is known today.

At this conference the MCP leaders 'agreed to co-operate fully with the Allied Commander-in-Chief for the purposes of defeating the Japanese *and* during the period when the Allied Armies should be responsible for the maintenance of peace and order in the country. We – representing South East Asia Command – agreed to supply arms, finance, training and medical facilities.'[24] It is clear that relations between the British and the MCP were by no means satisfactory; sometimes they were marked by hostility, but anyway the Japanese surrender prevented this alliance from being put militarily to the test.

However, though the armed MCP, the Malayan People's Anti-Japanese Army, was scarcely more than an irritant militarily to the Japanese and concentrated the better part of its operations against puppets, the political kudos earned by it during these years should not be underestimated. As in China, the Japanese occupation authorities singled out the Communists as their chief enemy, which indeed they were. The result of this policy has been vividly described by a non-Communist Chinese:

> Everyone, everywhere, feared and respected the 'communists', not knowing where they were or who they were. This fear of the unseen permeated even into Japanese consciousness. They began to suspect that 'communists' must be everywhere ... So great was this Japanese obsession, and so complete was Japanese hatred for communists, that anyone who had the slightest pro-Allied sentiment, anyone who made the slighest criticism against the Axis powers, anyone who listened to a short-wave radio ... anyone who talked about the evils of military scrip ... anyone who belittled the virtues of the Savings Campaigns ... anyone who did not respect Nipponzin, *must be a communist*![25]

24. Spencer Chapman, op. cit., p. 167.
25. Chin Kee Onn, *Malaya Upside Down*, Singapore, 1946, pp. 118–19.

In this manner a very small organization of dedicated revolutionaries, probably no more than 5,000 strong,[26] gained much wider support than would have been possible in other circumstances and doubtless a very widespread sympathy amongst Malayan Chinese. Since the Malays in general acquiesced in the Japanese occupation, and considerable numbers served as auxiliaries – as did some Chinese and Indians – this period saw ugly manifestations of racial strife that were portents of what was to happen in the way of alliances when the overwhelmingly Chinese MCP mounted its insurgency in 1948.

Indeed the immediate post-war activities of the MCP particularly in the States of Johore, Selangor, Perak and Negri Sembilan, included 'Wreaking vendetta on Malays who had stirred up anti-Chinese hatred which had resulted in huge massacres of Chinese in Johore and Perak just prior to the surrender'.[27] But more importantly, the MCP at this time took temporary control of a large number of small towns and villages, in order both to settle scores and to mount an exercise in armed propaganda. As Mr Chin Kee Onn put it, 'a brief reign of terror ensued!' There were also set up People's Courts, the proceedings of which may have been fair, though the punishments were often public executions of a very ugly kind.[28] The groundwork was thus laid for an atmosphere in which collaborators or even non-co-operators knew most vividly what 'people's justice' looked like. This brief reign of terror was doubtless remembered by many three years later when the insurgency was mounted.

Nevertheless authority was quickly reasserted; the Malayan People's Anti-Japanese Army surrendered at least as many arms as it had received from South East Asia Command (though very considerable caches of arms remained hidden, so great was the arms loss during the Japanese invasion); and members of the MPAJA marched in the victory parade in London. But the MCP set up a new organization, the MPAJA Ex-Comrades

26. Hanrahan, op. cit., p. 25.

27. Chin Kee Onn, op. cit., p. 202. For the Japanese exploitation of Malay nationalism, see Brimmell, op. cit., pp. 199–200.

28. Chin Kee Onn, op. cit., pp. 203–4.

Association in order to retain its army in potential. It also served a demand on the British for immediate self-rule.

Meanwhile it set about trying to establish a United National Front (with the programme of 1946 mentioned above) and concentrated its attention also upon the trade-union movement in both Singapore and Malaya. Racial suspicions caused a failure in the attempt to unite the MCP with left-wing Malay groups; and Indian racial suspicion of the Chinese leadership caused trouble for the MCP in the trade-union movement. However, 'For months the communists went about their task of building up successful unions. Thus winning confidence, they took over key positions, obtained more power. In due course nearly the whole of the labour movement in Malaya was under their control.'[29]

But in May 1948 the Malayan administration enacted an ordinance that decisively weakened the position of political agents in trade-union affairs. A general strike was ordered in Singapore but arrests and a lack of rank-and-file enthusiasm prevented its implementation.[30] The Singapore administration then also introduced legislation designed to disable MCP political agents in the union movement. Even so, the MCP had built up a very strong base in the unions. Thus the conversation in Singapore, lasting two weeks, between MCP leaders and Lawrence Sharkey, fresh from the Calcutta Conference, may be presumed to have been very significant in relation to the decision to opt for 'armed struggle'. It is also reasonable to presume that had this decision been made with more forethought, then the insurgency would not have been initiated so badly by the MCP.[31]

29. Alex Josey, *Trade Unionism in Malaya*, Donald Moore, Singapore, 1958, p. 23.

30. It should be said that a by no means minor part in the campaign against MCP control of trade unions was played by British employers' organizations, for commercial rather than political reasons. On the other hand, it was the MCP 'stand-over' tactics that enabled the British employers' organizations to make their point with the Administration to the extent they managed to do. For the period leading up to the armed struggle, see M. R. Stenson, *Industrial Conflict in Malaya*, Oxford University Press, 1970.

31. A combination of treachery on a high level and the youthfulness of the MCP leadership has also been adduced as a cause of ill-prepared embarkation upon armed struggle. But such a rationale is altogether un-Leninist.

Anyway, some 4–5,000 armed Communists, with perhaps 50,000 active supporters,[32] set about trying to create such fear, confusion and administrative and economic dislocation as would create conditions of anarchy conducive to a seizure of power by totalitarian party. In terms of dislocating the economy the MCP made the mistake, first, of gradually increasing the rate of terrorist acts and, secondly, of failing to annihilate quickly a significant number of European planters and tin miners. As Anthony Short has written, 'It would not have been a difficult task to murder practically every European planter and tin miner in the country. Had it been done, had a number of government officials been assassinated and had there been more acts of sabotage, particularly demolition, the economic mechanism of Malaya would have come to a halt.'[33] Certainly, having been awarded the advantage of surprise, the armed MCP did 'strike fiercely as and when they wanted; they operated in groups of 100–200, which were strong enough to overrun isolated police posts, and there was little the government could do'.[34]

But though they could and did do this, killing some 900 people in 1948 (more of them civilians than members of the security forces), by 1949 they were manifestly failing in their intended purpose, which was the much more ambitious one of establishing 'liberated areas'. The liberated areas were gradually to have been linked, a provisional revolutionary government of the Yenan kind proclaimed, and Communist politico-military power expanded throughout the country.

On the other hand, looking at the beginning of the insurgency from the point of view of the British administration, it clearly should and could have been prevented from assuming the proportions and longevity it did. The only truly effective counter-insurgency campaign is one that has prevented an insurgency developing. In this task the role of Intelligence is crucial. The

32. Robert Thompson, Introduction to Clutterbuck, op. cit., p. viii. Figures vary considerably; as did the degree of active support later supplied by 'active supporters'.

33. In Wang Gungwu, op. cit., p. 153.

34. Paget, op. cit.

Malayan Intelligence system was in a parlous state and the tiny bureau (the Malayan Security Service), operating only in the main centres of population, apparently took no appropriate notice of reports of increased Communist militancy.[35] The police did not have a Special Branch until 1949 and it took years before that eventually admirable service was fully adequate to the task. The police force itself was still well under strength and by 1948 was barely capable of dealing properly with the general lawlessness that followed the Japanese occupation, let alone handle a potential insurgency as well.

The armed forces, a battalion of Seaforths, of Devons, and of the Yorkshire Light Infantry, plus a Royal Artillery Regiment, five Gurkha and two Malay battalions, were on the whole untrained for the kind of small-unit warfare which ensued; and the British battalions were under strength. A Brigade of Guards arrived as reinforcements in December; and of course later the resources of various Commonwealth armies were tapped. But in the meantime the Malayan Races Liberation Army (as the armed MCP came to be called for racial propaganda reasons) was able to operate in a manner disturbing to the administration and civilians alike, and with an apparent efficacy deeply subversive of the morale of the police. This was a dangerous situation, since revolutionary warfare and its countering is basically a competition in government. The aim of the revolutionary guerrillas is to create a kind of administrative vacuum into which it can insert its own 'parallel hierarchies' or 'alternative government'.

Such a struggle is not, as is so often imagined, a competition in popularity but in authority. It is perfectly true that 'popular support' is crucial, but this is something that has different meanings at different stages of the struggle. Of course if the population-at-large is treated with indiscriminate harshness or savagery by (particularly) a *newly* foreign administration, then – as was the case in China – the revolutionary guerrilla organization may be turned to in terms of genuine popular support in the sense it is understood in the West.

35. The author owes this point, and much else, to Lt. Col. H. J. Coates, M.B.E.

It is reasonable to believe that the MCP did have quite a large measure of support initially of this kind. But MCP tactics, which can justly be called the tactics of terrorism,[36] engendered a kind of support that could be sustained only by a clear belief on the part of the population-at-large that the MCP was winning. The MCP itself admitted this error, as will be shown. Even so, for some time the MCP's terrorist tactics were efficacious in a negative sense: people would not inform the administration of what it needed to know about the Communist Terrorists (CTs as they were designated by the administration).

It is very difficult for the citizens of Western democracies to understand quite what terrorism means, let alone grasp the efficacy of this tactic in situations where an unaware administration has been thrown into some confusion. So long as the eventual outcome of an armed struggle remains doubtful, then a very few terrorists can achieve a great deal in the negative sense of closing people's mouths. As Mr Harry Miller put it:

> In the north the rich island of Penang was held in thrall by a group of fifteen men who formed a killer squad. This was a strange but stark fact. Nearly 200,000 people on this island, among them men earning incomes of 12,000 dollars a month, declined to give any information whatever about the terrorists.[37]

Or as an equally keen and militarily expert student of the Malayan Emergency, General Richard Clutterbuck, put it:

> This threat, in fact, faced Malayan government officials in the early stages of the war. The number of civilians killed in Malaya in the three years 1948–50 (500, 700, and 1,200) was on a similar scale to that in South Vietnam in 1957–9 (700, 1,200, and 2,500) bearing in mind that South Vietnam has double Malaya's population. In Malaya, these killings were down in 1951 to 1,000; but in South Vietnam in 1960, they soared to 4,000 and they have gone on rising,

36. It cannot be too often emphasized that 'terrorism' is a loaded word: one man's terrorist is another man's freedom fighter. It is intended to convey by the above use of the term the employment of apparently indiscriminate violence, involving victims on rubber estates and attacks on their means of livelihood for reasons that were not made intelligible to their fellows.

37. Harry Miller, *Menace in Malaya*, Harrap, 1954, p. 180.

sometimes reaching more than 100 a day. Once this terror begins to get out of hand, it becomes progressively harder to restore confidence and reverse the trend.[38]

But restoring confidence and reversing the trend is the task of an administration that has allowed, as the Malayan administration had certainly allowed, a revolutionary insurgency to develop. Luckily for the British administration, there were available a quite large number of soldiers, even if most of them were untrained for the particular task in hand. By adopting small-unit tactics fairly quickly, they could, and did, harry the guerrillas, even if actual contact between them and the guerrillas was a matter more of luck than good management. Though this helped the administration stave off catastrophe, which otherwise might have faced it at this time (1948–50), such activities did not in themselves 'restore confidence and reverse the trend', since they were not addressing themselves to what gradually came to be seen as *the* problem: cutting the links between the guerrillas and what has come to be called their 'infrastructure' in the Chinese village society itself. What had to be realized was something foreign to a normal military approach: that is, what was vital was not the guerrillas out in the jungle but the political organization that sustained them with food and medical supplies, information and recruits.

The British administration did in time begin to understand that killing armed guerrilla fighters was not in itself of primary importance so long as fresh recruits could be obtained and so long as the total politico-military apparatus could be kept substantially in being.

The point being made here must not be exaggerated. It is of course important to keep killing guerrillas, since this begins slowly to erode the quality of the middle-level leadership particularly, which had been pointed out by Spencer Chapman as the armed MCP's weakest link. It also begins to predispose guerrillas to surrender, provided the situation is correctly exploited. Moreover, provided the kill-ratio, to use that disagree-

38. *The Long Long War*, op. cit., p. 70.

able term, is favourable, then this becomes a morale-booster to the armed forces of the incumbent government.

Nevertheless this is certainly not fundamental in countering a revolutionary guerrilla war, for the simple reason that the revolutionary 'society' created long before the fighting has begun is much less susceptible to statistics of killed and wounded than is the society (if it is Western) involved in giving its young men to what so often appears an inconclusive and hence futile struggle.

The statistical approach was peculiarly misleading in the Malayan Emergency context – and it was used in order to mislead friends of the guerrillas. As General Clutterbuck has said:

> Much nonsense is heard on the subject of tie-down ratios in guerrilla warfare – that ten to twelve government troops are needed to tie down a single guerrilla, for instance. This is a dangerous illusion, arising from a disregard of the facts. It is quite true that, if the total figure of armed policemen and soldiers are balanced against armed guerrillas in any such war, the difference is large. This does not, however, represent the difference *in the jungle* . . .[39]

This goes to the heart of the matter: the competition in government. The security forces as a whole are not, or should not be, primarily concerned with killing guerrillas but in preventing the guerrillas subserving the political aims of the revolutionary organization. So long as armed guerrillas or their armed comrades within the village society can continue to give the impression that authority lies rather with the revolutionary organization than with the incumbent administration, then so long are they winning. The statistics of killed or wounded and surrendering are relevant only within the frame of reference imposed by the politico-military strategy. Which 'government' is being continually weakened? This is the big question. Everything else is subordinate to it.

In General Clutterbuck's exemplary study it is made plain that by 1950 the security forces were killing some fifty to sixty

39. ibid., p. 43.

guerrillas a month and inducing some twenty to thirty surrenders. But this loss could be more than made up for by an efficient recruiting service. Whereas the army was killing six guerrillas for every one man lost on their side, the police posts were still so vulnerable that their losses were worse than the MCP's.[40] More than a hundred civilians were being murdered each month. There was thus a very serious crisis of confidence.[41] The question being asked was: which side is likely to win in the end? The answer can have been by no means clear in the minds of the great mass of uncommitted people.

The reason why such a situation had developed was basically a failure to produce a plan for meeting a prolonged Emergency; a failure also to devise a means of persistent co-ordination between the various government agencies: to treat the struggle as a competition in government. It was the great achievement of General Briggs who arrived (in a civilian capacity) in 1950 to understand the nature of the struggle and to lay down the appropriate government guidelines for effectively waging it.

As Director of Operations (a post that should have been instituted much earlier) General Briggs insisted that the task of first priority must be the resettling of the Chinese 'squatters' in order that the guerrillas in the jungle should be cut off from their most accessible source of supply, information and general backing. It was no use the government having draconic regulations for the punishment of consorting with the terrorists in a situation where exposed squatters had no choice in the matter. Reprisals against informers were utterly savage, as was observed by a British officer:

> The man's body was slumped over in a heap at the back of the sleeping-bench. Blood had flowed from a number of wounds in his stomach and lay in a half-congealed pool on the bench. The little girl, shot through the heart, was lying on her back just in front of him, her left arm stretched out above her head, with the small hand

40. Intelligence should again be emphasized. It was estimated that in the jungle a quarter of the contacts with the guerrillas was the result of chance, three quarters the result of Intelligence.

41. ibid., p. 55.

hanging open over the edge of the bench. A small woolly doll had fallen out of it on to the body of her mother. It was obvious from the way the bodies lay that the woman had been killed first, then the child and lastly, Ah Chong [the informer] himself. A seething carpet of hungry flies covered them.[42]

Ah Chong's neighbours could validly argue that they had no choice in such a situation. Until such a choice is provided, then the often misunderstood slogan about such a struggle being 'a battle for the hearts and minds of men' is altogether meaningless. The forcible resettlement of the squatters was undoubtedly a measure involving harshness. But as one of the architects of the British success, Sir Robert Thompson, has put it,

There are many who will criticize the harshness of the measures which may have to be used. This is a mistaken attitude. What the peasant wants to know is: Does the government mean to win the war? Because if not, he will have to support the insurgent. The government must show its determination to win. Only in that way will it instil the confidence that it is going to win ... People will stand very harsh measures indeed, provided they are strictly enforced and fairly applied to all, are effective in achieving their purpose and are seen to be so.[43]

In the long run this does seem to be the case with the great majority of people involved in a protracted insurgency. But though the squatters in Malaya were engaged in a primitive and destructive mode of agriculture, and though they were not (as in, say, Vietnam) living in 'cohesive social units' with attachments to a past sanctified by a special geographical area,[44] the actual resettlement was very far from popular. Clutterbuck goes so far as to say that 'There is no doubt, in fact, that popular support for Communism in the New Villages was initially far stronger than it ever was among the South Vietnamese peasants.'

42. Arthur Campbell, *Jungle Green*, Allen & Unwin, 1953, pp. 27–8.

43. Robert Thompson, *Defeating Communist Insurgency*, Chatto & Windus, 1966, p. 146.

44. See Milton E. Osborne, *Strategic Hamlets in South Viet-Nam: A Survey and Comparison*, Department of Asian Studies, Cornell University, New York, 1965, for a comparison between Malaya's New Villages and South Vietnam's Strategic Hamlets.

Indeed a severe critic of Administration policy believed that the propaganda advantage still lay with the MCP despite the pains taken to site the so-called New Villages at places accessible to agricultural land or employment opportunities (and indeed to provide amenities on a scale that might have caused dangerous political reactions among the Malays had it been attempted by any other than an authoritarian government of this particular kind).[45] The point the critic in question, Victor Purcell, a great authority on the Chinese of Malaya, made is in varying forms relevant to all revolutionary guerrilla campaigns:

> This is the great conundrum facing the Emergency Information Services. The Communist slogans have at least a promise in them which only the experience of Communist rule can confirm or contradict. The promises of the Federal Government are subject to a more immediate test. It is no good telling a family of eleven living in a shed with an earthen floor, relying for a living on an unstable rubber market that they would be worse off under Communism. They will not believe it.[46]

However, although the Federal government did jazz up its approaches to making propaganda in 1950, including obtaining the services of Mr (now Sir) Hugh Carleton Greene, increasing its mechanical equipment and using surrendered 'bandits' (as they were still called), the main thrust of its operation was resettlement. By the end of that year 67,000 squatters from priority areas had been resettled and 50,000 from other areas. By the middle of 1951 the greater part of the squatter communities in priority areas had been resettled.[47] By 1953 the government campaign had swung into its counter-offensive.

This counter-offensive involved four elements contained in the Briggs Plan. Besides isolating the armed guerrillas from their supply base amongst the hitherto exposed population, the re-

45. This point is made in John J. McCuen, *The Art of Counter-Revolutionary War*, Faber & Faber, 1966, pp. 163 ff.

46. *Malaya: Communist or Free?*, Gollancz, 1953, p. 82.

47. '. . . by the end of 1952 some 470,000 persons, 85 per cent of them Chinese, had been brought under control. Altogether, between 1950 and 1960 some 530,000 persons were relocated in the New Villages . . .' (Osborne, op. cit., p. 13).

settlement scheme aimed to produce feelings of security conducive to the supply of information to the administration; thirdly, it sought to create conditions that would permit the break-up of the vital Communist political organization (or infrastructure, as it is known nowadays); and lastly, it was designed to compel the guerrillas either to attack the vastly strengthened security forces or to wither away in their jungle fastnesses.

However, it would be mistaken to imagine that the creation of security and the provision of an impressive list of amenities simply won a 'battle for the hearts and minds of men', with the consequence that there was a shift in public opinion analogous to that found in Western-style democracies. The process was nothing like that. It was far more complex and arduous. The movement of people and supplies of all kinds was extremely rigorously imposed; and the penalties for assisting, or getting oneself into the position to assist, the guerrillas were very harsh indeed.

For example, during 1950 Emergency Regulations brought in or developed included:

*Emergency Regulation 4 C*
The demanding, collecting or receiving of certain essential supplies from any other persons raising a reasonable presumption that the person making the demand or the person for whom the supplies were intended is a terrorist was made a capital offence.

*Emergency Regulation 4 C*
The possession of terrorist documents or of supplies for which the possessor cannot satisfactorily account was also made a capital offence.

*Emergency Regulation 17 FA*
Power to declare certain areas to be controlled areas and residential areas was vested in the State and Settlement executive officers. No person in a controlled area may reside except in a residential part or be at large in the controlled area during curfew hours.

*Emergency Regulation 17 DA*
Power to impose a collective fine on the residents of any village, area or district, to order the complete or partial closing of shops or the quartering of additional police therein, was conferred on the State and Settlement executive authorities, if they were satisfied, after inquiry by a competent authority appointed for the purpose, that the inhabitants had aided, abetted or consorted with bandits, suppressed evidence relating to offences against the Emergency Regulations, failed to give information to the police concerning bandit activities or failed to take steps to prevent the escape of bandits.[48]

This kind of approach is surely better described as the employment of (legalistic) force against the minds and wills of men rather than a (propaganda) battle for their 'hearts and minds'.[49] This approach adopted in Malaya was very much a part of the British imperial tradition of 'pacification'. The enemy was not being engaged in some kind of ideological contest involving violence, he really was in an important sense regarded as a bandit to be disarmed if possible, killed if not – but killed on the battlefield or hanged after a proper trial, not beaten to pulp or assassinated on the ground that he was (ideologically) a Communist. The point being made here will be elaborated later. It

48. *Federation of Malaya: Annual Report 1950*, op. cit., p. 11. By the end of 1950, 8,508 persons were held in preventative detention; 887 Chinese were in 1950 deported to China, a process that was coming to a close because of the attitude of the Peking Government; 225 detainees were repatriated to India that year (ibid., pp. 12, 13). 6,000 Chinese were deported under Emergency Regulations (Short, op. cit., p. 155). For 'Emergency' regulations, see particularly P. B. G. Walker, *A Study of the Emergency Regulations of Malaya, 1948-1960*, Stanford Research Unit, Menlo, California, March 1967. See also W. G. Stefaniak, 'Malayan Emergency: A Reconsideration of British Counterinsurgency Methods', *Spectrum*, Vol. 2, No. 1, October 1973, Bangkok.

49. Though collective punishment ofrecalcitrant communities had long been used in British imperial pacifications, it was the use of this device by General Templer later that occasioned the harshest criticisms in the British press and Parliament. On the whole, however, the British Administration received great support in England, a fact of some psychological importance.

is being made here in order to suggest that there was something curiously old-fashioned about the Malayan Administration's war against the revolutionary guerrillas; something old-fashionedly possible only in an imperial context, quite impossible where *both* sides are consciously trying to assert their own legitimacy in the quite new political arena created by liberation from imperial rule.

This legalistic approach, with regulations empowering every facet of counter-insurgent activities ranging from weapons control to defoliating roadsides in order to remove ambush points, should also have guided even propaganda, according to Sir Robert Thompson: no polemics or direct argument with the enemy for a number of reasons but particularly because 'the people are placed in the position of a neutral audience for whose attention two equal parties are contending, instead of it being taken for granted that people and government are one and indivisible against the enemy'.[50]

But a very important aspect of the British counter-insurgency in Malaya was the marrying of this approach with extreme thoroughness in the more pedestrian side of population-control: the identity-card system. An identity card had to be produced in order to acquire the very necessities of life. (The same thoroughness was observed in the practice of positively identifying every guerrilla killed so that his name could be removed from the Special Branch Wanted List. 'This often involved carrying a corpse miles through the jungle to a police station or post'.[51])

The identity-card system was also of great value in checking on people who moved outside their normal areas of work and might therefore be contact men – and might also therefore be usable as double-agents if handled rightly. But above all, as General Clutterbuck has made clear, because such a system of separating the people-at-large from the guerrillas meant that the latter had to 'make prearranged contacts with their supporters'.[52]

50. Thompson, op. cit., pp. 96–7.

51. Edgar O'Ballance, *Malaya: The Communist Insurgent War, 1948–1960*, Faber & Faber, 1966, p. 149.

52. Clutterbuck, op. cit., p. 38.

It was the art of handling a certain kind of supporter thus observed, and turning them into double-agents, along with patient, careful police Intelligence work, that slowly began to weaken the MCP organization as a whole. The manner in which this was done is described in general terms in Chapter 11 of General Clutterbuck's *The Long Long War*.[53] The technical details are hardly germane to this study, but two points should be underlined: first, torture was rejected because it was regarded as morally wrong and *also* because it was regarded as inefficacious in the long run.[54]

Secondly, it was this kind of activity, allied with the exploitation of surrendered guerrillas (Surrendered Enemy Personnel, SEPs, as they were known), which gradually began to destroy the MCP organization and not, as is so often imagined, the appeals of propaganda, 'the hearts and minds' game. Propaganda, though lavish and often polished, never achieved anything to speak of in itself; it could only reinforce an apparently irreversible trend that was engendered in those other ways. The SEPs will be discussed when considering motivation in a later chapter. Suffice to remark here that a desire to revenge themselves against leaders they had come to hate, a greed for the very large monetary awards put on the heads of leading guerrillas, and sometimes the possibility of having charges carrying the severest penalties waived, 'motivated' the SEPs used in this task.[55]

Another very important feature of General Briggs's approach was the establishment of what has come to be known generally as the 'committee system' of day-to-day co-ordination of the various agencies concerned with the counter-insurgency. At the top of the hierarchy, a Federal War Council was established;

53. It is also treated, vividly and satisfactorily, in Noel Barber, *The War of the Running Dogs*, Collins, 1971.

54. Torture, or, as the French delicately called it, 'special methods', came to be justified in situations of urban terrorism where speed of reaction was required. See for example Roger Trinquier, *Modern Warfare*, Pall Mall Press, 1964, pp. 22–3. Quick results could not be, and were not, expected in Malayan conditions.

55. See especially Lucian Pye, *Guerrilla Communism in Malaya*, op. cit., for SEPs.

below it on each level a committee combined civil, police and military activities. For example, on the State War Executive Committee the civilian component was the State Prime Minister, the Executive Secretary and the Information Officer. The police component was the Chief Police Officer, the Head of the Special Branch, the Military Intelligence Officer, the Home Guard Officer. The military were represented by the local Brigade Commander.[56] The control was civilian on all levels; and on the district level the Special Branch officer dominated the military so far as operations were concerned. Thus the approach was Intelligence-orientated. This avoided the military tendency towards a rough-shoot approach to disabling the guerrillas.

On the other hand the constant harrying of the guerrillas, particularly in the form of ambush patrols mounted as a result of sound Intelligence, was very important. 'Tactically, the army's job was to dominate the jungle up to about five hour's journey from the guerrilla supply areas with the object of forcing them to fight, disintegrate, or leave the area.'[57] This form of protracted attack was relentlessly pressed. Moreover, the guerrillas were not only cut off from the population-at-large; later they were cut off from the aboriginals they tried themselves to use as Intelligence screens and as sources of food-production. The guerrillas' own food production was also attacked by chemical warfare. 'In one and a half years ... the Communists cultivated hundreds of little vegetable-gardens in the deep recesses of the mountain range and in the forests of every State. It was a formidable accomplishment ... Many of these gardens could be seen from the air. They were plotted. In the course of time they were destroyed, either by ground forces or by chemicals sprayed by aircraft.'[58] This constant harrying of the guerrillas – killing them, wounding them, and thus inducing the surrender of others – was an essential part of the slow process of opening up what came to be called 'white areas' in which people could go about their lives in reasonable peace.

56. Clutterbuck, op. cit., p. 58, supplies a table illustrating the 'committee system'.

57. Short, op. cit., p. 54.

58. Miller, op. cit., p. 226.

After four years of struggle the armed MCP had clearly failed in their original objective. They had lost more than 4,000 men by the end of 1952 (two thirds of these, significantly, having been killed in action); this took a heavy toll of their leadership and also began to have a deleterious effect on the morale of rank-and-file: by 1953 surrenders were at their highest since the Emergency began.[59] Nevertheless what was in process was very much a long haul. It is probable that General Briggs, when he died in October 1952 in Cyprus, was not particularly sanguine about the ultimate result.

The control mechanism, so far as supreme direction was concerned, remained inadequate to the task. This was only finally rectified with the appointment of General Sir Gerald Templer as both High Commissioner and Director of Operations. He came armed with the greatest powers enjoyed by a British soldier since Cromwell and he was determined to exercise those powers to the utmost. A sensitive and gifted man, he spoke of winning that 'battle for the hearts and minds of men' but employed for the most part a language of extreme insensitivity clearly designed to shape the minds and wills of men; to bend them to a single task wherever possible, to break them if necessary.[60]

It has often been argued that one of the most important weapons, if not the most important, in Sir Gerald Templer's political armoury was the section of the policy directive appointing him supreme overlord which announced the British government's intention 'that Malaya should in due course become a fully self-governing nation'. It is true that he laid great stress on what might be called nation-building activities. He was

59. Hanrahan, op. cit., p. 70. By June 1953, over 6,000 Communist terrorists, to use a later designation, had been killed or captured, or had surrendered. Nearly 3,000 civilians had been killed by the CT's and nearly 1,600 members of the security forces.

60. His most spectacular exploit in this regard was his sentencing of the town of Tanjong Malim to a twenty-two-hour curfew in March 1952. The locals had obviously been assisting the guerrillas, who in that area had a very high score of recent ambushes, attacks on army and police patrols, slashing of rubber trees and intimidation of labour, not to speak of murders. See Miller, op. cit., p. 209.

responsible *inter alia* for emphasizing the necessity for a police force that would be respected by all communities; the formation of an all-races Federation Regiment; a national education system; a common form of citizenship,[61] and a considerable development of the elective system on the various political levels. But at least in his first year he was concerned to emphasize again and again that there was no point whatsoever in discussing self-government except in terms of the complete defeat of the insurgency.

Since the ability of Communist parties elsewhere to represent themselves as the vanguard of nationalism and/or anti-colonialism was so important (in China and Vietnam especially), doubtless the declared prospect of self-government was of some propaganda benefit to the Malayan Chinese Association, which was increasingly associated with the Administration's policy towards the MCP; and doubtless also the opening-up, even if in the indeterminate future, of an alternative mode of nationalist politics and its effects on the educated young. Nevertheless the destruction of the armed MCP and its political organization in the village society was what was crucial.[62]

Looking at this problem from the MCP point of view, certain factors may be clearly observed. Having catastrophically failed in their intention of setting up base areas from which to expand their politico-military control, the MCP Central Committee recognized as early as 1949 that 'Our greatest weakness is that we have not sufficient strength to protect co-operative vil-

61. In September 1952 all aliens born in Malaya were given full citizenship: 1,200,000 Chinese and 180,000 Indians; regulations were relaxed in order to make it easier for other residents to become citizens (O'Ballance, op. cit., p. 119).

62. Self-government and democracy were to be a consequence of establishing political stability and economic viability. 'They represented a risk . . . because they meant giving political power to the Malays. They had little appeal to the Chinese, who were at the root of the insurgency problem; and if given prematurely, might have given the Malayan Communist Party, itself almost entirely Chinese, a chance of becoming the political champion of the Chinese against the Malays, which would have been fatal' (Robert Thompson, *Foreign Affairs*, April 1968).

lagers. Therefore our environment becomes more and more difficult, especially from the provision supply aspects. We suffer from unreliable information, non-co-operation of the people and difficulty of movement.'[63] In other words, even during the period when trained British observers believed that the Administration was losing the struggle, the MCP was admitting extreme difficulties. The difficulties cited then were of course hugely compounded by the resettlement programme.

But the MCP's gradual isolation from the people-at-large was in part the result of its own terrorist policy, as was tacitly admitted in a Politbureau directive of October 1951. This directive reminded MCP members that their chief duty was to 'expand and consolidate the organization of the masses' rather than concentrate on purely military objectives. It went on to admit that terrorism had alienated the people in many cases and ordered that henceforth terrorism was to be curtailed unless of a strictly military kind; indeed it laid down that the masses must not even be submitted to unnecessary loss or inconvenience. Significantly in the context of revolutionary guerrilla thinking *à la* Mao, the directive also suggested that more attention must be paid to urban organization.[64]

But the MCP's future was not being determined simply, or even chiefly, in terms of what the Central Committee might regard as a newly 'correct' policy. The armed MCP – the Malayan Races Liberation Army and the partly armed Min Yuen service corps – numbered about 7,000 at its numerical height in 1950–51.[65] In the course of time, some 300,000 armed men were brought to bear against it. Apart from the fact that recruiting was to become more and more difficult, the armed MCP began to lose what Hanrahan has called 'the war of the cadres'; that is, it suffered a steady decline of its junior leadership. A force that was deteriorating in a qualitative way was also weakened by an inadequate central command system. This was largely the result of slowness of communications: directives from the Central

63. Quoted in Osborne, op. cit., p. 15.
64. Quoted in Hanrahan, op. cit., pp. 73–4.
65. See table in Short, op. cit., p. 160.

Committee often took six months to reach local branches and MRLA platoons.[66] Thus small units were left pretty much to their own devices, conducting operations according to how their leaders viewed local conditions.

This in turn began to raise problems of morale. While not discounting idealism, it is fairly clear from Pye's study of a rather better-educated, therefore cadre-material, sample of Surrendered Enemy Personnel that they saw in the MCP a career open to talent and a kind of patronal organization. 'They saw the movement as being essentially concerned with its own people, even though it had to ask them to suffer much before they could realize a better life.'[67] Despite the fact that even today a small hard-core element of the MCP struggles on with impressive fortitude, it may fairly be said for most men the appeals of Communism can be sustained only in so far as the future really does seem to be opening up in the promised manner. In Malaya this was manifestly not the case by the beginning of the 1950s: the guerrilla bands, far from coalescing in increasingly larger operations, were about to be submitted to ever stronger pressures. In time they were to be the harried and the hunted rather than the liberators. In conditions of increasing discomfiture, intensifying mutual mistrust and failing leadership, the surrenders grew to the eventual figure of no less than 2,700, nearly half as many as were killed in action, slightly more than the civilians murdered by the MCP.[68]

Though the MCP leadership had expounded a Maoist line of protracted revolutionary warfare in the countryside, the Party was not in fact bound in any one form of struggle. Thus in 1955, by which time the true pacification of the countryside was well under way and two thirds of the guerrilla strength had been annihilated, Chin Peng attempted to retrieve at truce talks something of what he was definitively losing through armed struggle: room for manoeuvre. But these talks in December 1955 between him and Tunku Abdul Rahman, Chief Minister of a by now

66. Clutterbuck, op. cit., p. 90.
67. Pye, op. cit., p. 227.
68. Short, op. cit., p. 160.

effectively independent Malaya, broke down over the Tunku's refusal to go back to square one, so to speak, that is to recognize the MCP as a legal political party.

In the context of General Templer's political legacy of self-government elections (Templer returned to England in June 1954), the Tunku very wisely relied upon the surrender developments and the fashioning of amnesty terms appropriate to the aim of detaching people from the MCP rather than trying to end the suffering quickly by permitting the MCP to return to the 'legal struggle'.

By 1959 the creation of 'White areas'[69] had developed to the point where only a few hard-core areas of MCP resistance remained. But even in this closing stage of the insurgency, the erosion of the armed MCP's position in the country was as much, if not more, the result of exploiting the surrender of high-ranking armed MCP commanders than of the political prospects that had been opened up by the formal declaration of Malayan independence on 31 August 1957. When the Emergency itself was formally declared ended in 1960, Chin Peng was left with a comparatively small group (probably about 500) of hard-core guerrillas based on the Malayan-Thai border area. There is no reason to suppose that the promise of political independence for Malaya was in itself the most important factor at work.

Now, as will be shown, the British experience in Malaya – it was of course much more than British – was later on to be cited as having revealed certain principles of counter-insurgency that were applicable in similar (or apparently similar) situations elsewhere; particularly was this held to be the case in South Vietnam in the early 1960s. Here the writer would only like to say (some of it at the risk of repetitiveness) that though there

69. Communities which had co-operated to the extent of permitting their territory to be designated a 'white area' had a vested interest in continuing co-operation in order to remain free of the onerous restrictions that were in force in the non-white areas. No 'white area' reverted to its former state, a fact of great importance to the steady phasing of the counter-insurgency. But this was possible only because of the inability of the guerrillas to re-infiltrate areas in force, as has occurred so many times in South Vietnam.

are indeed *tactical* principles, many of them learned from, or polished in, the Malayan Emergency, which are more or less universally applicable, the *strategic* problem in a newly politically independent state is altogether different from that facing a colonial-type administration. Moreover, in independent nations of the South East Asian kind, certain factors assume immense importance which are to a large extent subsumed in the total impact a colonial administration makes upon the society it seeks to dominate.

The most obvious example in Malaya has already been touched upon briefly: the communal or, if it is preferred, racial problem. Had the MCP engaged in insurgency against an independent Malaysian government, its task would have been very much easier in this regard. It could have appealed to the politically disappointed Chinese (and, possibly, Indians) in terms of offering them opportunities of advancement that otherwise might have appeared unavailable. So long as a colonial administration held sway, then it determined the avenues of advancement and could demarcate the legal from the subversive areas of activity in a way not open to a politically independent regime seeking to establish its own authority (and indeed legitimacy) in a new social situation.

So long as the colonial administration could preserve its own, very special kind of authority, the power struggle was only meaningful (aside from joining the insurgency) in terms of supporting the administration. Politics in the Western sense of the term just could not exist in that politico-social context. But the moment the communal groupings begin to contest the 'spoils system' that always accompanies the acquisition of national independence in countries of the South East Asian kind, the nature of politics is transformed.[70]

It is transformed not only because all kinds of political, social and economic possibilities (or the appearance thereof) for one's

70. It has indeed been persuasively argued in Milton Osborne, *Region of Revolt*, Penguin Books, 1971, p. 175, that the Malayan Chinese were not really won over to *approval* of the established political system, which involves permanent Malay political domination.

own communal racial group are created, if only some kind of fairly definitive position of power can be attained, but also because of the intense feeling of being threatened by the other community or communities, a feeling previously disguised by the political framework created by the utterly foreign colonial overlord. So long as the colonial administration persists, then all local politics are of a very limited nature – except for the insurgency itself. The insurgency may have an appeal to a certain kind of ambitious politician so long as it seems to be increasing in politico-military intensity. But the implementation of efficient counter-insurgent measures by the colonial administration makes it extraordinarily difficult and dangerous for an ordinarily, civilianly ambitious would-be politician to make or keep contact with the insurgents. It is not nearly so difficult, as will be shown, for ambitious men and groups of this kind to blur the distinction between armed insurgent and legal subversive when there is in power not an administration of a supranational kind but an independent *government* seeking to justify its measures in a purely national political context.

Aside from this fundamental difference between the Malayan Emergency and, say, the situation in South Vietnam from the late 1950s onwards, there is the fact, unpalatable as it may be to liberal feelings in the West, that a Western colonial bureaucracy was just much more efficient as a *machine* than the bureaucracies that have come into being since political independence.[71] To some extent this relates to the quite new political situation that has just been touched upon. It also relates to the debilitating effects upon the indigenous bureaucracy that flows from its having been directed for a very long time, at the highest levels of administration, by foreigners belonging to a civilization that had developed the civilian mode of ordering public affairs to a degree of cold efficiency undreamed-of by the bureaucracies of the past.

Aside from this, in turn, there was the fact of a superior technology being brought to bear – in good time. There is a point,

71. The notable exception is of course the Communist mode of ordering affairs.

as will be shown in the case of South Vietnam, beyond which the *political* intensity of the Communist idea-organization has developed to such an extent as to render nugatory – at least at a politically (or even humanly) acceptable price – the employment of Western technology. But that point was never anything like nearly reached by the Malayan Communist Party and its front organizations. This aspect of the struggle cannot be explored in detail here; some facets of it, for example chemical warfare against food production, have been touched upon. Another example may usefully be cited: the introduction of the helicopter meant that a new ratio of time between technological and humanly physical movement had been established: ten minutes by helicopter equalled ten hours on foot.[72] But this was important largely because the armed MCP was being isolated from its base amongst the population at large.

There were other features of the Malayan Emergency that were of some significance: the armed MCP received virtually no cadre infiltrators to stiffen its resistance and it appears to have received virtually no arms and supplies from outside. The matter of infiltration can be exaggerated: the capacity to absorb infiltrators into a guerrilla movement – and they must be absorbed into the movement to be effective – is a measure of the indigenous movement's politico-military success up to that point. But nor did the armed MCP enjoy a privileged sanctuary outside the country for training and recuperation. And as the weaponry of its enemy steadily increased in intensity and efficiency, the MCP had to go on making do, for the most part, with what it had at the beginning of the insurgency.[73]

Thus, looked at from the point of view of both sides, the phases of the insurgency can be fairly clearly marked. The armed MCP never really got beyond the terrorist stage to that of guerrilla warfare proper; and never came within crying dis-

72. Paget, op. cit., p. 175.

73. The symbiotic relationship that has been such an important feature – perhaps the central feature – of other recent revolutionary struggles never developed: the parasite was increasingly isolated from the host until it withered away.

tance of moving into the third, mobile-warfare phase. This was to some extent obscured from the British by lack of high-level Intelligence and perhaps by the fact that 1950 and 1951 were what Short calls 'the years of hope' for Asian Communists: the hopes being provided by the huge victory in China, and its apparently likely consequences elsewhere, and the temporarily successful Chinese intervention in Korea.

From the British point of view the phases were these: first, the various kinds of incapacity displayed pre-Briggs made for an attrition struggle until as late as 1950–51 and the appearance of losing the war for the confidence of the people-at-large. The second phase, which developed from 1952 onwards, saw the bringing to bear against the armed MCP of a series of measures, a weight of armed force and a mode of inter-agency co-ordination that was appropriate to the task of isolating the armed guerrillas, subverting the MCP infrastructure in the village society and thereby laying the groundwork for the destruction of the revolutionary guerrilla movement as a whole. The full implementation of this offensive policy took some eight years but by 1955 the MCP leader, Chin Peng, was so persuaded of its efficacy as to try to gain for the MCP the opportunity to wage a different form of struggle through truce talks.

The Malayan Emergency was chosen for more detailed study not because it was intrinsically more important than the other insurgencies which followed the Calcutta Conference in South East Asia, but for quite other reasons: it has been analysed more carefully than any other insurgency in the region; it has a clear beginning and end; the overwhelmingly Chinese make-up of the movement conferred upon it much clearer politico-social outlines than are to be found elsewhere; and the colonial police state nature of the counter-insurgency serves to make it reveal the technical problems involved in such an operation much more vividly than is the case in countries where insurgencies have coincided with struggles for power in the constitutional arena.

And yet the writer finds himself increasingly persuaded that there remain gaps in most of the now standard accounts of the

Malayan Emergency especially in so far as the British success has been represented as a model of counter-insurgency of general applicability to such situations. It is scarcely surprising that a guerrilla force which never numbered more than 8,000 men, which never received infusions of weaponry from abroad, which was deprived of an active sanctuary and which based itself altogether too much upon a removable population of squatters was eventually defeated by a force of 40,000 British and Commonwealth troops, 45,000 regular and special police, and a quarter of a million part-time Home Guards[74] in a country half of whose population were implacably opposed to what it saw as an attempt to establish Chinese hegemony.[75]

What is less easy to understand is why the MCP did not receive greater support from the Chinese population. This surely cannot be explained only in terms of the MCP adopting a Maoist policy of concentrating on the countryside. After all the Chinese, though enjoying a higher living standard than anywhere else in South East Asia, had been disabled from the point of view of citizenship by the failure of the immediately post-Second World War Malayan Union proposals; and yet those proposals met with 'no more than a lukewarm reception among the Chinese journalists of Malaya'.[76] Certainly the MCP did not like the form

74. Richard Meirs, *Shoot to Kill*, Faber & Faber, 1959, p. 32.

75. *Estimated Population of Malaya, Mid-1953*

| | Malaysians | Chinese | Indians and Pakistanis | All others | Total (Millions) |
|---|---|---|---|---|---|
| Federation | 2·80 | 2·15 | 0·67 | 0·08 | 5·70 |
| (% of total) | (49) | (38) | (12) | (1) | (100) |
| Singapore | 0·14 | 0·86 | 0·08 | 0·04 | 1·12 |
| (% of total) | (12) | (77) | (8) | (3) | (100) |
| | 2·94 | 3·01 | 0·75 | 0·12 | 6·82 |
| (% of total) | (43) | (44) | (11) | (2) | (100) |

*Source:* Registrar of Statistics, Government of Malaya.

76. Victor Purcell, *The Chinese in Southeast Asia*, Oxford University Press, 1948, p. 322.

the Union was to take and the Kuomintang thought of local politics in terms of Chinese mainland politics.

Nevertheless for decades the Chinese community had in effect been educated in their own schools nationalistically, indeed communistically in large part because of the staffing by 'poorly paid (and therefore leftist) teachers'.[77] They had suffered grievously at Japanese hands, men whose political stance varied from being supporters of Tan Kah-kee's leftist China relief fund to those regarded as pro-British were executed in considerable numbers, and the community in general had been intensively financially oppressed. This situation was the result of abysmal British failure to protect them in 1942.

They were deprived of a stake in the rice-growing economy, this being a Malaysian preserve (using the term Malaysian to denote Malays and 'Indonesians'), and thus deprived of the basic peasant stake in an Asian country. It was only as a result of the resettlement programme that they received titles to plots of land suitably close to the New Villages, which certainly resulted in a stable section of the rural economy and, when the Special Branch had done their work, a politically quiescent society as well.

Does one clue to MCP difficulties in building a political base outside the squatter community and, earlier, in the trade union movement, lie in the nature of the Malayan Chinese society itself? Considered as a community of a homogeneous kind, it had by 1937 acquired a useful spread of occupations upon which to build a political base: Chinese comprised 78 per cent of the miners, 21 per cent of the rubber tappers (though working for the overwhelming part on Chinese holdings) and 79 per cent of factory labour.[78] This did mean, of course, that the crucial estate rubber industry, in which a comparatively docile Indian labour force was predominant, lay outside the area of 'natural' support for the MCP.

However, considering the possible Chinese base of support, it must first be noticed that the distribution of Chinese varied

77. ibid., p. 278.

78. Virginia Thompson, *Labor Problems in Southeast Asia*, Yale University Press, New Haven, 1947, pp. 76–7.

widely from state to state[79] and, secondly, that the different clans or 'tribes', as they used to be called in British reports, were distributed in different ways. The Hokkiens, whose leader Tan Kah-kee was a Communist sympathizer, were on the whole concentrated in the urbanized Straits Settlements – and in Johore, one of the very worst centres of insurgency. The MCP's adoption of rural guerrilla warfare and consequent concentration of arms in the countryside permitted the virtual 'neutralization' of the cities and large towns by the British. Hakkas and Cantonese far outnumbered Hokkiens in the Federation, Hakkas supplying the bulk of mine workers; Hailams were in urban areas predominant amongst domestic servants while mostly being rubber tappers in rural areas; the Cantonese spread their occupational activities much more widely in both urban and rural areas.[80]

Since the MCP naturally made no distinction between clans, too much should not be made of this. But when it is remembered that in many years before the Second World War about the

79. The estimated population, as on 30 June 1950, was distributed by race group and territory as follows:

| Territory | Malaysians | Chinese | Indians and Pakistanis | All others | Total |
|---|---|---|---|---|---|
| Penang | 144,120 | 263,390 | 59,298 | 6,419 | 473,227 |
| Malacca | 131,069 | 102,641 | 21,098 | 3,700 | 258,508 |
| Perak | 386,486 | 473,622 | 149,160 | 9,335 | 1,018,603 |
| Selangor | 203,783 | 388,245 | 155,273 | 16,981 | 764,282 |
| Negri Sembilan | 118,872 | 122,919 | 41,663 | 5,094 | 288,548 |
| Pahang | 141,761 | 103,900 | 15,695 | 2,512 | 263,868 |
| Johore | 354,120 | 379,009 | 59,458 | 5,355 | 797,942 |
| Kedah | 399,887 | 124,314 | 54,105 | 10,894 | 589,200 |
| Kelantan | 426,622 | 24,162 | 5,242 | 8,287 | 464,313 |
| Trengganu | 214,493 | 16,417 | 1,726 | 535 | 233,171 |
| Perlis | 58,701 | 12,453 | 1,736 | 1,997 | 74,887 |
| Total | 2,579,914 | 2,011,072 | 564,454 | 71,109 | 5,226,549 |

The distribution has not altered significantly since the taking of the 1947 census.

Federation of Malaya Annual Report 1950, p. 17.

80. Virginia Thompson, op. cit.

same number of Chinese were leaving Malaya as were entering it and that during the war the MCP were hunted men chiefly concerned to eliminate collaborators and/or opponents when opportunity offered, it is reasonable to assume that it needed a far longer time than it had before embarking on insurgency to create the very widespread and in-depth infrastructure that was slowly built up in Vietnam. The exigencies of the trade-union strategy also seems probably to have left intact the traditional secret societies, some of which were used to defend mines and other businesses during the Emergency. Indeed so pervasive were the post-war activities of these societies that the depleted police Intelligence service was apt to see in them the chief threat to the future along with pan-Malayan extremists.

The result of inadequate preparation of an alternative government or 'parallel hierarchies' outside the squatter population was, on the Party's own admission, a far too large reliance upon activities that may properly be called terrorist in the early phase of the war, a fact which was cleverly exploited by the British in persistently designating the MCP guerrillas as the Communist Terrorist Organization (CTO). If by this term is meant that over the worst years of the insurgency more civilians than members of the security services were killed and wounded, then the figures cited overleaf, taken from the *Federation of Malaya Annual Report 1956*, do not bear them out. Moreover, the fact that the guerrillas suffered far more casualties than either security forces or civilians, casualties that can scarcely have been suffered while terrorizing civilians, suggest that the guerrillas were far more than mere terrorists.

On the other hand, there is no evidence that the MCP effectively represented, in terms of genuine popular support, the aspirations of the Chinese community, a community which appears to have lacked the social cohesiveness, even in the squatter areas for that matter, to be moved willingly to revolt. Whatever the British might have done constitutionally at the end of the Second World War, there is no reason whatsoever to suppose that the MCP, any more than any other Communist party with arms at its disposal, would have been prepared to share power. A

*Communist Terrorist, Security Forces and Civilian Casualties 1948–56*

| | 1948 | 1949 | | 1950 | | 1951 | | 1952 | | 1953 | | 1954 | | 1955 | | 90 months Average to | 1956 | | Total |
|---|---|---|---|---|---|---|---|---|---|---|---|---|---|---|---|---|---|---|---|
| Half-year | II | I | II | I | II | I | II | I | II | I | II | I | II | I | II | 31–12–55 | I | II | 102 months |
| *Terrorists:* | | | | | | | | | | | | | | | | | | | |
| Killed | 62·3 | 52·8 | 50·3 | 50·0 | 58·0 | 88·5 | 91·0 | 94·8 | 96·5 | 73·3 | 84·5 | 66·5 | 51·6 | 38·3 | 29·3 | 65·8 | 26·8 | 21·0 | 6,215 |
| Captured | 43·8 | 30·2 | 26·0 | 12·7 | 11·8 | 9·7 | 10·5 | 9·0 | 11·5 | 6·8 | 5·3 | 4·8 | 3·7 | 6·0 | 3·0 | 12·9 | 3·0 | 5·6 | 1,221 |
| Surrendered | 9·3 | 13·2 | 28·7 | 17·0 | 7·5 | 16·5 | 17·0 | 17·8 | 24·8 | 29·5 | 32·5 | 19·2 | 16·0 | 25·2 | 16·3 | 19·3 | 13·2 | 9·2 | 1,877 |
| | | | | | | | | | | | | | | | | Total No. of Eliminations | | | 9,313 |
| Wounded | NR,† | NR | NR | NR | NR | 53·0 | 55·2 | 52·8 | 46·5 | 20·7 | 27·8 | 18·8 | 16·7 | 18·5 | 8·5 | 43·5* | 10·8 | 8·7 | 2,724 |
| | | | | | | | | | | | | | | | | | Total | | 12,037 |
| *Security Forces:* | | | | | | | | | | | | | | | | | | | |
| Killed | 24·8 | 17·7 | 20·5 | 33·8 | 31·7 | 43·5 | 40·5 | 29·2 | 14·7 | 6·7 | 8·7 | 7·0 | 7·5 | 6·8 | 6·3 | 19·9 | 3·7 | 4·2 | 1,843 |
| Wounded | 35·2 | 17·2 | 24·0 | 39·2 | 43·5 | 56·7 | 58·5 | 41·0 | 25·8 | 7·0 | 12·5 | 12·5 | 13·2 | 10·2 | 7·0 | 26·8 | 7·0 | 6·2 | 2,499 |
| | | | | | | | | | | | | | | | | | Total | | 4,342 |
| *Civilians:* | | | | | | | | | | | | | | | | | | | |
| Killed | 52·5 | 22·3 | 33·3 | 52·7 | 55·0 | 46·8 | 42·0 | 40·5 | 16·7 | 6·2 | 8·0 | 9·0 | 7·2 | 6·5 | 3·8 | 26·8 | 3·0 | 2·0 | 2,445 |
| Wounded | 24·8 | 10·7 | 22·7 | 36·8 | 31·3 | 31·2 | 28·2 | 19·3 | 7·0 | 1·2 | 1·3 | 2·7 | 2·5 | 2·7 | 1·3 | 14·9 | 4·8 | 1·2 | 1,378 |
| | | | | | | | | | | | | | | | | | Total | | 3,823 |
| *Contacts* | NR | NR | NR | 56·2 | 107·7 | 156·5 | 162·0 | 156·7 | 154·7 | 118·5 | 116·0 | 90·5 | 75·0 | 58·5 | 35·7 | 107·3‡ | 42·2 | 88·8 | 8,213 |

* Over 60 months only – January 1951 to December 1955. † NR = No monthly record maintained. ‡ Over 72 months only – January 1950 to December 1955. The above figures are monthly averages calculated per half-year. Adjustments made up to 31 December 1956 are incorporated.

totalitarian party which acted impetuously in trying to mount an insurgency was defeated by the superior skills and overwhelming numbers brought to bear by an imperial autocracy. Though certain innovations were introduced by the British, the Emergency was to a large extent the last of a long series of colonial pacifications. The same methods were attempted in Cyprus with much less obvious success; indeed on a very different terrain, social as well as geographical, many of the methods proved counter-productive. The same methods are being applied in Northern Ireland in a situation of communal hatred not wholly dissimilar to Malaya, though altogether dissimilar as to an active sanctuary (until the turn of 1973) and infusions of modern weapons which were denied to the MCP guerrillas.

But there is no blueprint. As one of the greatest counter-insurgency experts has put it recently: 'The process is a sort of game based on intense mental activity allied to a determination to find things out and an ability to regard everything on its merits without regard to customs, doctrine or drill.'[81] And yet of course the things found out may be intractable in certain situations; Malaya happened not to be one of those situations.[82]

The extent of communal or minority rivalries and the limited competence of recently independent governments – themselves striving to attain a recognition of legitimacy – may cause a situation in which insurgency is never really mastered over decades. Burma is a case in point. The insurgency mounted by the Burma Communist Party (BCP), in answer to 'the big drum beaten in Calcutta', as the then Premier, U Nu, put it, was led by a Communist party which, though it had participated in the 'anti-Japanese Resistance' (such as it was, which was not much), had gained no great reputation or power out of the movement since it had participated as part of a nationalist coalition.

Like the MCP, it had turned from trade-union struggle to revolutionary guerrilla warfare. The insurgency was aimed at

81. Frank Kitson, *Low Intensity Operations*, Faber & Faber, 1971, p. 131.

82. Richard Clutterbuck's *Riot and Revolution in Singapore and Malaya, 1945-1963*, Faber, 1973, received after the above was written, answers many of the questions raised here.

the Anti-Fascist People's Freedom League (AFPFL), a nationalist coalition dominated by the Burma Socialist Party. The AFPFL claimed to be the liberators of Burma from British rule and they set about trying in effect (though not in constitutional theory) to establish one-party rule through control of the trade-union congress, the All-Burma Peasant Organization and State monopolies, especially of the all-important rice industry. They sought thereby to create a vast spoils system. They also controlled in a directly political fashion the armed forces. They were committed to a social democratic programme of almost incredible optimism,[83] including an ambitious land redistribution scheme that was made easier over large areas because of the resumption of land by alien Indian moneylenders in British Burma.

The AFPFL's disadvantage, as it was the disadvantage of the BCP, was to appear as a 'Burman chauvinist' party in the eyes of the minority communities. The communal or racial problem in Burma was altogether different from that of Malaya, where the two major communities, the Malays and the Chinese, both enjoyed advantages and strengths of different kinds. In Burma the minorities were fully exposed to the superior power of the Burman majority.[84] It was not long before significant personalities and groups in the minority areas, most of which were formally States within the Union of Burma, began to believe that their new overlords were much more oppressive than the British had ever been. The oppression was held to exist in a number of forms, ranging from economic exploitation to the overbearing behaviour of the army and the Union Military Police.

83. For example, U Nu's speech on mass education, 18 October 1949: 'Therefore, many branches of knowledge such as relativity, eugenics, quantum theory, laissez-faire, surplus value, utilitarianism, geopolitics and so on . . . will be within easy reach of our cowherds, cultivators, hewers of wood, and drawers of water.'

84. There were in 1957 nearly 13 million Burmans; 1,800,000 Karens; 1,500,000 Shans; 450,000 Kachins; 400,000 Chins, 400,000 Mons, plus other indigenous minority groups and sizable Indian and Chinese groups, according to the estimate made by C. A. Fisher in his *A Social, Economic, and Political Geography of South-East Asia*, Methuen, 1964, p. 468.

The dangers to the AFPFL government were compounded by the fact that some of the disaffected minority groups, the Karens and Kachins in particular, belonged to peoples the British had designated as martial and had accordingly used in preference to Burmans in the armed services. The task of the BCP therefore was to exploit these 'contradictions' in the new Union and to form a united front of all disaffected elements against the AFPFL government in Rangoon, which, apart from the disadvantages cited, suffered from the very important disadvantage suffered by every seat of central government in South East Asia: the distrust of village society for what was called government (not the government) or, even more sinisterly, the Centre. This distrust was very often exacerbated by the behaviour of Burman officials, civilian and military, who regarded service in the countryside as a form of exile and took out their rancour on the locals. This is a feature of the region that is of great importance to the Communist cadres who are prepared to forgo the comforts of urban living in order to serve the people, as they would put it, in the rural backwaters. That they doubtless hope for positions of power in a totalitarian apparatus at the conclusion of the struggle is not to the point while the struggle lasts. Thakin Than Tun and the BCP leaders were prepared to endure great and protracted hardships in waging 'people's war' against a formally 'progressive', if extraordinarily incompetent, social democratic government simply because it had been designated semi-colonial by the Cominform. Some of these leaders still were waging this struggle in 1973, despite a number of opportunities provided by government amnesties to return to 'the legal fold'.

The Burmese insurgent scene has throughout been complicated by the participation in one way or another of Communists within the constitutional arena as well. At first this was done through a legal political party, without, of course, the word Communist in its title; later through a front party; and later still through individual participation in the present one-party regime, ostensibly on the ground that such individuals had lost their allegiance to the armed insurgent BCP. This detachment of individuals of substance from the armed ranks through offering them opportunities within the legal regime doubtless has had some effect upon insurgent morale.

But the BCP suffered graver disadvantages from the outset. The British had never attempted to sponsor and arm a Burman resistance movement of the Malayan type; such use of Burmese as was made was confined to the martial races, the Karens and Kachins in particular.[85] Thus the BCP began as a very ill-armed organization (unlike the MCP and also unlike the Vietminh, as will be shown).

Though insurgencies of varying intensity developed amongst the Karens, the Kachins and the Mons, the size and geographical configuration of Burma made co-ordination extremely difficult.[86] Regional conservatism and distrust of Burmans of any political persuasion greatly compounded the BCP's difficulties in this regard. It established certain base areas and on occasion a united front was proclaimed; but the base areas did not expand and the fronts were of extreme frailty. The numbers of insurgents were quite large at the end of the 1940s – Rangoon very nearly fell to the Karen insurgents – but the failure to co-ordinate activities resulted by 1953–4 in severe setbacks, quite large surrender figures and an offer by the BCP to suspend hostilities

85. During the Second World War Wingate's Chindits, waging guerrilla warfare against Japanese communications behind the British lines in Burma, engaged Kachins in their task. Though the two Chindit expeditions do not properly belong to the kind of guerrilla warfare with which the author is primarily concerned, they are of considerable interest. See particularly: Sir William Slim, *Defeat into Victory*, Cassell, 1956; Bernard Fergusson, *Beyond the Chindwin*, Collins, 1951; Michael Calvert, *Prisoners of Hope*, Cape, 1952. In his foreword to Sir Bernard Fergusson's book, the late Field Marshal Lord Wavell remarks: 'Be it noted too, that though we had passed through Northern Burma in defeat, though the land had been under Japanese occupation and propaganda for a year, we found more friends and helpers than did our enemies' (p. 14). It must be presumed that he is referring particularly to the Kachins. British officers also led Karen guerrillas during the Second World War. Such Karens suffered terrible reprisals from Burman forces.

86. Cf. Burma's area of 261,789 square miles with Malaya's (West Malaysia's) 50,700 square miles.

if it would be taken into a coalition with the AFPFL.[87] By the end of 1953 BCP agents were moving in and out of China, but perhaps because of the very considerable distance between the BCP bases in Burma proper and China (or perhaps because the BCP was not 'doing its own thing' well enough in Peking eyes) the BCP did not receive effective assistance.

The various insurgencies continue in some form or other to this day. There has since been added a Shan insurgency and, towards the end of 1970, the proclamation of a new insurgency led by U Nu, long since displaced by General Ne Win's military regime. Once again, this new insurgent leadership seeks to unite the minority people against a 'Burman chauvinist' regime. It grandiosely calls itself the United National Liberation Front; how, or if, it will progress is impossible to determine. But it is of interest, amongst other things, in its demonstration of how a man who as Premier of Burma sincerely denounced what he called 'the cult of the gun', in the name of Buddhist gentleness is now prepared to make his devotions to – the Armalite rifle.

The Burmese insurgencies for the most part provide an antidote to the belief that in South East Asia the Communists everywhere have a lien on this kind of politico-military activity. Most of the insurgencies in Burma have arisen out of the fact that the British created a kind of State which they alone could fairly easily control and drew boundaries that were meaningful only in terms of the colonial era. For example, in northern Burma the Kachin and Shan peoples straddle the Sino-Burmese border. As a result, though the conservative leadership of the Shan insurgency looks (unavailingly) to their conservative 'cousins' in Thailand (the Shans correctly call themselves Thai) and eschews any support from the Chinese, there is in existence a considerable Kachin insurgent force which appears to be significantly

87. It was estimated in *The Nation*, Rangoon, in April 1953 that the BCP insurgents numbered some 2,500 and the Karens some 3,700 early that year. The total number of variegated insurgents in the field early in 1952 was estimated to be of the order of 37,000 (*Australia's Neighbours*, Melbourne, March 1954).

composed of Kachins drawn from militia units of China's Yunnan province.[88]

The extreme left-wing military government of Burma thus faces, after over twenty years of political independence for the country, a crippling internal defence burden, a decaying economy (part of which deterioration must be attributed to the insurgencies) and two particular insurgent threats: the Peking-sponsored, though locally engendered, Kachin movement in the north and the Karen-based United National Liberation Front in the south-east.

In the Philippines, on the other hand, the Communist (Hukbalahap) insurgency, which in 1950 looked as though it might well spread catastrophically for the government in Manila, has in fact been chiefly confined to two very poor and landlord-ridden provinces in central Luzon. It seems probable that the maiming, though by no means the destruction, of the Huk movement may be attributed to the only counter-insurgent to acquire the status of hero in the eyes of large numbers of people, the late Ramon Magsaysay, himself once a guerrilla hero. As Secretary of Defence and later as President, he provided the kind of leadership, humanly speaking, that was provided by General Templer in Malaya.

Though aspects of the Filipino insurgency will be touched upon when discussing the various features of revolutionary warfare, it is desirable briefly to mention some aspects of Magsaysay's strategy at this point. Magsaysay stressed that his policy was one of 'All-out Friendship or All-out Force'; he was concerned to compel the people at large to choose sides. This was done chiefly through a judicious mixture of relentless struggle against the armed guerrillas, which was carried out with very great technical skill, and the indoctrination of the armed forces in how to carry out what are these days known as 'civic action' programmes. Magsaysay's indefatigable energies were devoted towards personally seeing to the thoroughness with which such a dual policy simply must be implemented. This thoroughness

88. *Far Eastern Economic Review*, 12 December 1970.

was also a feature of the co-ordination between the various counter-insurgent agencies.

Though the Huks were seeking to exploit the glaring 'contradictions' existing between the rich and the masses of very poor, particularly in Pampanga and Tarlac provinces, Magsaysay did not, as is sometimes imagined, attempt a large-scale land reform. What he did was to offer land and rehabilitation to Huks who would surrender, on terms comparable to those enjoyed by returned soldiers (retired veterans). This was undoubtedly a shrewd move. But of the only sample of surrenderers interviewed, so far as the author is aware, 61 per cent cited hardships in the mountains and no less than 45 per cent cited their belief in the losing nature of their cause as reasons for surrendering. Once again, as in Malaya, it was war against the wills and minds of men that was crucial.[89] In the process of breaking the will of the Communist revolutionary guerrilla movement, nearly 10,000 Huks had to be killed, over 1,500 wounded and over 4,000 captured.[90]

Moreover, Magsaysay was enormously assisted in his task by what was probably the greatest Intelligence success in the history of counter-insurgency: the capture late in 1950 of the headquarters of the politbureau of the Communist Party of the Philippines, a large part of the Huk top leadership and almost certainly important Huk plans. The fact that such a capture was of such importance to the counter-insurgent effort throws a harsh light on the theory that Communist revolutionary insurgencies are simply spontaneous risings of the peasantry against injustices felt to have grown intolerable.

By the same token, the deterioration of standards of pacification and of civic ethics in general since the death of Magsaysay throws a harsh light on the theory that revolutionary guerrilla

89. See Alvin A. Scarf, *The Philippine Answer to Communism*, Stanford University Press.

90. Maximo V. Soliven, in S. N. Ray (ed.), *Vietnam: Seen From East and West*, Nelson (Australia), 1966, states that at the height of the insurrection the Huks had no more than 12,800 men in action, with less than 10,000 arms amongst them (p. 114).

warfare is simply a matter of sinister Communist conspiracy. The recrudescence of Huk activity to the point where it has established a symbiotic relationship with the larger Philippines society, the younger elements of which are increasingly disillusioned by the corrupt use of Western parliamentary forms by self-seeking individuals and groups, is proof that taking appropriate measures against a revolutionary insurgency over a period of years is not in itself a solution of the 'contradictions' which the revolutionary movement sought to exploit for its own totalitarian ends.

Looking at South East Asia in general since the Second World War, it is clear that there have been four kinds of insurgency. First, there is the insurgency mounted by elements (usually conservative) of minority peoples who feel themselves oppressed in various ways by the majority people within a 'nation-state' whose boundaries were defined by the Western imperialists and whose modern-style nationality was never completed, was held in abeyance indeed, by the fact and to some extent by the policies of the utterly foreign (and very small) colonial overlord group. Such insurgencies have occurred, with varying intensity and on disparate levels of political consciousness, not only in Burma but in Sumatra and East Indonesia. They have occurred, under French and American auspices, in the tribal areas of Laos and Vietnam. One appears to be occurring amongst the Muslim Malay population of southern Thailand. North-eastern India is also an area where local (tribal) resentment has resulted in protracted insurgency; now Mindanao in the Philippines is another.

Secondly, there is the insurgency mounted within a racially and culturally homogeneous society by an armed Communist party which affects to believe that political independence in the form of a Western-style liberal-capitalist democracy is a sham. It has been suggested that the claim that capitalist-democratic independence is a sham has not – in the long run – been only the result of international Communist pronouncements but has also been based upon certain social realities in the countryside that have seemed to make independence a sham for the people-at-large, at least in some rural areas.

Thirdly, there is the insurgency mounted by a Communist party affecting to represent the people-at-large against a colonial regime but in fact representing only one special group within one community of a plural society. Such was the case with the Malayan Communist Party. To some extent, it may be supposed, the MCP 'represented', albeit under quite false colours, the 'rights' of the squatters to their unauthorized way of life on the jungle fringes. But such representation as ever existed was clearly of a fortuitous and temporary nature, since virtually the whole of the resettled squatter population has accepted the fact of its resettlement.

Indeed the more the Malayan 'Emergency' is considered, the more a-typical it seems to have been, quite apart from the peculiar sociological make-up of the society. Denied a privileged sanctuary and infusions of weaponry; paying lip-service to the notion of protracted revolutionary warfare, and so failing to launch a conceivably successful politico-military blitzkrieg and instead engaging in the silliest kinds of terrorization; launching a muddled form of campaign with very inadequate political preparation and chiefly relying on a socially peripheral popular political base; confronting an efficient colonial government defending commercial interests quite vital to the dollar earnings of the homeland on a terrain marked by excellent communications – the MCP appears in retrospect to have acted absurdly. And yet the question remains, a question that is reinforced by the Burmese experience, whether revolutionary guerrilla warfare, however careful the political preparations, however clever the tactics employed, can succeed where communal problems are central.

Lastly, and immeasurably most formidable, there is the insurgency mounted by an armed Communist party which can stake a plausible claim to be *the* politico-military expression of an all-embracing nationalism against a foreign invader or against a foreign regime. If such a claim can be embodied in a front organization that is ostensibly non-Communist; and if it is directed against a colonial administration that has quite recently lost all power in a humiliating manner, then the insurgency is likely to be extraordinarily difficult to combat.

Such was the case in Vietnam between 1946 and 1954; and so what is now called the First Indo-China War deserves some attention.

## CHAPTER 5

# THE FIRST INDO-CHINA WAR

Most of the Vietnamese strong points are political; most French strong points are military.

TRUONG CHINH

The Indochina war became deadlocked politically in 1948, when the French political hesitations failed to make the Vietnamese nationalists an effective counterforce in the psychological struggle. It became strategically hopeless when the Chinese Reds arrived on Indochina's borders late in 1949 and China thus became a 'sanctuary' where Viet-Minh military forces could be trained and refitted. It was lost militarily as of 1953 when the cease-fire in Korea allowed the concentration of the whole Asian Communist war effort on the Indochinese theatre.

BERNARD FALL

REVOLT against French colonialism did not of course begin with the foundation of the Vietminh Front during the Second World War. It may be said that from the beginning of the French conquest – of Cochinchina in the south in 1862 – combined qualities of diplomatic and guerrilla resistance were in evidence.[1] Resistance was also encountered, in a protracted guerrilla form, when the conquest was later extended to Annam (central Vietnam) and Tongking.[2] Incidents of armed opposition to the French in Cochinchina continued throughout the sixties and seventies, 'Often the underlying motivations of the Vietnamese participants are difficult to judge. Much of the opposition seems

1. P. J. Honey, *Genesis of a Tragedy*, Benn, 1968, p. 45.

2. See for example Joseph Buttinger, *Vietnam: A Political History*, Praeger, 1968, Ch. III. For Cochinchina, see particularly Milton E. Osborne, *The French Presence in Cochinchina and Cambodia, 1859–1905*, Cornell University Press, 1969. Dennis J. Duncanson, *Government and Revolution in Vietnam*, Oxford University Press, 1968, is essential reading.

to have been fundamental: the reactions of peasants against a foreign presence that contributed to unstable conditions in the countryside.'[3]

But it is necessary also to notice that amongst the educated classes resisters were matched by loyal collaborators with the French. The latter did not by any means all act out of considerations of political expediency; some genuinely believed that French rule represented a 'liberation movement', so to speak – at any rate in the spheres of intellect and imagination. It has been argued with authority that 'In both North and South there are many signs that the French still dominate the conceptual framework in educated peoples' minds.'[4] Such a result naturally engendered very ambivalent feelings towards the West (or *la geste française*) on the part of Vietnamese who embraced both the (rather vague) notion of 'modernization' *and* the idea of 'national' revolt against the source of modernizing attitudes of mind. One of the appeals of Communism to Asian intellectuals placed in such a mental situation is a belief that, while it too is of Western provenance, it promises a surpassing of Western civilization.[5]

Despite evidence of a spirit of revolt persisting in various areas of the country, the French colonial apparatus was able to control Vietnam without very much difficulty up to the Japanese occupation during the Second World War.[6] The Kuomintang-style VNQDD nationalist party, founded in the late 1920s, and the Communist Party of Indo-China, which was also on the scene by that time, staged abortive revolts in 1930. The revolts were repressed with savagery by the French administration. However, it is of some significance that this repression of what

3. Osborne, op. cit., pp. 64–5. But see Duncanson, op. cit., pp. 136–7.

4. Duncanson, op. cit., p. 71.

5. For the masses, as Paul Mus remarked long ago, it can resemble the comprehensive and cohesive State religion of yesteryear. See his *Viêt-Nam: Sociologie d'une guerre*, Éditions du Seuil, Paris, 1952.

6. About 11,000 French troops, 16,000 indigenous militia and 507 French police agents kept the country pacified until 1940 (John T. McAlister *Vietnam: The Origins of the Revolution*, Allen Lane The Penguin Press, 1969, p. 50). The Vietnamese population was then about 19 million.

was widely regarded in France as a nationalist uprising engendered such anger in that country that all those detained without trial were released quite soon.[7] At this time the VNQDD and the ICP were both small clandestine parties and the latter was concerned with the class rather than the nationalist struggle. Though the infrastructure established by the Communist party was too difficult for the colonial administration to destroy, the counter-intelligence and police services did what was necessary to keep the country effectively pacified.[8]

Both the French-orientated class of civil servants in the South and their mandarinal counterparts in the North had a serious complaint in the very fact that though Indo-China had about one twelfth the population of British India it had three times as many expatriate officials.[9] High political ambitions could be fulfilled only by a very few, and then only in advisory councils. As to the people at large, though Indo-China was not a particularly good economic deal for France, except for a few special interests,[10] French rule did little to advance popular living standards, while dislocating the old village system and imposing an onerous system of imposts and state monopolies in opium, alcohol and salt of an odious kind.[11] Whether French colonial economic policy was on the whole more severe or disabling than that of other imperial powers is arguable, though it certainly failed to incl'ide Vietnamese in a share of indigenous agriculture of the export kind, while fostering large-scale European involvement, and its protectionist policy prevented the Vietnamese from developing their own industries. There was indeed

7. ibid., p. 130.

8. The VNQDD suffered more terribly during the French repression partly because of its tactics and inferior organizational techniques, and was not revived until helped back by the Chinese army after the Second World War.

9. Honey, op. cit., p. 51.

10. D. K. Fieldhouse, *The Colonial Empires*, Weidenfeld & Nicolson, 1966, pp. 387–8, shows that the margin between interest on government stock at home and abroad was small.

11. See Le Thanh Khoi, *Le Viet-Nam*, Éditions de Minuit, Paris, 1955, pp. 417–18.

a considerable irrigation achievement and the introduction of a certain amount of economic infrastructure for industrialization: roads, railways and so on.[12] But modernization was definitely not extended to indigenous farming, the occupation of the overwhelming mass of the population.[13]

This, however, is not to say that a rural situation existed in which revolutionaries could throughout the country lead a peasant revolt based on the slogan 'land to the tillers'. In Tonkin and Annam a very large percentage of the peasantry owned some land: the problem lay in its subdivision. It was in Cochinchina in the south, where the French vastly increased the acreage under cultivation, that some two thirds of cultivators were tenants paying up to 40 per cent of their crop in rent.[14] It was not there but in north and central Vietnam that the ICP's Vietminh Front was to score its great success.

However, in the 1930s there appeared to be no prospect whatsoever of the ICP coming to power in the lifetime of any member of the Communist Party. A rising in 1940 in Cochinchina

12. Another cause for complaint was the very small number indeed of Vietnamese who were 'assimilated' as French citizens. Only 2,746 were classified as French by naturalization in 1937 against over 36,000 French-born residents. (A considerable number of the former were Indians from Pondicherry.) Charles Robequain, *The Economic Development of French Indo-China*, Oxford University Press, 1944, provides tables, Ch. I.

13. Rice cultivation in Cochinchina was quadrupled between 1880 and 1939. But this was the result of the French promotion of large-scale farming.

14. But the Cochinese was much better fed than his brothers in Annam and Tongking, whose 'ownership' did not make them much better than tenants *vis-à-vis* the moneylender. The French geographer Pierre Gourou described the situation in Tongking thus: 'The peasant is led to borrow by poverty; when he has exhausted his resources following a bad harvest, he has to borrow. The interest on cash loans is extremely variable, 3 to 10 per cent per month. The lender covers himself by a mortgage on the harvest or goods of the borrower. For loans in kind the interest paid (also in kind) varies from 30 per cent to 50 per cent for one rice-growing season, that is to say, from 60 per cent to 100 per cent per annum.' Robequain saw population as 'the fundamental problem, the one on whose solution depend all the others'. For the problem of landless labourers in Annam and Tongking, see Donald Lancaster, *The Emancipation of French Indochina*, Oxford University Press, 1961, pp. 65–6. Also Eric H. Jacoby, *Agrarian Unrest in Southeast Asia*, Asia Publishing House, 1961, p. 180.

was put down in less than a fortnight, its repression again involving great cruelty.[15] But by then the Japanese were edging onto the scene. In mid-1941 the French Administration accepted an integration of Indo-China with the Japanese military system in East Asia. In return for permitting the Japanese to make do with very small forces, the Vichy-aligned Administration was granted a decent semblance of autonomy.

Apart from the quality of some of its leaders – which was not generally evident at this time – the hopes of the ICP had to rest on events over which they had no control. An extraordinary concatenation of circumstances and events placed this leadership, known only to colonial Intelligence services in 1941, at the head of an independent Vietnamese government only four years later – without a struggle.[16] And yet to put it like that, though it is true in a formal sense, is not to give sufficient emphasis to the great skill with which the ICP, under the guidance of Ho Chi Minh, exploited whatever opportunities offered. The first important breakthrough was to have the Vietminh subsidized and supported by the Kuomintang administration in South China as its Intelligence agency in Vietnam, for example, but the forming of the Vietminh Front in the border area in mid-1941 was a clever preparation for the future, and the Vietminh earned the Chinese auspices through being manifestly superior to the Vietnamese movement previously employed. Even so, this front organization formed by an exiled Communist party, led by a Comintern agent who had only recently rejoined its ranks,[17] still had to organize a show of resistance and obtain arms for the future if it was to stake a claim to be *the* nationalist movement – should the moment arise in which such a claim could be meaningfully staked, which was by no means certain until shortly before it came to power in August 1945.

15. Philippe Devillers, *Histoire du Viet-Nam de 1940 à 1942*. Éditions du Seuil, Paris, 1952, pp. 78–9.

16. 'Le 20 [August, 1945], le Viêt-Minh, sans lutte, est maître de toute l'administration, de tous les services de Hanoi' (ibid., p. 137).

17. Jean Lacouture, *Ho Chi Minh*, Penguin Books, 1967, is a very sympathetic study of this extraordinary man.

Considered as a purely political movement, the Vietminh was a national united front controlled by the ICP and making the kind of appeal based on patriotism (and rigorously eschewing any discussion of the 'social question') that was deemed most likely to make for a fairly rapid expansion – provided the organizational tactics were properly carried out. It was rivalled by the grouping known as the Dai Viet and the surviving VNQDD, which naturally had been patronized by the Kuomintang administration. The military strength of the Vietminh by the end of 1941 was only about one hundred soldiers, though volunteers were beginning to flock towards the training quarters of the man who was to become so well known as General Vo Nguyen Giap, at this time better known as a propagandist but long since a student of the military arts. It is of interest to notice that as Mao began to build a people's army out of 'declassed elements', the Vietminh began to build its people's army out of non-Vietnamese tribals, many of whom were later to serve the French with equal aplomb;[18] and city workers and petty civil servants.

The early Vietminh 'army' was a force chiefly concerned with armed propaganda, including terrorism against those who co-operated with the French Administration.[19] It would be fairly generally agreed that the Vietminh could claim two things in their favour during the immediate future: the cell organization and command system which enabled decisions 'reached in northern Tonkin to be put into effect in the Central Highlands of Annam and in the Mekong Delta';[20] and the movement of its cadres into Vietnam while the other contenders for political power remained in south China waiting upon future events. This is analogous with the KMT–CCP differences of approach towards Japanese-occupied areas in northern China; and it would be neither sensible nor decent for a student of guerrilla warfare to underplay the role of courage exemplified by men who felt the future was in their bones and acted accordingly.

18. Robert J. O'Neill, *General Giap: Politician and Strategist*, Cassell (Australia), 1969, p. 14.

19. Devillers, op. cit., p. 105; O'Neill, op. cit., p. 29.

20. O'Neill, op. cit., p. 29.

But it is also necessary to emphasize yet again the very great appropriateness for this kind of situation of Communist organization. The organizational skills of the ICP (which was very much in evidence despite its imminent tactical dissolution in order to further the claims of the Vietminh Front and in order to bemuse its allies) were shown at their most efficacious in the months leading up to the 'August Revolution' of August 1945. In the meantime these skills, particularly in the propaganda field, had reaped a valuable harvest of a kind more than somewhat ironic in retrospect: the support of the American Office of Strategic Services, father of the Central Intelligence Agency. The naïveté of American official circles in regard to anti-colonial movements at this time has been briefly touched upon in regard to China.[21] But the rhetorical questions asked by Ho Chi Minh, a Comintern agent with decades of experience, of a member of the OSS mission surely bespeak a contemptuous assessment of American intelligence: 'Am I any different from Nehru, Quezon – even George Washington? Was not Washington considered a revolutionary too?'[22] The contempt was well founded: the Americans were taken in, and the French administration began to realize that its problems included dangers from Sino-American ploys as the War began to draw to a close.

Meanwhile the decision had at first been made by the Vietminh Front leadership to prepare for guerrilla warfare rather than an armed general uprising. The shape of future strategy in this regard was revealed in Ho Chi Minh's instructions given out in December 1944:

1. The Viet-Nam Propaganda Unit for National Liberation shows by its name that greater importance should be attached to the political side than to the military side ... To act successfully, in the military field, the main principle is concentration of forces. Therefore, in accordance with the new instruction of the Organization [i.e. the ICP, now masquerading as the Vietnam Workers' Party], most resolute and energetic officers and men will be picked out of the ranks of the guerrilla units in Cao Bang, Bac Can, and Lang/Son [i.e.

21. See Bernard Fall, *The Two Vietnams*, Pall Mall Press, 1963, pp. 51–4, for a French view of American official attitudes to colonialism.

22. René J. Defourneaux, *Look* magazine, 9 August 1966.

in the Vietnam–China border areas] and a great amount of weapons will be concentrated to establish our main force.

Because ours is a national resistance by the whole people, we must mobilize and arm the whole people. Therefore, when concentrating our forces to set up the first unit, we must maintain the local armed forces, co-ordinate their operations and assist each other in all aspects. On its part, the main unit has the duty to guide the cadres of the local unit, assist them in drilling, and supply them with weapons if possible, thus helping these units to grow unceasingly.

2. With regard to local armed units, we will father their cadres for training, send trained cadres to various localities to exchange experience, maintain liaison, and co-ordinate military operations.

3. Concerning tactics, we will apply guerrilla warfare, which consists in being secret, rapid, active, now in the East, now in the West, arriving unexpectedly and leaving unnoticed.

The Viet-Nam Propaganda Unit for National Liberation is the first-born unit. It is hoped that other units will soon come into being. At first its size is small, however, its prospect is brilliant. It is the embryo of the Liberation Army and can move from North to South, throughout Vietnam.[23]

Its prospect indeed proved to have been brilliant, but this could not have been really evident at that time. However, in March 1945 another stroke of good fortune for the Vietminh occurred when the Japanese staged a *coup d'état* against the French Administration. During the war the Administration had used various devices to try to retain an influence over Indo-China, some of which were quite enlightened, but the policy was fundamentally one of encouraging various particularisms within an Indo-Chinese (not Vietnamese) frame of reference. There was a French anti-Japanese resistance but the general hope was placed in an American landing and then a joint Franco-American 'liberation' of Indo-China. The Japanese *coup* of 9 March put paid to such hopes. 'Individual Frenchmen demonstrated great bravery and suffered cruelly, but, for the Indochinese, French rule had ended.'[24] The titular Vietnamese

23. Ho Chi Minh, *On Revolution: Selected Writings, 1920–66*, Pall Mall Press, 1967, pp. 139–40.

24. Ellen J. Hammer, *The Struggle for Indochina*, Stanford University Press, 1954, p. 41.

Emperor, Bao Dai, announced the independence of Annam and its unification with Tonkin, though only Bao Dai abdicated: the rulers of Cambodia and Laos otherwise followed suit in declaring independence. The event was catastrophic for French prestige in Indo-China, but this was not realized in France. Within days de Gaulle in Paris was emphasizing France's determination that Indo-China would remain French. Indo-China was to have a 'special place' in 'the organization of the French community'.[25] French divisions were put in preparation for their own 'liberation' of Indo-China. Self-government for Indo-China was ruled right out.

However, the atom bombs and Japan's capitulation on 19 August put paid to that scheme too. Between the Japanese *coup* in March and the August capitulation the leadership of the Vietminh Front had been very carefully analysing the direction of events. The Japanese *coup* was noticed cautiously: 'Conditions are not yet sufficiently ripe for insurrection'; 'except for certain regions with favourable terrain which are already occupied by armed contingents, elsewhere in the entire country the progressive elements are preparing an insurrection, but as yet they are not ready for fighting and for sacrificing themselves'; the 'neutral' section of the population would take time to become anti-Japanese; there would certainly be an Allied landing in Indo-China. Thus: co-operation before the landings with the French against the new (and temporary) 'main enemy', the Japanese. Frenchmen who fought against the Japanese would have their property, freedom of trade etc. guaranteed as 'inviolable'.[26]

The main policy stresses were laid upon forms of struggle and organization. 'Utilizing the hatred caused by famine, we must develop agitation among the masses and draw them into the struggle (we must organize demonstrations to demand rice and other foodstuffs or to seize rice granaries ...)' But most important of all was 'The organization of power. We must

25. Rima Rathausky (ed.), *Documents of the August 1945 Revolution in Vietnam*, Australian National University, Canberra, 1963, p. vi.

26. ibid., pp. 4–6.

establish liberation Committees in factories, villages, on the properties of big landlords, in city streets, military barracks, schools, public and private services, etc. These Committees will acquire the character of a broad United National Anti-Japanese Front; on the other hand, they will be a sort of "provisional local administrative organ" in each factory, each village etc.'[27]

A note of Communist caution was sounded: 'the movement must not be allowed to develop in breadth to the detriment of its development in depth; therefore, simultaneously with organizing the movement it is extremely important to get things going in the sphere of political education and military instruction in accordance with the programme put forward by the Viet Minh.'

At this time (12 March 1945) the plan was to wait until the Allied forces had not only landed, but had made 'some progress', before launching a general insurrection designed to seize the initiative in the struggle.[28] The organizational preparation for the events of the following August, particularly in Tonkin, was masterly; so were the analyses of Allied situations liable to present 'contradictions' that could be exploited. For example, Free French forces were to be 'boycotted and isolated' while British, American and Chinese troops were to be welcomed – but also submitted to persistent nationalist propaganda.

Our policy is aimed at avoiding isolation in the face of the united Allied forces (China, France, Great Britain and the United States) which might invade our country and impose upon us a puppet government constituted by the French, or some other puppet government which does not answer to the aspirations of our people. That is why we must attract to our side the Soviet Union and the United States, because we shall then be able to offer resistance to the en-

27. ibid., pp. 7–8. It was at this time that the Communist Party began to show its extraordinary skill in fleshing out all manner of organizations, ranging from 'Peasants' National Salvation Associations' to 'Women's National Salvation Associations', all belong to the Vietnam Front under effective ICP leadership. See particularly Milton Sacks in Frank N. Trager (ed.), *Marxism in Southeast Asia*, Rand, New York, 1955, and Huyhn Kim Khan, 'The Vietnamese August Revolution', in *Journal of Asian Studies*, Vol. XXX, No. 4, August 1971.

28. Rathausky, op. cit., p. 9.

croachments of the French, who intend to establish their former position in Indo-China, and also the manoeuvres of certain Chinese militarists, who want to annex our country ... We must establish close contact with the Chinese and French peoples and obtain their support.[29]

In the meantime, the last word rested with the Japanese: would they hand over to their conquerors, the Allies, or to those who could best continue their role of ridding Asia of the white imperialists?[30] 'The Japanese forces of occupation – defeated, but still in control – were prepared to turn a blind eye ... Asian revolution was preferable to European *revanche*.'[31] The Vietminh occupied Hanoi and quickly secured the abdication of the Emperor Bao Dai at Hue. The implication was clear: the Vietminh Front government proclaimed in Hanoi had succeeded to the long line of Vietnamese rulers. The significance of this August Revolution can scarcely be overestimated, though it has often been underestimated. Though chances undreamed of a few years back had eased the Vietminh's path to power, M. Lacouture is surely right in arguing that:

It was a triumph for the techniques of Communism: streamers, leaflets, microphones, slogans chanted in rhythm until the chanters were out of breath. The crowd was taken over, conditioned, moulded, while the Vietminh's shock-troops occupied the public buildings and seized the arms and ammunition of the Indochinese Guard. The nationalist organizations seemed to have vanished. The students' union became loosely affiliated with the Vietminh. On 20 August Ho and his associates were in control of the city.[32]

Ho Chi Minh's appeal for this 'general uprising', issued on 16 August, was a masterpiece of succinct national front rhetoric: the Japanese army was crushed, the Vietminh numbered millions – intellectuals, workers, peasants, businessmen, soldiers, all the tribals; it had appointed a Liberation Committee to lead 'the entire people'. 'Our struggle will be a long and hard one. Because the Japanese are defeated, we shall not be liberated over-

29. ibid., pp. 47, 48.
30. Devillers, op. cit., p. 136.
31. Lacouture, op. cit., p. 90.
32. ibid., p. 91.

night. We still have to make further efforts ... Only a united struggle will bring us independence ... Join the Viet Minh Front, support it, make it greater and stronger!'[33] Thousands of Vietnamese, particularly the young, most of them non-Communists, were prepared to support this Front the programme of which was so very moderate.[34]

Moderate too, and slanted, with quite deliberate deception, towards the ideals of Western liberty, was the Declaration of Independence of 2 September 1945.[35] Or more precisely, it was moderate in the impression it gave of the kind of Vietnamese society the Vietminh wanted to create: a society informed by the principles of the American Declaration of Independence and the French Rights of Man, both of which were explicitly cited. On the other hand, it was uncompromising on the matter of complete political independence. This was wholly understandable; what is of interest about it is the way in which it was clearly related to an appeal to 'the Allies who have recognized the principles of equality of peoples at the Conference of Teheran and San Francisco'.

Ho Chi Minh, the chief signer as President, was one of the most intelligent Leninists of all. Though he had earlier opted for guerrilla warfare, when the situation seemed propitious for it, he was certainly not going to tie the Vietminh to one form of struggle. For some time after the Declaration of Independence the form of struggle adopted was necessarily diplomatic. The Vietminh could not possibly prevent the landing of British imperial troops in the South or Kuomintang Chinese troops in the North. All that could be done was to try to exploit 'contradictions' between the Allies and between the various groupings in France (at a time when the French government included a very significant Communist component).

33. Ho Chi Minh, op. cit., pp. 141–2.

34. Rathausky, op. cit., pp. 49–50. The programme was clearly designed to appeal to all sections of the community; it was Western democratic politically; so far as the 'land question' was concerned, it promised only a reduction of rents and of usurious rates of interest.

35. Harold R. Isaacs, *New Cycle in Asia* (Selected Documents), Macmillan, New York, 1947, pp. 163–5.

This is not to say that there was not a brief reign of terror directed against the French in Vietnam, both in the North and the South. The terror was worst in Saigon, seven hundred and fifty miles from the seat of independent government.

For a month on end life there was like a nightmare ... At dusk there began a strange migration: neighbouring families gathered stealthily in one of the houses – never the same – and there they united their joint lack of power. Every time it was the same interminable night. The darkness outside was full of prowling Vietminh. Their harsh, shrill voices could be heard coming from everywhere, their cruel laughter, their shouts and the sound of their whistles. Sometimes an assault group would go by, padding along to the *moc ai* rhythm, one-two, one-two: and then, when they stopped, that was the sign that a villa was going to be attacked ... The horror reached its culminating point in the massacre at the block called the Cité Hérault, where some hundred Frenchmen were dismembered, slashed to pieces, in unimaginably horrible circumstances.[36]

Then came the Gurkhas to 'restore order'. With them came French paras. Then General Leclerc, with one of the most famous armoured divisions in the world. He had in all some 50,000 men with whom to pacify Cochinchina and no promise (rather the reverse) of reinforcements. 'Presently captured French soldiers were found hacked to pieces, and presently Annamese villages went up in flames. For violence answered violence ... In a series of destructive thrusts the French retook Cochinchina, Cambodia, Laos, central and southern Annam. But the Red [guerrilla platoons] and all the guerrilla formations continually reappeared, as though they sprang from their own ashes.'[37]

There is a large variance in estimates of the Vietminh armed strength in the early days of the struggle. Tanham cites an estimate of some 60,000 men possessing only 40,000 rifles.[38] Fall

36. Lucien Bodard, *The Quicksand War: Prelude to Vietnam*, Faber & Faber, 1967, pp. 10, 11. Throughout this period, it seems clear, terror was also applied against rival political groups. See for example Vu Van Thai in *Asia*, No. 4, New York, Winter 1966.

37. Bodard, pp. 11–12.

38. George K. Tanham, *Communist Revolutionary Warfare: The Vietminh in Indochina*, Praeger, New York, 1961, p. 9.

stated that 'Although the Viet-Minh did not seize all Japanese equipment in Viet-Nam, it nevertheless succeeded in obtaining 35,000 rifles, 1,350 automatic weapons, 200 mortars, 54 cannon, and even 18 tanks from Japanese sources, French booty stocks, and American airdrops. This should dispose of the myth that the Viet-Minh began the war against the French almost bare-handed.'[39]

Nevertheless it is clear that at first the French were able to penetrate most areas of the country very easily, except for the Vietminh base area in the mountainous Viet Bac forest area in northern Tonkin – though by January 1947 General Leclerc was predicting that it would take a force of 500,000 men to put down the armed Vietminh quickly.[40] However, it must be understood that a complex series of diplomatic discussions finally broke down only at the end of 1946 and so the decision to seek a total military solution was made only after that date. The details of the diplomatic phase cannot be discussed here: each side believed the other guilty of bad faith. In Devillers' opinion, 'The Vietminh's fourteen months of power had paid off in bloody failure.'[41] The Chinese occupation army had been got out of the North (at the price of allowing a returning French foothold), but the Vietminh was isolated on the international stage and unsupported by the French Communist Party, whose presumed future successes probably heavily influenced the Vietminh concentration in 1946 on diplomatic struggle.

The Vietminh had also, since as early as 1945, been preparing a regular army. It was not ready for combat by early 1947 – regulars were not used until 1949 – and so the Vietminh had to adopt the strategic defensive in order to preserve their hard-core forces. In the words of Tanham, 'Giap clearly recognized the

39. Introduction to Truong Chinh, *Primer for Revolt*, Praeger, New York, 1963, footnote, p. 37. Truong Chinh argues (p. 37) that during the August Revolution the Vietminh Front failed to acquire as many Japanese arms as it might have.

40. Philippe Devillers and Jean Lacouture, *End of a War*, Pall Mall Press, 1969, p. 19.

41. W. L. Holland (ed.), *Asian Nationalism and the West*, Macmillan, New York, 1953, p. 202.

weaknesses of the French situation. He predicted that, as the war wore on, the French would have to use colonial troops and even Vietnamese, that they would never have adequate manpower or supplies, and that their morale would decline.'[42] (French law precluded the employment of conscripts outside France.)

In the meantime the French, in classic fashion, would begin to overextend their communications and supply lines. Popular bases would continue to be established by the Vietminh through armed propaganda; the regular army would grow in strength and the movement under ICP direction would continue to expand. 'Free Vietnam is first of all an army', as Giap put it; but if the army incarnated the people, it was in turn wholly informed and directed by the ICP. 'The People's Army is the instrument of the Party and the revolutionary State for the accomplishment, in armed form, of the tasks of the revolution ... Therefore, the political work in its ranks is of the first importance. *It is the soul of the army.*'[43]

Since the French had 115,000 men, a force likely to be reduced in future, instead of the 500,000 mentioned by General Leclerc, the high command perhaps understandably tried to smash the Vietminh in its northern base area in one fell swoop in 1947 with a combined force of 15,000 men. As Giap's biographer has written, 'Its task was to find and defeat a force of 60,000 men in an area of 7,500 square miles of jungle-covered peaks. By the standards of more recent operations in Vietnam, a reasonable task for such a force would have been to defeat a force of 3,000 guerrillas within an area of 400 square miles. What-

42. *Communist Revolutionary Warfare*, op. cit., p. 19.

43. *People's War, People's Army*, p. 55. Though it can be argued that this book is chiefly propagandistic, it is perhaps worthwhile emphasizing Giap's point further: 'The Vietnamese People's Army has been created by the Party, which ceaselessly trains and educates it. It has always been and will always be under the *leadership of the Party* which, alone, has made it into a revolutionary army, a true people's army . . . The army has always had its political commissars. In the units, the military and political chiefs assume their responsibilities under the leadership of the Party Committee at the corresponding echelon' (pp. 54–5).

ever the French may have lacked in their operational thinking, it was certainly not the spirit of boldness.'[44] The inevitable failure in the Viet Bac to destroy the Vietminh mainforce left the initiative with Giap, since the French forces were thinly spread in an attempt to hold altogether too many places deemed to be 'vital'.

It has been widely argued that the French at this time were starting to lose a struggle that was as much political as military through their failure to offer opponents of the Vietminh alternative opportunities of political activity. There is obviously truth in this: a great Vietnamese, Ngo Dinh Diem, more than once refused to serve as Premier of a Vietnam that did not have at least the equivalent of India's Dominion Status[45] (which was of course complete independence). It is likely that the lack of an attractive alternative, not to speak of the often very arrogant behaviour of the French, caused significent numbers of Vietnamese to rally to the Vietminh Front, or, equally often, to take no part in the struggle at all.

And yet it is very doubtful whether the situation was nearly as simple as that. First of all, there was the prodigious fact of Vietnamese history that in August 1945 there had come to power in Hanoi and Hue and Saigon – and over a very wide area of the country – an independent Vietnamese government, which in December 1946 had been assaulted at its Hanoi seat by French arms.[46] Secondly, there was the nature of the administration, even if clandestine, that had been established to some extent or other over such a wide area of the country. The development of the parallel hierarchies was of very great importance. These took two forms: the infiltration of existing organizations and the creation of new ones. Fall cites part of a French report on this parallel organization:

44. O'Neill, op. cit., p. 53.

45. Robert Shaplen, *The Lost Revolution: Vietnam 1945–65*, André Deutsch, 1966, p. 63.

46. The question of which side was responsible for the outbreak of hostilities in December 1946 has not been discussed because it is a matter of argument of a kind not strictly germane to the subject matter of this book. But it may be said that French conduct could not have been regarded as in good faith by Vietnamese nationalists.

The Lien-Viet (organization of Viet-Minh subsidiary groups) included youth groups, groups for mothers, farmers, workers, 'resistant' Catholics, war veterans, etc. It could just as well have included associations of flute players or bicycle racers; the important point was that no one escaped regimentation and that the (normal) territorial hierarchy was thus complemented by another which watched the former and was in turn watched by it – both of them being watched in turn from the outside and inside by the security services and the Party. The individual caught in the fine mesh of such a net has no chance whatever of preserving his independence.[47]

Thirdly, there was the fact that in so far as there were recognizable political parties of a non-Communist kind in Vietnam they were in many ways more like secret societies and for the most part were not possessed of organizational skills appropriate to 'mass mobilization'. Fourthly, the most important of these parties had been severely weakened by Vietminh terror and assassinations or by a joint Vietminh–French process of elimination. To quote a writer who has always sought to comment from a position 'above the struggle',

By propaganda, by threats and acts of terror, the Vietminh also tried to paralyse all who would leave the 'Democratic' Front or play an independent game. Adversaries who could not be reached, guerrilla units that rebelled against the Central Committee's orders, were even denounced to the French political police as dangerous Vietminh members, and the French authorities took over the task of eliminating them. The Vietminh also used a succession of rumours of a coming offensive to keep from secession those who still hesitated to come to terms with the French, and who asked themselves whether France would not one day send its forces home and so leave them in an exposed isolation.[48]

The author finds it very difficult not to agree with the verdict of Bernard Fall:

Self-styled specialists and professional anti-colonialists assert today that the Viet-Minh Communists would never have won control over even North Viet-Nam, had the French granted 'real independ-

47. *The Two Vietnams*, p. 134.
48. Phillippe Devillers in *Asian Nationalism and the West*, pp. 214–15.

ence' to the three Indochinese states in 1945. This is, of course, an extremely tempting theory. Its only trouble is that it omits one single hard fact: the Communist government of Ho Chi Minh was in full control of the country's administration as of VJ-day. Until the French returned to Hanoi in March 1946, it used its unhindered control to liquidate hundreds of Vietnamese anti-Communist nationalists likely to get in the way. For the French to grant independence to such a government would have, without the slightest doubt, resulted in a solidly Communist Vietnamese State at the latest by the time the Chinese Reds occupied the areas bordering on Viet-Nam in December 1949.[49]

This is not to suggest that the French were other than tardy in granting the non-Communists some of the attributes of a semi-independent State nor to argue that they did not lose much support during the period of tardiness. It is rather to suggest that they were in a very difficult predicament politically. They attempted to extricate themselves from it by representing their military effort in Vietnam as part of a world-wide struggle against Communist expansion. Viewed internationally, they were perfectly correct in making this claim but such a claim, in the Vietnamese context, was to beg the question of nationalism – which the Vietminh Front claimed to represent ... and which in a certain sense they clearly did politically represent in the colonial context. It would be as ludicrous to suggest that Ho Chi Minh was not a Vietnamese nationalist as it would be to argue that his greatest wish was not to see the whole world brought under Communist rule – as his last testament makes plain.

There were French generals like Raoul Salan who knew perfectly well that the French would win 'on the day when the peasants and bourgeoisie of Vietnam make common cause with us against the communists' but the making of that common cause did not, after the August Revolution, only involve the raising of the question, Why should we? but also the question, Is a French victory so reasonably certain that we can risk taking such a step?

49. *Street Without Joy*, Pall Mall Press, 1964, p. 382. Cf. O'Neill, op. cit., p. 59: 'Yet even this threat [of granting a 'moderate degree of independence to the political opponents of the Viet Minh'] could be countered by expert use of a reliable weapon – terror'.

This latter question was a peculiarly acute one in the villages of Vietnam where the action was taking place. Jean Lacouture's description of the pacification problem – at a later date, in the Red River Delta – presents the dilemma everywhere so long as the Vietminh could continue to make good their claim of being '*partout et nul partout*', everywhere and nowhere. 'The villagers are interrogated in the normal way: "Who fired on us?" The village chief bows, trembling, but saying nothing – there are at least two or three members of the Viet-Minh cell amongst the apparently terrified group behind him. If the chief talks he will be killed that evening when the French move on to occupy the next village. If he keeps silent, will [the French] shoot him? No, but he will be harassed, bullied, and certainly humiliated, and, more often than not, turned into an implacable enemy.'[50]

So far as the military struggle was concerned (while remembering that in revolutionary warfare the political and the military are strictly inextricable), 1949 saw the end of the Vietminh's strategic defensive period, the shifting of very large numbers of French troops to the North, not least because of the Red Army's conquest of China, and the creation of an 'internally sovereign' State of Vietnam.[51] Giap himself has acknowledged the significant change that was brought about by the completion of the Chinese Communist conquest. From this time onwards, though huge armies of coolies were to remain very important in the Vietminh logistical system, the promise of aid and arms necessary for the Vietminh regular formations was there – provided Giap could destroy the French border forts.[52] By the end of 1950 the whole Sino-Vietnamese border was cleared of French-

50. *Politique Étrangère*, Paris, May–July 1953.

51. See Allan B. Cole, *Conflict in Indo-China and International Repercussions: A Documentary History, 1945–1955*, pp. 73–80, for the text of the 8 March 1949 Agreement granting the exercise of 'all the attributions and prerogatives arising from internal sovereignty' to the State of Vietnam.

52. Tanham, op. cit., pp. 68–9 supplies figures. In 1951 the flow of aid from China was about 10–20 tons per month; 250 tons by the end of 1952; an average of between 400 and 600 tons in 1953; by the end, June 1954, it was reportedly 4,000 tons per month. By the end of 1953, the Vietminh reportedly had about 1,000 trucks but porterage remained vital. The Vietminh army of 300,000 required 1 million porters.

held forts. The French began to fear for the safety of the Red River Delta itself.

Giap's successes were considerable, but for the Vietminh Front the real battle had to be won in the areas of dense population in the South and in the North, both of which were still held by the French. A Communist army that never exceeded 300,000 including more than 150,000 guerrillas was opposed by 115,000 troops of the French army (including African colonial groups and the Foreign Legion) and in the course of time 300,000 Indo-Chinese (overwhelmingly Vietnamese) troops.[53] It was there, among the delta millions, that the Vietminh Front's claim to represent Vietnamese nationalism had to be made good. Forgetting the now endlessly vaunted principles of 'people's war' (Giap's army was in fact only a fraction of one per cent of the people), Giap decided to take the French head-on in the Red River Delta.

January 1951 saw Giap thrust out from the hills against Vinh Yen, only about thirty miles from Hanoi. The Tet (the Vietnamese New Year) was not to be celebrated in Hanoi: the attack failed. A second failure followed at Mao Khe in March. But through local recruiting and infiltration guerrilla mainforce units began to form within the French-held delta. An offensive on the Day River also failed in May. 'By July 1951 the Viet Minh had lost over 20,000 killed and wounded as a result of the delta battles. Giap had ... lost [the initiative] within six months.' Marshal de Lattre seemed to have saved the situation. In July a Mobilization Ordinance drafted men of between twenty and forty-five years, the Vietminh having attempted conscription a good deal earlier. De Lattre insisted that those Vietnamese who wanted to be 'real men' must choose their sides. The remark was understandable from a man who had only recently lost his only son in battle. But it should be remarked that the First Indo-China War, like the Second, was marked by a deplorable unfairness toward those Vietnamese fighting against the Communists: all publicity was concentrated on the activities of French units, just as it was later all to be concentrated on the

53. O'Neill, op. cit., p. 69.

exploits of American units. It came as a surprise when it was shown in 1953 that during the previous year the dead and missing from metropolitan France were 1,860 in number; 4,049 were from the Legion and African units – while 7,730 were Vietnamese soldiers fighting the Communists.[54] Fall argued that the neglect of the Vietnamese effort was 'because the truth clashes with official dogma and widespread prejudice'. Of the 1,800 volunteers to drop into Dien Bien Phu during the last days of the battle, nearly 800 were Vietnamese.[55]

However, what was most fundamental in the situation was the fact that the French command just did not have sufficient men to keep most of the country pacified *and* defeat Giap's army. Meanwhile the totalitarian State which the People's Army served was by 1953 clearly coming into being under the guise of 'land reform'. The instrument was in fact State terrorism the purpose of which was, as Duncanson put it, 'less the elimination of any particular class of people than eradication from everyone's mind, without distinction of class, any desire to own private property or to pursue any private purpose'.[56] 1953 saw the worst outburst of 'land reform' – that is to say, the inducing of denunciations of neighbours, the farce of 'people's courts', and a general shattering of village morale in a deliberately created atmosphere of hysteria – before the major 'land reform' of 1956.

It was also during 1953 that it became clear that this inconclusive war was beginning to look dirty in the eyes of many Frenchmen at home: dirty in its fighting methods in the eyes of the left, dirty in its fortune-making techniques for certain

54. Donald Lancaster, *The Emancipation of French Indochina*, Oxford University Press, 1961. Between 1945 and July 1954, the total Vietnamese casualties were the largest by far of any component of the French Expeditionary Corps, and to this figure there would have to be added the very considerable casualties suffered by the army of the State of Vietnam. See Cole, op. cit., p. 259. The same unfairness has marked American reporting of the Second Indo-China war, in which, almost every single month, Vietnamese government forces have suffered the heaviest casualties – a fact widely unknown in the West.

55. *The Two Vietnams*, op. cit., p. 105.

56. Duncanson, op. cit., p. 173.

interest groups in the eyes of liberals. Napalm and the traffic in piastres became the two symbols of metropolitan disgust.[57] The United States was certainly paying a larger and larger share of the costs of the war and by 1954 was paying about 80 per cent of the total costs.[58] But this did not alter the fact of stalemate. Talk of negotiations began to increase in frequency. The problem was: how to negotiate from a position of strength?

The attempt to solve this problem, allied with a belief that Laos must be protected from the Vietminh and a belief that all would be well if only the People's Army could be induced to fight a positional battle, resulted in a politico-military catastrophe for the French at Dien Bien Phu. The new French Commander, General Navarre, was aware that Giap had already thrust into Laos and was likely to do so again. Dien Bien Phu stood in the way; it could of course be bypassed, but might not Giap be induced to try to take it by storm? Certainly Giap had argued in his book, *La Guerre de la libération et l'armée populaire*, published in 1950, that it had been a basic strategic mistake to have ignored Laos and Cambodia.[59] Navarre believed it was his job to defend Laos and to induce a battle of a kind he believed – on the basis of a false analogy with the fortified camp at Na San and very erroneous Intelligence – would certainly be of great propaganda value to France for any forthcoming negotiations.

Giap asked himself one simple question about the fortified camp of Dien Bien Phu: 'Could we be certain of victory in attacking it? Our decision had to depend on this consideration

57. The special issue of *Les Temps Modernes*, August–September 1953, eloquently exemplifies the first kind of disgust; Jacques Despuech, *Le Trafic de piastres*, Deux Rives, Paris 1953, the second kind. There were also Frenchmen like Claude Göeldhieux, *Quinze Mois prisonniers chez les Viets*, René Julliard, 1953, who recognized that the Vietminh had 'the gift of the gab'. But they were few in number.

58. Hammer, op. cit., p. 313. Cole, op. cit., p. 260, supplies figures of US aid for the whole war (military and civilian): nearly $US 10 billion. That was about a third of the annual cost to the USA of the Second Indo-China War according to widely accepted estimates.

59. Quoted in Tanham, op. cit., p. 55.

alone.'[60] It was to be a battle for political rather than military stakes, since the Vietminh Front also was prepared to enter into negotiations and wanted the best position of strength from which to proceed. Once again, like good Leninists, the ICP high command did not feel themselves tied to one form of struggle; indeed it seems that the ICP's great patrons wanted negotiations and, in view of Giap's revelations about the uncertainty of morale for a time during the siege of Dien Bien Phu, it may well have been deemed necessary by the ICP to seek negotiations (see below).

However, Giap was not concerned only with Dien Bien Phu; he knew that Navarre also was not concerned only with Dien Bien Phu but with a generally offensive stance, including a large offensive operation in Central Vietnam. As Giap stated it,

> In the carrying-out of this plan, the enemy met a great contradiction, a serious difficulty: if they kept their forces scattered in order to occupy territory, it would be impossible for them to organize a strong mobile force; but if they reduced their occupation forces to regroup them, our guerrillas would take advantage of the new weakness of their position to increase their activity, their posts and garrisons would be threatened or annihilated, the local puppet authorities overthrown, and the occupied zones reduced.[61]

Giap goes on to say that Navarre was trying to get round this problem by organizing fifty-four new battalions of puppet troops but contents himself with some scathing remarks about their lack of quality. It is not impossible, however, that the threat of this new mobilization also tended to make the Vietminh favour negotiations – provided they could be entered into from a position of strength. It should be noticed that Giap launched

60. Quoted in O'Neill, op. cit., p. 139. For the battle of Dien Bien Phu. see O'Neill, op. cit.; Bernard Fall, *Hell is a Very Small Place*, J. B. Lippincott, Philadelphia, 1966; and Jules Roy, *The Battle of Dien Bien Phu*, Faber & Faber, 1964.

61. *People's War, People's Army*, op. cit., p. 194. General Navarre found that in the Red River delta, 100,000 French Union troops were immobilized in garrisoning 917 posts while the Vietminh were estimated to control, completely or partially, 5,000 out of the 7,000 delta villages. Lancaster op. cit., p. 265.

a large number of diversionary attacks while preparing for the – logistically very formidable – task of reducing the fortified encampment at Dien Bien Phu. Such diversionary attacks undoubtedly were greatly aided by local guerrilla forces and the careful political propagandizing of the villages. The effect of these diversionary attacks on French military minds seems to have been the feeling that this meant Giap could not implement a truly massive attack on Dien Bien Phu. The defence of Dien Bien Phu was based on the belief that a French Expeditionary Division could maul, and hold out against, two Vietminh divisions. The defenders found themselves far more greatly outnumbered than that; they also found themselves altogether outgunned and in a situation (topographically and weather-wise) very unfavourable for air supply.

And so, while the representatives of the great powers were preparing for the discussions at Geneva, the world watched a contest being fought out in the Thai country of north-west Vietnam. Displays of marvellous courage on the French side and immensely brave self-sacrifice by the Vietminh Front soldiers were the order of the day. But it was the political result that counted: the Vietminh victory, bought so very heavily in human lives, was a victory in Europe as well as in Asia. The era in which European statesmen had been able to say that 'Asian questions are settled in Europe' had clearly ended. And yet, had it really? some people perhaps asked themselves at the diplomatic aftermath in Geneva.

Here a different kind of question must be raised: What did the First Indo-China War reveal about the efficacy of revolutionary guerrilla warfare? It is not quite as simply answered as might appear at first. It did of course provide a clear demonstration of how formidable a Communist Front organization could be in circumstances which permitted it plausibly to represent itself as *the* organization of nationalism in the country. The significance of the struggle in this regard is delineated by Giap in an interesting manner:

> Our national war ended with a great victory which showed the very clear-sighted and heroic leadership of our Party. This was a great victory of Marx–Leninism in the liberation war of a small and

heroic nation. Our people could say with pride: under the leadership of our Party headed by President Ho Chi Minh we established a great historic truth: *a colonized and weak people once it has risen up and is united in the struggle and determined to fight for its independence and peace, has the full power to defeat the strong aggressive army of an imperialist country.*[62]

There is no reason whatsoever to believe that the people at large rose up united in support of the Vietminh Front against the French or later against the State of Vietnam. If this had been so, the position of the French would have been untenable throughout; and the Vietminh's elaborate measures taken to destroy other political parties, not to speak of its very widespread employment of coercion and indeed terror, would not have been necessary. The number of permanently *active* supporters of the Vietminh Front was probably a comparatively small section of the population. Nevertheless its mobilization of the people was immeasurably more successful than that of its opponents. The reason for this is several-fold. From the point of view of the Communists leading the Vietminh and the wider Lien-Viet Front, the factors in their favour were these: their past establishment of an apparently widely based and widely legitimized Vietnamese government; the geographical situation and the nature of the terrain which permitted the retention of the base area throughout; outside aid and an active sanctuary for training regular divisions in China from 1950 onwards; leadership of a national united front appropriate to the mobilizing of very disparate sections of the population and a profound understanding of how to enmesh the people on a very large scale through agitational-propaganda (or, if it is preferred, political educational) techniques.

The French militarily were trying to pacify an area four times as large as that attempted later by the Americans and their allies with less French soldiers than the Americans had even by the end of 1965.[63] As time passed, they found themselves attempting with far too few men – partly because of their tardiness in build-

62. ibid., p. 187.

63. Jean Lartéguy, *Un Million de Dollars Le Viet*, Raoul Solar, Paris, 1965, p. 23.

ing a Vietnamese army – both to pacify the heavily populated areas and to destroy the growing Vietminh mainforce. The attempt to achieve the former task let the Vietminh regular units into the Red River Delta, the famous de Lattre line of blockhouses proving no barrier.

Moreover, they were attempting the North African method of 'oil slick' ('*tache d'huile*') technique that was inappropriate to heavily populated areas unless huge numbers of security troops were available. The gridding (*quadrillage*), followed by the raking over (*ratissage*), of selected areas just did not work on a terrain, physical and social, which afforded opportunities for all manner of concealment devices.[64] The 'oil-slick' method is effective only if it results in the destruction of the local political infrastructure as well as local guerrillas and guarantees such future security from major re-infiltration of guerrillas to nerve the locals to undertake their own defence.

Compared with the impossibility of success for this method, though it was persisted in for most of the war, the lack of co-ordinated psychological warfare activities can easily be exaggerated. Moreover, most Frenchmen, unlike their American successors, did not see themselves as representatives of an alternative revolution until the Algerian war afterwards; rather they were torn between conflicting notions of colonial warfare, defending part of the world against a then presumedly monolithic Communism, and ancient military honour. The politicians at home did little to resolve their confusion; if anything they added to it. But apart from this, the task of destroying the Vietminh politico-military apparatus on the village level was one that could have been tackled on the village level only by Vietnamese.

And not even by them, it may well be argued, after the infiltration of the Vietminh regulars into the delta; or anyway not without attempting to replicate the organizational modes and political tactics of the Vietminh – an attempt that was made eventually during the Second Indo-China War. The regulars

64. These are excellently described in Phillipe de Pirey, *Operation Waste*, Arco Publications, London, 1954. The counter-productive methods of large-scale French pacification drives are excellently described in Warner, op. cit.

who infiltrated the delta were indeed educated, in the Maoist manner, to 'respect, help, and defend' the people; and they undoubtedly did often help constructively with village tasks.

But the rottening (*pourrissement*) of the delta, as the French called it, was not quite as amiable a process as that; nor simply a result of the inadequacies of French pacification. A French analysis should be considered:

> Entire regiments infiltrate into the very interior of the protected zone ... Cleverly dispersed, these 'regulars', according to the consecrated expression, 'encyst' themselves in small groups, in underground posts hidden from the air and in reconnaissance patrols, establishing arms and ammunition depots, supply dumps, stations for the wounded ... The population, feeling no longer safely protected by the Franco–Vietnamese army, falls to the mercy of the rebels, who know how to exploit both persuasion and terror ... The village chief and the 'notables' faithful to the Bao Dai government are assassinated. Viet Minh functionaries are substituted to surround and keep careful watch over the citizens. A schoolteacher instructs the children in Marxist doctrines. The young men are raked over in the search for soldiers. And Communist cells partition each little citadel, imprisoning it in their espionage net.[65]

The importance of Communist organization will doubtless be disputed by those in the West who still see this kind of struggle as a spontaneous rising by a united people. Two things should be said about this. First, important areas of all three parts of Vietnam contain significant ethnic or sectarian minorities which had been living unto themselves and felt no natural attraction to a Vietnamese nation led by a Communist Front. Apart from this, family, clan, village and regional loyalties added up to a far more real complex of loyalties than is easily understood by Westerners. Such loyalties could only be permanently subsumed into a politically effective 'higher loyalty' where the writ of the totalitarian Communist Front counter-State actually ran.

Secondly, it must be pointed out that General Giap himself

65. Yvonne Pagniez, *Choses vues au Viet-nam*, Paris, 1954 quoted in George Armstrong Kelly, *Lost Soldiers*, MIT Press, Cambridge, Mass., 1965, p. 87.

supplies clear evidence of the overwhelming importance of the Communist idea-organization even within the regular army itself. Two quotations must suffice:

To maintain and consolidate the absolute leadership of the Party in the army, to increase political work as the sinews of our army, to intensify proletarian ideological education for officers and men, to implement the principle of internal unity, solidarity between the army and people and international solidarity ... are fundamental principles of the building of our army and an essential safeguard for it to maintain its people's nature, for its development and success.[66]

Second:

Our combatants' *determination to fight and win ... came from the revolutionary nature of our army and the painstaking education of the Party. It had been enhanced in battle and in the ideological remoulding classes.* This does not mean that, even when the Dien Bien Phu battle was at its height, negative factors never appeared. *To maintain and develop this determination to fight and win was a whole process of unremitting and patient education and struggle,* tireless and patient efforts in political work on the front line. This was a great achievement of the Party's organizations and branches and cadres ... This ideological struggle was very successful. This was one of the greatest achievements in political work in our army's history. It led the Dien Bien Phu campaign to complete victory.[67]

This fusion of the political and military was certainly not emphasized only by Giap. Truong Chinh, a much more important theoretician, states the Communist understanding very clearly in this passage:

Those who rely on politics often do not realize the important role of armed force in history, do not realize that sometimes armed force must be used to fight the internal enemy or external aggressors. Internally, such people often accept reconciliation contrary to principle. In foreign relations, they are liable to surrender, or make diplomatic concessions. Again, those who have a tendency only to rely on military action are inclined to militarism. They tend to believe that

66. *People's War, People's Army,* op. cit., p. 131.
67. ibid., pp. 180–81.

everything can be settled by armed force; they do not apply political mobilization, are unwilling to give explanations and to convince people; they even use threats, or bring pressure to bear on the people. Or, fighting spiritedly, they neglect political work; they do not seek ways of building ties of affection between officers and men, do not act in such a way that the army and the people can wholeheartedly help one another; and they neglect propaganda directed to the breaking of the morale of the enemy troops. Such people know only how to fight; they fail to consolidate the National United Front, fail to seek new allies outside the country, and neglect the study of the internal and world situation, which is indispensable to the development of correct internal and foreign policies.[68]

It was this fusion of the political and military that proved crucial. For example, the French in Tonkin proved themselves very fine leaders of guerrilla bands made up from ethnic minority peoples and they almost certainly tied down very large Vietminh security forces (about which Giap is utterly silent).[69] But this was not meshed in with a political strategy and so the bands achieved nothing more. The Vietminh knew precisely what they wanted to achieve; the French did not. The Indo-Chinese Communist Party never lost sight of the fact that the Vietminh Front existed as a way of mobilizing vast numbers of people under the Party's totalitarian control. Certainly it was also fighting for the political independence of Vietnam from the French, but the struggle was phased according to the requirements of the first objective, not the second.

It is perfectly true that 1953–4 saw a greater and greater infiltration of Vietminh fighters[70] into the heavily populated areas and an increasingly effective use of large-scale ambushes in Central Vietnam. By the early months of 1954 the French were beginning to appreciate the threat to the Red River Delta itself and had been made all too shatteringly aware of how a mobile task force could be destroyed by ambushes involving

68. *Primer for Revolt*, op. cit., p. 179.

69. See Roger Trinquier, *Modern Warfare*, Pall Mall Press, 1964.

70. Denis Warner, *Out of the Gun*, Hutchinson, 1956, p. 148, cites a French HQ estimate that, by the end of 1953, they held 1,960 hamlets in the Red River Delta against the Vietminh's 3,266.

mines and superior mobility in the Central Highlands.[71] But so far as the general military situation was concerned, it was the deteriorating situation in the North that weighed most heavily. When America declined to intervene at Dien Bien Phu with massive air power and the fortified camp fell, the result was not catastrophic militarily. Nearly half a million anti-Communist forces were still in the field, including 280,000 Vietnamese. And yet politically the French undoubtedly were politico-militarily defeated: a stalemate is a victory for a revolutionary guerrilla army in such circumstances.

The cease-fire, which was signed only by representatives of the two military commands, was a humiliating business for France and, as Duncanson has remarked, it 'tended to confirm Vietnamese scepticism about the political institutions and principles of government cherished in the West – a scepticism that has marked the conduct of public affairs ever since Geneva, in the South almost as much as in the North'.[72]

There were many officers of the French Union forces, whose killed, missing and wounded amounted to almost 150,000 men, who also came to be very sceptical about the politicians and political institutions of France.

There were also a number of Algerians serving in Indo-China who were impressed by this new kind of army against which they had fought. Bernard Fall met one of them years later after he had joined the anti-French liberation army. The Algerian in question was captured at Dien Bien Phu. When he inquired of a Vietminh officer how he was to obey the instruction to move north out of the fortified camp across the barbed wire, the officer replied, 'Just walk across the bodies of our men.' As the prisoners began to move off they halted before a dying Vietminh soldier who was looking up at them and trying to speak. 'Get going,' the officer said. 'You can step on him. He has done his duty for the Democratic Republic of Viet-Nam.'[73] The Algerian was deeply impressed.

71. See *Street Without Joy*, Ch. 4, 'End of a Task Force'.

72. Duncanson, op. cit., p. 203.

73. *Viet-Nam Eyewitness, 1953–66*, Praeger, New York, 1966, pp. 244–5.

The French army found itself faced by another revolutionary war in Algeria. Some of the veterans of Indo-China, including a few who had been subjected to Communist indoctrination as prisoners of war after Dien Bien Phu, came to believe that they now really understood what this kind of war was 'all about'. Armed with this understanding, they believed they could atone for Indo-China by ensuring that French Algeria (as it was, according to French law) would not be lost by 'the forces of order' to the 'forces of international Communism'.

Algeria was about four times the size of France (though the vast Saharan territories were peripheral to the struggle); contained 1,200,000 Europeans, mostly French, many of whose families had been long settled in the country; but was mainly settled by some nine million Muslims, most of them Arabs. The overwhelming number of European Algerians lived in cities and towns, which of course held large numbers of both communities. The overwhelming proportion of Arab Algerians eked out a bare livelihood and their only abiding experience in the liberation struggle was that of risking starvation or a chance explosive. The fighting men of the Algerian nationalist movement never exceeded about 40,000.[74]

It is not altogether difficult to understand how the French military theorists of revolutionary warfare (or modern warfare, as one of the most distinguished of them insisted upon calling it),[75] believed they were again engaged in a struggle against international Communism. The Algerian liberation movement (FLN) was, like so many 'liberation movements' since, to some extent an organizational replica of the Communist model, in its command structure, cells and so on. Joint action was taken by nationalist and Communist cells; 'at the height of the terror it was not uncommon for the Sûreté to uncover FLN bombs with timing mechanisms coming from Communist sources of manufacture.'[76] The FLN, though it argued in general terms that it sought only a politically independent Algeria, had an

74. George Armstrong Kelly, op. cit., p. 144.
75. Trinquier, op. cit.
76. Kelly, op. cit., p. 161.

élitist leadership which also used the Marx–Leninist explanations for its struggle against capitalist exploitation.[77] Moreover, it received considerable aid from Egypt, which could plausibly be represented as an agent of international Communist expansion.

But the French military theorists of *la guerre révolutionnaire* went far beyond this more or less intelligible area of understanding. They became the agents and victims of what elsewhere in this study has been called the 'replication effect'. That is, they abstracted from their experiences of Communist revolutionary warfare certain factors that seemed to them indispensable for defeating it; they then tried to introduce those factors – in policy form – into the struggle against the FLN. The literature that grew up around this determination not to be bested again (for that is what it really amounted to 'motivation'-wise) ranged from the provision of profound insights to the inflaming of febrile energies. Justice to the range of it cannot be done here; it has been analysed in two excellent studies in English.[78]

The gist of the doctrine seems to the author to be this: the problem of countering modern warfare is basically unrelated to the specific economic, political and social conditions in a given country. This is because it is fundamentally a problem of a certain kind of organization which, though it exploits those conditions, does not in any real way owe its existence to those conditions. It is autonomous, this kind of organization, and hence the struggle is all about techniques – techniques which obviously, by definition, can be replicated.

This understanding of what revolutionary warfare is 'all about' is not as foolish as it may seem when adumbrated in this way. After all, it was none other than Lenin who insisted that 'Organization is everything'. But it was also Lenin who insisted that every situation must be analysed in terms of its own particularities and in terms of its alteration from week to week (or, in

77. This is certainly not to say that the Algerian leadership was Communist; Communists played a minor part in the struggle.

78. See Kelly, op. cit., and Peter Paret, *French Revolutionary Warfare from Indochina to Algeria*, Pall Mall Press, 1964.

truly revolutionary situations, from day to day, from hour to hour).[79] The situation also had to be analysed all the time – as Giap and Truong Chinh insisted – in international terms. It would be quite untrue to argue that the French 'Milites', as they were called, were unaware of this international component. The most famous story illustrating their viewpoint ends on the note that the greatest ally (the USA) will be the greatest opponent.[80]

This was very clever so far as it went, but it did not take account of the possibility that the greatest opponent would in fact come from the very epicentre of the French tradition: General de Gaulle (who later read the international situation differently). It must also be said that the 'Milites' also failed to take account of the real aims of the FLN, whatever its rhetoric might be. This was based upon drawing a false analogy between Vietnam and Algeria. Vietnam did not have an important labour force earning valuable francs in France, as Algeria did; nor did Vietnam have very valuable oil resources which could conveniently be exploited only by French technicians – nor was the FLN a Communist movement.

The upshot was a 'victory' in Algeria in terms of counter-insurgency, in the sense that the French army and its auxiliaries had put down the terrorist movement in the cities – a very important element in this particular revolutionary guerrilla war – and had prevented the armed movement expanding as planned. The French even dealt effectively with the privileged sanctuary in Tunisia in so far as it was a factor in the armed Algerian struggle. But this is to take altogether too narrow a view of counter-insurgency: in international and Gaullist terms, all the FLN leadership had to do was to remain in being – and even half a million security forces could not prevent that.

79. So for that matter have the best amongst British counter-insurgents 'French military thinkers, true to their national intellectual traditions, attempted to formulate *une doctrine* ... the pragmatic British, whose cumulative experience of counter-insurgency campaigning was no less than that of the French, thought more modestly in terms of "techniques"' (Michael Howard, *Studies in War and Peace*, Temple Smith, 1970, p. 180).

80. Quoted in Paret, op. cit., pp. 3–4.

Once again a situation of stalemate was reached. As a Tunisian put it at the United Nations in 1959: 'Though it is impossible for the French military forces to gain decisive victory over the National Liberation Army of Algeria, it is equally unlikely that our Algerian brethren can triumph over the powerful and well-trained army of France.' Thus negotiations were possible – on the basis of self-determination – and General de Gaulle was prepared to negotiate, not simply because he saw a stalemate but because he saw a quite different role for France on the European sub-continent.

This situation came about despite the employment of over half of the French army, the recruitment of 150,000 Muslim irregulars (about four times as many as in the armed units of the FLN), a resettlement of some two million Algerians, and a rigorous attempt to apply what might be called counter-Maoism to the struggle. As Paret has stated the case, 'Whatever her policies or methods, France after 1954 could have maintained her dominance over Algeria only if the political system and intent of the country had been reshaped along totalitarian lines, and if her allies had become far less flexible in their dealings with the Communist powers. A totalitarian nation within the framework of an aggressively anti-Russian and anti-Chinese alliance might well have won the revolutionary war in Algeria.'[81]

The world was not like that in 1954, when the revolt began (as the French government discovered when the Americans refused to intervene at Dien Bien Phu, using the British reluctance to participate as alibi); it was even less like that at the beginning of the 1960s, when the struggle moved on to the plane of full-scale negotiations. One result was the corruption of significant numbers of brave, honourable and very able French officers. It was the corruption engendered by the pursuit of the impossible (to employ Michael Oakeshott's phrase). The process began with the admirable seconding of officers in a civilian capacity to work among the people in what today would be called civic action programmes; but without being able to link these programmes, in which many Muslims participated, to any kind of Arab Algerian

81. ibid., p. 123.

government. It developed the use of psychological techniques that were based on an ugly Pavlovian theory about human behaviour; and it ended with 'special methods', as torture was delicately called, and an attitude towards France that can only be called quasi-Fascist – at any rate in its élitist and activist contempt for the institutions and modes of political behaviour which informed the French Republic.

Finally some of them tried to bring down the Republic itself in a very dramatic manner. They did not do this because they really liked or even sympathized with the French Algerian *colons* with whom they became politically allied. The reason was much more sinister than that: the officer-theorists of the colonial *paras* and their comrades in other jobs had become a distorted mirror-image of a Communist party, a counter-Communist party, so to speak. They saw themselves as a vanguard group who alone understood political realities; who stood above the squalid self-seeking of the democratic market-place and hence had been chosen (by History, just like the Communists) to use whatever methods were necessary in order to win what was for them a Manichaean contest between Light and Darkness. All the necessary methods could be used only if liberal-capitalist democracy was forced to make way for a monolithic state. The development of this replication-effect in the French army, and the politico-military skulduggery that it engendered amongst exceptionally brave and honourable men, shows very vividly the extreme dangers to liberal democracy should revolutionary warfare have appeared during the next decade to be 'encircling' what Lin Piao calls 'the cities of the world'. An American special forces officer is supposed to have said, 'Our Algeria will be in Latin America.' It is to be hoped not. The First Indo-China War ended with the Commander-in-Chief, General Navarre, writing about 'treason and its ally defeatism'; the Algerian War ended with a former C.-in-C., General Salan, on trial for his life on a charge of treason against the French State.

## CHAPTER 6

# THE SECOND INDO-CHINA WAR

The enemy will pass slowly from the offensive to the defensive. Thus, the enemy will be caught in a dilemma: He has to drag out the war in order to win it and does not possess, on the other hand, the psychological and political means to fight a long-drawn-out war . . .

VO NGUYEN GIAP

I feel the fate of Asia – South and South-East Asia – will be decided in the next few years by what happens out in Vietnam . . . I am convinced that by seeing this struggle through now, in Vietnam, we are reducing the chances of a larger war – perhaps a nuclear war.

LYNDON BAINES JOHNSON

SINCE the commitment of American forces *en masse* to South Vietnam in 1965, the Second Indo-China War has become so overlaid with propaganda and the diplomatic ambiguities that are inherent in appealing to domestic and 'world' opinion that it is difficult to discuss the revolutionary war itself at all briefly without simplifying its origins and course to the point of distortion. Certainly the verbal war has been an exceedingly important component of the struggle since 1965. General Giap's statement cited at the head of the chapter continues in a fashion summarized by Bernard Fall: 'In all likelihood, Giap concludes, public opinion in the democracy will demand an end to the "useless bloodshed", or its legislature will insist on knowing for how long it will have to vote astronomical credits without a clear-cut victory in sight. This is what eternally compels the military leaders of democratic armies to promise a quick end to the war – to "bring the boys home by Christmas" – or forces the democratic politicians to agree to almost any kind of humiliating compromise rather than accept the idea of a semi-permanent anti-guerrilla operation.'[1]

In the early stages of the war one of the chief propaganda arguments advanced in support of the revolutionary guerrillas was that the Hanoi government, the Democratic Republic of Vietnam (DRV), had been deprived of its just expectations under the Geneva Accords of 1954. Since this argument directly relates to the origin and course of the revolutionary war, it must be briefly discussed. The Geneva Accords were the result of a conference co-chaired by the United Kingdom and the Soviet Union, designed to establish the conditions for the settlement of Vietnamese political and military affairs. Neither the USA nor the Saigon government (GVN) signed the Accords. Both Vietnamese governments claimed sovereignty over the whole of Vietnam.[2]

One of the very important provisions of the Geneva Accords was paragraph 7, stipulating that 'general elections shall be held in July 1956 under the supervision of an international commission...'[3] The refusal of the GVN to hold these elections was again and again represented before 'world opinion' as a cheating of the DRV of rightful expectations and sometimes as a breach of international law by the GVN. The legal arguments are beyond the competence of the author to judge and are not strictly germane to this study.[4] What is germane is the fact that not only was a 'justification' for the revolutionary war provided but it was often implied that it was the failure to hold these elections that impelled the DRV gradually to consider other means of attaining the unification of the country – which undoubtedly was the intention of the Geneva Accords.

1. *The Two Viet-Nams*, op. cit., p. 113.

2. Both governments were later recognized by considerable numbers of countries, the GVN by thirty-six countries by 1955.

3. Cited in George McTurnan Kahin and John W. Lewis, *The United States in Vietnam*, Delta Books, 1966, p. 52.

4. Different interpretations are offered in Richard A. Falk (ed.), *The Vietnam War and International Law*, Princeton University Press, 1968. See also Alan Watt, *Vietnam: An Australian Analysis*, Cheshire, Melbourne, 1968, Ch. III.

The question is: were DRV expectations disappointed? Was the failure to hold elections a cause of the Second Indo-China War? A recent study of the available evidence suggests quite clearly that the DRV never expected the elections to be held, although, according to a high-ranking defector, 'this was not discussed below province level within the Party in the interest of morale and also so as not to interfere with the Party's public stance that the Geneva Accords were a great victory for the Revolution'.[5]

By the same token, nor was revolutionary war being contemplated at this time. The bulk of Vietminh fighting units were withdrawn to the North to be formed into special military units. But a considerable number of military units were secretly maintained in the South, principally located on the Cambodian border and deep in the Delta. 'Large quantities of the newest weapons were cached in the South to support . . . military activity if necessary.'[6] The Communist apparatus in the South had been since 1951, when the Communist Party was officially reactivated as the Laodong (Workers' Party), organized by the Central Office for South Vietnam (COSVN). COSVN's head was Le Duan, a prominent member of the Laodong Politbureau, his deputy, Le Duc Tho, also being a Politbureau member. The organization was divided into two 'interzones'. Interzone 5 (Trung Bo) was the northern and central part of South Vietnam; Interzone Nam Bo encompassed the southern and south-western part, including the Mekong Delta. There was a special Saigon regional apparatus. As a cadre's account put it, 'The Party apparatus in South Viet-Nam . . . became covert. The organization and methods of the Party were changed in order to guarantee the leadership and focus forces of the Party under the new struggle condition.'[7]

5. Jeffrey Race, 'The Origins of the Second Indochina War', *Asian Survey*, May 1970, p. 361. Race's article is based on captured Communist documents in the Secret Police (Cong An) Archives of the Diem regime and extensive interviews with two particularly senior NLF defectors. It might be noticed that by 1957 the Soviet Union proposed to admit both Vietnams and both Koreas into the United Nations. See Falk, op. cit., p. 406.

6. Race, op. cit., p. 362.

7. Testimony of an unidentified cadre whose 23,000-word review written

'The new struggle condition' was the regime of Ngo Dinh Diem, a noted administrator and patriot, and a Catholic who lacked a popular political base and hence drew upon the skills of Vietnamese Catholics (including refugees from the North, numbering at least 800,000, most of them Catholic). Diem was not expected by most observers to last very long at all and so the Party could, and apparently did, reasonably hope for a *coup d'état* or conditions of anarchy that it could exploit.[8] Diem had an American following and U S advisers were early on the scene. However, he seemed to have little substantial going for him:

> ... except for his family and a few Vietnamese friends and his American supporters, he literally stood alone. As the French hastily withdrew most of their public servants, there was scarcely any administrative talent left, and disorder, abetted by banditry, mounted in the countryside. Communications everywhere were in a state of collapse, the Vietminh having sabotaged the railroads and set up obstacles on the roads and canals. Vietnamese soldiers were deserting by the thousands, and for a time Diem's authority scarcely extended beyond Saigon itself, where he had only a single battalion of loyal troops upon which he could completely depend.[9]

Apart from plots against him, Diem had to deal with three hostile private armies: The Binh Xuyen gangster movement, and

---

about 1963 has become known as the CRIMP document. Cited in Albert E. Palmerlee, *The Central Office of South Viet-Nam, Viet-Nam Documents and Research Notes*, United States Mission in Vietnam, No. 40. See also *Viet-Nam Documents and Research Notes*, Nos. 36–37. Henceforth these documents will be designated VNDRN.

8. Race, op. cit., p. 361. It may also be cogently argued that the nature of the so-called 'land reform' of 1953–6, chiefly affecting what was to become the DRV at Geneva, itself made elections out of the question. This reign of terror, later admitted by the Communists to have been a 'grave error', in which 30 per cent of persons liquidated were admitted by the Party journal, *Nhan Dan* (see Duncanson, footnote b, p. 174), to have owned no land, provided an adequate excuse for the Diem Government to refuse participation in nation-wide elections. What government would have participated in conditions in which a clear majority, including people in the northern provinces of South Vietnam, had, many of them very recently, been subjected to a reign of terror? See also footnote 13.

9. Robert Shaplen, *The Lost Revolution*, Deutsch, 1966, p. 115.

the armies of the Cao Dai and Hoa Hao sects, which virtually ran their own little states. Diem won this struggle but at the cost of making elements of the sects ready to join the National Liberation Front (NLF) later. Some informed observers have maintained that Diem's determination to try conclusions with the sects was one of his major errors.

Having put down these immediate threats, Diem decided to force the abdication of the Emperor Bao Dai, who in 1945 had been forced to abdicate by the Vietminh. This was done by way of what was clearly a rigged referendum. The next target was to be the Vietminh apparatus in the South: Diem was resolved utterly to destroy it if he could because he knew perfectly well that it would destroy him if he did not.

But before discussing this campaign it should be pointed out that Diem and his brother Ngo Dinh Nhu were clearly determined also to establish a regime for their purposes which was an organizationally imperfect replica of the Vietminh. There was an ideology of sorts, derived from French Personalism, and a secret élite party, the Can Lao. While Diem's emphasis seems to have been Confucian-authoritarian, his powerful brother clearly saw himself as something of a revolutionary. As Denis Warner says, 'Nhu ... was so much of an anti-Communist, and knew so much about Communist tactics that he often turned to the Communist method ...'[10]

The regime that was established was very arbitrary indeed. As Duncanson described it, by 1956: '[Diem] and his brothers had every cause to congratulate themselves on their recipe for power and on their judicious mixing of its ingredients – intrigue, nepotism, simony, public humbug and private intimidation. But henceforward it was a question of exercising the power they had won. Unhappily, they determined to carry on as they had begun ...'[11]

Looking at it from the Communist point of view, the regime displayed obvious 'contradictions' that could be exploited – provided the Party could survive physically. There was the old

10. Denis Warner, *The Last Confucian*, Penguin Books, 1964, p. 103.
11. Duncanson, op. cit., p. 225.

regional problem reflected in the administrative dominance of Northerners and men from Central Vietnam over Southerners.[12] There was the subversion of the administration by the Diem circle's addiction to favouritism – or reliance on personal loyalty, if it is preferred – in the matter of promotions. There was a disregard for the processes of law and a promiscuous use of arbitrary powers in the attempt to destroy the Communist apparatus, which created disaffection in non-Communist circles – not that many of those circles were any more democratic than that of the Ngos.

There were also the very unsatisfactory aspects of the land reform: dilatoriness in getting it under way, disguised rents being paid despite the stipulated lowering to 25 per cent, a tenderness for the susceptibilities of even absentee landlords, collection of rent on abandoned land by the security services, not the Land Office, and for a percentage, to mention only some failings.[13] On the other hand, Duncanson points out that 'In the

12. Robert Scigliano, *South Vietnam: Nation Under Stress*, Houghton Mifflin, Boston, 1963, p. 51, provides figures.

13. See Scigliano, op. cit., Ch. 5, and Duncanson, op. cit., pp. 242–7, for discussions on land reform. It should be noticed again that a very different kind of 'land reform' was carried out in the North during the time before the nation-wide election was scheduled. It was in fact a reign of terror in which large numbers of people were done to death in atrocious circumstances; for example: 'Those unfortunates who were sentenced to death were shot immediately after sentence had been passed. Before the tribunal began, a hole was dug nearby to receive the bodies of the victims . . . a cadre stood behind the accused, ready as soon as the sentence had been passed to thrust a piece of cloth into his mouth and drag him away . . . it frequently happened [because of bad shooting] that the victims were buried alive . . . A huge parade was organized on the occasion of a landlord's execution, with small children beating drums and the adults shouting the usual slogans. The crowd had to clap their hands when the victims fell down . . . The landlord was a scapegoat to satisfy the cruel instincts of a few fanatics and to strike terror into the heart of the whole of the population' (Hoang Van Chi, *From Colonialism to Communism: A Case History of North Vietnam*, Pall Mall Press, 1964, p. 189). Cf. Duncanson, op. cit., pp. 258–9, where he points out that there were thirty-three 'verified unjudicial executions attributable to the [Diem] regime', twenty of the victims having been mown down in a panic during a prison riot.

short run, the results of the work done on rent reduction did come quickly and were very rewarding: by 'mid-1959 four-fifths of all tenanted land had been brought under the new controls and 800,000 contracts registered'. But by 1962, of an estimated 1 to 1.2 million tenant households existing in 1955 only about 10 per cent obtained land under the government's land-transfer programme.

However, the unsatisfactory aspects of the land-reform programme should not be over-estimated in regard to the rebuilding of the Communist Front apparatus. This for an old reason of which Lenin had been very aware and which was stated by the NLF when describing the struggle for control of a village in the Mekong Delta: 'Though the Party correctly based its actions on the people's interests – especially with respect to land – and persuaded them to join the mass movement, it did not know how to profit from the opportunity to teach the people that their rights and interests must be subordinated to the national interests of independence, peace, and reunification, or that they must focus all their resentment on, and fight against the US–Diem clique.' The NLF report then adds perhaps its most significant sentence: 'Consequently, once the people are satisfied about land, the movement degenerates.'[14] The 'mobilization of the masses' was clearly to be a much more difficult business than simply telling peasants that they now owned their plots on abandoned holdings in Communist territory.

According to one distinguished authority, M. Philippe Devillers, it was the indiscriminately repressive measures of the Diem regime from 1957 onwards that started the Second Indo-China War.

In 1958 the situation grew worse. Round-ups of 'dissidents' became more frequent and more brutal . . . A certain sequence of events became almost classical: denunciation, encirclement of villages, searches and raids, arrest of suspects, plundering interrogations enlivened sometimes by torture (even of innocent people), deportation, and 'regrouping' of populations suspected of intelligence with the rebels . . . In the course of [December 1958] and the following Janu-

14. Quoted in Warner, op. cit., p. 150.

ary armed bands sprang into being almost everywhere. The ground was well prepared; many villages fell under their control and were immediately transformed into bases ... at the end of March 1959, M. Diem told the correspondent to *Figaro* that 'at the present time Vietnam is a nation at war'.[15]

Whatever the excesses of the Diem regime may have been – and there are grounds for believing that the rural administration was much weaker than Devillers' picture would suggest – and whatever Diem may have thought in March 1959, the second revolutionary war had not begun that early. Of course, in such a situation it all depends upon what is meant by the word 'war'. Duncanson points out, on the basis of statements by Nguyen Huu Tho (later titular leader of the NLF) and General Giap, that 'Communist action to obstruct, and ultimately destroy, the Diem regime was initiated within ten days of the signing of the Geneva Agreements.'[16] So far as the Party was concerned the struggle had never ended at all. But despite a recrudescence of terrorism by 1958, the second revolutionary guerrilla war was not decided upon until the middle of 1959; and the end of that year was regarded as a quite desperate time for the Party.[17] The decision for revolutionary war was made by the Politbureau of the Laodong (Communist) Party in Hanoi.[18] Though there had been many complaints by cadres under grave stress in the South, the Party had remained one and indivisible. As a former high-ranking Communist expressed it, 'There never were clear factions or groups within the Party demanding armed activity which might have broken off from the Party in the South or from the Central Committee in Hanoi – that could never happen.'[19]

There can be no doubt that the nature of the promiscuous attack on likely political enemies, of whom the Communists were

15. 'Ngo Dinh Diem and the Struggle for Reunification', in Marvin E. Gettleman, *Vietnam: History, Documents, and Opinions on a Major World Crisis*, Penguin Books, 1965, pp. 232–5.

16. Duncanson, op. cit., p. 251.

17. See document in Race, op. cit., pp. 372–3.

18. See Le Duan's statement, VNDRN No. 40, p. 4.

19. Quoted in Race, op. cit., p. 372.

only one, by Diem's forces helped to provide conditions of disaffection which could be exploited in order to build yet another 'united front', this time entitled the National Liberation Front of South Vietnam (NLFSV);[20] nor can there be any doubt that the success of this attempt to smash the Communist apparatus in the South put the southern branch of the Party in dire jeopardy unless an armed struggle were to be mounted. But there is also no doubt whatever that the strategic decision was made in Hanoi and that the high command was the Politbureau in Hanoi acting through a refurbished COSVN in Nam Bo and probably more directly controlled further north in South Vietnam.

However, though the NLF was designed to serve 'the supreme interests of the Fatherland', that is, bring about reunification through armed struggle, it was to be a Front fleshed out in terms of *southern* conditions and its chief strength was to derive from an organized exploitation of those conditions, not from infiltrations from the North for a number of years. The various facets of the nature of the NLF are established by Pike as follows:

> ... the NLF was not simply an indigenous organization in which Communists played a part. Neither was it simply a robot-like instrument of the DRV. The Communists formed the NLF to establish a single organization around which all anti-Diem activity could cluster and create a bipolar political condition. This met several of their needs. They needed a mass base, since the Lao Doñg Party [Communist Party] was not a mass-based organization in South Vietnam. They needed a skeletal, standby governmental structure for possible future use. They needed an opportunity to infiltrate non-Communist organizations, and participation in the Front obviously provided good access to these groups. They also needed a divisive wedge, and the NLF organization allowed the Communists to play one group against another, forcing individual members to choose sides against each other rather than against the Communists.[21]

20. Douglas Pike, *The Viet Cong*, MIT Press, Cambridge, Mass., 1966, p. 81, cites a Laodong statement of 1960 designed for Party members which makes it clear that the NLF was a successor of earlier Front movements dating back to 1941.

21. ibid., p. 82.

At the same time it must be said that reinfiltration of cadres which had regrouped in the North did begin in or before 1960. Most of those who went North appear to have come from the poor coastal provinces of Phu Yen, Binh Dinh and Quang Ngai, an area which had been very much under Vietminh control during the earlier struggle and was to be very important in activating the second war. But there were also cadres from most other areas. And, as has been remarked, there were considerable quantities of the most modern light and medium weapons available, despite the fact that between 1955 and 1960 the GVN had recovered 307 caches of arms. From 1959 onwards the preparation of the Ho Chi Minh trail network was being prepared through Laos. But, as in the first war, great store was set upon capturing arms from the enemy; and many were captured early in 1960.

As a distinguished observer unsympathetic to the Diem regime has also pointed out, 'This was a period of deliberate and premeditated terror directed at all officials in the countryside who were either unjust administrators or who, by their good example, served the government well ... They killed both bad officials and good officials: the mediocre, those who saw and heard no evil (in the Viet Cong), survived. It was an effective tactic.'[22] A reasonable estimate puts assassinations of officials – which included malarial eradication officers and even schoolmasters – at 20,000 during the nine years of Diem's rule, which is the equivalent of an annual murder in every administrative village.[23]

The effects of such a terrorist campaign of course were felt far beyond the confines of the victim's family. As one of the terrorist informants of the Australian NLF sympathizer, Wilfred Burchett, put it,

> Many of those 'pardoned' found ways of contacting us, thanking us on their knees for the pardon. Many offered to serve us while pretending to serve the enemy. In fact, we knew in most cases they

22. Warner, op. cit., pp. 160–61.
23. Duncanson, op. cit., p. 252.

would continue to serve the enemy as well. But we counted on the people exercising strict control over them in the future so we could accept this. Unrepentant sinners . . . would leave the village and operate from the nearest military post, visiting the village only in daytime.[24]

However, the corollary to terrorism was the positive activity of building in the countryside Front organizations, three of which were regarded by the NLF as of central importance: the Farmers' Liberation Association, the Youth Liberation Association and the Women's Liberation Association. In the opinion of the Westerner who has most intensively examined the documents, Douglas Pike, the NLF's chief triumph between 1962 and 1965–6 was a sheer organizational one: the building up of an organization of some 300,000 by 1962.[25] This mobilizing of the masses occurred in a peculiar manner: '[The NLF] sprang full-blown into existence and then was fleshed out. The grievances were developed or manufactured almost as a necessary afterthought. The creation of the NLF was an accomplishment of such skill, precision, and refinement that when one thinks of who the master planner must have been, only one name comes to mind: Vietnam's organizational genius, Ho Chi Minh.'[26]

This is not to say that Pike underestimates the role of terror. Far from it: 'Terror destroys the structure of authority which normally stands for security. Terror, especially in an isolated village, causes fright, anxiety, and despair ... Terror isolates. The villager sees himself alone, in anguish and impotent ...' Indeed Pike lays a bigger charge against the Vietcong terrorists

24. Wilfred Burchett, *Vietnam: Inside Story of the Guerrilla War*, International Publishers, New York, 1965, p. 147.

25. Pike, op. cit., p. 115. Pike states that in 1965–6 the NLF membership stood at between 250,000 and 300,000, in a population of some 13 millions.

26. ibid., p. 76. An Englishman who served under Winston Churchill, saw Roosevelt and Stalin in conference action, met Mao Tse-tung, and later stayed with Ho Chi Minh, told the author that he formed the impression that Ho was much the cleverest man of them all, so Pike's judgement may well be right. But the I C P leadership was and is collective.

than any other writer: 'Many villages by 1966 were virtually depopulated of their natural leaders, who are the single most important element in any society. They represent a human resource of incalculable value. This loss to Vietnam is inestimable, and it will take a generation or more to repair the damage to the society. By any definition, the NLF action against village leaders amounts to genocide.'[27]

The NLF announced a ten-point programme at the time of its official foundation on 20 December 1960. Apart from provisions for the confiscation of land 'owned by American imperialists and their servants', the thrust of the document is to establish what it calls a 'largely liberal and democratic regime'. As with the foundation of the Vietminh Front (and later the wider Lien-Viet Front), the objectives of the Lao Dong Party are altogether hidden. In the much longer programme of 1967 it is promised that 'The state will negotiate the purchase of land from landlords who possess upwards of a certain amount, varying with the situation in each locality.' In the first programme the emphasis is placed upon overthrowing the 'American-Diem clique'; in the second it is naturally placed more upon the 'American imperialists'. Neither programme bears any relation to ultimate objectives.[28]

The Diem regime's response to the reactivation of revolutionary guerrilla warfare was two-fold in the countryside: the

27. ibid., p. 248. What the Communists call, in some ways more correctly, their policy of 'repression' is but one instrument amongst many of mutually supporting kinds, designed 'to eliminate, neutralize, and "reform" their known enemies in the Government of South Vietnam as well as others whom they suspect of being hostile or unsympathetic to their movement' (Stephen T. Hosmer, *Vietcong Repression and Its Implications for the Future*, Rand, Santa Monica, 1970, p. 1. This is the most thorough examination of what is loosely known as Vietcong 'terrorism'.)

28. See *Political Program of the South Vietnam National Liberation Front*, US Mission in Vietnam, Saigon, October 1967, which contains the 1960 and 1967 programmes. The 1967 programme, like its predecessor, advocates 'a broad and progressive democratic regime', which will embrace 'the most representative persons among the various social strata, nationalities, religious communities, patriotic and democratic parties . . .' etc. The objective of the Lao Dong still remains hidden.

use of the armed forces – army, Civil Guard and Self-Defence Corps – in counter-insurgent activities and, in the latter half of 1961, the development of an altogether overly ambitious programme of building strategic hamlets. The army and security forces totalled about 250,000 men and were built up by another 120,000 men by 1962.[29] The police, who numbered well under 10,000 at the beginning and were under three commands until 1962, and the Civil Guards, a volunteer organization, had not been retrained as a rural police force as was advised by some Americans. Thus the Diem regime was ill-equipped to prevent the *beginnings* of revolutionary guerrilla warfare.[30]

The 150,000-strong army (in 1961) had on American advice been trained to meet invasion by regular forces and therefore was not prepared for the sort of war which now faced it.[31] As a result, its counter-insurgent activities were very often counter-productive.[32] It is true that in mid-1960 US specialists in counter-insurgency arrived and began to train companies of anti-guerrillas along the lines of the US Rangers, the Civil Guards began to be retrained, and the wretched Self-Defence Corps began to receive American aid.

Opposed to them were some 5,500 Vietcong Mainforce troops and about 30,000 regional and local guerrillas by the end of 1960. They were commanded by a reactivated COSVN and by high-ranking Communists within the NLF Committee, whose non-Communist members were Front men of no political consequence in South Vietnam. Infiltration, as has been said, was not large, but it began to grow in numbers – and was mostly composed of officers and NCOs, virtually all of whom were of

29. Scigliano, op. cit., p. 118. Army strength was 150,000 up to 1961 (Duncanson, op. cit., p. 289).

30. See Duncanson, op. cit., pp. 254–9, 281.

31. One reason for this concern with invasion by DRV regulars was the fact, disclosed by Sir Anthony Eden in the House of Commons on 8 November 1954, that by the end of that year the Vietminh/DRV would have twice as many regular field formations as at the time of the Geneva Agreement (B. S. N. Murti, *Vietnam Divided: The Unfinished Struggle*, Asia Publishing House, 1964, p. 49).

32. Warner, op. cit., pp. 151–3, gives an important example of this.

Southern origin until late 1963.[33] A great deal of trouble was taken by the Communist Party, including the planting of evidence, to disguise the fact of the war's command from Hanoi.

If a date had to be selected for the beginning of the war proper it would be 13–15 January 1960, the period of the Vietnamese New Year (Tet) celebrations. This saw a major exercise in armed propaganda: a wave of assassinations and attacks. Race has described this in Long An province as follows:

> While the government as a whole did not collapse, the great majority of local officials who lived among the people – hamlet and village chiefs, police agents, information cadres – either stopped working or fled to market towns where outposts were located. At the same time that the government withdrew from the rural areas into outposts and towns the Party apparatus, previously forced to lead an underground existence, surfaced and took the place of the Saigon authorities. Thus the Party actually *became* the government in considerable areas as early as 1960, gradually expanding and consolidating its grip in the following years.[34]

However, the struggle was to be a grim one. Apart from retraining the security forces and attempting to bring the bulk of

33. Infiltration figures supplied by Mr Averell Harriman on 27 May 1968 at the Paris talks were as follows:

| Year | Confirmed | Probable | Total |
|---|---|---|---|
| 1959–60 | 4,556 | 26 | 4,582 |
| 1961 | 4,118 | 2,177 | 6,295 |
| 1962 | 5,362 | 7,495 | 12,857 |
| 1963 | 4,726 | 3,180 | 7,906 |
| | 18,762 | 12,878 | 31,640 |

Source: VNDRD Nos. 36–37, p. 10.

But cf. Fall, *Street Without Joy*, pp. 347–8: '. . . the hard fact is that, save for a few specialized anti-aircraft and anti-tank weapons and cadre personnel not exceeding perhaps 3,000 to 4,000 a year or less, the VC operation inside South Viet-Nam's foreign borders has become self-sustaining. And while the complete closing of the South Vietnamese border to infiltrators certainly remains a worthwhile objective, to achieve it along 700 miles of jungle-covered mountains and swamp would just about absorb the totality of South Viet-Nam's 1964 forces of 250,000 regulars and 250,000 para-military troops of various kinds.'

34. Race, op. cit., p. 380.

the population under government control through the creation of very large numbers of strategic hamlets,[35] the Diem regime evidenced a clear tendency towards what has elsewhere been called the replication of the enemy Communist society or counter-State. The National Revolutionary Movement, the government's 'mass party', was supposed to reinforce the village administration with indoctrinal and propaganda skills, as well as providing a kind of counter-Intelligence service. There was a counterpart for the administration itself in the National Revolutionary Civil Servants League. There was also the Republican Youth and Madame Nhu's women's organization; and there were the hundreds of devoted young men of the Commissariat for Civic Action. It was also attempted to organize the people into neighbourhood-control groups in an obvious replication of Communist organization.[36]

A battle had been joined that was a contest partly for the 'hearts and minds' of men but much more for control over their wills.

In retrospect it is easy to see the mistakes the GVN made in the years 1961–3: the over-extension of the hamlet programme; the failure to provide adequate defence and communications; the failure adequately to communicate their purpose to the people;[37] the failures in getting huge doses of economic aid from the USA to the villages, in many cases;[38] the failures to avoid ambush, to harry mainforce units sufficiently, to ration-

35. See below.

36. Scigliano, op. cit., pp. 168–70.

37. For example: 'The peasants were asked to erect their own thatch-roofed houses, dig a protective ditch around the site and crown it with a mud wall and barbed wire. In spite of various government subsidies and other inducements of better living conditions, it had been difficult to persuade peasants to leave their ancestral plots for other areas. There were a number of incidents where over-zealous officials rounded up peasants and put them to work without pay, and such people easily believed the guerrillas when they described the fortified villages as concentration camps' (Murti, op. cit., pp. 193–4). But the reducing of strategic hamlets was often a tactical problem, the solution of one being vividly described in Burchett, op. cit., pp. 191–2.

38. Probably the most intelligently specific analysis of these failures in pacification is William A. Nighswonger, *Rural Pacification in Vietnam*, Praeger, New York, 1966.

alize the time spent on duty by the Self-Defence Corps, to mention but a few mistakes. It is therefore easy enough to castigate overly optimistic statements made by U S advisers.

However, it is by no means simple in the midst of the fray to judge which way the tide of events is flowing in this kind of war. This is borne out very clearly by the testimony of Vietcong leaders in interviews with the Australian Communist sympathizer, Wilfred Burchett, who was in the field. After citing an example of the great ingenuity the Vietcong displayed in breaching hamlets in Phu Yen province on the coastal strip, Burchett continues:

> The struggle could not develop everywhere as in Phu Yen. Although it had the most unfavourable conditions for guerrilla warfare in Central Vietnam, it was a paradise as compared to the flat Mekong Delta, with no mountains at all and forest only in the unpopulated mangrove swamps bordering the coastal areas. During 1962, helicopter-borne troops took a fairly heavy toll of resistance fighters and there was a period when the Front leadership almost decided the price was too high, that resistance in the Delta should cease and regular Front armed forces should withdraw to bases in the mountains ...
>
> It is clear that the situation at the end of 1962 was critical in one sense for the Front. Diem had not been able to set up his 16,000 strategic hamlets but he had set up many thousands and re-established some sort of nominal control in regions which a year previously had been solidly Front-controlled ... The 'tug-of-war' struggle never ceased ... In terms of territory and population, Diem made a considerable comeback in 1962; in terms of winning popular support, he lost out heavily. In strictly military terms, the U S-Diemist forces registered a number of successes and held the strategic and tactical initiative. But this situation was dramatically reversed in the very first days of 1963.[39]

This last reference is to the battle of Ap Bac, a cluster of hamlets in the Mekong Delta some forty miles south-west of Saigon, on 2–3 January 1963. This was a propaganda victory for the NLF at home and abroad, and the battle became a propaganda point of considerable significance in the USA. A bitter opponent of the Diem regime, Mr David Halberstam, of the

39. Burchett, op. cit., pp. 192–3.

*New York Times*, who visited the scene afterwards, wrote a story in which he said, amongst other things, that the American advisers in the Mekong Delta 'feel that what happened at Ap Bac goes far deeper than one battle and is tied directly to the question of whether the Vietnamese are really interested in having American advisers and listening to them . . .'[40]

What was assumed to have happened at Ap Bac was widely publicized in the USA as typical of a struggle that was being lost because of the nature of the Diem regime. But two equally distinguished American journalists later wrote about Ap Bac, which was indeed a failure to contain and destroy a trapped Vietcong mainforce, in a rather different manner. Mr Malcolm Browne pointed out that the Vietcong unit in question, the 514th battalion, was 'probably the most dangerous fighting unit in the country', that it prepared its positions at Ap Bac very well, that it was for the first time in the war ordered to stand its ground and that the chief failure revealed was one pertaining to weaponry: the M113 personnel carrier, which was wrongly used as a tank, paratroopers having missed the dropping zone. The course of the battle was therefore not necessarily typical of anything in particular.[41]

Secondly, the late Marguerite Higgins drew attention to the fact that Ap Bac was not the only battle fought in the first half of 1963. While fully conceding that Vietnamese officers had displayed 'incredibly bad leadership, prompting Lieutenant Colonel John Vann, the brilliant and idealistic US adviser at the time, to complain bitterly', Marguerite Higgins pointed out that a success quite as great as the failure at Ap Bac – a battle in Quang Ngai, which cost the Vietcong over 226 dead and Chinese and Czech machine guns – received nothing like equivalent reportage in the USA.[42]

The formation of the operational MACV (Military Assist-

40. Cited in David Halberstam, *The Making of a Quagmire*, Bodley Head, 1965, p. 155.

41. Malcolm W. Browne, *The New Face of War: A Report on a Communist Guerrilla Campaign*, Cassell, 1965, pp. 10–13.

42. Marguerite Higgins, *Our Vietnam Nightmare*, Harper & Row, New York, 1965, pp. 127–30.

ance Command, Vietnam) early in 1962, following a large expansion in military aid and training undertakings, may be said to have begun the real US involvement in the Second Indo-China War, since American military prestige was now linked to the fortunes of that war. Indeed, it has been argued that General Maxwell Taylor 'had written the victory plan for Vietnam'[43]; and it was he who appointed General Harkins, whose expressions of optimism about the way the war was going later came in for much criticism.

Most conspicuously opposed to the optimistic view was Colonel John Vann, who eventually quit the Army as a result of the dispute, but returned to become the most senior and respected US adviser until his death in 1972. The argument in a sense was one about criteria: which criteria were indicative of progress? MACV pointed, for example, to increased Vietcong casualties; Vann pointed to a lack of combativeness on the part of the regulars (the ARVN), the promiscuous use of 'hardware', the generally static strategy (if there really was a strategy at this time).

There was argument about the Vietcong capacity to recruit; and argument about ratios between weapons lost and weapons recovered. These were very serious arguments: casualties cannot be crucial so long as they can be made up by recruiting, and they clearly were made up at this time. The capacity to recruit is in turn indicative of a government failure to control the population – and strategic hamlets were being most talked about in official circles and in propaganda as an answer to the guerrilla threat.

The arms ratio too was a very serious question, since the art of revolutionary guerrilla warfare – however vital fusions of high-quality weapons are for the final counter-offensive phase – is to build up one's strength by living off the enemy. The argument here was less conclusive.[44]

Severe Intelligence failings; an apparent inability to introduce

43. Halberstam, op. cit., p. 169.

44. Higgins, op. cit., p. 126 cites figures given by Robert S. McNamara showing that between 1960 and April 1965 the NLF had received 85 per cent of their arms from outside. Thompson, op. cit., p. 40, supplies figures showing a net loss of weapons to the Vietcong of about 12,000, the bulk of them from the 'Buddhist crisis' onwards but particularly in 1964 after Diem's death.

population and resources control (that is, the inability to stop the easy movement of people and supplies by the Vietcong); a propensity to be lured into occasional grisly and large-scale ambushes (itself a sign that the Vietcong were not being harried sufficiently to prevent large-scale co-ordination of their units); and an increasing dislocation of the communications systems – these too were ominous signs. Some of these failures were the result of defects in the nature of the regime. Clearly, the suspicions of a clique government affected very deleteriously the employment of the many Intelligence agencies, just as it deleteriously affected relations between senior armed service officers.

However, it should be noticed that though there were many signs in 1963 that the U S–Diem (as it by then was) counter-insurgency campaign was not winning, and in the long term was possibly losing, this was also a campaign against an attempt to engender what the Vietnamese Communists call a 'general uprising'. Hanoi was not simply masterminding a protracted revolutionary war. The mastermind of this 'general uprising' strategy was Truong Chinh, and the strategy was at least in part based upon the experience of the August Revolution of 1945 when, as a result of special circumstances as well as remarkable organization, the people-at-large did rise on a wide scale, in the towns just as much as in the countryside.

Pike has described the concept of *Khoi Nghia*, or general uprising, as follows:

> The NLF social myth, *Khoi Nghia*, quite clearly is traceable to the myth of the General Strike. It is the general strike in an agrarian setting. Briefly it is this: by various means, political and military, the revolutionary consciousness of the Vietnamese people gradually is raised and intensified until it no longer can be contained and suddenly, one golden morning, explodes through the nation. The people rise, indomitably, and march into power. *Khoi Nghia* is accomplished.[45]

45. Pike, *Politics of the Vietcong*, op. cit., p. 27. It has been argued by other experts that the term has been made too much of by Douglas Pike. It is probably truer to say that it has sometimes been made too much of by Truong Chinh.

The 'revolutionary consciousness' of the people, according to this theory, is 'raised and intensified' through facets of the 'struggle movement' (an activity which Pike says is composed of 'commitment, hatred, ambition, grievance, revenge and aspiration', a heady brew). Different kinds of struggle are carried out: within NLF-held territory, in the GVN-controlled areas, and amongst the GVN security forces ('enemy proselytizing').

He provides a superb instance of political struggle in GVN territory. A woman, it appears, was killed by the security forces. Her family and relatives assembled to mourn. The hamlet's NLF executive decided the opportunity was too good to miss and so invited the family to spread the mourning and turn it into a protest movement. But they were all too afraid, except for an uncle, so the executive 'decided to refrigerate the body and send runners in sampans to other hamlets to gather people for the struggle'. A delegation was formed and moved in sampans towed by a motor boat to Camau city. There boats began to gather around the victim's mother, who had begun to cry very loudly. Some 200 people came down to the wharf from the market. The mother told her story. A petition was presented. Then the corpse was laid out in the market-place and, predictably, the police intervened, removed the boat and the body, arrested a number of people, including children, and generally made themselves disagreeable. All in all it was quite a good propaganda show.

However, the operation was analysed very coolly and purposefully in the Vietcong report written later:

> The strong points of the struggle were these: There was good leadership; the village executive committee acted quickly . . .; the struggle was well planned, and no difficulties were encountered in getting the body to the market-place . . .; the timing was correct; early morning in the market-place was the correct time for the struggle . . .; there was [follow-up] . . .; when the hamlet people returned to their village more demonstrations were held . . . Medical care was given to those injured during the demonstration . . .
>
> The weak points of the struggle were these: The executive committee was not prepared for an immediate struggle but had to send people to other hamlets for assistance . . . When the police came to

suppress the demonstration, those from the village did not stand up and admit they were from the village, but in fact they denied it ... Unfortunately the only member of the victim's family at the market-place was the girl's mother; the rest got 'cold feet' when approaching Camau and turned back ... It was necessary therefore for us to supply a 'make-believe sister and children' to accompany the mother ... No one argued when the police came to take away the body ... The petition to the officials only asked for the correction of an injustice, and did not include demands, such as an end to the strategic-hamlet program ... There was a lack of firmness in requesting the release of those arrested during the demonstration.[46]

However, zealous as the struggle movement was, theorists of the general uprising, unlike the theorists of Maoist-style protracted war, needed to heighten the 'revolutionary consciousness' of those in the cities as well as in the countryside. From June 1963 a situation began to develop that proved ultimately fatal to the Ngos but did not in the event engender the hoped-for general uprising. This was the so-called 'Buddhist crisis'.

Buddhists suffered from institutional disabilities under a law having nothing to do with the Diem regime. But by skilful manipulation of dissident elements and the press, particularly the Western press, militant Buddhists managed to create the impression that they were being *persecuted* by a Catholic-dominated government. There never was at any time any persecution of Buddhists[47] and the militants were centred in Saigon and Hue – a specifically Buddhist 'consciousness' being absent from the countryside, except in Cambodian minority regions – but American officials, many of whom were anyway exasperated by Diem, began to be persuaded that this 'persecution' could afford the pretext for bringing him down.

Firing in Hue and the ostentatious self-immolation of monks, nearly always in the presence of forewarned Western pressmen and photographers, created the right atmosphere. Nhu gave it the final touch by raiding the command-centre of the Buddhist

46. Pike, *The Vietcong*, op. cit., pp. 395–7.

47. Some Buddhists have, however, insisted to the author that Buddhists were disabled in regard to advancement in the regime; and sometimes felt themselves to be 'second-class' citizens.

militant campaign, the Xa Loi pagoda, a move which might have saved the situation had it not been for 'pressure coming from overseas, which further fed the flames in Saigon and Hue'.[48] More demonstrations and arrests occurred. Diem and his regime were brought down by an army *coup* supported by the US Government.[49]

Diem and Nhu, who were done to death at this time, had made very serious mistakes and on occasion silly misjudgements but the NLF, which claimed to have manipulated the 'Buddhist crisis', knew better than the Americans (including President Kennedy) who brought him down. Wilfred Burchett quotes a member of the People's Revolutionary Party (the southern branch of the Indo-Chinese Communist Party):

> ... in fact they will search in vain for a more efficient horse than Diem. With all his faults and criminal stupidities, in nine years Diem did succeed in setting up and maintaining an army, an administration and some sort of a political machine, with all the reins of power in his hands ... Over 100 officers up to the rank of colonel were kicked out of the army. At provincial and district level, many officials faithful to Diem were eliminated. The whole apparatus of the secret police was dissolved ... It [the aftermath of Diem] explains also how we were able to exploit the situation for large-scale activities in the countryside and in Saigon itself. Many hundreds of 'strategic hamlets' were liberated in groups of ten and twenty at a time and we scored important victories on all fronts. In Saigon factories, universities and schools there was a big upsurge of activity ... A new and important development is the very strong movement for 'peace and neutrality' among different sections of the urban population.[50]

And yet the expected general uprising did not occur, as it did not occur during the 1968 Tet Offensive, simply because the

48. Duncanson, op. cit., p. 337. It is of interest that Buddhist monks who burned themselves *after* Diem's downfall were of no concern to Western pressmen and photographers.

49. It now seems clear from Chester L. Cooper, *The Lost Crusade*, MacGibbon & Kee, 1971, Ch. IX, and from the famous *Pentagon Papers*, Bantam Books, New York, 1971, that tortured American liberals pursued a tortuous course ultimately predicated upon the capacity of a group of generals to stage a coup that would issue in a viable government.

50. Burchett, op. cit., pp. 217–18.

NLF did not have the degree of genuine popular support it claimed. Nor did the army, though some of its units began to get chewed up, then begin to disintegrate as a result of 'troop proselytizing'. (The army desertions that have figured so large in journalists' reports had little or nothing to do with the political attractions of the NLF – it was the attractions of the home hamlet that were at work.)

The failure of the general uprising, which probably was very much Truong Chinh's brainchild, resulted in Giap coming back to the epicentre of the politico-military stage. Though the ARVN did not disintegrate according to plan, it did begin to crumble. 'Clearly victory was now a feasible prospect for the insurgents, provided that it could be achieved without provoking massive American military involvement. Giap stepped up the pace of operations in a bid to cut the South into two pieces for easy digestion.'[51] By the end of 1964 this operation had not quite been brought off.[52] The Americans intervened *en masse*.

Why they did so at this time cannot be usefully investigated here. In part it was because their prestige had for several years been directly involved in the outcome of the Second Indo-China War; partly because since 1961 'special warfare' (under the aegis of President Kennedy) had been very greatly upgraded as an alternative to both nuclear holocaust and global retreat; partly, as Mr Dean Rusk was prone to emphasize (rightly at that time, in the author's opinion), because the whole American alliance system had been put on the line; partly because the liberal intellectuals who had come to the fore in the administration (even if some of them quit as soon as the going got rough) had come to accept the philosophy of the late Ernest Hemingway's Jordan, hero of the Spanish Civil War, that 'if we stop them here, we will stop them everywhere'; partly because the then

51. O'Neill, op. cit., p. 190.

52. But 'By late Spring of 1965 the South Vietnamese Army was losing almost one infantry battalion a week to enemy action . . . the enemy was gaining control of at least one district capital town each week . . . the Government of South Vietnam could not survive this mounting . . . offensive for more than six months unless the United States chose to increase its military commitment' (General Westmoreland, quoted in Cooper, op. cit., p. 279).

Secretary of State for Defense, Mr Robert McNamara, believed that he had a mathematical answer to the problem, predicated on a wrong estimation of the 'Aggression from the North' thesis, and of the efficacy of the grandiosely named 'strategy of measured response'; and partly because of the ill-named 'Domino Theory', which really implied a recognition of the fact (the author would maintain) that South East Asia was the victim of interlocking crises – and a Communist victory in South Vietnam would unlock the situation in a manner catastrophically unfavourable to the nations of the area and deeply deleterious to the fortunes of the free world.

But of course the struggle was not going to be waged in terms of intellectual justification. The early 'Vietnam debates', the teach-ins and so on, were important only in terms of a protracted war: they cast doubt upon the enterprise, certainly, but such doubts would have been assuaged easily enough if a comparatively quick victory could have been achieved. Or, put more precisely: if a comparatively quick and cheap victory could have been achieved.[53]

General Giap knew better than this: he understood American psychology and he was aware that no more than about 600,000 troops could be brought to bear against the Vietcong and (by this time) North Vietnamese regular forces. There were some 500,000 South Vietnamese government troops, but there were 200,000 Vietcong fighting men and he could use at least a fifth of his North Vietnamese Army (100,000) in operations in the South. Given the Hanoi appreciation of American 'contradictions', this was not really a very frightening prospect.[54]

It was to be, on the psychological plane, a battle of wills and institutions and modes of thought. As Professor Robert Scalapino said when the struggle was really joined, 'Vietnam is a major test of American institutions and American political behaviour. Can our people endure a long, complicated, intricate

53. For example, the majority of American students did not oppose the war until mid-1968. See Seymour M. Lipset, 'Polls and Protests', *Foreign Affairs*, April 1971.

54. O'Neill, op. cit., pp. 191–2.

game which must not be played at 0 or 100? Can they adjust to playing at 46, and being willing to go to 63 – but no more? Or down to 8, but no lower?'[55] The American quantifiers seemed for a while to have come into their own. They were enormously intelligent men – mathematically – but, like some of the academic intellectuals who buzzed around the White House while the going was good, they began to address themselves to very different subjects once it became abundantly clear that the war was going to be long, messy and somewhat vague as to goals.

The problem was really a qualitative one. It was stated by another kind of intellectual who became attached to President Johnson's staff, Mr John P. Roche:

> [Whatever the distortions of the media and the critics may have been] Vietnam poisoned our atmosphere for a far more fundamental reason than a failure of communication between the Johnson Administration and the people.
>
> The basic issue in Vietnam was this: Could a free society fight a limited war? That is, a strategic war, a war without hate, a war without massive popular involvement? To put it differently, the War in Vietnam was being fought for an abstraction: American national interest in a non-totalitarian Asian future. And it was being fought by a new set of rules, rules which began to emerge during the Korean War, but were forgotten in subsequent years. It was very difficult to tell a young soldier, 'Go out there and fight, perhaps die, for a good bargaining position.' It was almost impossible to explain to a Congressman that Vietnam was a crucial testing ground – on the one side for a brilliantly mounted 'war of liberation'; on the other, for the American capacity to cope with (and, in future, deter) such liberators . . . But Lyndon Johnson flatly refused to whoop up yahoo chauvinism . . . Ho Chi Minh was always a problem. While we may have been fighting a limited war against him, he had declared total war against us – and he played his hand brilliantly. His central goal . . . was to escalate the war in Vietnam to the point where it became *politically* unjustifiable in the United States.[56]

Looking at the situation in South Vietnam from the American point of view, it may be said that they found themselves honour-

55. Robert Scalapino, in *The New York Times Magazine*, 11 December 1966.

56. John P. Roche, in *The Bulletin*, Sydney, 16 November 1968.

ing a commitment made by the late President Kennedy on 3 August 1961: 'The United States is determined that the Republic of Vietnam shall not be lost to the Communists for lack of any support the United States can render.'[57] What was intended was, in the words of Robert S. McNamara, to 'force the Communists to move from the battlefield to the conference table'. This was to be done by the so-called strategy of measured response: put vulgarly, the Americans would continue to raise its response to a point beyond which the Vietnamese Communists would not have the capacity to go. This military strategy involved four chief kinds of tactical operation: search-and-destroy, clear-and-hold, mobile reactive and operations designed to defend vital government centres; the logistic support of the South Vietnamese armed forces; aerial and naval bombardment of North Vietnam short of blockade measures; aerial bombardment of the network of Communist supply and reinforcement trails through southern Laos, but no 'hot pursuit' of Communist forces using Laos and Cambodia as sanctuaries – and certainly no ground attack on North Vietnam. The North Vietnamese regime was guaranteed against ground attacks from the beginning because of fear of Chinese intervention in a war intended to be a very limited operation.

But, as General Maxwell Taylor was to write later, '. . . apart from all other requirements, one major condition must be met if we are to expect Hanoi to withdraw from the lists. It is to convince that leadership that under no circumstances will the United States change its present policy and vary from its determination to attain the basic objective which we have proclaimed before the whole world.'[58] The objective was spelt out by President Johnson on 28 July 1965 as follows:

These steps [reinforcement and appropriation], like our actions in the past, are carefully measured to what must be done to bring an end to aggression and a peaceful settlement. We do not want an expanding struggle with consequences that no one can perceive, nor will we bluster or bully or flaunt our power, but we will not sur-

57. When convenient, a note from Eisenhower to Diem of 1954 was adverted to.

58. *New York Times Weekly Review*, 15 October 1967.

render and we will not retreat, for behind our American pledge lies the determination and resources, I believe, of all the American nation. Second, once the Communists know, as we know, that a violent solution is impossible, then a peaceful solution is inevitable. We are ready now, as we always have been, to move from the battleground to the conference table ... but we insist and we always shall insist that the people of South Vietnam shall have the right of choice, the right to shape their own destiny in free elections in the South or throughout all Vietnam under international supervision, and they shall not have any government imposed upon them by force and terror.

Therefore, the first 'theory of victory' amounted to an attempt to show the enemy that he could not win. But there was not of course a theory of victory at all, since, as Herman Kahn was to remark later, 'if preventing North Vietnam and the VC from winning is the best the United States can do, the enemy can plausibly claim the same capability and the war is reduced to a competition in staying power, motivation, morale, discipline, etc.'. Indeed, that was all the Communists needed to do in order that their expectations about American morale should be fulfilled. If they could create the impression of a stalemate, they reasoned (and it would obviously be a very expensive stalemate for the Americans), then American public opinion would tire of the war.

The American commander, General Westmoreland, did have a military theory of victory which he explained to the National Press Club in Washington on 21 November 1967. He divided the war into phases. The first phase was 1965 to mid-1966, a period in which a South Vietnamese collapse was prevented, bases were built and US troops deployed. The second phase began in mid-1966 and lasted throughout 1967. During this phase, General Westmoreland claimed, the enemy divisions had been 'driven back to sanctuary or in hiding'; the ARVN had been trained, expanded and improved in quality; enemy base areas had been entered and his supplies destroyed; enemy losses had been raised beyond 'his input capability'; free elections had been completed in South Vietnam and a civilian government installed; prices had been stabilized and communications opened; enemy defection had been encouraged; the enemy's battle plans had been discovered and so thwarted before they could be implemented; and the U S had improved the pacification effort. That phase, he said, would be completed by the end of 1967.

During Phase III, beginning in 1968, the U S forces would begin to concentrate their advisory efforts on the Regional and Popular Forces; revitalize the ARVN to take an increasing share of the war through re-equipment; continue pressure on the North to 'prevent rebuilding'; increase U S support in the Mekong Delta area of heaviest population; 'Help the Government of Vietnam single out and destroy the Communist Shadow Government', isolate the guerrillas from the population, and strengthen the police force, as well as continuing to open up more communications and help to improve the economy and standard of living.

Phase IV, the final phase, was not dated in any way as to beginning or end. It envisaged a slowing-down of infiltration, a cutting-up of the infrastructure, governmental stability, an improvement in Regional and Popular Forces, a gradual 'Vietnamization' (as it later came to be called) of the war, and an ultimate 'mopping-up' by the Vietnamese armed forces of the Vietcong, 'which will probably last several years'. He concluded by saying, 'It lies within our grasp – the enemy's hopes are bankrupt. With your support we will give you a success that will impact not only on South Vietnam, but on every emerging nation in the world.'[59]

Had the problem been a purely military one – had no account had to be taken of American public opinion, not just the moralistic dissenters, but the hard-headed section more aware of the annual $30 billion cost – then General Westmoreland's 'theory of victory' might not have been altogether unsound ... in the long run; and if it had not been for the mentality of commanders sent to South Vietnam for only one year, which, in Sir Robert Thompson's words, they regarded as 'an opportunity to

59. Quoted in Armbruster, Gastil, Kahn, Piaff and Stillman, *Can We Win in Vietnam? The American Dilemma*, Pall Mall Press, 1968, pp. 198–201.

indulge in a year's big-game shooting from their helicopter howdahs at government expense'; and if the enemy had been different and the quantifiers more humanly perceptive and if ... but: if is a king, as the French say.

There is no doubt whatever that the American search-and-destroy operations hurt the North Vietnamese Army (NVA)/Vietcong mainforce units in the period leading up to the Communist Tet Offensive early in 1968. While General Giap could persist in *his* Phase III use of large formations in the easily supplied northern I Corps zone, the base area for what was to be an attack on Saigon itself was destroyed by a major operation dubbed 'Cedar Falls'; the so-called Iron Triangle some thirty miles north of Saigon was surrounded in January 1967 by a multi-division force, severe casualties inflicted, an 'underground city' destroyed and sufficient rice captured or destroyed to feed 3,000 men for a full year.[60]

Late in February that year the largest battle so far was fought in Tay Ninh and Binh Long provinces, the area in which the COSVN high command was located, an area known as War Zone C. This joint US/ARVN operation was known as 'Junction City'. Like 'Cedar Falls' it was accompanied by a tremendous use of airpower: 4,000 close air-support strikes. It resulted in a loss of 2,700 men to the NVA/VC and almost 100 crew-served weapons.[61]

In the view of O'Neill these two operations in III Corps caused Giap 'to raise the stakes of the war by opening up a new and bloody series of desperate attacks in I Corps, which forced General Westmoreland to transfer to the northern provinces a great part of those divisions and regiments which had comprised his mobile striking force in the southern region'.[62] The establishment of Marine bases at Con Thien and Khe Sanh in the North began to evoke notions in the Western press of another Dien Bien Phu, more particularly in the case of the latter base. As to the former, lying only fourteen miles from the

60. *1967 Wrap-Up: A Year of Progress*, MACOI, US Army, n.d., p. 43.
61. ibid., pp. 45–6.
62. O'Neill, op. cit., p. 195.

Demilitarized Zone (DMZ) between the two Vietnams, MACV reported at the end of 1967 that though it had received 'the heaviest shelling of the war', its enemy received 'one of the greatest massings of firepower in support of a single division in the history of modern warfare'.[63] The analogies with Dien Bien Phu were later shown as having been altogether false in the case of Khe Sanh.

But what did this – and other fierce battles in border areas such as the struggle for Dak To – really amount to in terms of General Westmoreland's 'theory of victory'? First, it meant that some two thirds of the US forces in-country (as the saying is) were *up-country,* engaged either at bases or in search-and-destroy operations. There was no strategic reserve: the marvellous pipeline into South Vietnam had, up to this time, acted as a kind of strategic reserve. The result, whether deliberately managed by Giap or not, was that the American and ARVN forces were to such an extent employed far forward as to permit the preparation for a NVA/Vietcong attack on the areas of pacification, particularly the cities.

There had grown up the false notion that there were two wars in South Vietnam: the big-unit, search-and-destroy war and the politico-military pacification effort. Indeed, to the distress of Sir Robert Thompson, later special Adviser to President Nixon, pacification came to be referred to as 'the other war'. Officially, it was called 'rural development' and was carried out under Robert Komer, who held ambassadorial rank. In September 1966 Komer issued a report on its objectives and its progress.

The objectives were large:

> Both governments are mounting a growing effort to protect the countryside, revive its economic health, and provide it with modern services. Our efforts will not end when communist aggression ceases, but will remain as the foundation of a modern nation ... In the midst of war, the GVN has courageously sought to bring its economic house in order – devaluing its currency, overhauling its fiscal

63. *Year-End Wrap-Up Report CY67,* USMACV, ABPO San Francisco 96222, 12 February 1968.

system, and employing budgetary restraints ... The US has put increasing emphasis on helping to meet the health and educational needs of Vietnam's people, and on caring for the impoverished refugees who are tragic victims of the war.

Stress was also laid on the Chieu Hoi (Open Arms) amnesty programme; the steps that had been taken towards representative government – the election in which it was claimed some 80 per cent of the population participated; and, particularly, the problem of security.

The Komer Report recognized very frankly that the task being essayed was exceedingly difficult. It had to be carried out in conditions of organized violence that had resulted in two thirds of Vietnam's able-bodied young men between the ages of twenty and thirty being removed from productive occupations; and also in conditions where 'the Viet Cong have been able to sink their roots deep into the fabric of rural Vietnam. Insecurity, poverty, low health standards, lack of opportunity, social injustice, and land inequities have enabled the VC to exploit a rural feeling of alienation from the government.'

'The Revolutionary Development programme must change all that,' the Komer Report insisted, 'or ultimately be judged a failure like its predecessors ... it focuses on gradually securing the countryside, eliminating terror and intimidation, and producing radical and constructive change in the lives of the people. Its aim is to dry up the source of VC local support and build a strong and progressive society from the hamlet up.' The difficulties lying in the way of implementing the programme were to the point: first, the enemy regarded this campaign as crucial; secondly, officers and cadres had to be adequately trained, and this was not going to be achieved quickly; thirdly, and very importantly, this was the successor to other ambitious pacification campaigns which had failed; lastly, the build-up of enemy mainforce units had drawn significant numbers of ARVN and US troops away from protection duties.

The intention was to establish more and more secured areas through the agency of the army, destroy the political infrastructure, and use Regional and Popular Forces (RF/PF) for local security, aided by the Police Field Force (a mobile para-military force) and a greatly expanded National Police Force. Within secured areas, the new Revolutionary Development cadres, working in fifty-nine-man teams, all of them arms-trained, were to be the agents of village-level 'modernization', being employed whenever possible in home areas. The programme for expanding the secure areas was stated modestly. Some 55 per cent of the population was held to be living in secured areas: the tentative goal for 1967 was to secure another half million people. At the end of 1967 MACV claimed that during the year the secure areas had increased from 62 to 67 per cent, secure hamlets from 4,702 at the beginning of the year to 5,340 at the end.[64]

But the big question was: What precisely was meant by security?

The Hamlet Evaluation Scheme (HES) got under way at the beginning of 1967. The past system had been found unsatisfactory for a number of reasons; ranging from the fact of up-country advisers having too much paperwork to an overly narrow choice of criteria by which to assess the progress (or lack of progress) of pacification.

Pacification has been officially defined as follows: The military, economic and social process of establishing or re-establishing local government responsive to, and involving the participation of, the people. It includes the provision of sustained, credible territorial security, the destruction of the enemy's underground government, the assertion or re-assertion of political control and involvement of the people in government, and the initiation of economic and social activity capable of self-sustenance and expansion. The economic element of pacification includes the opening of roads and waterways and the maintenance of lines of communication important to economic and military activity.

It was also believed necessary to concentrate more precise

64. The RD cadres were – and are – trained by a very remarkable Vietnamese, Colonel Nguyen Be, who developed a theory of People's War, as he calls it, 'where everyone becomes a citizen-soldier, though not a member of a standing army'. See his *Revolutionary Development Cadre Program*, Chi-Linh, February 1968.

attention on the hamlet instead of making provincial estimates. Lastly, the Government of Vietnam (GVN) began to concentrate on the hamlet, as distinct from the village (a group of hamlets), as the appropriate target for pacification.

The forty-four provinces of South Vietnam were divided into 244 districts containing over 2,000 villages and some 12,750 hamlets. US advisory teams went down to district level.

Clearly, the subjective elements in this method of assessment are important, as a perusal of a HES worksheet will show to some extent. It is true that provision is made for the district adviser to record the level of confidence he places in the validity of information on which his evaluation ratings for each factor are made. But though he is encouraged to visit each hamlet during the month, as well as to gather information from his team about hamlet conditions, a good deal of the information must necessarily come from the GVN district chief (his opposite number) and his staff, and from other US and GVN sources. Normally, the Vietnamese provide the largest amount and the greatest variety of information for the HES; and it may be presumed that many of these Vietnamese must be well aware that their own 'face' and future prospects are involved in assessments of progress. Thus the categorizing of hamlets into A or B or C etc. is to a significant extent at the mercy of those factors which, so long as the struggle lasts, cannot be quantified.

It can even be argued that this quantifying approach tends to obscure the fact that in this kind of struggle – a struggle in which people can be reminded, at least on occasion, by exemplary acts of terrorism, however highly rated their hamlet might be, that the Communist apparatus has not been finally eliminated – it is often impossible adequately to gauge those *qualitative* factors that are so vital immediately the pacification programme is submitted, even if only temporarily, to real stress: confidence, fear, resolution, solidarity, resentment – morale, in a word.

Nevertheless, the HES does provide an indication of outward trends and these outward trends themselves significantly affect the inward direction of men's minds; after all, most men and women are not intrinsically heroic and therefore – particularly in a struggle that has attained vast dimensions – their attitudes are, to a large degree, shaped by signs of which side *seems* to be the more likely ultimately to triumph.

The real point of the HES is surely this: it is quite impossible to generalize about the indicators chosen for the HES or about the problems central to successful pacification on the basis of sampling. Through the HES a picture of trends, built up hamlet by hamlet and centrally computerized, is produced of a kind which can be produced in no other manageable way. The HES permits examination of the pacification situation at various levels and enables analyses of trends throughout the period in which the system has been in operation.[65]

The apparatus of the NLF counter-State in the Delta was described by an American expert as follows:

> The strength of the apparatus in a Delta province of 500,000 persons would be something like this: members of the Farmers' Liberation Association, the chief front organization, 25,000; members of the Women's Liberation Association, the second most important front organization, 2,000 members; members of the third most important front group, the Youth Liberation Association, 2,500; other liberation associations' membership – those linking workers, students and cultural or professional persons – 500; cadres, about 1,500; PRP [Communist] members, 500; PRP Youth League members, 450; local guerrillas, around 3,000; regionals or territorials, 2,000 or less; probably no Main Force units. There would of course be overlapping in these categories ... In communist-organized 'struggle movements' perhaps as many as 90,000 persons could be reached. Thus only something like 20 to 25 per cent of the population of the typical province is in any way engaged in the struggle and only a fraction of these are

65. But it cannot be stressed too strongly that a computer is only as good as the information fed into it; and the information depends upon the collection, collation and evaluation of Intelligence. Sir Robert Thompson claimed to have found in Saigon seventeen different Intelligence organizations 'most of them not talking to each other', before 1966 (*Canberra Times*, 25 February 1970). It was not until after the 1968 Tet Offensive that police Intelligence, under the so-called Phoenix programme, which was primarily one of adequate co-ordination of agencies, in order to 'eliminate' the NLF, insured that the NLF infrastructure began systematically to be eroded.

committed. The manpower pool, therefore, is not large, by any measurement.[66]

That this infrastructure, as it has come to be called, was not being effectively destroyed in supposedly secured areas in 1967 was proved during the famous Tet Offensive of early 1968. But before discussing that great exercise in armed propaganda, it is desirable to observe some of the other indicators which at the end of that year persuaded General Westmoreland to adumbrate his 'theory of victory' with apparent confidence. That the American command was optimistic is proved by the following extract from the MACV annual report on 1967:

> The friendly picture gives rise to an optimistic outlook for CY1968 [Calendar Year 1968]. In CY67 the logistics base and increased forces permitted Allied Forces to assume a fully offensive posture. With ground forces, TAC-air, B-52s, and Naval gunfire support ships working together, continuous pressure was applied against the enemy. An improved intelligence system frequently enabled Allied Forces to concentrate and preempt enemy military initiatives. Material and tactical innovations have been further developed and employed: Air-inserted reconnaissance patrols, aerial reconnaissance means, new O-24 observation aircraft, Roman Plows, C-47 (Spooky) gunships, airmobile operations and the Mobile Riverine Force (MRF) to name a few. The helicopter has established itself as perhaps the single most important tool in this war. Air support in both RVN and NVN contributed much to the overall accomplishment.

The report then engages in the numbers game: enemy losses showed an increase of 56.7 per cent over 1966; their weapons loss increased 68.6 per cent. (Friendly losses of men increased by 36.7 per cent.) The enemy 'had about 90,000' killed in action and 'probably' lost another 55,000 in other ways. 'Heavy losses by the enemy plus increased control of the population by the RVN Government has reduced the number of physically fit males available to the VC. In-country recruiting declined from

66. *A Study of the Prospects for the Viet Cong*, United States Mission, Saigon, December 1966, pp. 24–5. Internal evidence suggests that the author was Douglas Pike.

an estimated 7,000 per month in CY66 to 3,500 by 1 January 1967 ... Intelligence reports indicate that the VC are recruiting males as young as 13 and as old as 55.'

The bombing of the North was held by the American army to have been effective, General Westmoreland arguing that 'In my opinion bombing of the North has hurt the enemy very much ... It has retarded the infiltration of men, equipment and supplies. It has destroyed a great deal of ammunition that would otherwise have been used against our troops ... And although he could send more men to the South, he would be hard pressed to support these men logistically as long as our air campaign continues.' In the MACV Report it was claimed that in every month of 1967 the enemy forces in South Vietnam had sustained losses 'greater than input'.

Such reports could hardly be expected to relate the bombing of the North and the use of massed firepower in the South to public opinion in the USA – as these activities were transmitted by the pressmen and cameramen and above all by the television teams. And yet it is the relating of the military to the political that is so vitally important in modern warfare.

It was against this background of US military optimism that the concerted attack on the cities, known as the Tet Offensive in the world press, but called the Winter–Spring Offensive by the Communists, was conceived in Hanoi. Though the concept of general uprising had proved a will-o'-the-wisp even during the crumbling of the GVN administration after Diem's downfall, it was decided to attempt once again to engender one by attacking the hitherto secure urban areas. Such at any rate was the *maximum* objective sought: this was borne out by Vietcong assessments that were captured. But the Tet Offensive may well have been viewed primarily as an exercise in armed propaganda, an exercise in which the Vietnamese townsfolk, especially the privileged middle class, would be a target, but in which the main target would be the American public.

It seems that the order to prepare for this general uprising/general offensive was transmitted from Hanoi to high-ranking cadres in the South in July 1967. Between July and December the NVA/VC organized forward headquarters; they organized and strengthened city forces by

> assigning experienced officers to the city units and giving these cadre priority in their choice of personnel. Additional sapper companies and battalions were activated and equipped with sufficient weapons. Special-action units were also strengthened. Operating units conducted a crash training program at bases located in and out of South Vietnam. Sapper tactics were stressed. Supposedly, the battlefield was prepared; yet evidence indicates that thorough planning and control were lacking.[67]

This is true: the sappers did in the event prove to lack support. Nevertheless, the attacks launched against twenty-eight urban centres, including Saigon (where the US Embassy itself was attacked), were quite sufficiently co-ordinated to make the US-ARVN look very foolish and 'theories of victory' appear absurd.[68] Certainly the mass media, particularly television, acquiesced in General Giap's campaign for the eyes and minds of men far away in the USA and the impression created was deeply misleading in terms of the war in South Vietnam. Apart from Saigon and Hue, the Vietcong attacks were quite quickly repulsed, though sometimes in an appallingly destructive manner; and the losses sustained by the Vietcong, who had used the New Year truce and its attendant crescendos of fire-crackers to penetrate the cities, suffered very severely indeed – especially in terms of high-quality people.

Figures of losses in an atmosphere dominated by the misconceived 'numbers game' are apt to be very inaccurately reported. But the following estimate would appear to be not too inaccurate:

> Prior to the offensive Communist strength was estimated around 323,000 troops of all types. According to a table of estimated Viet Cong strength early in March, the Communists lost about 45,000 men as follows: 18,600 combat troops, 4,000 support troops, 12,400

67. *The Impact of the Sapper on the Viet-Nam War*, US Mission, Saigon, October 1969.

68. Twenty-eight out of the forty-eight cities and provincial towns of South Vietnam were seriously attacked, the remaining twenty recorded only mortar attacks or small harassing actions and some were left alone.

guerrillas, 5,000 political cadres, 5,000 civilians and laborers. Communist strength after 29 February was estimated to be *circa* 283,500 broken out as follows: 110,600 combat troops, 33,700 support troops, 60,200 guerrilla, and 79,000 political cadres.[69]

Figures as such were misleading, as always. Sir Robert Thompson has pointed out that 'by the end of 1967, when nearly 800 aircraft had been lost over the North and more than 1,000,000 tons of bombs had been dropped, the prestige of air power was at stake. Infiltration was still estimated at 6,000 a month and there was no indication at all that the bombing would bring Hanoi to the conference table.'[70] The numbers lost by the NVA/VC – they were in fact overwhelmingly VC – could obviously be made up in much less than a year. But what was important was the loss of specialized élite troops and political cadres of high calibre. (Others had surfaced and were identified.) Continued infusions of NVA troops, even if they made up the numbers lost, and more, were not of comparable usefulness. As a result of the past history of regionalism, NVA troops simply could not be assimilated into the clandestine counter-State apparatus at all appropriately: they were very often looked upon as foreigners by the locals and they were not usually equipped to understand local problems.

But there was another factor at work as a result of the Tet Offensive of a very different kind. Though the Hanoi command may well have thought in terms of maximum and minimum objectives, middle- and lowel-level VC commanders and cadres undoubtedly had been given to understand that they were engaged in a 'general uprising', that the people would rise on behalf of the NLF organization which for so long had claimed to be the only true representative of the South Vietnamese people. The people did not rise in support. Another important element in the preparation for the 1968 Tet Offensive had been 'troop proselytizing' – and the inculcation of the belief among VC rank-and-file that the ARVN would crumble under the

69. Pham Van Son and Le Van Duong (eds.), *The Viet 'Tet' Offensive (1968)*, ARVN, Saigon, 1969, p. 41.

70. *No Exit from Vietnam*, Chatto & Windus, 1969, p. 96.

politico-military assault. Not only did the ARVN do nothing of the kind, even the despised National Police stood their ground and shot it out bravely with the VC infiltrators of the cities. While recalling that the Rural Development programme was the successor to failures, it should also be remembered that this general uprising was the successor to an earlier failure too.

But such factors were not uppermost in the minds of most Westerners on the spot at the time.[71] There was a period of acute dismay in official circles, particularly in Washington; and there was a period of appalled shock throughout a good deal of the American nation. Henceforth the protest movement was to be a very important factor indeed in the struggle. For reasons the precise details of which will doubtless be disputed for a long time, President Johnson announced on 31 March 1968 that he would not seek another term of office and would devote his remaining time in office to the pursuit of peace negotiations. US bombing of the North was to be limited to special interdiction in the south and west, apparently on the understanding that Hanoi would not take advantage of this cessation to increase the rate of infiltration.

The DRV quickly stated its 'readiness to appoint its representatives to contact the US representative with a view toward determining with the American side the unconditional cessation of the US bombing raids and all other acts of war against the Democratic Republic of Vietnam that talks may start.' But at the same time Communist troops in South Vietnam were informed that the offer was a 'deceitful scheme' and so 'we must closely co-ordinate our military and political struggle with diplomatic offensives'.[72] Fighting-while-negotiating was to be the order of the day. At the same time yet another front was floated to widen the area of appeal at a time of confusion and doubts

71. There were notable exceptions. In the immediate aftermath of the offensive in Saigon the author found Mr Robert Komer correctly sanguine about the situation in the countryside, which he was exploring by helicopter; Brigadier Serong predicted the results with uncanny accuracy; and Sir Robert Thompson was as unflappable as always.

72. Directive of Political Staff of 3 NVA Division, 4 April 1968, Press Release, 29 April 1969, US Mission, Saigon.

about American staying-power.[73] There also began a subtle shift in NLF attitudes towards a coalition government in South Vietnam; there was a lessening of the propaganda emphasis upon the claim that the NLF was 'the only legitimate representative of the people in South Vietnam', though the claim was of course reiterated in NLF internal statements. In the meantime the general uprising/offensive was to continue in further waves of violence, including the deliberately indiscriminate attacks on populated areas by heavy mortars, an activity that evoked no comment from the protest movement in the USA and elsewhere in the West.

The shock of the Tet Offensive and the apparently unilateral nature of President Johnson's concessions, which were accompanied by a decision not to build up American troop numbers any further, gave even very experienced observers to believe that 'the odds favoured a sell-out'. But this proved not to be a prospect in the near future at all. A new commander, General Creighton Abrams, was sent to South Vietnam to implement a new strategic policy. Henceforth the relationship between forward (search-and-destroy) deployment and rear (security) deployment was to be reversed: two thirds of the forces were now to be devoted to security, this force in future to provide the strategic reserve now that the manpower pipeline had been cut off except for replacements. Small-unit operations, which had long been advocated by many experts but had all too often been prevented by the career ambitions of field commanders, were from now on to be the normal order of the day. It was represented to President Nixon that 300,000 men in this manner could do what had been done by 540,000. This permitted politically necessary withdrawals of American troops (12,500 per month) without in any way jeopardizing security in South Vietnam.

Looking at the situation politically, though a phased withdrawal was necessary for US domestic reasons, the new Administration, by assuming a posture of tailoring military operations

73. Viet-Nam Alliance of National Democratic and Peace Forces. See VNDRN No. 42; also VNDRN No. 21.

to public opinion, was able to argue that what came to be called its 'Vietnamization' programme had to be implemented in such a way as to avoid giving the impression of a scuttle out of South Vietnam. 'The limits of American commitment can be expressed in two propositions,' the man who was to become President Nixon's chief adviser argued: 'first, the United States cannot accept a military defeat, or a change in the political structure of South Viet Nam brought about by external military force; second, once North Vietnamese forces and pressures are removed, the United States has no obligation to maintain a government in Saigon by force.'[74]

In the long run, everything was staked on the effectiveness of Vietnamization. But in the shorter run, Hanoi was warned that the US would take 'strong and effective measures' should Hanoi escalate the fighting during the American withdrawal.[75] By the same token, Defense Secretary Laird declared that such strong and effective measures would be undertaken for only one purpose: to provide security for US forces during the withdrawal.

Thus a great deal clearly was going to depend upon how Vietnamization progressed. Since the South Vietnamese had taken the heaviest casualties in almost every month of the struggle, the term was hardly a happy one, but it was designed for US domestic consumption. It was to involve first of all a re-equipment of the ARVN, which had been neglected while US commanders charged their large units up and down the country; and much of its infantry had found itself outgunned by the Communist Tet attackers who had been re-equipped for that purpose with the latest infantry weapons. The security forces were to be expanded as a whole, with a very strong emphasis on the hamlet militia. This was to be meshed in with a 'mobilization of the masses' for military and economic purposes in hamlets that had elected their own officials. Ninety per cent of the hamlets held elections in 1969.

74. Henry A. Kissinger, *Foreign Affairs*, January 1969, p. 230.

75. See *Forum World Features*, 20 December 1969, Brian Crozier interview of Sir Robert Thompson, who was by then a Special Presidential Adviser.

This vast process, which also involved an ugly, though not atrocious[76] effort to weed out the VC infrastructure, a major hamlet-level propaganda campaign, the resettlement of very large numbers of refugees, innumerable self-help programmes selected by the hamlets themselves, and the denial of recruiting facilities to the Vietcong, was predicated on a belief that – in terms of internal war in South Vietnam – the struggle had begun to be decisively won.

This belief was not grounded only on the Hamlet Evaluation System's claim that by 1969 some 92 per cent of the population lived in areas that were 'relatively secure' (*vis-à-vis* 70 per cent in October 1968) or upon estimates that perhaps three quarters of enemy mainforce units were composed of North Vietnamese. It was also grounded upon assessments of captured Vietcong documents, which seemed to suggest that the Communists had been forced back to small-scale guerrilla warfare and terrorism.

The most important document was a resolution issued by the 9th Conference of COSVN in July 1969. Despite some grandiose claims, such as having 'upset the Americans' global anti-revolutionary strategy', the resolution did admit very serious deficiencies in the general uprising/offensive. For example,

> We have failed to promote a *strong political tide* suitable to the requirements of the General Offensive and Uprising phase and the great political opportunity now prevailing; our *military proselyting* spearhead is weak . . . *guerrilla warfare* has developed slowly and unevenly; our territorial forces at provincial and district levels, and even some units of our main forces at region level did not fight in good directions and according to good methods, and their combat efficiency is still low; the replenishment of forces, especially for units at region level and even for many provincial units, is still beset with prolonged difficulties; the building of political forces . . . is making slow progress; the operations ensuring material support to the front lines are deficient and many areas still have difficulties (in getting material supplies). Those are problems which had been discussed at the beginning of the General Offensive and Uprising; although we

76. That it was ugly rather than atrocious as a weeding-out campaign was later indicated by the large numbers of political prisoners claimed after the signing of the Cessation of Hostilities Agreement by the NLF.

had made efforts to overcome them and had scored some progress, this progress was still slow compared to our requirements.[77]

Nevertheless, however well the pacification struggle might be progressing in South Vietnam, there remained the fact of North Vietnamese invasion and its supply through Cambodia and Laos, particularly the former by this stage. The two privileged sanctuaries had been left free from ground attack throughout the war. Since the war had become primarily an invasion by the North Vietnamese Army, these sanctuaries were vital for its continuance: there could be no question of the NVA establishing a symbiotic relationship with the target society in the way the indigenous movement had in the past.

In March 1970 Prince Sihanouk, who had increasingly acquiesced in North Vietnamese purposes out of a belief that they must ultimately prevail, was overthrown. The NVA/VC forces in Cambodia immediately started to undermine the successor government and attack its forces.[78] No protest movement in the West had ever made the least complaint about Vietnamese Communist forces occupying large areas of Cambodian territory, but when President Nixon ordered a short operation against Communist base areas in Cambodia, he was immediately accused of escalating the war and the US protest movement received a new lease of life. Hanoi then engaged in the solemn farce of calling together what was called the Indo-Chinese People's Summit Conference, which was attended by the exiled Prince Norodom Sihanouk and Mr Chou En-lai.

Amongst other things, the parties to the Conference stated their respect for 'the fundamental principles of the 1954 Geneva Agreements on Indo-China and the 1962 Geneva Agreements on Laos'.[79] Under the latter agreements, Laos was supposed to

77. COSVN Resolution No. 9, n.p., n.d., received from the GVN delegation to the Peace Conference, Paris, January 1970. See also VNDRN Nos. 64, 68 and 81.

78. Speech of Yem Sambur, Cambodian Justice Minister, at Jakarta, *Vietnam Digest*, Canberra, No. 5, November 1970. See also VNDRN No. 88.

79. VNDRN, No. 80.

have been neutralized, but in fact simply served as the pipeline to South Vietnam. As a Laotian government White Paper put it in 1968,

. . . today there are at least four North Vietnamese Divisions in Laos, operating alongside the Neo Lao Hak Xat. The Ho Chi Minh Trail has become the Ho Chi Minh Road . . . We call the attention of the international audience that this road runs through Laos for several hundred kilometers . . . the North Vietnamese weapons, aircraft, dead, defectors and wounded counted on Lao soil are not fiction. The 600,000 refugees coming from the Neo Lao Hak Xat [Communist] areas cannot all be liars and the facts they report cannot honestly be doubted.[80]

And so in mid-February 1971 the South Vietnamese army at long last moved into southern Laos in a very hazardous operation designed to destroy supplies and choke the supply line. It could not be a permanent success if the totalitarian government in Hanoi, headed by the men who founded the Indo-Chinese Communist Party over forty years ago, were determined to press home what advantage they still saw in the situation. But what was certain by 1971 was that the South Vietnamese anti-Communists could only be defeated by North Vietnamese invasion – or defeat themselves through exercises in suicidal factionalism. It was no longer a guerrilla war of any consequence, though political and economic failure on the part of Saigon could see it all begin again.

But it did not happen like that. Pacification, which had begun as long ago as 1954 by way of Civic Action teams, later through refugee resettlement, land reform, the building of *agrovilles* (rural towns), to strategic hamlets in Diem's day, continued despite setbacks regarded at the time as crippling and defects seen by many throughout as subversive of any form of pacification – corruption and ineptitude in particular on the grass-roots level. Pacification went under many names, partly in order to disguise past failures, partly in order to gird loins anew. Sometimes the

80. *White Book on the Violations of the Geneva Accords of 1962 by the Government of North Vietnam*, Ministry of Foreign Affairs of Laos, Vientiane, 1968.

emphasis seemed to be on security, at others on creating a social revolution that would undercut the appeal of the NLF social revolution.

More and more techniques were brought into play, ranging from more sensible ways of involving the villagers in material endeavours, through providing funds for projects chosen by the villagers themselves to which they had to contribute, to an ever more intense and sophisticated propaganda reinforcement of material aims through hamlet television sets. It was estimated that the Saigon TV station by 1972 had the potentiality to reach 75 per cent of the population through 500,000 sets.[81] Aid to villages was linked to their creation of democratic local self-government and local elections, while the thrust of rural development was to link it to the presumed benevolence of the central government.

It is scarcely too much to say that a kind of imperfect replication of Communist techniques of popular manipulation and population controls was being slowly improved over the years, especially after the 1968 Tet Offensive, though beginning well before that, combined with the creation of a liberal-capitalist ethos in the countryside. The combination may at first sight appear very odd indeed. But in fact is was engendered by the nature of the struggle.

The NLF's organization had become so deeply implanted in rural society that institutional modes of countering it, necessarily similar to that of the Communists in some ways during the struggle, had to be used while the NLF's own infrastructure was being destroyed. Otherwise the necessary command structure, reaching from Saigon down to the hamlet, could not be made viable. The anti-Communist regime was intent upon removing from the NLF what has come to be widely regarded as its greatest source of strength: a virtual monopoly of *influence* over many of the people. In times of revolutionary warfare on a vast scale, this can only be done by substituting another virtual monopoly and in some senses it must resemble a replication of the Communist organizational technique.

81. Alex Carey, *The Clockwork Vietnam*, unpublished paper, University of New South Wales, 1972, p. 31.

But what must be emphasized is that the 'imperfections' of the replication are not simply the result of human frailties and organizational ineptitudes; they also flow from the fact that what is being attempted by the GVN is something designed specifically to meet the exigencies of a very special kind of war. Put simply, such methods are being adopted to defeat a totalitarian enemy; they are not designed, as is the case with the NLF, to create a totalitarian society.

And this is where the combination of these present politico-military techniques with the development of liberal-capitalist opportunity in the countryside might well ultimately make sense. After all, from the point of view of the Vietnamese (or any other) peasant when faced by the prospect of Communist domination, the one ultimate issue, if he is enabled to perceive it, is between some kind of individual farming and agricultural collectivization. He is concerned to preserve at least some measure of economic freedom, since from that alone flows the possibility of his being able to preserve at least some measure of family autonomy. If, as is now the case in the most heavily populated agricultural areas, the government offers – certainly very dilatorily in the case of South Vietnam – not only the prospect of a reasonably secure tenure of land but quite quickly increasing opportunities of a better livelihood on the land, then he has no reason genuinely to accept NLF promises for the future – the NLF's promises at this stage being, as was the case with the Vietminh, promises of individual holdings – promises that are broken the moment the Communists are in power.

But so long as the NLF infrastructure, backed by its armed squads, remains in being, then the issue of the future is less surely presented to the peasants' minds. This is peculiarly the case where past rural development-cum-pacification campaigns have failed in their purpose and the NLF parallel government has reasserted itself with all the attendant exercises in repression, ranging from public executions to secret bullying (or political re-indoctrination, if it is preferred). The recognition of this fact gave rise to what has been described earlier as an ugly but not atrocious weeding-out process known popularly as Operation Phoenix. It was not in fact an operation but a slow development, quickening from 1968 onwards, of the means of adequately tackling the problem presented by the abiding NLF parallel government. It undoubtedly did involve replication of the NLF 'Moral Persuasion' squads in the form of Provisional Reconnaissance Units. But on the whole it has been misrepresented in the Western press.

Though many NLF cadres have been reported to have been killed, usually without reference to the circumstances of their deaths, the fact that the Communists and their supporters in the West claim that as many as 200-300,000 political cadres are held prisoner in South Vietnamese gaols and detention centres strongly suggests that preventive detention, rather than assassination, has been the GVN policy.

On the other hand, since the Vietnamese Communists' use of statistics – they claim to have 'knocked out' 290,000 enemy troops, including 128,000 'US and satellite troops' in the 1965–6 and 1966–7 dry season fighting[82] – is so propagandistic in intent, such figures may be regarded as essentially meaningless. So in all probability are the figures relating to NLF cadres 'neutralized' or killed, cited from time to time in the Western press. If they were anything like accurate, the NLF infrastructure would have been wiped out completely. It is difficult to escape the conclusion that both sides have used figures as psychologically reinforcing symbols in a vast contest in political Couéism.

Nevertheless, quite clearly the infrastructure has been terribly damaged by the GVN Intelligence operations of the Special Branch kind amongst others. Otherwise, the employment of the bulk of the North Vietnamese army in invading South Vietnam at the end of March 1972, at a time when American troop withdrawals were fast reaching their conclusion – at a time when American ground troops were no longer being used except for garrison duties – would make no sense. If the villagers of South Vietnam, by now armed with something like a million small-arms, were really disaffected by the GVN, why, in the wake of the American withdrawal, was it necessary to invade South Vietnam at this time?

82. 'Forty Years of Party History', VNDRN No. 76, p. 87.

Since the Paris peace negotiations which eventually issued out of President Johnson's refusal to stand for office again, and were sustained by President Nixon's promise to extricate American ground forces, were obviously designed to permit the US 'to get out from under', why this offensive? It did not in the event cause very serious setbacks to pacification except in five or six out of forty-four South Vietnamese provinces; despite disposing of greatly superior tank and artillery forces, which were significantly neutralized by US airpower at certain points, the North Vietnamese army was fought to a standstill by the ARVN.

The name of the game seemed to have changed dramatically: in the past General Giap had proclaimed the superiority of (Communist) men over (Capitalist) weapons. On this occasion he apparently relied upon the superiority of Russian over American weapons. This is hardly revolutionary warfare, at first sight. And yet it was: it was an attempt to establish a 'capital' for the so-called Provincial Revolutionary Government of South Vietnam whose creation was announced in 1969 as a maximum objective; as a minimum objective it was an attempt to implant in South Vietnam the presence of the North Vietnamese army at a time when Hanoi believed that a cease-fire was consonant with its ultimate objective: to subjugate South Vietnam. Knowing full well by early 1972, if not a good deal earlier, that there was no question of a 'people's war' prevailing in South Vietnam, even at the end of the American withdrawal of ground troops, Hanoi clearly decided that the Cessation of Hostilities Agreement must be signed in conditions where its regular army was deep inside South Vietnam.

And such was the situation when the Agreement was signed in Paris on 27 January 1973. What Hanoi and the NLF did not get, though they very nearly did get it in late 1972, was a disguised form of coalition government. The US bombing of North Vietnam and the mining of its harbours prevented that. It did not get nearly as wide a diplomatic recognition of the so-called Provisional Government of South Vietnam as it may well have hoped for.

But what it did get, above all, amongst other things, was what the Americans always claimed they would never allow: a 'Peace Agreement' which permitted the North Vietnamese army to remain in South Vietnam. This army is very conservatively estimated at 145,000 men, but is probably nearer 200,000 men in fact, not to speak of its 'fillers' in depleted NLF (Vietcong) units. It also got an undertaking that the cadres, 'the political prisoners', would be released in order, in fact, that they should be enabled to reassert their parallel government under the aegis of the North Vietnamese army. This has been delayed to some extent.

In the meanwhile, the Communists make no real attempt to observe other terms of the 'Peace Treaty'; in Cambodia their recently created 'national liberation front' continues to undermine the authority of the Cambodian government in flagrant disregard of the Agreement; in Laos its Pathet Lao satellite politico-military organization continues to increase its pressures on the Laotian government; in South Vietnam its forces bid fair to induce the withdrawal at least of those Western and pro-Western representatives on the Control Commission.

This is a not unimpressive achievement on the part of a Communist Party and its various Front movements which, quite deliberately, 'took on' the materially most powerful nation on earth. Of course it relied upon Soviet and Chinese arms and supplies, but they were comparatively small compared with what the US expended: a mere fraction of the $136,000 millions the war had cost the USA by October 1972.

According to Pentagon figures, cited in the *Sun-Herald* of Sydney on 29 October 1972, nearly 46,000 Americans died, some 186,000 South Vietnamese soldiers (though one would hardly have realized this from reading the Western press), about 5,000 other Allied soldiers, and nearly 877,000 North Vietnamese and Vietcong soldiers: a military total of dead, allowing for errors, of about a million. Probably about 400,000 civilians were killed in South Vietnam by the end of 1972; and refugees were numbered in millions.

What has equally horrified many who have protested against the US and Allied involvement has been the immense weight of destructive technology brought to bear upon a small country: roughly three and a half times the tonnage of explosives used by the Allies in the Second World War, according to one estimate,[83] by October 1972, not to speak of the very widespread use of herbicides and defoliants. When it can be argued that 'The effective response ... is ... forced-draft urbanization and modernization which rapidly brings the country ... out of the phase in which a rural revolutionary movement can hope to generate sufficient strength to come to power',[84] then the sense of horror is compounded.

But never in all the writings of the Vietnamese Communists is there to be found any hint of official regret that the implacable resolve of the Hanoi politbureau to impose its will upon the South was responsible, and continues to be responsible, for bringing down upon the Vietnamese people such deep suffering. As it has been put most moderately by an authority on the two Indo-China wars, 'While Ho had little chance of altering his emphasis from Communism to Nationalism in the early 1950s, his subsequent actions incline one to the belief that, fundamentally, Ho and his followers are more interested in a type of government than in the people who are to be governed. It is this factor which has inflicted a double round of suffering on Vietnam.'[85]

It is to be noticed that in his Last Testament, Ho Chi Minh again and again referred to 'the Party' before going to join, as he put it, 'Karl Marx, Lenin and other revolutionary elders', not the heroes of Vietnamese history.[86] This tradition of seeing in the Second Indo-China War an exemplary struggle of universal relevance is carried on by Le Duan, for example, the Politbureau member most involved in planning the Second Indo-China War:

> They [the American neo-fascists] are severely condemned throughout the world, and in the United States itself. Their dominant posi-

83. *Sun-Herald*, Sydney, 29 October 1972.

84. S. P. Huntingdon, *Foreign Affairs*, July 1968.

85. Robert J. O'Neill, *Indo-China Tragedy 1945–1954*, Cheshire, Melbourne, 1968, pp. 53–4.

86. Quoted in full in *The Tribune*, Sydney, 17 September 1969.

tion in the capitalist world has grown more wobbly and is visibly on the wane. The Vietnamese people's resistance to American aggression for their national salvation is the crest of the wave of the people's struggle the world over against imperialism headed by US imperialism.[87]

General Giap is reported to have said, 'Every minute hundreds of thousands of men die all over the world. The life and death of . . . tens of thousands of men, even if they are our compatriots, means little.'[88] He and his fellow-members of the Hanoi politbureau continue insouciantly to proceed upon that assumption to continue with a war which in a sense began at the turn of the 1930s and by now has destroyed the flower of Vietnamese youth.

Now it can be argued, immensely persuasively with the benefit of hindsight, that by 1965 the politico-military situation in South Vietnam was so bad that it could only be redressed at a cost in human lives altogether unacceptable to the public opinion of Western (or 'Eastern') democracies. It can even be argued that 'It was not in any sense a victory; it was a tragic defeat for America. Not in the military terms of the battlefield, but a defeat for our political authority and moral influence abroad and for our sense of mission and cohesion at home.'[89]

It can also be argued, as Lee Kuan Yew, the Prime Minister of Singapore, has often argued, that the American intervention in Vietnam had 'broken a hypnotic spell that had led other South-east Asian countries to believe that Communism is the irresistible wave of history'.[90] Or it can be argued, as it has been argued by Mochtar Lubis, a heroic figure and careful mind in the development of Indonesia, in the following manner:

The American presence in Asia and the Pacific since the end of the Second World War has had ambiguous results. On the one hand

87. Le Duan, *The Vietnamese Revolution*, International Publishers, New York, 1971, p. 148.

88. Quoted in Bernard Fall, *Le Viet-Minh*, Librairie Armand Colin, Paris, 1960, p. 184.

89. George W. Ball, *New York Times Weekly Review*, 1 April 1973.

90. Quoted in *News-Weekly*, Melbourne, 25 April 1973.

it sharpened the conflicts and confrontations between the communist and non-communist forces in Asia ... This situation made it most difficult to achieve settlements and compromises. At the same time the American presence for example in South Viet-Nam had certainly bought time for the democratic forces in Indonesia. The non-communist forces in Indonesia, in or outside the army would [have] lost heart and confidence in themselves, had the American forces left Vietnam before 1965. Most people would otherwise have become persuaded that the communists held the future in their hands in Asia. The communist coup in October 1965 would have succeeded, and the position of the non-communist regimes in Thailand, Malaysia and Singapore would [have] become untenable.[91]

It is not to the purpose of this brief study to explore the validity of such arguments. But what may be stated with certainty is this: whereas even those Western democrats who supported American intervention (itself a loaded word *vis-à-vis* Hanoi's planning and controlling the war in the South, something that was not denied at the time even by the sternest critics of American policy amongst the American press corps) have been possessed by the gravest misgivings as to the manner in which the war was conducted, the other side has never expressed any ethical misgivings whatsoever. This may in part explain why it is so 'well motivated', as the current jargon puts it. But it is as well that the implications of this be understood. The Nazi army was not defeated because of the superior 'motivation' of the Allies but because of an immensely superior firepower, based on a vastly greater industrial complex, being brought into play. The wretched Lieutenant Calley of My Lai was represented as somehow typical of American democracy abroad; the destruction of Dresden did not attract the same kind of argument. In that contrast lies embedded the essential secret of revolutionary warfare as it is waged – in the form of psychological warfare – in the democratic world today. Which should not in any way stop a man from weeping over the Second Indo-China War.

It has been a tragedy. It has resulted in terrible suffering

91. *Prospects in Asia in the 1970s*, Papers presented at Airlie House, Warrenton, Virginia, May 1971.

for the Vietnamese, who throughout have been the main contestants, it should never be forgotten. The second Indo-China War would have been inconceivable had it not been for rivalries deeply embedded in Vietnamese history and had it not been for the implacable determination of the Communist leaders in Hanoi to sacrifice a generation in order to unify the country under their totalitarian rule.

Those who are not Vietnamese and yet weep over that awful struggle; those especially who prefer to engage in expressions of moral outrage at the fact that the war reached such ghastly intensity – such people might well ask themselves a simple question: why is the bulk of the regular army of North Vietnam deployed in the South without this fact ever having been *admitted* by the Hanoi Government? If the cause of the North were as just as it is so widely presumed to be in influential circles in the West, why this subterfuge? The answer to what revolutionary warfare is really 'all about' lies embedded in that very question. It is one thing to weep or grow angry about human suffering; it is quite another thing to remain wilfully ignorant about being manipulated by a form of psychological judo.

## CHAPTER 7

# CUBA AND ALL THAT

> Every day my admiration for Lenin grows. The more I know about his work and his life and above all the more I understand the revolution, the more I admire Lenin. Only now can I grasp the difficulties Lenin had to overcome and the magnitude of the heritage he bequeathed humanity – It's not the same thing to talk about revolution in theory – and actually to carry one out oneself.
>
> FIDEL CASTRO, 1961

> Twelve men, each with a rifle and ten cartridges hidden on a mountain top.
>
> An Army, Navy, and Air Force consisting of 30,000 men equipped with the finest weapons . . .
>
> HUBERMAN AND SWEEZY

> So far as the different classes of Cuba are concerned, the revolution looks like this: Throughout it has been, and it is, led by this young intelligentsia . . .
>
> A CUBAN STUDENT

EVERY revolutionary guerrilla war is in some ways different from the others. But some are more different than others. Cuba most certainly was. Despite this fact, attempts were made to universalize the Cuban revolutionary experience; and they were made with an uncritical zeal that must have made great exponents like Mao Tse-tung and Vo Nguyen Giap gasp in horrified amazement. There were in all likelihood a number of reasons for the literary happenings designed to stake out great claims for Castro and his band. First, there was the important fact that, if Peron's regime is set aside as being of dubious meaning, Mexico was the only Latin American country to have experienced a real, social revolution in the whole of the first half of the twentieth century. Secondly, Señor Castro came to assume the role of Jack-the-Giant-Killer *vis-à-vis* the USA, a role attractive to many understandably jaundiced Latin American eyes. Thirdly, the Cuban leadership for a time seems to have suffered from *folie de grandeur* – perhaps in a desperate attempt to see to it that Latin American revolution should not be as evocative of comic opera as more reactionary political activities had long been. Lastly it seems possible that the course of this struggle was so bizarre – the collapse of an army in the face of a few hundred guerrillas – that the chief participants were themselves somewhat blinded to what had really happened.

The Cuban struggle has become so overlaid by theorizing glosses of a universalizing tendency that it is by no means simple to establish precisely what it was 'all about'. The most thorough analysis is Professor Hugh Thomas's book.[1]

Quite clearly, the debate about the nature of the Cuban revolutionary war is of considerable significance for the future. Guevara's failure in Bolivia may still prove to have been less meaningful than the Cuban success. The present outbreak of urban guerrilla terrorism is not necessarily the revolutionary wave of the future. That kind of revolutionary activity may in time revolutionize the counter-revolution just as much as Castro's kind is believed to have done.

The debate is of peculiar importance because Latin America as a whole is at last involved in a great revolt. As Professor Humphreys has stated,

> the traditional organization of society in Latin America has been challenged: not only what was bad in it, but what was good; not only the tyranny of the great estate, but, at its best, the old paternal relation between *patron* and peasant . . . This is not simply one more expression of the tradition of revolt at work in Latin America, though of that, too, examples enough can be found: it is a revolt against tradition.[2]

If the Cuban revolutionary guerrilla war really was as the chief participants claim, a peasant-based revolution, then it would at first sight seem to offer a model for the area as a whole. According to the United Nations Economic Commission for Latin America, eighteen countries being considered in the

1. *Cuba, or The Pursuit of Freedom*, Eyre & Spottiswoode, 1971.

2. R. A. Humphreys, *Tradition and Revolt in Latin America*, Creighton Lecture in History 1964, University of London, 1965, p. 20.

competition, over 70 per cent of the total farm area was in 1961 owned by 1.2 per cent of the farming population. Nearly three quarters of farms were under 20 hectares (about 50 acres) but this class of holding comprised only 2.9 per cent of the total farmed land.[3]

However, if the populations of Latin American countries are being considered as a whole, as they must be, such figures are apt to be misleading. Latin America has for a very long time been an area of great urbanization – urbanization of a pre-industrial kind. 'In most Latin American countries 50 per cent or more of the total population lived in three or four major cities... Even today the degree of urban concentration in centres of 100,000 or more inhabitants is greater in Latin America than in Europe or the Soviet Union.'[4] The result has been the continuing growth of *villas miserias*, 'slum tenements, infested by rats and vermin and lacking all sanitary facilities, that make New York's Harlem look like a couch of luxury'.[5] Hence, in part, the argument for urban guerrilla warfare rather than the mobilization of the peasantry.

What light does the Cuban revolutionary war throw upon the great debate between the proponents of the two kinds of struggle? Was it a peasant-based war? Or was it, as Theodore Draper has argued, '... essentially a middle-class revolution that has been used to destroy the middle class'?[6] Was it in fact really more of an urban than a rural guerrilla war, as Hugh Thomas has argued?[7]

3. Cited in John Gerrasi, *The Great Fear in Latin America*, Collier Books, New York, 1967, p. 35. Cuba and Bolivia, which had carried out major 'land reforms', were not included in the list of countries.

4. Claudio Veliz (ed.), *Obstacles to Social Change in Latin America*, Oxford University Press, 1965, p. 3.

5. Tad Szulc, *The Winds of Revolution, Latin America Today – and Tomorrow*, Praeger, New York, 1963, pp. 53–4. Szulc estimates that 10 per cent of landlords own 90 per cent of Latin American farmed land. See note 3, above.

6. Theodore Draper, *Castro's Revolution: Myths and Realities*, Praeger, New York, 1962, p. 10.

7. In Claudio Veliz, *The Politics of Conformity in Latin America*, Oxford University Press, 1967, p. 266: 'As a movement which worried away, day in and day out, at the regime by placing bombs, staging demonstrations, show-

It may first be said that Cuba under the military dictator Batista, whose regime had been established a few years before Castro's band landed from Mexico in December 1956, enjoyed a standard of living, an urbanization, a literacy rate, and so on, that was very high on the Latin American scale and in some particulars by no means terribly low on a European scale – if the population was to be averaged out, or perhaps more precisely averaged in. But as Hugh Thomas has remarked, '... such statistics do not mean that the country had got beyond the stage where a sense of outrage led people to dream of violent and radical changes'.[8] In the context of the revolutionary guerrilla war that was begun by the landing in Cuba at the end of 1956 – or rather by the establishment of a *foco* in the mountains by the ten to nineteen survivors of the initial disaster upon landing – who were the people who dreamed of violent and radical change?

Obviously there was the small group under Castro. Since Castro had already led the abortive attack on the Moncada barracks and had been imprisoned for it, it may be assumed that those who landed with him were men of violence: they came armed, though whether it was with the intention of starting a protracted rural insurgency appears somewhat doubtful.[9] There were those who later engaged in guerrilla terrorism in the cities. What about the peasants?

It is perhaps desirable to recall at this point that in the case of immeasurably greater guerrilla wars than the one Cuba saw – China and Vietnam, for example – the struggle was not initi-

---

ing flags, [the movement in the cities] really waged guerrilla war more than did Castro. But Castro remained the leader of these urban *guerrilleros*, though few of them knew of him ...'

8. ibid., p. 255.

9. According to Draper, the landing in December 1956 was supposed to spark an uprising in Santiago de Cuba; 'and a country-wide campaign of sabotage and agitation was to culminate in a general strike' (*Castroism: Theory and Practice*, Praeger, New York, 1965, p. 23). Draper refers to an admission by Castro to the effect that so little did he envisage protracted guerrilla warfare that, not only had he not attempted to establish an organization there, but he had not even bothered to study the geography of the guerrilla area (p. 23).

ally launched through the agency of a peasantry but rather through what Mao called 'declassed elements'. The term peasantry has become a very misleading one, not least because of revolutionary propaganda. As has been pointed out, the number of people *actively* engaged in a revolutionary war is always a very small proportion of the rural population indeed. In the case of Cuba, the numbers appear to have been minute: some 300 fighters, most of the time, out of a population of five millions. It is true that the figure 300 may have been selected by the revolutionaries because of its nice clean arithmetical ratio with the estimated 30,000 government forces. Even so, it is a very odd claim for Maoist-type rural revolutionary guerrillas to make (and afterwards Ernesto Guevara did argue that, instinctively of course, and not through imitation, the Castroite movement had indeed trodden the Mao–Giap trail).

It was an odd claim for two reasons. First, though the ratio business is misleading, as is pointed out elsewhere, there has never in the history of guerrilla warfare been another case of guerrillas prevailing from such a position of numerical disadvantage. In Greece, where the 'forces of order' won, the ratio was 8:1. In Algeria, where the 'forces of order' did not quite win, even in purely local terms, the ratio was 16:1. In Indo-China, where the struggle had been grim and protracted, the ratio was 6:4.[10] Here the ratio between the 'forces of order' and the guerrillas at the critical stage – that is, the one major Batista government counter-offensive in mid-1958 – is held to have been 100:1.

But, secondly, it is a peculiarly odd claim to be made by those who saw themselves (in retrospect?) as the leaders of a 'peasant revolution'. The Chinese Communist Party, at the conclusion of the First World War, could claim with some justice a 'constituency' of 100 millions, nearly all of them peasants. As a matter of fact, Guevara admitted by implication, during a talk in January 1959, that the guerrillas had not 'fully identified themselves with the peasants until after the April 1958 strike failure, only nine months from the end of the war'.

10. Kelly, *The Lost Soldiers*, op. cit., p. 115.

Why then was the claim made? The answer might seem obvious: this very small band of adventurers became so intoxicated with success that its spokesmen felt it necessary to universalize what was for the most part a most extraordinary fluke.

However, there was another reason: the Cuban Communists, gathered together in the Popular Socialist Party, though they had in the past made arrangements with the Batista regime, later tried to jump on the Castroite bandwaggon; and later still the Communists tried to argue that the revolution had been brought about, not by the peasantry but by the working class; the working class, 'had been, as a class, the leader'.[11]

Such arguments prove nothing in themselves about the guerrilla struggle but it is necessary to mention them in order to show the kind of difficulties that lie in the way of understanding the Cuban struggle. To return to the struggle itself: The group which survived the initial attack, which was very nearly catastrophic, were tyros. Guevara guided it towards the Sierra Maestra by what he imagined was the North Star but later found was not! The first period of the guerrilla war was described by Guevara thus: 'Our small group, basically non-military, lived in the Sierra Maestra but was not adjusted to it: we went from hut to hut, we ate only when we could pay for it, we were tolerated but nothing more ... We spent several months like this, wandering amongst the highest mountains of the Sierra Maestra, descending from time to time on brief raids, and returning at once to the *maquis*. Life was very hard there.'[12]

When Robert Taber visited the Castroite base in April 1957 the band numbered about one hundred, half of them having arrived recently from Santiago.[13] But even at this time the small raids were yielding badly needed weapons. This was to be a

11. Anibal Escalante's argument, *Castroism: Theory and Practice*, pp. 92–5.

12. Quoted in Luis Mercier Vega, *Guerrillas in Latin America*, Pall Mall Press, 1969, p. 75.

13. Robert Taber, *The War of the Flea: A Study of Guerrilla Warfare Theory and Practice*, Paladin, 1970, p. 38.

persistent feature of the war. Which is not to say that infusions of arms from the city and abroad were not important. Huberman and Sweezy refer to the 'tremendously' helpful air supply of automatic weapons, mortar shells, and .50 machine guns early in 1958 at the very time the Movement became sure it would win.[14] Nevertheless it seems that the garrison strategy of the Batista army allowed large numbers of arms to be lost, and later the increased ambush skills of the guerrillas enabled them to capture more and more arms.

According to one observer, the guerrillas were notable chiefly for their will to fight: 'All of Castro's fighting men were terror victims to the extent that they believed they would be killed if they went back to their homes while Batista remained in power ... most of them expressed [the conviction] that they as individuals could not expect to live if they did not destroy the *Batistianos* who were then still policing their home communities.'[15] In contrast, captured Batista soldiers were set free, after receiving a lecture to the effect that they would be freed, again and again, should they return to the fight.

The basic make-up of the original guerrilla army was therefore urban, not rural; nor was it middle-class as has often been suggested. The chief motivation was this knowledge that either the Movement or Batista would go under. Its raids were complemented by acts of sabotage and terror in the cities. This had the required result: 'Batista's answer to the terror was counter-terror. The army and secret police struck back blindly, indiscriminately, senselessly. The students, blamed as the chief troublemakers, were the chief victims. It became safer for young men to take to the hills than to walk the streets. The orgy of murders, tortures, and brutalities sent tremors of fear and horror through the entire Cuban people and especially the middle-class

14. Leo Huberman and Paul M. Sweezy, *Cuba: Anatomy of a Revolution*, Routledge & Kegan Paul, 1961, p. 62. But cf. Dickey Chapelle, in T. N. Greene (ed.), *The Guerrilla – and How to fight Him*, Praeger, New York, 1962, p. 229, where she accepts Castro's statement that only 15 per cent of arms were infused from outside. Of course, much depends upon the quality of the arms delivered, which seems to have been high.

15. Chappelle, op. cit., p. 222.

students.'[16] Sufferers from this repression in the cities far outnumbered casualties amongst the Castroite guerrilla band.

But what about the peasants? Well, though it has been said many times that Castroite Intelligence was very good because the peasants saw in him something of a saviour, Ernesto Guevara, who seems to have been usually an honest man, was a good deal more reserved in his description of the peasants' role in the revolutionary war. He saw the situation of the guerrilla band *vis-à-vis* the peasantry (using that term in a loose fashion) very much in terms explicated theoretically by Debray later on in his *Revolution in the Revolution?*. That is, Guevara, though he emphasized the Movement's attempt always to be just towards the rural population, argued that it was a recognition of 'the invincibility of the guerrillas and the long duration of the struggle' that made peasants act 'logically' and join the guerrilla force. As he put it, somewhat grimly, but as it has been put in regard to so many struggles of this kind: 'Denouncing us did violence to their own conscience and, in any case, put them in danger, since revolutionary justice was speedy.'[17]

For Guevara, the 'secret of victory' did not really lie in peasant revolt but rather in the tactics of the struggle: the fact that the guerrillas could, through the careful concentration of forces, destroy small barracks with such deadly efficacy that the exceedingly poor Batista troops felt impelled to withdraw into larger fortifications – in which many of them remained until the end of the struggle.[18] A clue to Castro's success does seem to lie in the condition of Batista's army, which was of course a reflection of the shoddy makeshift nature of his regime, the inception of

16. *Castro's Revolution: Myths and Realities*, p. 14. Cf. Crozier, *The Rebels*, 'From the first . . . Batista ruled through fear of the police and army. Opposition to the regime . . . rested on the triple grounds of illegality, corruption and depravity, and the tyrannical exercise of power . . . [But] the full rigours of official terrorism were imposed only *after* the rebellion had been launched and as a method of repressing it; before that, the regime had been relatively moderate' (p. 71).

17. Ernesto Che Guevara, *Reminiscences of the Cuban Revolutionary War* Allen & Unwin, 1968, p. 197.

18. ibid., p. 118.

which in 1952 had been made possible only by the apparently incorrigible inability of the liberal political groupings to act in concert. Though Guevara in his chivalrous way gives credit to the bravery of Batista troops on occasion, it can scarcely be doubted that Draper is substantially correct when he argues that a 'general revulsion' against Batista's promiscuous counter-terrorism 'penetrated and permeated his own army and made it incapable of carrying out the offensive it launched in May (1958) against Castro's hideout'.[19] But due credit should go to Castro's very skilful manner of troop proselytizing. His explanation on Radio Rebelde of why captured Batista troops were released was nicely put: 'We do not wish to deprive these Cubans of the company of their loving families. Nor, for practical reasons, can we keep them, as our food, cigarettes, and other commodities are in short supply. We hope the people of Cuba will understand our position in this respect.'

But if the condition of the army and the garrison mentality were important factors in explaining Castro's victory, so was the terrain and the skilful use of it that the guerrillas gradually learned. Batista appears to have hoped for quite a long time that the guerrillas up in the thinly populated mountains would either starve or weary of a seemingly futile campaign. Castro was thus for long permitted a secure base area which became a recruiting centre and, as the force grew, a take-off point for raids into the foothills. Propaganda and a widespread popular malaise permitted Castro's talk of a 'total war' in March 1958 to sound as though he had far more than his two to three hundred men deployed in grandiosely styled 'Columns'.

The 5,000 Batista troops deployed to cordon off the area were wholly inadequate to the task. As Robert Taber has neatly described it:

> The Sierra runs more than one hundred miles east and west and is fifteen to twenty-five miles deep. Simple arithmetic shows how impossible was the task set for the army, given a trackless terrain of precipitous and thickly wooded mountains. It would have been impossible with twice the number of troops.

19. *Myths and Realities*, p. 14.

Aircraft were used against the guerrillas, but as Castro noted, the thick, wet woods blotted out the effects of high explosive bombs and napalm within twenty-five to fifty yards. There was little danger even had the bombardiers been accurate and the location of the guerrillas known – and neither of these 'ifs' ever prevailed.[20]

Early in May 1958 Batista's forces launched their one major offensive against the guerrilla base area. The political background to this offensive was the failure of a projected general strike and of an expected civic resistance movement in Havana.[21] By this time the apparently somewhat mysterious civilian Directorate was firmly under the guerrilla command, which had become the focus of hope and of leadership for all disaffected elements in town and country – the former being much the more important. But whereas civilian resistance, particularly the projected general strike, had proved a fiasco, the guerrillas skilfully handled this offensive and according to some accounts actually turned it into a guerrilla counter-offensive. What appears clear is that by July the Batista effort had spent itself and that by September Castro's columns fanned out from the mountains. In October the Communist PSP successfully jumped on the band-waggon of success, though as late as June it had still been pursuing the 'Moscow' line of peaceful mass struggle and the search for a coalition. The respectable began to get on-side too and Batista prepared to flee, which he did at the beginning of January 1959 in conditions of complete breakdown of authority.

But what about the peasants? it may well be asked again. Well, when describing events as late as the September 1958 breakout from the mountains Guevara wrote that 'we had increasingly to avoid populated areas as we moved beyond Oriente Province'. He continued:

In the midst of our troubles we never lacked for support from the peasants. There was always one to serve as a guide or keep us from starving. To be sure, we did not find unanimous support such as that

20. Taber, op. cit., pp. 39–40.

21. See Herbert L. Matthews, *The Cuban Story*, George Braziller, New York, 1961, p. 77, and Andres Suarez, *Cuba: Castroism and Communism, 1958–1966*, MIT Press, Cambridge, Mass., 1967, p. 25.

given us by the population of Oriente, but nonetheless there were always people to help us. Sometimes we were betrayed, while passing through an estate. This by no means signified a concerted peasant action against us. It must be understood that their conditions of existence turned these men into slaves. Terrified at the thought of losing their daily crust, they would inform the proprietor that we were passing through the estate property, and he had nothing better to do than warn the military authorities.[22]

It was the fact that some half of Cuba's cultivatable land was devoted to the growing of sugar cane (along with the apparently not very politically important fact that about a third of the population was Negro) that prompted Hugh Thomas to suggest that Cuba should be considered as a Caribbean rather than a Latin American country.[23] Since over a third of the sugar was under US control, it is reasonable to suppose the Castroite movement attracted considerable nationalist feeling towards it. But this is not directly a peasant issue except in the face of an occupying army, as in the case of China in the 1930s.

What Castro did do was to promulgate in October 1950 from the Sierra a land law granting ownership rights to peasant farmers with 165 acres or less.[24] This was of course ultimately to prove to have been only the normal Communist-style first step towards agricultural collectivization but at the time it doubtless had its propaganda value. The extent of this propaganda effect would, however, seem to be of dubious significance so far as the population-at-large was concerned. Suarez has pointed out that the poor peasant – those owning less than 25 hectares – constituted some 111,000 out of an 'economically active' population of over two millions. He concludes that 'It is difficult to see how a segment that did not amount to 6 per cent of the economically active population and plainly did not have the avid hunger for land that was discovered by observers (when Guevara started the myth of peasant revolution) could have made an important contribution to the revolutionary situation in 1959.'[25]

It seems fairly clear that Batista's regime owed what little

22. *Reminiscences*, pp. 246–7.
23. Veliz, op. cit., pp. 249–52.
24. Suarez, op. cit., p. 38.
25. ibid., p. 36.

authority it enjoyed for a few years to the organizational ineptitude of the conservative and liberal political groupings; and to a sordid spoils system designed to exploit members of interest groups that had lost faith in their capacity radically to modernize a society plagued by corruption (in the modern meaning of the term). It was not, therefore, very difficult to provoke the regime into destroying itself; to provoke the kind of blind striking out at enemies, imagined as well as real, which in turn created a consensus of opposition that came increasingly to accept Castroite leadership. Armed struggle – in the cities more than the countryside, though orientated towards the leadership in the countryside – broke up the situation of squalid group manoeuvres which Batista had presided over rather than politically mastered.

But from the point of view of guerrilla warfare, some 300 (perhaps 1,500 during the last five months of the struggle) had 'triumphed' over at least 30,000 'forces of order'. And they had done so in a politically quite different manner from the Chinese or Vietnamese revolutionary guerrillas. The Castroite Movement had a programme of sorts: democracy (of the old but betrayed kind); land reform with compensation; moderate nationalization of utilities, and so on. The programme bore no resemblance to what was put into practice after victory; and so in that regard it was similar to that of the Chinese and Vietminh movements. Like those movements, the Movement of 26 July sought to represent a consensus of hopes, which were swiftly betrayed by the armed political apparatus once it was in power. (Whether the 26 July Movement or various of its leaders were crypto-Communist cannot be discussed here. The question became scholastic very quickly, since the Movement-as-government was Leninist in all essential particulars.)

But where the revolutionary guerrilla war inverted the principles of Mao and Giap was in the organizational and propaganda field. According to the Cuban theory, as a clever sympathizer has put it, 'The incumbent government is outfought before it is outadministered.'[26] Señor Castro apparently did not hold a

26. Ahmad Eqbal in Leo Huberman and Paul M. Sweezy (eds.), *Debray and the Latin American Revolution*, Monthly Review Press, New York and London, 1968, p. 77.

single political rally in his zone of operations during the two years of struggle.

In the flush of victory, it did not take long for two myths to be propagated very widely: first, the technical skills in rural warfare of the Castroite Movement had resulted in the rout of a hugely larger army; secondly, a peasant revolution had displaced Batista. The relationship between the two myths was kept hazy for polemical reasons; the fact that both myths were false was not realized for some time, and the failure to realize this cost Guevara his life in Bolivia ... not to speak of the setback his Bolivian fiasco gave to the Cuban thesis. ('Che lives!' may have been a very moving slogan to privileged young people in liberal-capitalist universities, but the late Major Ernesto Guevara himself had seen quite plainly that what was important to 'the peasantry' was a complete confidence that the guerrillas were *winning* the military struggle.)

The lessons Guevara drew from the Cuban experience revealed 'three fundamental conclusions about armed revolution in the Americas'. They were these: popular forces can win a war against an army; one does not necessarily have to wait for all the conditions of a revolutionary situation to arise – it can be created; and in the under-developed countries of the Americas, rural areas are the best battlefields for revolution.[27] The second claim was not as incautious as it may sound, since he added the rider that 'Certain minimum pre-conditions are needed to kindle the first spark. The people must be shown that social wrongs are not going to be redressed by civil means alone. And it is desirable to have the oppressor, wittingly or not, to break the peace first.'

He did not, as is sometimes supposed, underrate the value of urban guerrilla struggle.

> The importance of suburban struggle has usually been underestimated; it is really very great. A good operation of this type extended over a wide area paralyses almost completely the commercial and industrial life of the sector and places the entire population in a situation of unrest, of anguish, almost of impatience for the development of violent events that will relieve the period of suspense. If from

27. Mao Tse-Tung and Che Guevara, *Guerrilla Warfare*, Cassell, 1965, p. 111.

the first moment of the war thought is taken for the future possibility of this type of fight and an organization of specialists started, a much more rapid action will be assured, and with it a saving of lives and of the priceless time of the nation.[28]

But the emphasis lay on the word 'specialists'; the revolutionary command had to lie with the leaders of the armed guerrilla movement in the countryside, since it was there he believed the 'ideal conditions for the fight' were offering. It is also clear that Guevara thought that an urban guerrilla movement was much more vulnerable to detection and penetration by the forces of order. But over and above these considerations, there was his exalted vision of the rural guerrilla fighter who, 'as a person conscious of a role in the vanguard of the people, must have a moral conduct that shows him to be a true priest of the reform to which he aspires. To the stoicism imposed by the difficult conditions of warfare should be added an austerity born of rigid self-control that will prevent a single excess, a single slip, whatever the circumstances. The guerrilla soldier should be an ascetic.'

Though he was not unmindful of the necessity to establish a counter-State, including 'courts', in the guerrilla-controlled zones, the thrust of his argument was very much more military than political. This comes out clearly in the following passage which deals with 'enemy territory':

There small groups begin to penetrate, assaulting the roads, destroying bridges, planting mines, sowing disquiet. With the ups and downs characteristic of warfare the movement begins to grow; by this time the extensive work among the masses makes easy movement of

28. Che Guevara, *Guerrilla Warfare*, Penguin Books, 1969, p. 43. It should be remarked that another factor placing the population in a position of unrest is the withdrawal of aid to the incumbent government by its patron. 'The effect [of propaganda], on the political and economic level, was to bring about an American arms embargo against the government of Fulgencio Batista, to discourage investment and restrict credits to such an extent as to put a severe strain on the regime, and to cause, gradually, a failure of nerve within the administration that spread to the military and made it practically impotent long before most of the troops had ever heard a rifle shot' (Taber, op. cit., p. 38).

the forces possible in unfavourable territory and so opens the final stage, which is suburban guerrilla warfare.

Sabotage increases considerably in the whole zone. Life is paralysed; the zone is conquered. The guerrillas then go into other zones, where they fight with the enemy army along defined fronts; by now heavy arms have been captured, perhaps even some tanks; the fight is more equal. The enemy falls when the process of partial victories becomes transformed into final victories, that is to say, when the enemy is brought to accept battle in conditions imposed by the guerrilla band; there he is annihilated and his surrender compelled.[29]

Compared with the Chinese Communist or Vietminh/Vietcong approach, this is really pretty slap-happy, both politically and militarily. 'Extensive work among the masses' in a Leninist-style revolutionary war is not simply designed to facilitate ease of movement – though that is certainly important – but also, and more importantly, to mobilize the masses in a different kind of society from that which is being attacked: an ideologically and organizationally stronger society which can endure during the ebb and flow of the struggle. This seems to have been where the Cuban experience was very misleading. From the military point of view, neither Mao nor Giap would have contemplated pitting guerrillas against a regular army in pitched battles. Here again the Cuban experience – in which the opposing army simply 'evaporated', as C. Wright Mills once put it – was very misleading.

However, Guevara was a man who could truly say that 'I risk my neck to prove my platitudes' and so he took a small band of men to Bolivia for that purpose; or, as he also put it, much more grandiosely, for the purpose of making 'not one but several Vietnams' in the Americas. The band of Cubans, Bolivian Communists, Argentinians and Peruvians got off to a flying start with a successful ambush. But most of the remainder of Guevara's diary, kept from the arrival on 7 November 1966 at a farmhouse in the Bolivian highlands until the day before his capture and murder on 8 October 1967, is a sad tale of inefficiency and

29. Quoted in Vega, op. cit., p. 228.

woe. It is also a tale of great heroism so far as the asthmatic Guevara is concerned.

A wrong theory was applied to a most unsuitable society – doubtless partly for geopolitical reasons: Bolivia as a base for penetrating neighbouring countries; also probably in the expectation of a miners' revolt and urban violence. Though Bolivia was poor and predominantly agricultural, it had in the 1950s undergone one of Latin America's only three social revolutions, including a land reform and the reconstruction of the army into an educationally progressive force in part. Guevara's opponent, Barrientos, was no Batista but a man of impressive qualities. Guevara plunged his foreign band into action in this vast and inhospitable land with reckless insouciance about local attitudes.

The guerrilla band was far from ascetic in its treatment of food stores and was so weakened by the physical environment – incessant rains, swamplands, malaria, food-poisoning, malnutrition – as to lose much of its heart. 'Peasant support' from the Indians was just not forthcoming since they had recently enjoyed a land reform; the Moscow-line Communist Party of Bolivia would not accept direction of the campaign by the guerrilla leadership and turned hostile; the supposedly hard-core of the revolution began to disintegrate as a result of defections and enemy arms. Guevara just floundered about in a vast and inhospitable area until armed forces trained by American counter-insurgent experts caught up with him and killed him.[30]

In view of the singularly ill-chosen terrain it is doubtful whether Guevara's fiasco in Bolivia proved anything very much one way or the other about the possibilities of rural-based revolutionary warfare elsewhere in Latin America. But it is a fact that only disasters have been met with since the great Cuban success, and this despite the fact that rural guerrilla movements did start up in many Latin American countries in the 1960s. Some, particularly those in Colombia, Venezuela and Guatemala, were not inconsiderable efforts for a time; and they were based on a belief that the iniquitous land-tenure systems would produce peasant support.

30. See Che Guevara, *Bolivian Diary*, Cape/Lorrimer, 1968.

But these failures do not prove, in the author's opinion, that there is not a future for rural insurgencies. It is fairly clear that the Cuban myth of a few men with guns being able to take on 'the forces of order' resulted in a rash of voluntarism of an absurdly ill-prepared kind. At the same time the forces of order, under American instruction, were very greatly improving their tactics, their weaponry and their communications. More than that, Latin American armies began to see themselves as the modernizing agency of their countries; to the extent that some of them could claim with justice to understand the problems of the rural poor, particularly the Indian population, better than the guerrilla intellectuals did.

As M. Régis Debray said, the revolution can revolutionize the counter-revolution. Debray thus set out, arguing very much from the Cuban experience, to revolutionize the revolution. His solution to the rural revolutionary problem was very much in accord with Guevara's disastrous policy in Bolivia. The guerrilla *foco* was to be the 'small motor' which set the 'big motor' of revolution going. Whereas Giap believed the Party was the soul and guide of the revolutionary army, Debray believed that the guerrilla band was the Party in embryo; and yet, like Guevara, he was weak on political organization. Like Guevara again, but much more starkly, he emphasizes the propaganda of the military deed:

> The destruction of a troop transport truck or the public execution of a police torturer is more effective propaganda for the local population than a hundred speeches. Such conduct convinces them of the essential: that the Revolution is on the march, that the enemy is no longer invulnerable. It convinces them, to begin with, that the soldier is an enemy – their enemy – and that a war is under way, the progress of which is dependent on their daily activities. Afterwards, speeches may be made and will be heeded. In the process of such raids the fighters collect arms, reduce the enemy's military potential, acquire experience, demoralize enemy troops, and renew the hopes of militants throughout the country. The agitational and propagandistic impact resides in this very concentration of effects.[31]

31. *Revolution in the Revolution?* ,op. cit., pp. 53–4.

However, though Debray is formally aware of the need for agitational propaganda – after the military action – his emphasis lies upon the 'concentration of effects'. This springs from his ultra-élitist views on the guerrilla vanguard: 'And the irony of history has willed, by virtue of the social situation of many Latin American countries, the assignment of precisely this vanguard role to students and revolutionary intellectuals, who have had to unleash, or rather initiate, the highest forms of class struggle.'[32] The watchwords of the intellectual shock troops are to be: constant vigilance, constant mistrust, constant mobility.

Though much lip-service is paid to popular support, it is fairly clear that the real contest is between the educated and idealistic guerrilla fighters, purged of city corruption and 'proletarianized' by the good clean mountain air, and the armed forces of order. 'The protection of the population depends on the progressive destruction of the enemy's military potential ... this objective requires that the guerrilla *foco* be independent of the families residing in the zone of operations ...'[33] 'The population will be safe when the opposing forces are completely defeated.'

What Debray fails to explain is how this guerrilla band, whose 'base of support' in the initial stage 'is in the guerrilla's knapsack', survives the initial phase without having created a popular base. The answer appears to be terrorism, though the matter is treated somewhat obliquely: 'In many areas of the Sierra Maestra, it was eventually more dangerous to help the government than to help the rebels, unlike in the later war in Bolivia, where Che was perpetually betrayed by peasants he could not control or terrorize into silence. In the Cuban War, however, Che noted of the peasants: "Denouncing us did violence to their conscience and, in any case, put them in danger, since revolutionary justice was speedy."'

Though Debray's approach has had a wide appeal to certain intellectual circles, as has Guevara's, it clearly does not offer a feasible mode of making rural revolution in Latin America. The

32. ibid., p. 21. 33. ibid., pp. 41–2.

deaths of many young students and intellectuals who tried to start their 'small motors' in remote places is testimony to this. It is not possible to wage revolutionary guerrilla warfare while playing fast and loose with the questions of political organization and political indoctrination, unless the regime under attack is quite peculiarly weak, as was the case in Cuba. Revolution (or the threat thereof) has indeed revolutionized the counter-revolution.

Hence the recent emphasis placed on what is called urban guerrilla warfare. The terrorist groups who rob banks and kidnap officials (in order to obtain the release of incarcerated comrades) do indeed succeed in widely publicizing their cause in a way that is not open to rural guerrillas; and this propaganda of deeds may well attract some adherents to the cause. It may also, by invoking promiscuous 'police' activities, draw world attention to the shortcomings (or in some cases the cruelty) of the incumbent regimes. But one of the urban guerrillas' troubles is that they are often 'attacking' the kind of regime that does not have to care much about world opinion; or alternatively risk evoking an authoritarian response behind which their behaviour has pushed the support of a very large segment of public opinion.

The aim of urban guerrilla warfare is of course to provoke the repressive activities of the State and then say, 'This is what we told you the State is *really* like.' But ordinary people do not always – or probably even usually – react in this way. The terrorization of a city is a very different problem from the terrorization of a village society. It cannot be an instrument of 'pin-point coercion' so far as the citizens-at-large are concerned; nor can it induce the same kind of neurosis as terrorization of a village can. The 'anonymity' of city life cuts both ways: it can protect the terrorist's identity while he goes about his work of murder but it also imposes anonymity on the terrorist organization in a way that is politically frustrating to it: either the organization continues to give the impression of diffused violence, with which most citizens cannot possibly identify themselves, or it risks complete destruction at the hands of the police by attempting widespread recruiting and propagandizing.

The point should not be pushed too far: it may be that those *villas miserias*, those terrible slums, of Latin America will afford a new kind of 'terrain' for guerrillas to exploit – but not according to the élitist, small-group approach that seems to be *de rigueur* at present. The epidemic of kidnapping of hostages is essentially a defensive strategy: to rescue comrades and to keep the movement in being through publicizing its existence. Such groups could doubtless be of very great importance in a political crisis, but unless they can engender a crisis then their first really revolutionary step is a political, organizational one: recruiting a 'mass movement'. Even the most awful slum can scarcely be a base area in the sense that the Viet Bac was for the Vietminh or the Sierra Maestra for Castro's movement.[34]

The overthrow of the Allende regime, which in power was a mixture of the constitutional, the 'Front', and the (unofficially) violent approaches to social revolution, will doubtless initially reinforce the argument of those who see in the directly and centrally violent approach the only feasible revolutionary policy.

But clearly the matter is less simple than that. Western theorists and commentators sympathetic to revolutionary violence are bad guides in this regard, since their personal attitudes, compounded of vicarious romanticism and anomically violent propensities, often flavoured by wishful thinking, are not attuned to the complex realities out of which political violence erupts. Cruel repression, including that ultimate obscenity, torture, is beginning to proliferate in increasingly efficient forms; and barring a truly grave recession in the West, the exploration of the possibilities of the so-called multi-polar international balance of power is likely to militate against Great Power support for revolutionary movements. But the variables are such as to make predictions quite futile.

34. This was beginning to be proved in Belfast before the Londonderry shooting, early in 1972, though partly because the IRA Provisionals relied too much upon gunmanship as a mass-mobilizing technique. When, at Londonderry, the terrorists acted in concert with a trained mass gathering, the consequent deaths were very effective in mobilizing the Catholic masses, as never before.

It would seem that the exponents of the rural revolutionary approach have not yet been put out of court, however wrong some of them may have been about the role of political organization *vis-à-vis* the role of military contention. What would be most effective in Latin America and in an increasingly urbanized Asia would be a marrying of the urban and guerrilla struggles, but even then the revolutionary guerrillas would have to find more appropriate ways of 'mobilizing the masses' than they have done so far in the cities.

The only safe, if very inconclusive, generalization that can be made so far was made by Robert Moss: '... the urban guerrilla is a political catalyst whose actions can radicalize a society and bring about the kind of social and economic confusion that will lead to a decline in popular belief in peaceful solutions. The end results may be indirect and will often take forms that neither the guerrillas nor the government anticipated.'[35]

35. *Urban Guerrilla Warfare*, op. cit., p. 16. Two very useful studies on guerrillas in Latin America appeared too late for their findings to be incorporated in this chapter: Richard Gott, *Guerrilla Movements in Latin America*, Nelson, 1970, a large study from a sympathetic point of view; and Robert Moss, *Urban Guerrillas in Latin America*, Institute for the Study of Conflict, London, 1970, a short study from the other point of view.

CHAPTER 8

# ASPECTS OF THE PROBLEM

## PROPAGANDA

CLAUSEWITZ believed that 'Public opinion is ultimately gained by great victories'. T. E. Lawrence argued that the printing press was 'the greatest weapon in the armoury of the modern commander'. Great victories are not possible in guerrilla wars; and the printing press is not at the disposal of the commander of a democratic army. The capacity to avoid the possibility of great defeats and to avail himself not only of his own press but of the enemy press as well is the privilege of the revolutionary guerrilla commander in the second half of the twentieth century (or, more precisely, of the regime the commander serves).

It is scarcely an exaggeration to say that 'Modern Communism is permanent psychological warfare in action'.[1] Propaganda on an international scale can only be effectively employed by totalitarian regimes against free societies. The converse is impossible, for the simple reason that 'Propaganda consists of the planned use of any forms of public or mass-produced communication designed to affect the minds and emotions of a given group for a specific public purpose, whether military, economic, or political.'[2] Only in conditions of declared war is such planning available to democratic governments.

From the Communist point of view this is only one component of political warfare; that is, 'all types of agitation, propaganda, subversion, economic manipulation, rioting, terror, diversionary diplomacy, guerrilla and para-military actions etc.: everything, in sum, short of the employment of the main formal armed forces'.[3] But in the international arena Communist propa-

1. Paul Linebarger, *Psychological Warfare*, op. cit., p. 75.

2. ibid., p. 39.

3. James Burnham in Franklin M. Osanka, *Modern Guerrilla Warfare*, Free Press of Glencoe, New York, 1962, p. 420.

ganda does have a life of its own, so to speak, as was acknowledged by General Vo Nguyen Giap when he wrote: '... efforts had to be made to win over the support of progressive people throughout the world, particularly to co-ordinate with the struggle of the French people and those in the French colonies against this dirty war'.[4] Such efforts are made not simply in the hope of affecting the beliefs and emotions of groups in the West but in the firm belief that they will certainly evoke a favourable response. In other words, this propaganda is designed to exploit conflict situations that are held already potentially to exist in the target societies. It was this belief that permitted Hanoi quite confidently to expect, from the very beginning of the Second Indo-China War, an unconditional American defeat:

> A staggering assessment of the United States and its leadership – so unreal as to defy discussion – grips the Communist North Vietnamese regime as an article of faith. Not only does the party, run by the aged Ho Chi-minh, believe it will win, unconditionally, the war in South Vietnam. It is also certain that President Johnson will be overthrown. It forecasts a divided USA tearing itself apart over the war. These conclusions, reached by the top Vietnamese leaders, have dumbfounded a recent spate of visitors. How do the North Vietnamese account for their belief that revolution is around the corner in America? 'Criticism in colleges and assorted debates always lead to revolution,' is the collective reply.[5]

In this, and in General Giap's prediction about a democratic public coming to demand an end to 'the useless bloodshed' and astronomical credits, there is no reference to the shocked revulsion evoked by the first full televised war or to the moral abhorrence with which so many Americans came to view the employment of the technology of war on a massive scale for de-

4. Vo Nguyen Giap, *People's War, People's Army*, op. cit., p. 97. Cf. Régis Debray, *Revolution in the Revolution*, op. cit., p. 47: '... the first nucleus of fighters will be divided into small propaganda patrols which will cover the mountain areas, going into villages, holding meetings ... Cells, public or underground, will be supported or initiated; and the program of the Revolution will be reiterated again and again. It is only at this stage ... that the guerrillas can pass over to direct action against the enemy.'

5. *The Australian*, 20 July 1965.

batable purposes. The picture of American society, and of Western liberal-capitalist society in general, upon which Communist propaganda is based is a picture of infirmity of will and internal dissension, not of moral conflict within the minds of individuals. The reference to 'useless bloodshed' is a reference to the supposedly base liberal capitalist obsession with success, not to moral susceptibilities as such; the reference to astronomical credits is also a reference to a presumed obsessive greed on the part of such a society, and not to any capacity they might have for coming to consider that in the context of Vietnam valid political ends were being swallowed up by the means employed.

Communist diplomacy, which is always very carefully meshed in with propaganda, is also predicated on a view of the base qualities of their enemies. As M. Jules Monnerot has remarked:

> Totalitarian diplomacy and propaganda frequently test the psychological resistance of the opponents they tend to disintegrate by suddenly switching from war talk to peace talk, in the hope of obtaining from 'cowardly relief' what they were unable to achieve through menaces. Another of their objectives is to enable their friends to maintain, without too great implausibility, that 'an agreement is possible' with the totalitarians . . .[6]

As with the armed propaganda squads and their terrorist auxiliaries in the villages of Asia, so on the international scene: propaganda is aimed against the minds and wills of men, not at the generosity of their feelings, nor even at their moral anxieties about the justice or injustice of great and terrible events. The language of humanity (or of neurosis for that matter) is not the language used by Communists actually engaged in revolutionary warfare, so far as the international scene is generally concerned.

That is the task of mediators within the West itself; and of course it is not for the most part set in any direct fashion by Communist manipulators. It is a self-assumed task on the part of many people who are quite unaware of the success over a long period of time of Communists and fellow travellers in the West who naturally have had to translate the jargon of totalitarian

6. Jules Monnerot, *Sociology of Communism*, Allen & Unwin, 1953, p. 242.

psychological warfare into the language of Western moral concern.

This legacy of decades of propaganda mediation is of very great benefit to revolutionary movements; this is proved by the assiduity with which they seek, from the very beginnings of their campaigns, any available news channels into democratic societies.[7] Such a search for access to democratic public opinion is only meaningful, could only be meaningful, if based on a belief that it will be of service to the revolution.

What are the grounds for this belief? First of all, there has grown up since the 1930s an influential body of opinion-makers in the West who are automatically and uncritically responsive to any appeal couched in the language of nationalism, whatever the ultimate aims or political behaviour of the movement making the appeal may be. The uncritical acceptance of the credentials of anti-Western nationalists from Sukarno to Nkrumah is now all too well known. (Indeed it was, for that matter, the presumed anti-French stance of Ngo Dinh Diem that endeared him for some time to a fairly influential number of American liberals.)

This response to the appeal of nationalist slogans and anti-imperialist sloganeers, however dishonest the slogans and however squalid or cruel the sloganeers, quite certainly developed out of a generous belief that the rule by white aliens of distant places was humanly subversive of both nations involved in the relationship; a belief too, though sometimes less well founded, that such rule was not only economically exploitative but was actually retarding the various facets of development of the subject people.

But this process was not simply one of a developing belief that nationalism was *ipso facto* good and progressive[8] and that

7. Howard R. Simpson, *US Naval Institute Proceedings*, August 1969, cites the directive of an Algerian FLN leader, as asking 'Is it better for our cause to kill ten of the enemy in the countryside of Telergma, where no one will speak of it, or one in Algeria that will be mentioned the next day in the American press?' The question was rhetorical; the propaganda of the deed was henceforth concentrated in Algiers.

8. Though this has been an extraordinary feature of recent years. 'Who, in the nineteenth century, would have predicted the rise of acute nationalism

imperialism was consequently bad and reactionary. (The logical relationship between the two beliefs was probably as often put the other way around.) The process came in time to be inextricably mixed in with guilt-feelings, very often expressed in a disagreeably meretricious fashion,[9] about what the democratic West really stood for and stands for *vis-à-vis* the non-European world. At first this world was chiefly 'Afro-Asia'; later terms like the Third World permitted the encompassing of a very different civilization, that of Latin America, in this guilt-neurosis as it surely may be termed, since its sloganeers have seldom, if ever, been amongst that great band of Europeans working to better the life of the people of the Third World. This guilt-neurosis may be traced in its growth through the change in terminology from 'undeveloped' to 'developing world'.

There is no evidence that the rule of the white imperial administrations was less humane towards the subject people-at-large than any, or almost any, independent government has proved to be; and their rule was certainly found much more agreeable by the vast masses of minority peoples of various kinds.[10] This is not in any way to suggest that European imperial rule in Asia and Africa created a humanly attractive relationship between peoples; it most certainly did not, and it did have its atrocious moments. But it is to say that the guilt-neurosis which has become embedded in so many educated Europeans' attitudes to

---

in Canada, in Pakistan . . . or in Wales or Brittany or Scotland or the Basque country?' (Sir Isaiah Berlin, 'The Bent Twig', in *Foreign Affairs*, Vol. 51, No. 1, October 1972).

9. Arthur Koestler, *Encounter*, Vol. 1, No. 2, November 1953, wittily describes this type. 'The slightest injustice in his own country wrings from him cries of anguish and despair, but he finds excuses for the most heinous crimes committed in the opposite camp. When a coloured tennis player is refused a room in a London luxury hotel he quivers with a spontaneous indignation; when millions spit out their lungs in Soviet Arctic mines and concentration camps, his sensitive conscience is silent. He is an inverted patriot, whose self-hatred and craving for punishment has turned into hatred for his country or social class and a yearning for the whip that will scourge it.'

10. For example, tens of millions of Indian Muslims were not prepared to chance their lot under Hindu-majority rule and instead insisted upon the partition of the sub-continent.

words like nationalism and imperialism and race *is* a neurosis in the sense that it is not grounded on substantial fact.

As is shown particularly in the case of the two Indo-China Wars, not to speak of the 'agrarian reformer' syndrome amongst writers on the Chinese Communists, the distinction between a nationalist movement and a Communist movement has been blurred to the great advantage of the Communists so far as world-wide propaganda is concerned. This blurring is not simply owing to a lack of precise discrimination and an evasion of the question of the command structure of Communist Front movements on the part of so many commentators in the West; it owes much to the great pains Communist revolutionary movements have taken to disguise the political nature of the many-faceted fronts which they control.

In recent years, in the vocabulary of revolutionary guerrilla movements from the Yemen to Algeria, from Jordan to Latin America, the word 'liberation' has been consistently added to the term 'front'. Thus a word that not very long ago connoted the relief of captive nations from Nazi tryranny, and the restoration of liberal democracy, has been appropriated by small groups of armed intellectuals who are out to shackle their countrymen in chains of a psychological, political and social strength and durability undreamed of by the European imperialists or by the often authoritarian regimes that have come to power in the wake of European disengagement from empire. Such 'liberation fronts' are not of course all Communist in ideology or in close alliance with the chief Communist States. But by adopting an élitist, one-party (the 'party of nationalism') stance, the organizational methods, the fighting tactics and the assiduous refusal to declare their ultimate aims, not to speak of the frequent acceptance of Communist politico-military instructors and weaponry, such movements do very often come to resemble Communist movements to all intents and purposes. This is very often particularly noticeable in a hate-filled stance towards the liberal-capitalist West.[11]

11. e.g. 'Leave this Europe where they are never done talking of Man, yet murder men everywhere they find them, at the corner of every one of their

It is perhaps in this regard that widespread sympathy in the West for movements which have appropriated the term 'liberation' is most easily intelligible. The West – and in recent years, much more obviously, the USA – has supported a number of regimes in the Third World that have been disreputable in various ways. But since such regimes have regularly been visited by Western correspondents, or very often have had resident Western correspondents in their capital cities, their unattractive features have all too often come to obscure, if not obliterate, the real aims and nature of the 'liberation movements' opposed to them. No Western correspondent covered the 1953–6 'Land Reform' in North Vietnam, for example; very few Western correspondents over a number of decades exposed the fact that twenty million Soviet 'citizens' were being done to death in the name of 'socialism'. As far as the author knows, no Western correspondent has covered any one of the thousands upon thousands of assassinations of South Vietnamese by agents of the National Liberation Front's violence programme.

National Liberation Front is of course the most potent of all the verbal combinations created in order to subserve the aims of the small groups of armed intellectuals engaged in the task of seizing total power for themselves. 'National' evokes an almost Pavlovian response from undiscriminating liberals in the West; 'liberation' exerts a profound emotional effect upon the young gormless engaged in a desperate quest for the formlessly pure; 'front' has curiously lost any precise meaning, except for the Communist or other totalitarian élitist leadership groups. The romantic designations for such movements also enable people in the West to participate vicariously in what they imagine to be a worldwide movement of human liberation. It is possible to imagine oneself a 'freedom fighter' by joining a demonstration in a city square at home. It seems that very few people in the West would understand quite what the Chinese Communist theoretician, Ai Ssu-chi, meant when he wrote, 'There are only

---

own streets, in all the corners of the globe. For centuries they have stifled almost the whole of humanity in the name of a so-called spiritual experience' (Frantz Fanon, *The Wretched of the Earth*, Penguin Books, 1967, p. 8).

two kinds of political task: one is the task of propaganda and education, and the other is the task of organization.'[12]

The point is nicely made by a profound student of Communist revolutionary warfare, Michael Eliott-Bateman:

> In Britain 'Committees of Peace for Vietnam' flourish under the chairmanship of respected non-Communist members of the community. The Committees are often initially prompted by Communists who provide lavish anti-American propaganda, but the majority of the organizers are merely deeply concerned over the war and are seeking for the truth. Attempts are made to produce a proper balance of opinion at the meetings, but American consulates in Britain foolishly ignore invitations to state their case. Thus, through American default, most meetings develop a strong anti-American flavour . . . The American hierarchy do not appear to be able to comprehend anything that cannot be expressed in terms of physical or financial power: they miss more than half of the game.[13]

It would not be argued here that the growth of feeling and political demonstration against the American involvement in Vietnam over the five years that have passed since the beginning of the commitment of American forces *en masse* is chiefly attributable to Communist propaganda through the agency of front organizations; nor would it be argued that the United States Information Agency had been remiss in its activities, though this may well have been the case with American Consulates in Britain. It is pretty obvious that a number of disparate factors have been at work producing different kinds of disillusionment in the USA itself. The picture of the USA 'tearing itself apart' over the war, which had been drawn in advance in Hanoi, was doubtless sufficient to make most natural sympathizers with the USA in Europe wonder what the war was all about. In France there was prevalent a shamelessly exposed hope that the Americans would not succeed where France had failed; in Britain there was a strong hangover of resentment against the power held responsible for the subversion of the

12. Quoted in S. P. Huntington, *Political Order in Changing Societies*, op. cit., p. 340.

13. *Defeat in the East*, op. cit., p. 164.

British Empire, along with the liberal British admiration for a giant-killer as Ho Chi Minh was held to be (just as Nasser had been held to be in 1956). It is not germane to this study to extend this kind of analysis: in plural societies there will naturally be a plurality of reactions to world events involving much suffering.

But what is germane to this study is the fact that even in the very early days of the commitment of American troops *en masse*, long before the television agencies began to present an unprecedentedly intense and highly selective 'coverage' of warfare, there had been put in train a formidable propaganda operation. This operation was carried out through the mediation of sympathizers with the National Liberation Front who sought to present it as an authentic expression of nationalism rather than what it really was: a front organization being used by a small group of armed intellectuals for the seizure of total and irreversible political power. Endless debates were held about the causes of the initial outbreaks of violence against the Saigon regime in 1957; about the various disaffected groupings that went to make up the NLF and the diplomatic ambiguities flowing from the Geneva Accords of 1954, and so on. What was not being discussed for the most part was the command system originating in Hanoi or the control mechanisms within the NLF or the nature of Communist front organizations; and it is these matters that are central to understanding a revolutionary war.

To what extent such debates were influenced by Communist propaganda is impossible to determine; and it is almost certainly unwise for any Western democrat, however deeply anti-Communist he may be, to be overly concerned with trying to determine such a matter. Nothing is more subversive of Western democratic modes of behaviour than a preoccupation with conspiracy theories of history in political contexts where they can be neither proved nor disproved.

Nevertheless it is fair to suggest that in subtle ways, for reasons adumbrated above, the debate was from the beginning framed in terms that could be of advantage only to the Communists. The promiscuous use of firepower by the USA reinforced doubts rather than created them; ratified a feeling of revulsion against U S technology rather than engendered it – in the minds of so many in the West. But at the same time a large number of the more articulate members of the variegated 'protest movement' were, or anyway seemed to be, unaware of the extent to which they had been conditioned to feel doubts and/or revulsion as a result of the very long-term Communist propaganda offensive directed against their societies.

This may be attributed to the fact that psychological warfare *à l'outrance*, as it is waged by the Communist world, is not only organizationally impossible within the framework of a democ- the needs of fanatically sought lusts for power, war co-ordinated racy, it is exceedingly difficult to comprehend. '... war turned to the *n*th degree, waged in the light of enemy opinion and aiming at the political and moral weaknesses of the enemy' is a skill and a privilege reserved to totalitarian State apparatuses.

The use of the Western press by the Vietnamese Communists has been described very clearly by Mr Dennis Duncanson:

> If we may judge by their publications the Communists soon came to realize that, if they played things carefully, they could put their trust in the foreign press. They invited a small number of sympathetic journalists to Hanoi, knowing the very rarity of the 'concession' would make the meeting a scoop in the West ... Similarly the Tet Offensive, mounted in 1968, an American election year, was a psychological campaign. In Vietnam, it achieved practically nothing, militarily or psychologically, but the impact of reports and films, shown with professional art, forced President Johnson to sue for peace and ... abdicate from his candidature for re-election. Henceforward the North Vietnamese could turn against their South Vietnamese adversaries, not only the latter's material resources, but the moral strength of the American forces as well ... Moreover, North Vietnam hoped that if America's morale dropped even lower, the American public could be led to force the South Vietnamese government into a capitulation which Communist arms alone could not force upon it. Liberation Radio welcomed the moratoriums as 'an autumn cyclone of the American people in smooth co-ordination with the autumn general offensive of our troops'.[14]

14. *History of the Twentieth Century*, ed. J. M. Roberts, Purnell, 1970, Vol. 7, Ch. 99, p. 75.

## MOTIVATION AND MOBILIZATION

A term that has appeared amongst those engaged in fighting against revolutionary movements in recent years is 'well motivated'. It has been applied particularly, and with justice, to the Vietcong on many occasions; and it has been used, often most unfairly, to suggest that the Vietcong are always superior in fighting quality to the government of Vietnam's forces. Further, the suggestion is often made – or anyway it is very often implied – that this presumed superior fighting quality on the part of Communist guerrillas in the Third World is testimony of a superior moral quality. The endurance and tenacity of the men out in the bush are contrasted with the corruption (favourite word of journalists from affluent countries who are hostile to incumbent regimes) and military unreliability of their uniformed enemies.

There has gradually been built up a picture of revolutionary guerrilla armies as being composed of idealists fighting the squalid and the corrupt; and the successes of movements like the Vietcong have been very widely attributed to this idealism, as though it were much the chief factor at work. The reality is much more complex than that. It is not in fact the experience of those who have engaged the Vietcong in protracted warfare that they are up against a monolithically superior kind of enemy. The testimony of an Australian Intelligence Officer in Vietnam is fairly typical:

> We had met the Vietcong and found them to be a widely varying force in terms of their proficiency. Their worst were rabble, their best were good fighters and cadre leaders by any standards. We pitied their miserable existence and the way in which their commanders were prepared to squander the lives of their men for very small military gains. We were revolted by their atrocities and amazed by their tactical ineptitudes such as the frequency with which they used lights for guiding their movement at night. They are a unique enemy, cunning in tactic but repetitive in strategy. They form part of an ideological crusade, but they are often pathetically ignorant of the doctrine on whose altar their lives are sacrificed. After we had come

to know them it was difficult to maintain a personal dislike against the Viet Cong for considering the forces to which they had been subjected, they were understandable. This did not make the goal of their masters any more tolerable, but we were much happier to capture a Viet Cong than to kill him.[15]

The author may perhaps be forgiven for citing at this point what he wrote after observing the cordon-and-search of a Vietnamese village, during which some Vietcong surrendered:

Coming down the road was a prisoner, a slight figure, escorted by a much taller soldier. One was oddly reminded of injured footballers being assisted off the field. He was sat down on a log beside, but a little way apart from, another prisoner, both of them blindfolded and bare-foot. He was given a cigarette and a drink of water and then was very quietly interrogated.

His mouth was full and soft, almost girlish. A very high forehead was crowned by strong, coarse black hair. One noticed the wide nostrils below the khaki handkerchief bound around his eyes. There was no slightest twitching of the big lips, no tic-ticking of a nervous pulse; a peaceful nose in a peaceful face breathed with decorum. He was alive; he knew that now, and doubtless realized that he was not going to be roughed up. His wide dust-covered feet turned upwards with the contentment of someone relaxing at the beach. He looked exceedingly young, but was estimated at about nineteen by the experienced New Zealand interrogator. He set about shopping his mates who were still out in the scrub, describing their numbers and their armament – revolvers as well as rocket launchers, I gathered – and explained where he had hidden his own equipment before surrendering, as he had been instructed by the aircraft's loud-hailer. Shopping one's mates was pretty normal drill during the shock of capture; and of courses there was a graduated scale of rewards for information leading to the discovery of VC arms. Some surrendered VC had retired from politico-military warfare to run a shop or some small business on the proceeds. The war was not always quite as the Common Room Guevaras at home imagined it to be.[16]

In considering the question of 'motivation' it is necessary to distinguish between the kind of people who join the revolution-

15. Robert J. O'Neill, *Vietnam Task*, Cassell (Australia), p. 248.
16. *Vietnam Digest*, No. 3, December 1969, Canberra.

ary movement at various stages, while remembering that most revolutionary guerrilla movements, including active supporters, have comprised only a very small section of the population. The first people on the scene are of course the cadres who in nearly all cases have learned about Communism in cities or towns. Such people very usually have had at least some secondary education. They are also, as a result, normally very aware of the special dislocation affecting particularly people like themselves; aware of what has been called 'the revolution of rising expectations' of which people like themselves are peculiarly the victims. That is, their expectations have been raised to heights far beyond that which the existing society can translate into reality. At the same time, very often, they see others not much better educated than themselves, if at all, advancing beyond them in the existing society through use of family connections or as a result of having concentrated on studies more immediately marketable in the existing society.

This is not to discount genuine idealism about the future or a genuine feeling of outrage against existing social injustices. But in order to understand the attractions of Communist revolutionary movements in the Third World it is necessary to understand the importance at all times of the idea-organization through which the idealist comes to confront the future. Whatever the original source of attraction to the Party may have been, the cadre comes to look at the future in terms of what he believes is an ineluctably expanding *society* or quasi-State, which offers career oportunities as well as opportunities for self-sacrifice.

His task on the local rural scene is to build this alternative society on the one hand, and weaken the existing society on the other hand. Thus he has to recruit and exploit local 'contradictions' at the same time. The emphasis placed on each task varies according to the state of the struggle. If he (almost invariably as part of a small band) is simply concerned slowly to build up the movement during the subversive stage, then the emphasis is usually placed on recruitment of the young, particularly, at first, in areas where something of an administrative vacuum exists.

The motivation of such young as join the movement is not in the least hard to understand. Boredom and frustration with a life often revealed by the transistor radio to be not the kind of life currently being lived by millions of others is quite sufficient to predispose many youths to seek more exhilarating outlets. Through farmers' associations and sporting clubs the cadres can easily begin to open up prospects of excitement and of advancement previously beyond the dreams of the local boys. Their new attitudes of mind will then doubtless bring them into a relationship of conflict, even if for some time disguised in nature, with their elders and thus there comes into existence an exploitable 'contradiction' for the day when political pressure is intensified.

In certain isolated areas the emphasis may be placed on motivating the whole hamlet towards support for the Communist movement by painstaking work on behalf of hamlet life in the form of introducing medicines or building a fishpond or nerving the villagers to resume abandoned land. It is not necessary to seek obscure sources of motivation in situations where a propaganda team is helping the villagers in such ways and offering promises of much more to come if only things are permitted to continue under cadre leadership.[17] Perhaps most importantly, such cadre groups are working *within* the village society in a fashion that has seldom in the past been adopted by the government agencies attempting to do the same kind of thing. The next step for the Communists in such a situation is to provoke government repression, if possible of a violent kind, that will solidify the hamlet around their leadership. A single sniper's bullet or booby trap can quite simply provoke the required government action.

An interesting example of how a small band operated in Vietnam is cited by Marguerite Higgins. A defector, Captain Ba, who later worked heartily against his former comrades, explained how his band was enjoined specifically not to use violence for the whole of their first year of agitational-propaganda activities. Instead they were to move from village to village

17. See, for example, the description of village X in Denis Warner, *The Last Confucian*, op. cit.

to learn the qualities of personality and character that could be turned to our purposes . . . The process is very simple. We go into a village and find out who is hated, and why. We find out who is vain and susceptible to being made to feel important. We find out who has stolen something or cheated his wife during a trip. When we are very sure of our assessment of the people, their faults and their secrets, then we go to work to recruit. With the vain man, we tell him that if he will work with us there is a chance to be a leader of the side that will win. In the case of a farmer who has cheated, we tell him that if he will not join our ranks and take our orders we will expose him. And so on. And once some village men come over to us, they can no longer get away. If they tried, then we would kill them or their families. And one or two deaths are usually enough to keep the rest of the villagers terrorized into obedience. Then once the villagers are actually involved in actions hostile to the government – an ambush, or digging traps for the army to fall into – then they are guilty, and so, in a sense, is the whole village. They are on the Viet Cong side, because having attacked the government, there is no going back.[18]

It is simply not true that the majority of those who take part in a revolutionary insurgency are particularly 'well-motivated' in the sense that they are idealists who have made a personal commitment to a great cause. They are for the most part *involved,* rather than *committed.* The fact that they often fight well is not attributable, so far as the rank-and-file and a good part of the middle leadership are concerned, to some superior kind of motivation. They have simply got themselves involved in a movement the leadership of which has, at a time of its own choosing, put them beyond the law. Certainly pride in their unit is often a feature of revolutionary guerrilla forces as it is of other forces. But other factors are also significantly at work: a belief in the inevitability of victory, at least for a time; fear of the consequences of deserting and a (deliberately inculcated) fear of what will happen to them if they surrender; a feeling of belonging only to this new society and having been fatally cut off from the old society. Hence the otherwise extraordinary regularity with which captured Vietcong guerrillas betray their com-

18. Higgins, *Our Vietnam Nightmare,* op. cit., pp. 141–2.

rades in the shock of loneliness attendant upon capture; and their susceptibility to bribes for revealing hideouts and arms caches thereafter. Another important factor in sustaining morale is the comparative infrequency of actual combat operations and the extreme thoroughness with which such operations are prepared.

The crucial period in terms of 'motivation', so far as the revolutionaries are concerned, provided that they can phase the development of the movement according to plan, is not that of armed contestation. It is the period of early recruitment; the period of subversion that precedes the armed struggle. It is in this sense that it may be said that the only truly successful counter-insurgency is one that has prevented an insurgency being got under way. Once the parallel hierarchies have been established in the villages to support the armed guerrilla organization in the jungle or fringe areas, then the revolutionaries can recruit through force and threats until their links are cut. Press-ganged guerrillas also often fight well, though they can hardly be regarded as 'well motivated' in terms of individual commitment to ideals.

Since the mounting of a revolutionary war requires comparatively very small numbers of active participants it is far from difficult to gather them in rural societies wherever the administration is weak. It is not necessary to seek to descry a great deal of idealism. As Sir Robert Thompson has put it, 'If the path from the discussion group to a jungle training camp is a gentle slope, it can be made more slippery by the prospect of excitement and action. There are not many boys who, when offered a rifle and told to fire at all passing aircraft, could possibly resist the temptation.'[19]

Nevertheless, in order to prepare the organization properly for the move from the subversive phase to that of guerrilla warfare, time and administrative weakness are necessary. The vital element in a revolutionary movement of this kind are the cadres, not the rank-and-file, and cadres take time to train. This is particularly the case when front groups are used as 'observation laboratories' to determine who is to be admitted into the Party

19. Thompson, op. cit., p. 36.

ranks and over what period of time. Pye points out that in Malaya it took an average of eighteen months' service in fronts before even those who later became functionaries were regarded as fledged revolutionaries, though some spent less than six months in front groups. The rank-and-file averaged more than two years in front groups before they were admitted to the party. Some took more than three years to graduate.[20]

Thus it is obvious that the success of a revolutionary guerrilla movement initially hinges on its ability to prepare the organization adequately before moving to the second phase. It is the organization that is vital for the future, not the nature of discontents as such; and the organization can only be brought into being if the administration permits it. Thus, on the political level, the outbreak of an insurgency very often is the result much more of administrative weakness than failures in economic and social policy.

Of course there are those who believe that the revolutionary insurgencies of the present day are spontaneous expressions of popular anger against economic and social and/or political oppression. Even the most cursory reading of revolutionary writings and study of the development of guerrilla movements will show that this view is simply untenable. Setting aside the emotional attitudes that are usually involved in the putting forward of this view, it must be said that it is based upon a fallacious understanding of political behaviour. As Oppenheimer has written:

> Even in the situation of a most spontaneous outbreak – for example, an urban riot – the rioters must then or later develop a more formal organization if their objectives are to have any longer-range meaning. Even within a riot, as it takes place, organization develops: tasks are allocated, a division of labour develops, guards are posted, certain groups have the job of tearing down the lattices which protect store windows, and the like.[21]

In the case of revolutionary guerrilla warfare, spontaneity is something that is to be carefully guarded against, since it en-

20. Pye, op. cit., pp. 220–21.
21. *Urban Guerrilla Warfare*, op. cit., p. 18.

dangers the movement at its early, most vulnerable stage – when a spontaneous outburst of violence can bring down repression on a scale and with an intensity that may well destroy all revolutionary hopes for many years to come. Spontaneity is also rigorously eschewed after the campaign has moved from the subversive to the guerrilla phase, since this kind of politico-military behaviour (which Mao Tse-tung called 'guerrillaism') is subversive of the revolutionary command structure and dangerous for the appropriate further phasing of the campaign into the final stage of mobile warfare or 'general counter-offensive'.

'Motivation' varies from person to person in the subversive stage during which the appeal to the 'hearts and minds' is often of great significance; in the guerrilla stage the situation is usually reached fairly quickly where each side tries to impose conformity with its strategic plans by the mobilization of large numbers of people in various ways and by the remote control or neutralization of the rest. As the struggle gathers intensity, the ebb and flow of it imposes its own pressures which virtually obliterate the possibility of individual choices being made on the basis of interior 'motivation'. The aim of the totalitarian revolutionary organization is of course to create within its own ranks conditions which deny individuals their solitude and hence opportunities for doubt. This is done through incessant indoctrination and self-criticism sessions, as is well known, but this 'brain-washing' process is normally very incomplete as long as the struggle lasts – so far as the rank-and-file are concerned, which is why so many 'Communist' guerrillas very quickly slough off their apparently superior conviction or 'motivation' the moment they are captured or are otherwise prised out of the Communist idea-organization.

So far as the villagers at large are concerned, the most important theme is not one devoted to 'hearts and minds' as that term has come to be understood in Western discussions of insurgency. As the Westerner who has studied the Vietcong most deeply has pointed out,

> The NLF leadership clearly recognizes that what it must do is not so much win voluntary support as to *convince the villager that the*

*NLF is going to win.* This is the certainty-of-victory theme in NLF propaganda and more attention is paid to it than all other themes combined ... The traditional villager does not think of the NLF and the [Government of Vietnam] in terms of who is good and bad, right and wrong – although he may have opinions on the subject – but *what is going to happen* and *how best should he adjust his behaviour accordingly.*[22]

## POPULAR SUPPORT

It is widely agreed that popular support is necessary for the effective functioning of a guerrilla movement, whether revolutionary or traditional in form. Without popular support the guerrillas are isolated and continually in danger of betrayal; bereft of Intelligence about enemy activities, hampered in their movement around the countryside, except in wild and isolated territory, they are denied the kind of initiative necessary to expand the movement and may be deprived of the supplies, some kinds of food and medical equipment that are necessary for long-term survival.

In general terms this is undoubtedly true, but to put the question in such general terms is to obscure the fact that popular support is of various kinds and its nature varies according to different stages in the struggle – and according to different areas within a country. There have been cases of recent invasions, involving promiscuous cruelty, but not encompassing an attempt at pacification of a deeply political kind, which have left a situation in which widespread popular support for nationalist guerrillas is very easily evoked. Ciano recognized this in the case of the Italian conquest of Abyssinia (Ethiopia) when he told Hitler:

> Although Abyssinia is almost pacified, the pacification is something external and superficial. In the event of a general war, a few British planes would only need to drop leaflets on Abyssinia announcing that the world had risen against Italy and that the Negus was going to return for rebellion to break out all over the country.[23]

22. *Politics of the Vietcong*, op. cit., p. 46.
23. Cited in Mergelen, *Surprise Warfare*, op. cit., p. 72.

His prediction was proved more or less accurate when war came and a very small British force raised part of the countryside with considerable ease (probably through bribery as much as anything else). This inadequate pacification is not only a feature of relations between white men and dark, though that has been the most typical form in much of the world over the last couple of centuries. At least in the negative form of a strong disinclination to betray one's blood-fellows to the overlord, popular support for guerrillas is often to be found amongst minority peoples in South and South East Asia. An illuminating example of this kind of situation comes from Nagaland on India's north-east border-land:

> It was so easy for a hostile to drop his weapon into a hole in the ground and to pose as an innocent villager, wrapping a Naga cloak around his shoulders and pretending to wield his ... planting hoe at the approach of any army patrol or convoy! Then there was no denying the fact that sections of the population, sometimes whole villages, were in active or passive support of the underground. The armed police and the army, on whom the responsibility of suppressing the movement rested, even had serious doubts regarding the bona fides of some Government Nagas, whom they suspected of dragging their feet when it came to active enforcement of the law. Even loyal Nagas could, under the circumstances, be excused for drawing a distinction between supporting the Government and betraying a fellow Naga.[24]

It may be said with some certainty that the more primitive (or, as the author would prefer to put it, the more traditional) the society afflicted by guerrilla war, the more difficult it is for a foreign overlord to detach local people as puppets or even to influence locals to the extent of getting them to supply information against their blood-fellows. But the overlord administration need not be foreign, in the sense of belonging to another nation or race, for this difficulty to be encountered. For example, North Vietnamese troops in South Vietnam which operate as distinct units are immeasurably more liable to betrayal than the Vietcong; to some extent officials who emigrated to North Viet-

24. P. D. Stracey, *Nagaland Nightmare*, Allied Publishers, Bombay, 1968, p. 116.

nam in 1954 and even officials from Central Vietnam encounter difficulties with the locals in the south.

It is too seldom understood that an unwillingness to supply information to the government on the part of villagers is not necessarily a sign of political support for the guerrillas, as ideologically or emotionally 'motivated' sympathizers in the West are apt to assume. It may of course be the result of the success of the Communist 'violence programme' (see 'Terrorism', below); or it may be a sign of a generalized local support for the guerrillas. But it may be much more basic and apolitical: an unwillingness to betray local boys (who are likely to be done to death in an ambush as a result of the betrayal) to a central administration viewed as alien to the village community. Hence the enormous importance in counter-insurgency of involving the locals in their own self-defence units. But this does depend upon an adequately timed response to subversion or, at the very least, to the early stage of violence (see 'Administration' and 'Phases', below). There is no value in mobilizing the locals in self-defence units that are unable to defend themselves against the kind of guerrilla forces that have already been created. (See also 'Strategic Hamlets', below.)

During the subversive stage, popular support can be won in the Western sense of the term; that is, free choices may be made to join the revolutionary movement, even if the choices may have been 'motivated' by a quite false appreciation of the ultimate aims of the movement or by quite false hopes of personal advancement. But as the movement grows in strength and influence its purpose is to narrow right down the area of choice and involve the locals willy-nilly in the struggle on the revolutionary side. This is done either through terror or through provoking government reprisals that will induce hatred of the government. This is a very different kind of 'popular support' from the first kind.

Thirdly, as the war grows in intensity a long and fluctuating period of contestation occurs in which the ebb and flow of politico-military control determines to a very large extent the 'popular support' to be found in different areas. The advantage the Communist revolutionary organization has in this kind of situation is that it has established a form of control mechanism within village society that is much more deeply implanted, and hence more enduring in its psychological effects, than the mere administrative covering of the area by the government. It only requires the existence of a small Communist cell to remind a large village, if necessary through exemplary acts of terrorism, that the parallel hierarchies still exist and one day will come into their own again. Such psychological control is of course immeasurably more effective if in the past the government has temporarily taken over the village but later withdrawn. Hence the enormous importance of Sir Robert Thompson's contention that it is necessary to secure *base areas first* and work out from them in such a carefully phased manner that no declared pacified area is ever left exposed to revolutionary vengeance. This was done in Malaya; it was not done under the frantic strategic hamlet-building programme of the Ngo brothers in South Vietnam.

Whenever claims to popular support are relayed from revolutionary leaders through the mediation of sympathetic or simply scoop-hungry journalists, readers in the West should ask themselves very carefully: What precisely is meant by popular support in this particular context? What sort of individual choice is available? What role is terror playing? To what extent is the support localized and the result of deliberately provoked government reprisals? To what sort of programme are the people being asked to offer their popular support? If the revolutionary leadership is Communist, the reader might well ask himself whether peasants really are assenting, in full knowledge, to the coming to power of a regime that will deprive them of any land they may have and brigade them into collective farms?

## ADMINISTRATION

It is often not adequately understood that '... economic development and political stability are two independent goals and progress towards one has no necessary connection with progress towards the other'.[25] The outbreak of an insurgency, revolutionary or otherwise, does not necessarily demonstrate economic and social failure on the part of the incumbent government. But it does indicate administrative failure. Practically every non-Communist government from Karachi to Taiwan, whether it is known as 'progressive' or 'reactionary', is armed with powers to deal with subversion. Preventive detention has been a commonly used power by governments widely regarded as 'progressive', such as India and Singapore. Such powers have frequently been used in the Middle East against Communist parties even by self-styled 'progressive' regimes; the same may be said of much of Africa and Latin America.

Such powers as preventive detention have been effective against subversive leadership groups, but they do not meet the case of rural subversion carried out in terms of protracted revolutionary warfare unless the administration has the means of identifying the agitational-propaganda teams or of itinerant agents such as travelling hairdressers, pedlars or medicine hawkers. The first necessity is a proper census, which is a very large undertaking in an administratively weak society. So it is very seldom carried out in good time; that is, during the stage of subversion, before the revolutionary organization has established its own quasi-State in the villages and set up its armed bases outside.

The census must be accompanied by the issue of identity cards of a comparatively foolproof kind; that is, including not only a photograph and relevant particulars (which can be altered) but a fingerprint. Such ID cards should be obligatory at least for everyone over sixteen years of age.[26] An index should be established at the various administrative levels. This is itself a considerable undertaking. The revolutionary organization will of course try to register its own personnel, but this can be made

25. S. P. Huntington, *Political Order in Changing Societies*, p. 6.

26. Since one of the many atrocious features of revolutionary insurgency has in recent years involved the increasing use of young children in terrorist or Intelligence activities, the age-limit should almost certainly be lower, disagreeable as the notion is.

dangerous by requiring that everyone who registers be vouched for by at least two local people outside his own family, with severe penalties for anyone supplying a false reference. Even assuming that an administration has the resources for carrying out such a measure of population control, which is a large assumption, it must, if it is to be truly effective, be carried out before the parallel hierarchies have been inserted into the villages. Otherwise the penalties threatened by the revolutionaries will always be at least equal to the worst penalty the government can threaten and almost invariably will be much more severe.

For such an identification system to be wholly effective in detecting the unusual movements or journeys of revolutionary agents, an efficient national police force enjoying decent relations with the village or hamlet community is also required. This again involves a great effort on the part of the administration to train its police force properly; and to see to it that neither the police nor other government (or quasi-government) officers enjoy undue privilege or exact undue remuneration from the people-at-large. There will always be a certain amount of 'present-giving' in poor societies; this kind of 'corruption' (as men from the affluent West like to call it) has a functional utility. But the moment it ceases to be a transaction and becomes an exaction by the privileged representative of a distant and distrusted 'Centre', then it creates a 'contradiction' that can easily be exploited by revolutionary agents. It is therefore obvious that the more a village society can be administered through the participation of locals the better.

It also makes it all the more important to break up the revolutionary organization in its embryonic stage and before arms have been made available to would-be insurgents. The government should at all costs try to avoid a situation which necessitates the appearance of the regular army. This for a simple reason: permanent policemen or other officials usually have to avoid undue rapacity or oppression towards the village society in order to establish some kind of tolerable life amongst the locals. Even if they do overstep the limits, since they are in the area for a considerable period, if they are not locals (and there are arguments against having local police), their misdemeanours have a chance of being detected by authority or the villagers have some chance of making persistent complaints.

With the appearance of the army, the situation is all too often dramatically transformed in the subversive organization's favour. Chickens are stolen, girls are molested, transistors disappear, bicycles are ridden away. The subversive revolutionary agents know that at all costs they must never behave in this way: they want men's souls, not their chickens. The trouble is that in countries where arms are available it is not very difficult to use them in such a way as to provoke the appearance of the army.

The next step, and it is a deadly one, is to persuade at least some of the outraged villagers to prepare booby traps for the next army visit; or to fire from cover on the army unit as it next approaches. Unless the army unit has been very well schooled in counter-insurgent techniques, it is all too likely to call for an air or artillery strike or at least use its own automatic weapons in a promiscuous fashion. The psychological damage done is exceedingly difficult to repair.

Thus the disarming of all 'private' elements in the population is a task of very great importance. But this has very often been impossible since the Second World War because of the arms lost or distributed during that war. It has therefore usually been possible in South East Asia – and in most subverted areas of Africa, the Middle East and Latin America for that matter – to back subversive activity in carefully chosen outback areas with armed propaganda, as the Communists call it.

In such a case the incumbent administration's task is doubly difficult: it risks either causing (or dramatically reinforcing) local disaffection by the rough entry of its forces into village life or, on the other hand, by failing to assert its armed authority, giving the impression of being so weak as to be unable to give protection against the expanding, armed quasi-society of the revolutionary guerrillas.[27]

27. '. . . it seems clear that the peasant's estimation of the Government's authority and desirability would hinge on the effectiveness of the administration. If the Government proved unable to protect him and his family, then it

Once the armed struggle is under way, a determined government, particularly of a fairly recently independent country, is apt to run a much more profound risk: the creation of a very unattractive, organizationally inferior replication of the armed revolutionary quasi-State against which it is fighting. This has been noticed in the case of the Kuomintang and discussed in the case of Diem's Vietnam.

This replication effect is extremely difficult to avoid once the struggle has reached the stage of widespread revolutionary guerrilla warfare, which is why it has been emphasized on a number of occasions that the only truly successful counter-insurgency is one that has prevented the insurgency occurring. The Malayan experience may seem to controvert this argument, but it does not really do so, since the situation in Malaya was never really other than a very adverse political situation with a high violence component. This would be the situation over most of South Vietnam today if it were not for the continued attempt at conquest by the North Vietnamese army. In the meantime however there has occurred this partial replication effect without being matched by a Communist-style command system at the centre of government; nor an ideological under-pinning.

To return to the problem of administration at the stage when subversion is being used to create the organization necessary for guerrilla warfare: clearly the struggle is not simply political and administrative; it is also at *this* stage a competition for 'hearts and minds', unless the government is prepared to leave the field open to the revolutionaries. What can the government do to cut the ground from under the revolutionary efforts on the economic and social plane?

Before attempting to discuss this, it must be realized that the revolutionaries have the great advantage of being able to make quite extravagant promises for the future, while plausibly insist-

---

was, presumably, no longer blessed by the 'mandate' [of Heaven] . . . Provided authority afforded protection, and did not interfere too closely in the daily habits of the village, it was acceptable' (Osborne, *Strategic Hamlets*, p. 20).

ing that the promises cannot be made good until the present administration has been got rid of. The administration, on the other hand, will be judged by the record it establishes, not by its promises. This means that in the matter of what has come to be called 'civic action' the government is likely to be faced with a task that will not only strain its administrative resources but be extremely expensive. It is a very dubious approach to concentrate civic action resources in certain narrowly defined areas in response to reports of subversion, since such concentration is likely to create a further 'contradiction' to be exploited, between the suddenly favoured areas and equally poor or otherwise disadvantaged areas in the vicinity. Moreover such responsive action might well seem to put a premium on expressions of disaffection. It is nevertheless sometimes deemed necessary.

There is another reason why narrowly conceived responsive exercises in civic action should whenever possible be eschewed: such responses are all too apt to be over-generous in the short run, thus raising expectations of a kind that could not possibly be fulfilled in the foreseeable future. Or, alternatively, such responses are apt to concentrate on an impressive but very temporary assembling of various forms of aid and assistance, which then have to be shuffled hurriedly elsewhere, leaving the original recipients more dissatisfied than ever.

However, to avoid this kind of mistake the government has, of course, to involve itself in undertakings of such a large and expensive kind as to create a national economic strain without extensive foreign assistance. (Which means the presence of foreign advisers, who introduce another 'contradiction' to be exploited by the revolutionaries, though discreet behaviour can mitigate this disadvantage.) But the government's problems do not end there; since most subversion nowadays is carried out through armed propaganda teams, the government has to spend very large sums in order that the people in friendly villages can protect themselves and where necessary be protected by government forces. No aid and assistance imaginable can stabilize a rural situation in which the people are helpless before armed reprisals, (see 'Terrorism', pp. 348–357).

Where agricultural distress is a major 'contradiction' to be exploited, as it is in so many vital areas of revolutionary campaigning, the expense involved in rectifying the situation is very considerable too. Even if the larger landholders are to be compensated chiefly through government bonds and penalized for past misdemeanours in the taxation field (as was done in at least one Latin American land re-distribution), the task allotted to the Land Office is likely to strain the resources of the bureaucracy, as is the creation of a proper system of rural credit (see 'Land and Peasantry', below).

On the other hand, the overheads of the revolutionaries are very small indeed. This is not just because they are, for the time being (as they believe), living 'selflessly' amongst the people without expecting any privileges. It is also, as has been pointed out, because their introduction of very moderate medical aids and their participation in bridge-repairing or harvest-gathering can quite convincingly be represented as only an earnest of much more to come once their organization has replaced the present regime. This position of psychological advantage also permits the revolutionaries to concentrate on carefully selected target areas in a way not open to the government.

It has been argued that there is an asymmetrical relationship between the revolutionary movement and the incumbent government in the sense that revolutionary wars or insurgent situations are created by the revolutionaries; the government responds but cannot initiate.[28] In a political sense this is doubtless true – true by definition, one might almost say – but at least to some extent it obscures the nature of the problem as it exists at the subversive stage, since the revolutionary organization undoubtedly builds itself in new localities through the exploitation of 'contradictions'. Many of these contradictions are inherent in the process of what is vaguely called 'modernization'; others are very unlikely to have been removed *in toto* by even the most energetic administration of a developing country – again, by definition, one might say, since one of the most important tests

28. See for example, David Galula, *Counter-Insurgency Warfare*, Pall Mall Press, 1964.

of development pertains to the quality of the administration itself.

But it can also be said with some certainty that one of the tests of development, or, if it is preferred, modernization, is the ability of the central government and its administration adequately to communicate with the people; to make it clear to the people-at-large that government policies are purposeful in a special sense: in the sense that they are responsive to the properly articulated needs of the people-at-large.

No Western democratic government, in this age of increasing bureaucratization and rising expectations, anything like succeeds in this task of communication for more than a few years. To succeed adequately in societies where the feeling of participation in the making of the larger national policies has never existed is something quite beyond any government. The Communist totalitarian governments do not have to be unduly troubled by this problem since their disposition of the agencies of State power, particularly those of an Intelligence-gathering kind and the coercive apparatus that complements them, is so overwhelming as to be able to destroy in advance any kind of disaffection at the lower levels of the command system. The only threat to such a regime lies in a 'palace revolution', as was the case with the Nazi regime.

The governments of countries, whether in South East Asia or Africa or Latin America, which are based upon some kind of consensus between groupings with their own special ambitions – however authoritarian such governments may appear to be in good liberal eyes – are not at all in the same position of power. And this is partly, though in an important sense, a problem of communication. The sort of government that is being considered may be achieving far more in economic and social terms for the people-at-large than a Communist government could. But it has inherited a tradition of extreme reserve, if not downright mistrust, on the part of village society towards *any* kind of central government. Thus when it interferes in village life, even for the most 'progressive' reasons, its interference is interpreted by the village society as an encroachment of central power of the traditional kind – which was of a kind generally concerned to increase oppression and central aggrandizement and was virtually never concerned with popular welfare as such (see 'Communications and Intelligence' below).

Now it may be argued that the government should approach this problem of communication with the villager in the way the Communist revolutionaries do; that is, through the implanting of agitational-propagandists on the grass-roots level. Superficially such an argument may appear attractive. But it is necessary to consider what would be involved in such an approach; and here one comes back to what has been described as the replication effect. How is it possible to adopt such an approach without creating another kind of totalitarian system?

It is perhaps worth spelling out this dilemma a little. If elements of the government apparatus – or quasi-governmental agencies created specially for the purpose – are to approach the issue of economic and social 'contradictions' in the countryside in the same way as the Communists do, then certain things follow: those invited to engage in such grass-roots agitational-propaganda activities must, most of them anyway, be indoctrinated in an ideology promising their advancement in a necessarily undefined future society of a kind they cannot expect in the existing society. Otherwise, why should they undergo the kind of privations that would be required of them? They have their futures already mapped out in terms of the existing order.

In order to indoctrinate men in such a way as counter-cadres, so to speak, the government – or rather a very small élite within it – would have to subvert in some way the existing consensus between variegated political groupings upon which the political stability of the regime was based. In order to do this it would have to move towards totalitarian control, conjure up an ersatz ideology and a new kind of 'party', and thereby subvert all the living traditions of the nation. Moreover, by creating this kind of cadre-organization it would destroy in village society every living link with the civilized modes of behaviour the society in question had evolved over hundreds of years of human experience. This would be so simply because traditional village society would be torn apart by the conflict between the two grass-roots totalitarian organizations. Even those modes of behaviour most susceptible of modification according to the needs of modernization would be utterly shattered; and everything noble and compassionate, or even indifferent, that had made life somewhat tolerable for the people-at-large would have been ground into dust under the feet of two competing totalitarian societies.

And yet the problem of communication remains in societies which are chiefly agricultural: the government's authority has for hundreds of years (in Asia anyway), except in the matters of 'taxation' or forced labour (*corvée*), been assumed to end at the village hedge or ditch.

## COMMUNICATIONS AND INTELLIGENCE

Jomini, writing of the Spanish guerrilla war, drew attention to certain facts of the situation:

> Each armed inhabitant knows the smallest paths and their connections; he finds everywhere a friend who aids him . . . and learning immediately the slightest movement on the part of the invader, can adopt the best measures to defeat his projects. The enemy, without information . . . and certain of safety only in the concentration of his own columns, is like a blind man . . . No army, however disciplined, can contend successfully against such a national resistance unless strong enough to hold all the essential points . . . cover its own communications and . . . furnish an active force sufficient to beat the enemy wherever he may present himself . . . If this force has a regular army . . . around which to rally the people, what force will be sufficient to be superior everywhere and to assure the safety of the long lines of communications?[29]

If Napoleon was right in arguing that modern war-making is based on the science of communications, then it may be said that this applies equally to revolutionary guerrilla warfare and counter-insurgency. The Second Indo-China War has very clearly demonstrated the inefficacy of large-scale 'search-and-destroy' operations against presumed enemy base areas, which

29. Quoted in Ropp, *War in the Modern World*, op. cit., p. 127.

have nearly always been substantially evacuated before the regular forces arrived on the scene. (Which is not to say that strong reactive forces may not have to be used in priority operations against revolutionary mainforce moves when the situation has deteriorated to the extent it had by 1965: the enemy then was beginning to mount the third, mobile-war phase of their attempt to subjugate the country. Nor is it to say that large-scale operations against fixed base areas in 'privileged sanctuaries' such as were provided by the former Cambodian regime are unwise. Such operations are essential; only political lunacy or the location of the sanctuaries inside the territory of a major power could delay them.)

If guerrillas are simply concerned to make life so uncomfortable for an occupying army as to induce it to go away, the communications problem is chiefly one for the occupying army. But this is not at all the case with revolutionary guerrilla warfare, in which the revolutionary guerrilla units' links with the political infrastructure are vital to the movement as a whole. To destroy the movement the counter-insurgent must master the science of communications in a number of different forms.

He must in the first place address himself to cutting communications between the villages and the guerrilla forces. This is certainly not done in the early stages by winning the 'hearts and minds' of the majority of people in the area and waiting for them to provide information. Information supplied in this way is a measure of the success of the counter-insurgent effort, but it does not for a long time contribute to that success. So long as the people-at-large feel themselves caught between two competing armed forces, with the outcome of this confrontation seeming unclear, people will not talk.

Security comes first; voluntary information comes later. In order to begin breaking the links between the village infrastructure and the armed guerrillas the first thing that must be done is to implement a rigorous system of population and resources control. This enables the security forces patiently to observe those locals who are behaving unusually, moving about at odd hours or in areas unconnected with their employment. If such people prove as a result of covert observation to be contacting guerrillas through a 'jungle post-box' or in other ways, then when the moment is judged ripe they are 'fingered' by the Special Branch or other counter-Intelligence organization and psychologically handled (most emphatically not tortured) in such a way as to induce their co-operation in building up a general picture of the two arms of the revolutionary movement and the links between them. What is done with such information is a highly technical art: it may be used for a long time only in order to fill out the general picture, then later to create more double-agents; later still come the arrests and the ambushes, the latter sometimes themselves being of great value in further building up the picture of the organization and detecting the contact points.

Resources control is important in a number of ways too. It not only can make life very miserable for the guerrillas in terms of food supplies and medical equipment but the checking system involved in controlling resources, if it is implemented very thoroughly, leads to the revealing of the identities of supporters who can be exploited as explained above. The central purpose of the various control and Intelligence activities must be directed towards the destruction of the clandestine organization, and towards nothing else. Thus it is absolutely essential that all the Intelligence-gathering agencies should be co-ordinated and centrally controlled in such a way that the political objective never becomes subordinated to the military.

This may seem obvious enough, but it does not by any means always work out this way. For example, military commanders have a natural bias towards using military Intelligence for purposes that will enhance their reputations and the reputations of their units. But this may be quite the wrong way of using information obtained by military Intelligence itself in terms of the central objective: to destroy the revolutionary organization. However, the situation in many countries of the Third World (though certainly not only of the Third World) is for a proliferating number of Intelligence agencies to compete and even to spend more time spying on each other than on the revolutionary organization. This was for a long time the situation in South Vietnam.

It is in this respect that the political stability and coherence of the incumbent regime is of very great importance. If various political factions are struggling for power in such a fashion as to make the future of a government under insurgent attack problematical or if such faction fighting fractures the loyal unity of members of the central government, then Intelligence agencies become wielders of power by ambitious individuals and co-ordination becomes impossible.[30] Once again it should be emphasized what a great organizational advantage is enjoyed by either a Communist *or* a colonial regime over the government of a country new to democracy yet committed to the democratic party system in conditions of insurgency. Equally, of course, in a new or quasi-democracy lacking a tradition of non-political bureaucratic service to the State, the concentration of secret Intelligence in the hands of one man is a very dangerous business. Hence the desirability of some kind of 'committee system' on the various levels of the counter-insurgent command system.

But even leaving aside the problems of human weakness, the co-ordinated collation, evaluation and use of Intelligence is not an easy thing to achieve. For example in the South Vietnamese province of Phuoc Tuy the following forces and agencies gathered Intelligence: the Australian Task Force, the Provincial Reconnaissance Unit, the Police Field Force, the National Police, the Police Special Branch, the Military Security Section, the Regional and Provincial Forces, the village Popular Self-Defence Forces, the Pacification Security Co-ordination, Revolutionary Development cadres, Information Service, Political Warfare Service, Psychological Operations, the Chieu Hoi (Surrenderers) Centre, and the PIOCC/DIOCC (the organization specifically assigned the task of winkling out the Vietcong infrastructure in the so-called 'Phoenix Programme'). It was late in 1970 before a Joint Intelligence Centre got under way, and then it was on a liaison basis rather than on a basis of adequate co-ordination and central direction.

30. This failure of co-ordination is much worse when *coups* are in the air.

Sometimes there are extremely important Intelligence coups – the capture of the Party headquarters in Manila, the seizure of the Mau Mau order of battle during a search in Nairobi in 1954 and the capture of a terrorist in Aden in 1965, for example[31] – but such happenings are rare. The destruction of a revolutionary movement is nearly always a very long-drawn-out business once the organization has inserted itself into the fabric of rural society. But the business is much more prolonged if efforts are dispersed.

However, an efficient Special Branch can prevent a subversive movement from developing into an armed insurgency if it knows what it is about. This was the case with one of the greatest of counter-Intelligence *coups* in South East Asia: the arrest of the Comintern agent Joseph Ducroux, in Singapore in 1930. He made a full confession and gave away the Communist network over a large area of East and South East Asia. The rebuilding of the networks took many years and fourteen leading Malayan Communists were arrested.[32]

It might be noticed again that one of the very unpleasant aspects of partisan warfare in recent decades has been the increasing extent to which young, sometimes very young, children have been recruited not only into Intelligence but also sabotage and booby-trap activities. The practice is not of course new in itself but the extent of it certainly is. It was a very common ploy amongst the Soviet partisans;[33] and its frequency in South Vietnam undoubtedly in part created the predisposing conditions for the My-Lai atrocity. (This is not in any way to offer an excuse for My-Lai, but it is to suggest very strongly that the 'mobilization' of children to throw hand-grenades into crowds, as has happened, is to go far beyond using them for Intelligence purposes. Unfortunately, no distinction has been drawn by the Viet Cong.) (See 'Terrorism', below.)

31. Paget, op. cit., p. 163.

32. Hanrahan, op. cit., p. 13. Cf. 'The first and most important of the prerequisites to success [in countering subversion] is, I regret to say, an efficient secret police, or "Special Branch" to use the delicate British colonial term for it' (Dr Goh Keng Swee, Singapore's Minister for Defence and Interior, in *Communism in Asia*, Australian Institute of Political Science, Angus & Robertson, Sydney, 1967, p. 53).

33. See for example, Dixon and Heilbrunn, op. cit., pp. 50–52.

So far as military communications are concerned, from the revolutionary guerrilla point of view, the aim is to use superior Intelligence, mobility and knowledge of the terrain to strike at the weak points of regular forces using modern transportation and dependent upon heavy infusions of weapons, ammunition and supplies. The ambush of convoys and even motorized columns of the French Expeditionary Corps was a major feature of the First Indo-China War.

It is now a century since partisans pitted themselves against an army relying in a very large way on technical developments. In the Franco-Prussian War bridges were numerously attacked, German army telephone wires cut and railway travel made so hazardous as to provoke the placing of French hostages of some notability on railway engines. 'The whole secret of the art of war lies in making oneself master of the communications' is a maxim difficult to apply in the case of a determined and well-organized guerrilla campaign, as another German army found in Russia. In July 1941 Hitler believed that 'The partisan war ... has some advantage for us; it enables us to eradicate everyone who opposes us.' But by September 1942 the reading of the situation was very different: 'The bands in the East have become an unbearable menace during the last few months, and are more seriously threatening the supply lines to the front.'[34]

However, where guerrillas have come to rely upon infusions of modern weaponry and infiltration of allied troops, they too have supply lines open to attack. As Sir Robert Thompson has pointed out, every two hundred men require at least five tons of rice (more in paddy form) per month on the march. 'This logistical problem is the weakest link in the infiltration chain and should be the government's initial target.'[35]

During the Second Indo-China War the infusion of arms became of very great importance indeed to the insurgent forces. Very large arms shipments were brought by sea to the port of Sihanoukville in neutral Cambodia, moved to privileged sanctuaries in the Cambodian–Vietnamese border area, and then moved to the fighting units in South Vietnam. The disruption of these

34. ibid., p. 55. 35. Thompson, op. cit., p. 154.

sanctuaries, though undertaken too late to be wholly effective (the lateness being the result of the great propaganda campaign on the U S home front), inflicted a severe setback to the North Vietnamese–Vietcong campaign to subjugate the country. But long before the Second Indo-China War attained its full fury, the so-called Ho Chi Minh Trail – really an intricate network of trails and roads – had been developed in order not only to infuse vast quantities of arms but very large numbers of North Vietnamese to subjugate the country. But growth in this traffic, after the destruction of the Cambodian bases, compelled President Nixon in December 1970 to order a great increase of bombing the network and to threaten to bomb military sites if Hanoi appeared to be developing a capacity to increase the fighting in the South. By that time the war in South Vietnam had become overwhelmingly a matter of outright invasion by North Vietnam, the Vietcong having been forced to return to low-profile guerrilla war of a kind that was by then basically really only a mass terrorist campaign.

The Vietcong has also developed the use of radio communications, as have the South Vietnamese local anti-guerrilla forces. This is a significant advance on the Malayan Emergency, in which Central Committee directives often took six months to reach the guerrilla platoons. It is also an advance since the days of Diem's regime, when strategic hamlets themselves had to rely on runners to summon aid in the case of a Vietcong attack.

The increased use of radio communications makes important the technique of monitoring. This too was a feature of partisan warfare in the Soviet Union during the Second World War. The partisans became so adept at monitoring German telephone conversations that the Germany army 'discouraged the use of the telephone altogether and imposed special security measures for telephone conversations'.[36]

The monitoring of government radio communications in rural outposts in South Vietnam throws light on the necessity of meshing agencies into the one command structure. On occasion three separate channels of radio communication were used, not

36. Dixon and Heilbrunn, op. cit., p. 64.

only back to various base headquarters but in order for the representatives of the three separate agencies/forces to communicate with each other *within* the base under attack!

Of course in a revolutionary guerrilla war the most important aspect of communications is not any of the technical devices employed but rather the total impact made upon the people by the contending forces. Whispered warnings after an exemplary assassination may be very much more effective in this regard than the loudest mechanical hailer ever invented. A Province Chief who really understands the people in his charge is a better communicator than millions of leaflets dropped from on high. The exploitation by word of mouth of an incident involving the ugly misbehaviour of an Allied soldier towards a Vietnamese girl may be far more effective than the provision of many truckloads of badly needed Allied supplies can ever be used to exploit contradictions between the people and the Vietcong.

However, the communications struggle is joined long before the armed insurgency is mounted. During the period of subversion the communications struggle on the village level is analogous to the later country-wide struggle: the government tries to communicate with the village leadership in such a way as to obtain their support in implementing its policies, while the revolutionary agents try to enlist villagers who are (normally) necessarily relatively far removed from the village ruling circle.

Villagers chosen by the revolutionaries are not chosen at random but as a result of careful study. Resentments, frustrations, ambitions, grievances are singled out for psychological exploitation. The source of the villager's discontent is patiently identified by the agent while he seeks to help the villager in practical ways. The aim of the operation is to make the villager believe that his grievance can be redressed or his frustration removed only by a radical alteration of the village system. Then he must be persuaded to commit himself, perhaps only in very innocuous ways at first, against the village system. The operation is completed when or if the villager is persuaded irretrievably to involve himself on the side of the revolutionary movement by committing an act explicitly and overtly hostile to the village system. It is this face-to-face communication that is truly effective. Other forms of propaganda, such as leaflets or 'information' transmitted by a clandestine radio station and received from now very widely owned transistor sets, are not of comparable significance, though they may help set the face-to-face communication in the right general 'atmosphere' (see also 'Motivation and Mobilization', above).

The communicational problem is much the same for the government. The propaganda media can create an atmosphere favourable to more direct forms of communication designed intimately to affect the views and behaviour of village leaders (provided it is consistently truthful about the situation, particularly in regard to security matters). But it is not the case that village leaders are interested in *national* plans as such: they are simply interested in how such plans are designed to help their own village. It is local irrigation, local marketing facilities, local grain prices and so on that are of interest. Hence the desirability of letting villages choose their own projects, wherever possible, as is now the case in South Vietnam, and supply funds and materials in proportion to the village's own contribution. It is very important for the communicational relationship between government and village leadership that the latter should feel they are themselves playing a somewhat constructive role.

This relationship cannot be established through the mass media; it can be established only by the government's representatives in the countryside and through face-to-face discussion in the village environment. But once again it has to be stressed, that if this relationship is to be altogether successful, it must be established before the village has been effectively penetrated by revolutionary parallel hierarchies allied with armed guerrilla units and disposing of terrorist squads – squads which are capable of exerting pinpoint coercion against individual members of a village leadership that seems to be lining up with the government, or organizing against the revolutionary organization in the name of the old traditional manner of ordering village affairs.

Communication between government and villages is usually effectively broken by the time the counter-insurgents are studying wall maps dotted with coloured pins, because '. . . a map does not indicate the gangrene which works in the mind of the inhabitants. It does not portray the real state of the country, the atmosphere in which the friendly or enemy units live and the population, sympathetic or hostile.'[37] Only persistent communication can do that.

## STRATEGIC HAMLETS

A decision to build strategic hamlets or 'new villages' on a large scale in heavily populated areas is an admission that the country has been deeply subverted and that the armed guerrilla forces *are* able to exert pinpoint coercion against village leadership. But, as Sir Robert Thompson has pointed out, they need not be defensive in concept: 'If the programme is strategically directed, and supported by the armed forces, it becomes an offensive advance which will wrest the military initiative from the enemy. This is far more aggressive, because it is effective, than launching thousands of operations with hundreds of troops in each, all wading through the paddy fields with their rifles cocked to no purpose.'[38]

In Malaya in the 1950s the strategy worked; in South Vietnam in the 1960s it did not. There were a number of reasons for the very different outcome of two schemes which were substantially of the same kind: timing, priority, scale, phasing, arming, communications, population control, hamlet security, central government authority and the working outwards from secure base areas. These factors varied in their application in the two campaigns, both designed to provide security through constructing defensible villages and cutting the links between the revolutionary infrastructure in the villages and the guerrillas outside, hence exposing the guerrillas to the full weight of the government's politico-military offensive.

In regard to timing, the difference was not so great. The decision to resettle some half a million people in the Malayan new

37. McCuen, *The Art of Counter-Revolutionary War*, op. cit., p. 78.
38. Thompson, op. cit., p. 126.

villages was dilatorily made as was the decision in South Vietnam. But timing has to be related to the capacity of the government to select priority areas and the proportion of the population involved in some manner or other in the insurgency. The fact that half the Malayan population could not be subverted by what was in effect a Chinese Communist party permitted a bad area like Johore to be selected as a priority target for resettlement.[39] In South Vietnam, where the revolutionary forces were proportionate to those in Malaya at the commencement of resettlement, it was deemed necessary to cover a very large proportion of the population. Thus, whereas it took three years in Malaya to get 500 new villages properly under way, the Diem government of South Vietnam attempted to build some 12,000 strategic hamlets in two years and did, after a fashion, build some 8,000 in under two years, the majority of them in the first nine months of 1963.[40] The planned total of 11–12,000 envisaged protecting the entire population. Vietnamese figures for this period are very unreliable, but claims that between 4½ and 7 millions were living in strategic hamlets, started or completed, were made in October 1962.[41] Thus a much *less* efficient administration was attempting something on a vastly *greater scale* than had been attempted in Malaya.

Consequently the programme was not properly phased: it was altogether over-extended and left many hamlets vulnerable to enemy attack. Sir Robert Thompson, as Head of the British Advisory Mission, disagreed with General Harkins, the American Chief, when the latter made his much-referred-to statement that the Vietcong was losing the war in 1963:

> Thompson did not agree with General Harkins's flat statement that 'the Viet Cong are losing' because he felt it was premature ... Thompson's experience with Communist insurgency in Malaya had impressed him with the volatility of a situation involving guerrilla

39. Even in the case of Johore there was a lapse of over two years before presentation of the first resettlement report and the completion of resettlement (Osborne, pp. 14–15).

40. Thompson, op. cit., p. 141.

41. Osborne, op. cit., p. 35.

war; the progress of one July could easily be reversed by the next – especially if Hanoi decided to increase dramatically the number of hard-core units sent south (as it so developed in 1964 and 1965). But Thompson certainly did not feel that the war in Vietnam was being lost. Indeed, [he] . . . said that the improvement in 1962 and 1963 was far greater than he had anticipated.

'The way I would put it,' said Thompson, 'is that at last I can see light at the end of the tunnel.'

In the delta, Thompson's principal concern was that the strategic hamlet program was overextended; too many had been established without prospect of adequate defense in case of attack . . . The spectacle of too many hamlets vulnerable to attack and too few troops to defend them finally persuaded the most ardent supporters of the hamlet scheme that Thompson was right.[42]

One consequence of this overall extension of the programme was inadequate arming of the villages and an inadequate organization and employment of the hamlet militia. Osborne even cites a proposal that strategic hamlets should be armed by the government for six months and then left to defend themselves with captured arms.[43] Thompson observed that hamlet militias were too often exposed to attacks of a kind with which they could not be expected to cope; were made to work too long hours for no pay in a rigid and unsupervised manner. 'Even so, they did their best, and over 150,000 volunteered. Although there were some defections and disasters, the vast majority fought valiantly and suffered heavy casualties.'

In the case of attack, communications were for some time by runner only; and even after radios were installed it was very often possible for the Vietcong to overrun ill-fortified hamlets so

42. Higgins, *Our Vietnam Nightmare*, op. cit., pp. 116–17.

43. In terms of revolutionary warfare the notion would not be altogether absurd: establishing a symbiotic relationship with the administration and its resources is part of the name of the game. But sedentary Home Guards, unless backed by an extremely good Intelligence service, in conditions where the army is constantly harassing the larger guerrilla formations, cannot be expected to gain many arms. This is simply because the guerrillas can carefully prepare attacks on selected villages with the appropriately overwhelming force.

quickly as to put the radio out of operation as the primary objective. Moreover, the creation of the strategic hamlets was not meshed in with a programme for controlling persons and supplies. This was an extremely serious gap in government strategy: agents and couriers moved at will and transport was freely used to move supplies.

But the defects of the programme did not end there. The criteria for the building of strategic hamlets were as follows: that the Communist infrastructure had been eliminated; that the local people had been organized into their own associations and knew precisely what the tasks assigned to them were; that the defensive fortifications had been completed; and that the hamlet management board had been elected and the Village Charter had been promulgated.

These criteria were very seldom implemented. The village infrastructure just was not eliminated; the people were inadequately organized in associations which the regime attempted to impose from above instead of building from below; the overall organization seldom did make people understand what their functions were, apart from the wretched militia; the fortifications very often were not properly completed; and the secret election of the hamlet boards did not jell with the politically authoritarian approach of the Diem regime. The hamlets just did not develop that new and better life that was provided for in the philosophical outpourings of the Ngo brothers when they spoke about the programme.

On the other hand, the Communists did find the conception most alarming and the implementation of it distinctly frustrating for some time. The Australian journalist Wilfred Burchett, covering the war from the Communist standpoint, testifies to this on the basis of talks with Vietcong leaders in the field: 'If 1963 was [Vietcong] year, 1962 must be largely credited to Saigon. With US aid in men and materials pouring in from the end of 1961, a major effort was made to destroy and isolate the Front's armed forces, to push Front influence back from the gates of Saigon, and other provincial capitals and to re-instal Diemist power in the countryside ... The drive to set up "strategic hamlets" was also a problem for the NLF organizers and additional hardship for the population.'[44]

The theory was sound enough; it was the timing and implementation that was gravely at fault. Later refinements of this mode of countering revolutionary warfare have been discussed in Chapter 6.

## LAND AND PEASANTRY

In a Communist revolutionary struggle in the Third World the road from promises of land-to-the-tiller to the enforced collectivization of agriculture by the 'people's army', including coercion by artillery where necessary, is a long and tortuous one in some cases. It is presumably a very corrupting one for the Communist leaders, who deliberately mislead the peasantry over many years in order to mobilize them into a totalitarian society against which they have no possibility of protesting in their own interest.

Nevertheless revolutionary guerrilla wars are still often taken to be spontaneous expressions of peasant unrest by liberal circles in the West. That the unrest is there in many areas and that it is all too often altogether intelligible to anyone who cares to look at conditions is also a fact in the situation. The debate about the morality of revolutionary wars, so far as their opponents are concerned, should hinge on what the Communists do with these conditions of unrest. The conditions themselves must not be insouciantly ignored; nor should peasant habits which exacerbate the misery of their conditions be ignored.

In Central Luzon, where the Filipino Communist movement continues to be important, over half the 'farmers' in rich rice country are just sharecroppers working land that is often owned by absentees. A perfervid attachment to ancestral locality makes for seemingly endless subdivision; any kind of emigration to open up new land is beyond the imagination – except perhaps in the form of horrific nightmares – of very many such peasants, even though they may be touched by modernity to the extent of

44. W. G. Burchett, *Vietnam: Inside Story of the Guerrilla War*, op. cit., p. 243.

borrowing in order to send their sons to school. But such a concession to modernity is more than offset by traditional outlays on festivals and gambling – a disease endemic throughout South East Asia and in many other peasant communities. The result is a crushing debt most times, interest rates being astronomical in comparison with those obtaining in the West. The 'peasant' is thus placed in a position not only of great poverty but of permanent disadvantage in transactions with other members of society, from the village shopkeeper upwards.

During the last few years the Communist Huks, despite a division of commands as a result of the Revisionist-Maoist controversy, have been rebuilding a mass base. At the same time the Filipino government has been trying to implement its Central Luzon Development Programme (CLDP) which was initiated in mid-1966. The CLDP is hampered by lack of adequate funds and by a plethora of different development agencies (over forty). The plan, on paper, includes the very ambitious measures of abolishing share cropping tenancies and establishing privately owned farms of a family size. As well, the range of the other activities is very wide: the provision of agricultural incentives, public works and water resources development, health, education, a speedier administration of justice and the promotion of self-help projects with the aid of the armed forces employed in a civic-action capacity.

The success or failure of this programme will not be clear for some time to come, but it would seem obvious that in an area of such inequalities and disabilities as exist in Central Luzon land reform is of very great importance in resisting the expansion of revolutionary guerrilla warfare. But as has been shown in the case of the Communist area in north China at the time of the Japanese invasion and in the case of Tongking, land *ownership* is not always a central problem. Means other than a promise of land-to-the-tiller had to be adopted in order to mobilize the peasant masses so that their own people's army should later deprive them of their land. In the case of the earlier Filipino government campaign against the Huks, the land reform embarked on by Magsaysay was marginal to the land question itself, though quite significant in terms of Huk members. About a thousand families directly benefited, but the projects were undertaken in different areas of the country and 'did not in themselves make a significant contribution to the economic or social welfare of the country'.[45]

Land reform can be exaggerated in terms of countering the growth of a revolutionary guerrilla movement: its implementation, if it is not efficient and relatively speedy, can create other 'contradictions' to be exploited; and except where it is a mere granting of tenure to peasants already in effective occupation it is a socially dislocating process. It can easily give rise to resentments between, say (to take the case of the Philippines), tenants, settlers who move to newly opened, underdeveloped public land, agricultural wage-earners including migrant workers, and owner-farmers who are working rather more land than is stipulated as the landowning ceiling under the reform Act. And of course such a programme can provide – usually does provide, one might say – large opportunities for bureaucratic graft and hence another 'contradiction' ready-made for exploitation.

The Communist command system enables it to phase its land reform during the struggle in a fashion that is not open to less politico-militarized regimes. For example, the Vietminh at first protected landowners, except those denoted 'traitors' because of their absence and their presumed co-operation with the French. It was not until 1953 that the Vietminh went beyond a policy of reducing land rents and rates of interest. By then the politico-military organization felt it 'necessary to promote the accomplishment of anti-feudal tasks', as General Giap put it;[46] that is, larger landowners were dispossessed in what was certainly a brutal fashion. But this was simply a clearing away for the Land Reform, which was described by a former Vietminh official as 'in effect, the establishment of the "dictatorship of the proletariat" by the imposition of the Agricultural Tax and by a wave of terror'.[47] In view of the failure of collectivized agriculture

45. Valeriano and Bohannan, op. cit., p. 221.
46. *People's War, People's Army*, op. cit., p. 22.
47. Hoang Van Chi, op. cit., p. 41.

elsewhere, there is no reason to believe that the crushing of the peasantry by the Communist State machine, in particular that people's army which Giap believes to be ensouled by the Communist Party of Indo-China, was done in order to increase agricultural productivity; rather it was done in order to confer absolute power on the small band of professional revolutionaries who had come together to found the Party a quarter of a century earlier.

In the Cuban revolutionary guerrilla war, the role of land and peasantry seems to be a good deal more obscure in the period between the founding of the guerrilla base and the collapse of the Batista regime. As in Central Luzon there were good grounds for agricultural unrest, however much better the life of urban dwellers may have been in comparison with most other Latin American countries. A writer deeply unsympathetic to the Cuban regime that emerged out of this struggle described the situation thus:

> ... the peasants of Cuba were little more than serfs in the sense that they were bound to the land ... they worked only ten or twelve weeks of the year, during harvest time. And half a million of them – in a total population of 6½ millions – never worked at all ... about 80 per cent (in value) of the island's exports consisted of sugar; only a fifth of the sugar cane was grown on small plots owned by their farmers; three-quarters of the sugar was grown by tenants whose plots were owned by the big companies which decided both the rent paid by the tenants and the price paid to them for the sugar they grew.[48]

Nevertheless there is little reason to believe that the Castroite success was in any real sense the result of leading a peasant revolt or a revolt of landless and/or unemployed agricultural labourers. It has indeed been persuasively argued that Castro and his guerrillas did not include promises about a radical land reform in their propaganda but concentrated rather on offering a peace in which even the 'honest military men' of Batista's army could share abundantly.[49] The weight of agitational propaganda does seem to have fallen on troop proselytizing. This is not to say that

48. Crozier, *The Rebels*, op. cit., pp. 73–4.
49. Suarez, op. cit., pp. 36–7.

a judicious mixture of blarney and terrorism did not win support from the peasantry where this was necessary to protect the existence of the movement (see 'Terrorism', below). It is true that Huberman and Sweezy argue that:

> As the revolutionary army spread out over more and more territory, it introduced agrarian reform measures. Fidel tells about one of the early instances: When we arrived at the Sierra Maestra, we executed a ranch foreman who had accused tenant farmers and peasants of being pro-rebel, and who had increased the holdings of his landlord from 10 acres to 400 acres by taking the land of those he denounced. So we tried him and executed him and won the affection of the peasants.[50]

While that is doubtless land reform of a sort, it looks very *ad hoc* compared with the systematic approach of the Vietminh. But then it is almost certainly to be revealed in time that the Cuban revolutionary war was a pretty rum sort of affair: the collapse of a shoddy regime rather than its purposeful subversion through the introduction and expansion of parallel hierarchies and the large-scale weakening of traditional village authority, through the application of 'pinpoint coercion' against thousands of headmen, as was the case with the Vietcong.

However, after victory the Castroite regime began to create a myth of peasant rebellion brought about by efficient unnerving of the government armed forces by ambushes and their psychological disarming by certain propaganda techniques. It was the attempt to re-enact this false myth in Bolivian conditions through the catalytic agency of a technically skilled band of guerrilla desperadoes, many of foreign provenance, that was to cost Major Guevara his life.

However, the concluding stage of the 'agrarian revolution' was carried out very much in accordance with earlier Communist 'solutions' to this question. According to the Agrarian Reform Law of 1959, the inefficiency of the old system rather than its injustices was what had to be rectified. The ceiling for landholdings was very high (as high as 3,000 acres in some cases,

50. ibid., p. 58.

though generally 1,000). But this of course was only the beginning. The National Institute of Agrarian Reform (INRA), acting under the auspices of, and directly supported by, the 'people's army' began to expropriate the people's holdings in order to form co-operatives. 'The whole transaction is completely informal; there are no hearings, no inventories, no receipts. In some cases, if the owners are willing to accept INRA's offer, they may get paid in cash. No one has yet seen any bonds; the government says they are being printed.'[51] The people of Cuba had been effectively taken in hand by the 'people's army' and the 'people's State' after a less than exacting revolutionary war but with the same totalitarian results as in a number of other countries.

The role of land reform in any particular revolutionary war requires careful scrutiny. But, though it is not necessarily a crucial issue in itself, it can easily become exceedingly important if it is incessantly emphasized by the insurgents – particularly if their redistribution in temporarily controlled areas is reversed by absentee landlords returning in the wake of government reconquest. This has happened in South Vietnam frequently in the past. But it is an exceedingly unwise practice, to put it mildly, in a situation where the government is seeking to create a constituency for itself amongst the people-at-large.

As an observer of the Diem regime's attempt to organize the countryside against the Vietcong has written:

> In South Viet-Nam the lack of any long tradition of association between the peasants and the Government did not prevent an awareness that the central authorities were supported by a foreign power. The Government manifested its presence chiefly through the army and through forced resettlement. And it was the Government which, in the peasants' minds, represented the absentee landlords who sought rent on lands which the peasants had farmed without charge over many years. While the Saigon government might speak of the horrors of 'land reform' in the north, this was merely an abstraction.

51. Theodore Draper, quoted in Huberman and Sweezy, op. cit., p. 118. By the end of 1960 some three fifths of agricultural lands had come under INRA control.

The threat of having the landlords' power restored or having to pay rents on land which was tilled without rent costs was immediate.[52]

This has at long last been understood in governing circles in South Vietnam. Though the government had since 1968 been distributing land more quickly than in the past and had been granting credit facilities to peasants wishing to buy the plots they were working, it had not faced up to the political problem that was presented by Vietcong re-distribution of land. A new law introduced early in 1970 laid it down that anyone working rented or vacated land could lay claim to 2½ acres in Central Vietnam and 7½ acres in the Mekong Delta. But beyond that, the new law makes it clear that a person granted land by the Vietcong will be permitted to go on cultivating it after the area has been pacified; and after establishing legal tenancy, a process estimated to take a year, he can claim ownership.[53]

Of course, such a title will be truly meaningful only if the pacification is permanently successful. It is not a substitute for security, though it may well contribute to making local security an easier task. To recognize this technically illegal re-distribution of land or to grant ownership to people who have themselves occupied abandoned land is not at all the same thing as trying to implement a general programme of government-planned re-distribution in conditions of insurgency. As has been suggested above, that is a much more tricky matter and indeed one survey in South Vietnam came up with some interesting findings: the area most amenable to government control was a province 'in which population density is high, cross-country mobility is low, few peasants operate their own land, the distribution of farms by size is unequal, large estates (formerly French-owned and now primarily GVN run) exist, and no land redistribution has taken place.'[54]

Whatever the general relevance of these findings may be – and in matters of peasant life generalizations are not easily to be

52. Osborne, op. cit., p. 55.

53. *Economist*, 11 April 1970.

54. Edward J. Mitchell, in *Asian Survey*, Vol. VII, No. 8, August 1967, p. 580.

made – there can be little doubt about the validity of the dictum of one of the most distinguished counter-insurgent experts, Dr George Tanham: 'Without security, social, economic, and political measures cannot be taken except in a very limited and sporadic manner.'[55] It is in the light of this truth that one of Tanham's team in South Vietnam defined pacification in this manner: '. . . selection and training of cadres to assist the farmers in organizing new life hamlets; decentralization of responsibility and funds for hamlet construction; and the holding of elections and training of local officials to gain popular support for and participation in government. These various programmes are commonly called pacification activities, since their purpose is to secure the countryside and win the support of the rural people.'

'Land reform' is a term that is often carelessly and/or emotionally employed to obscure a complex of problems varying from region to region. Land hunger may be 'political dynamite' but only to the extent that it is purposefully used by a revolutionary organization that knows what it is about. For example, the Indian National Congress in British days, particularly as a result of the influence of Jawaharlal Nehru, laid great stress on the inequities resulting from what was known as the *zamindari* system – basically (if simplistically) describable as a system of landlords. After independence, laws were enacted abolishing this system and it was held by the Congress that millions of tenants had thereby been given a new deal. But the problem was not as simple as that. Despite legal ceilings, large landholdings remained in many areas; they were for the most part leased to tenants on a verbal basis that precluded any kind of secure tenure. Such tenants were held in economic bondage while the army of landless labourers grew larger. And yet it took the application of Maoist agitational propaganda by the so-called Naxalites for these often appalling conditions to be translated into violent political activity.

It is true that Naxalite 'mobilization of the masses' coincided with an exacerbation of the tenants' anyway parlous condition in many areas by the consequences of the introduction of high-yielding seed: eviction of tenants by landlords seeing new

55. *War without Guns*, op. cit., p. 35.

economic possibilities in doing their own farming or by enhancing rents. But if revolutionary guerrilla wars were the spontaneous reactions of country people-at-large to intolerable social and economic conditions, then in places like India (and in Pakistan) such conditions may be said to have existed for a very long time without any such 'spontaneous' risings occurring.

Anyway, as has been pointed out or intimated on a number of occasions, spontaneity is not regarded by revolutionary guerrilla leaders as anything other than something to be guarded against, and not just because of the tactical dangers presented by such disorganized political behaviour: spontaneity is the last thing required by those who have arrogated to themselves the task of guiding mankind along carefully defined party 'lines' so as to create a new kind of human being. Spontaneity is all too Adamic and hence subversive of those alterations to the human psyche which are proposed by these violent improvers of mankind.

As Chairman Mao has said, 'We support the peasants' demand for equal distribution of the land in order to help the broad masses of peasants to abolish the system of ownership by the feudal landlord class, but we do not advocate absolute equalitarianism. Whoever advocates absolute equalitarianism is wrong.' Which may be interpreted as: We Communists support the demand for equal distribution of land in so far as it helps our Party to assume total power, at which time our total power will be used in armed form to ensure that private ownership of land in any form that might permit the persistence of individuality will be obliterated.

## PHASES

Since revolutionaries plan revolutionary wars and governments respond to them as best they can, in the matter of phases or stages it is necessary to consider first how the revolutionaries see the development of the struggle. General Giap has put it this way:

> The general law of a long revolutionary war is usually to go through three stages: defensive, equilibrium and offensive. Fundamentally, in the main directions, our Resistance War also followed

this general law. Of course, the reality on the battlefields unfolded in a more lively and complicated manner.[56]

Giap's brief description substantially derives from the Maoist version of how a 'people's war' should develop. It is not really true that the first phase is defensive except in the sense that armed guerrilla units obviously must not be risked before the political preparation – in particular the insertion of the parallel hierarchies – is well under way and base areas established. It is a period that has been described by Giap in this fashion:

> The most appropriate guiding principle for activities was *armed propaganda: political activities were more important than military activities, and fighting less important than propaganda;* armed activity was used to safeguard, consolidate and develop the political bases. Once the political bases were consolidated and developed, we proceeded one step further to the consolidation and development of the semi-armed and armed forces. These had to be in strict secrecy with central points for propaganda activity or for dealing with traitors. Their military attacks were strictly secret and carried out with rapidity. Their movements had to be phantom-like. A position of legal struggle was maintained for the broad masses.[57]

This describes activities before the Japanese *coup* against the Vichy French regime of 9 March 1945, but it does describe the kind of activities that may be expected to be found before guerrilla war proper is mounted: propaganda, terror, arming of units, creation of political bases for the forthcoming struggle.

The period of contention is that of revolutionary guerrilla warfare proper: the weakening or rupture of enemy communications, increasingly large ambushing of his forces; the building-up of larger revolutionary forces with captured and/or infused weaponry; the building-up of larger and larger regular forces which enable mobile warfare gradually to be insinuated into the struggle; the mobilization of larger and larger numbers of the population into the Communist quasi-State; and the continued exploitation of contradictions, both internally and internationally (see 'Propaganda', above). In the course of time two different states are in effect at war with each other, often in a manner

56. *People's War, People's Army*, op. cit., p. 101.
57. ibid., pp. 78–9.

so volatile as to make it difficult to determine at any given moment which side is critically expanding, which contracting.

At this stage outside support becomes of very considerable importance in terms of arms and supplies and in terms of offering privileged sanctuaries for training and recuperation. Even General Giap was constrained to admit that the victory of the Chinese Communists 'exerted a considerable influence on the war of liberation of the Vietnamese people'.[58] Sometimes, as in South Vietnam in 1962–3, the infiltration of cadres and specialists, later even armed units, may become of considerable significance. But everything that can significantly be introduced from the outside is subordinate to the development of the internal revolutionary movement itself: it is significant only in so far as it can be *absorbed* into the movement and employed as part of a general strategy.

Once a revolutionary war has reached this stage of contention the government is presented with difficult decisions. It must begin by securing its own base areas; that is axiomatic. But if the government has permitted the war to reach this stage then even the pacifying of base areas may be an exacting task, demanding a large concentration of its available forces, thus permitting the insurgents to get a hold over other very considerable areas of the countryside. Deciding the maximum feasible size of the base areas is not simple. This is particularly the case if the revolutionary movement has built up formidable armed regular units in privileged sanctuaries which, supported by an infrastructure established even earlier, can launch punitive expeditions against the peripheries of the base areas. The tendency then is to launch major reactive campaigns during which armed guerrilla formations often can infiltrate the base areas.[59]

It is also much simpler for the revolutionary forces to stage diversionary movements, since they are not compelled – quite often are not seeking – to establish the same *kind* of political control as that to which the government forces are committed

58. ibid., p. 22.

59. As has been pointed out, this was a crucial factor in enabling the Vietminh to establish its regular units in thousands of hamlets in the Red River Delta during the First Indo-China War.

should they seek to expand. The revolutionary movement can where necessary content itself with permanently inserting only such covert force as is required to frighten the locals away from co-operating with the government forces. The government, on the contrary, is committed to providing security in zones into which it expands – permanent security if its credibility is not soon to be deeply undermined. This requires vastly larger forces and resources than is required for covert control measures. Theories about the ratio of security forces to guerrillas are often stated simplistically and hence misleadingly: such a ratio changes according to the course of the struggle and is a measure of the direction of the struggle. But generally speaking the security forces required are, during this stage of contention, very large indeed compared with the revolutionary forces.

In Malaya something of the order of 300,000 security personnel were brought to bear against some 7,000 guerrillas. (This is not to say that the Home Guard, for example, operated as a whole all the time. The reference is to forces at the disposal of the government.) The most spectacular claim, perhaps not surprisingly, has been made for the Cuban struggle: 'the Rebel Army, its chief [Castro] tells us, became invincible when it reached a ratio of one to 500.'[60] In Algeria nearly 1½ millions served 'in the forces of law and order' over the five years up to the end of 1959 against insurgent forces of the order of 30,000 men.[61] Over 60,000 security forces were required to put paid to some 12–15,000 Mau Mau tribals in Kenya.[62]

60. *Revolution in the Revolution?*, op. cit., p. 76. 'The government must, since it is the government, protect property owners; the *guerrilleros* don't have to protect anything anywhere. They have no dead weight. Therefore the relation of forces cannot be measured in purely arithmetical terms. In Cuba, for example, Batista could never utilize more than 10,000 out of his 50,000 men against the guerrillas at any one time.'

61. 'Our army in Algeria is in excess of 300,000 men supplied with the most modern equipment; its adversary numbers some 30,000 in general poorly equipped with only light weapons' (Trinquier, *Modern Warfare*, op. cit., p. 8). By 1959 some 182,000 Algerian Muslims were fighting on the French side (De Gaulle, Press Conference, 10 November 1959, *International Review Service*, New York, Vol. 6, No. 55).

62. Paget, op. cit., p. 36.

Of course, the ratio between government and guerrilla forces is not only not very meaningful because of its shifting nature but because stated baldly it ignores the all-important factor of the political base. It is here that the exceedingly disagreeable 'body-count' approach to measuring the efficacy of counter-insurgent progress is peculiarly misleading. For example, in 1964 the Viet-cong fighting force was estimated at about 35,000; it was also estimated to have suffered casualties between 15,000 and 20,000 in each of the preceding two years. But its area of control by this time embraced something of the order of five million people and hence it could not only keep up its armed numbers but could actually expand them through recruitment.[63]

Provided the level of violence is below that of a revolutionary guerrilla war proper, then 'cordons-and-searches' can be used very effectively against large numbers of people in order to winkle out the support structure or at least cut the links between this infrastructure and the armed guerrilla forces. This is particularly the case with a large urban concentration. For example, when it was known that some 30,000 Mau Mau sympathizers had moved into Nairobi (population 200,000) and were establishing their own 'courts' to 'try' recalcitrant members of the Kikuyu tribe, five battalions and part of the Kenya Regiment provided a surrounding screen which permitted the police to test the credentials of about 30,000 people in two weeks, half of whom were detained. The second phase of the operation involved issuing 'forgery-proof' identity cards. The link was cut, the higher command disrupted severely, the movement's hold over the city was permanently severed and a great deal of information about the movement was discovered.[64]

But once the stage of what Giap calls 'contention' has been reached, mere security operations of this kind are often rendered virtually impossible, since in order to have raised the struggle to this level the revolutionary guerrilla movement clearly must have got a grip on the initiative to such an extent as to be able to compel the use of the government's security forces for much less immediately rewarding, reactive tasks. Thus it may be said

63. Thompson, op. cit., p. 41.

64. Paget, op. cit., pp. 97–9.

not only (as has been said already, perhaps *ad nauseam*) that the only truly effective counter-insurgency is one that has prevented the stage of insurgency being reached but also that an even approximately successful counter-insurgency requires the destruction, or anyway very serious weakening, of the revolutionary movement before the stage of contention is fully reached. For example, the last chance the government of South Vietnam had of avoiding a truly terrible war was in about 1959, when the armed guerrillas numbered some 5,000 and their supporters about 100,000. The great effort was required then, not in 1961–2. That is not to say that the Diem regime could not still have won the war had it been more patient and thorough – and had its command system been a less pale replication of the Communist (or colonial) command system. But it is to say that by 1961–2 the stage of contention was being approached and hence the struggle must thereafter have been a very costly one.

By that stage the question is not only costliness in terms of human suffering but costliness of administration. Imperial governments learnt long ago that revolts of most kinds are so costly as to cause doubts at the metropolitan seat of power whether the operation is justified politically. For example, in March 1921 a statement of the Arab case for independence pointed out that Iraq, with a population of no more than 2½ millions, had a very large British garrison; Palestine had 50,000 troops for a population of 600,000; regions of Syria whose population was some two millions were garrisoned by 160,000 troops of the French Empire. The Iraqi revolt which began in mid-1920 cost the British government 40 million pounds to suppress, which was four times what they had spent on the whole Arab Revolt against the Turkish Empire during the First World War.[65]

Revolts of the new revolutionary kind, specifically designed to be protracted as a result of careful political preparation, are enormously expensive to put down. The Algerian War was estimated to cost France £1 million a day.[66] Even for imperial

65. Suleiman Mousa, *T. E. Lawrence: An Arab View*, Oxford University Press, 1966, pp. 236–7.

66. Paget, op. cit., p. 17.

powers the cost could come to be regarded as excessive in terms of a continuing national interest:

> Once again, as in Algeria and elsewhere, one of the effects of terrorism in Palestine was to force the responsible power into ever-mounting expenditure. On 20 May 1947, the assistant Secretary for Economic Affairs in the Palestine Administration announced that security would rise to an estimated £8 million in 1947, compared with £4.5 million in 1945. Mounting costs might have been borne, terrorist harassment withstood and American pressure resisted *if retention of the Mandate had been essential to Britain's security or economic survival*. But demonstrably it was not.[67]

If campaigns of this order can trouble the governments of empires, then clearly the cost of winning a struggle against a revolutionary guerrilla movement that has reached the stage of contention is likely to be far beyond the resources of most governments of recently independent, small countries. But of course the moment the governments of small countries find themselves in the position of having to call upon the assistance (and so upon the advisory teams) of the USA, the only Western nation which in recent years has had both the resources and the will to undertake such a task, then at that moment they become propaganda targets for the insurgent armoury in quite a new way – the manner in which Vietcong and Hanoi propaganda consistently linked Diem with the USA is instructive in this regard. They also become targets in the Western press on the ground that such a situation could not have arisen had they not been hopelessly corrupt and inefficient.

There is of course a kind of truth in this assertion, the kind of truth that resides in all tautological statements. If, say, the Diem regime had met all the desires, hopes and aspirations of the Vietnamese people within two years of its coming to power in the most difficult circumstances, then, by definition, there would have been no 'contradictions' for the Communists to exploit.

But in terms of actuality this is not really a very helpful approach. If corruption and inefficiency were the only terms of the problem, most of Asia, Africa, the Middle East and Latin

67. Crozier, op. cit., p. 187.

America would be engulfed by revolutionary guerrilla warfare. This may of course occur, but even if it did it would in no way prove what the supporters of a theory of spontaneous peasant revolt want to prove, since conditions of life in very many areas of the world have been, and are, much worse than they were in Malaya in 1948 and worse than in South Vietnam in 1959. The same may be said about corruption and inefficiency.

The course of a revolutionary insurgency depends upon a large number of factors besides the quality of the government under attack: the political system obtaining is an important one of them. Most governments of recently independent countries affect to represent 'The Nation' rather than a definable constituency but at the same time do not have at their disposal a public opinion articulated either through political parties or a responsible press. Very often the groups that call themselves political parties (and, if they employ the appropriate rhetoric, get themselves accepted as such in the West) are simply gangs out to seize total power themselves. The press also is very often in the hands of men out for total political power. The conduct of both is therefore subversive of the counter-insurgency and clearly cannot be permitted complete licence during the period of contention. They are thus further alienated and liable to argue that they have no other recourse but to establish links with insurgent groups, usually Fronts.

Such disaffected groups will quite likely have friends amongst ambitious army commanders who can be persuaded that errors in the counter-insurgent campaign or even defeats by the enemy are attributable to the 'oppressive' central political leadership rather than to themselves. The government, knowing this, begins to shift generals around for reasons of its own safety rather than the requirements of war-making, and more tensions are set up. The result is a command system altogether inadequate to the task of wresting control from the revolutionary insurgents during the period of contention. Another result may well be a jealous or fearful constricting of the opportunities of the ablest commanders on the government side.

So far as the disloyal opposition politicians and their newspaper-owning allies are concerned, restrictions on debate and censorship of the press often provoke more sinisterly disloyal activities of the kind just mentioned. This will quite likely result in imprisonment, or anyway house arrest, and a closing down of newspapers. Such moves are liable to provoke raucous opposition, in the name of democratic principles singularly incongruent with the stage of guerrilla contention, on the part of students, academics, newspapermen and religious groups, not to speak of people from all ranks of society who belong to the very close-knit families of those imprisoned. The government begins to harry them, or at least spy on them; the circles of opposition begin to expand and in most newly independent countries such circles are at least potentially subversive, not least because a framework of national loyalty embodied in institutional traditions has not been firmly built.

The kind of people affected by what they will call 'persecution' are the kind of people likely to have contacts with Western pressmen whose very professional instinct is ready-made for exploitation in such a situation. If the 'persecution' can be represented to be of a religious nature, as it spuriously was in the case of Diem's activities in South Vietnam in 1963, its reporting in the West is especially damaging to the government, since it conjures up pictures of a 'medieval' atmosphere of an altogether febrilely sinister kind. But even if the repression is simply of a political nature it is easily represented (by setting it in a Western-style democratic frame of reference which does not in fact exist) as behaviour which cannot be condoned by a Western democratic ally. Such newspaper articles, if reprinted in local newspapers or retailed in bookstores, are very dangerous for the incumbent government: they not only reduce its prestige amongst the 'intelligentsia' at a time of widespread war when prestige is a major factor in the struggle, they also suggest that the government's position is becoming precarious *vis-à-vis* such Western allies or supporters as it may have. This is especially the case because in most countries of the world the major Western newspapers are presumed to be the preserve of the Establishment and hence reflect – or possibly anticipate – government policy. So reporters are expelled; the situation in this regard worsens.

Clearly a government under widespread guerrilla attack, which is also in this kind of political situation, is extremely unlikely to be able to address itself to the implementing of a counter-insurgent strategy with the necessary purposefulness and single-minded consistency.

In the case of South Vietnam a direct relationship can be established between the ratio of arms lost to arms captured or otherwise recovered and the political stability of the South Vietnamese society. The ratio in the period between September 1962 and March 1963, that is, before the 'Buddhist persecution' became a major source of political disruption, was not unfavourable to the government – and this ratio is an important gauge of how the war is going. But as the political crisis developed the ratio began to become increasingly unfavourable; it was much more unfavourable after the Ngo brothers were done to death and a period of plotting and *coups* set in.[68] The result was that the stage of contention began to develop critically in favour of the Vietcong and the North Vietnamese. By the time the Americans arrived *en masse* in 1965 the Communist high command was about to cut South Vietnam in half and was beginning to chew up large South Vietnamese regular formations.

It is not being suggested that the political system and the mode of political behaviour prevailing in a country is the only factor affecting the development of the second and third stages of a revolutionary warfare campaign. But it certainly must rank amongst the most important, especially when the stage of contention or all-out guerrilla warfare has been reached. Unless the government has been able to develop an efficient command system, the revolutionary movement need not necessarily strive to reach stage three. It can simply carry on guerrilla warfare, sowing political and economic disaffection, imposing a larger and larger financial burden on a government whose revenues are declining and whose grip on the price structure is slipping –

68. Thompson, op. cit., p. 40, provides tables of arms lost and recovered.

and wait for dissensions at the centre to develop. Such dissensions will not necessarily be of the oppositional kind described above; they are also likely to involve groups which are just as committed to the struggle as the incumbent government but believe they could run the war better. In order to get their way – either in order to negotiate, or to fight on, from a position of central authority – opposition groups claim the right to behave politically in a way that would not have been tolerated by any Western democracy during the Second World War, for example.

All sorts of other factors enter into the struggle at the stage of contention, some of them having been discussed, others such as the quality and kind of army at the disposal of the government being obvious enough. It is quite certain that no revolutionary insurgency that has reached this phase can be effectively countered unless the country is put on a war footing and directed by a command system at least as politically rigorous as was acceptable to Western democracies at war against the other great totalitarian threat of this century. This means, amongst other things, the imprisoning of men who consistently advocate the making of peace overtures. The period of contention may be a limited war for allies engaged in it; it is an altogether total war for the indigenous participants. In the case of a Communist revolutionary insurgency that is finally successful at either the second or third phase of the struggle, not only will the reprisals be frightful for hundreds of thousands, perhaps millions, of people, but the 'people's army' will foreclose the future of that country by collectivizing the peasantry, turning the trade unions into state agencies, purging the universities and the creative intelligentsia, transforming the press into a centralized propaganda agency and establishing Party stool-pigeons at every vantage point. The Western allies will soon forget the silence that has come down over the country if the revolutionary movement should succeed; those who support the government under attack are fighting against that silence, which they cannot escape should they lose the struggle.

Certainly one of the aims of the revolutionary movement always is to exploit contradictions in this field too: to hold out the offer to most groups on the opposing side of finding employment, and avoiding reprisals – if only they will throw off the present government leadership. This is done in the full knowledge that a removal of the leadership at the stage of contention is bound to be followed by political disruption which will seriously weaken the non-Communist society's capacity to resist.

This approach has not been successful in South Vietnam, perhaps because of the example of what followed the assassination of the Ngo brothers. But it might have been successful in 1971 had the government been opposed by a 'peace' bloc of candidates headed by General Minh. The factionalism endemic in South Vietnamese politics has been given a fairly long rein, at least partly because the USA has worked so hard to create democratic conditions, in the midst of the stage of contention, to a degree indeed that no Western democratic group would have asked from Madrid during the Spanish Civil War, for example.

Even if the non-Communist Vietnamese should defeat themselves in this manner, it is desirable to distinguish this kind of exploiting of contradictions, a necessarily devious and somewhat indirect operation, from the more direct kind of subversion involved in inducing defections, civil and military, from the non-Communist areas. It is a very interesting feature of the Second Indo-China War, considered politically, that despite the near-chaos following the assassination of the Ngo brothers, and despite the quite rabid factionalism of Saigonese politics, not to speak of religious and regional hostilities (contradictions open for exploitation if ever there were any), the National Liberation Front has never been able to boast of a defector, civil or military, of any national significance at all.

The government of South Vietnam, it is true, has not been able to boast of a civilian political defector to it of any significance either. But this is scarcely to have been expected in the case of a monolithic political apparatus which, at least until 1970, had no real reason to contemplate the possibility of permanent defeat. But there have been a considerable number of military commanders of some stature who have come over to the government side, especially since the militarily abortive, though propagandistically successful, 1968 Tet Offensive. Their defection has not been at all well exploited, partly because the Saigon government has since its inception been very bad at propagating its own cause; partly also because the Western press has on the whole been so vociferous in its predictions of a Communist victory in South Vietnam that it appears to dislike any evidence that might suggest it has been wrong in its predictions. The fact remains that, as General Giap once put it, 'Free Vietnam is first of all an army' and that 'troop proselytizing' has been an activity that has on the whole gone against the Communist militarized form of 'liberation'.

But 'troop proselytizing' can be an effective approach if the target government is feeble and fatuous enough. Such was the case in Cuba. If the propagandists are to be believed, the Cuban revolutionary war was indeed remarkable in terms of phases or stages. It began in this fashion: 'Twelve men, with a rifle and ten cartridges, hidden on a mountain top.'

'An Army, Navy, and Air Force consisting of 30,000 men equipped with the finest weapons ...'[69]

Then: 'On 5 May 1958, the invasion was launched. Twelve thousand men, more than a third of the regime's total armed strength, were thrown in ... tanks, jeeps, armoured cars, cannon, bazookas ... napalm bombs bought from Trujillo, Batista's counterpart in the Dominican Republic ... The odds were 40 to 1 – 12,000 Batista soldiers against 300 revolutionaries in uniform.'

Now it is not particularly difficult to believe that a large concentration of soldiers failed to trap the Cuban guerrillas. It is not unusual for a large concentration of soldiers to fail to trap a guerrilla band in mountainous country. It has indeed happened many times. But it has been claimed that not only did the band survive, '... 300 guerrilleros repulsed and routed 10,000 men. A general counter-offensive followed.'[70] This would indeed be

69. Hubermann and Sweezy, op. cit., p. 56.
70. *Revolution in the Revolution?*, op. cit., p. 57.

unique in the annals of revolutionary warfare. Normally the stage of contention is long and complex, a fact which is not regarded as disadvantageous by theoreticians like Mao and Truong Chinh because they see *in the struggle itself* an opportunity not only of expanding the totalitarian counter-State but of creating – out of the exigencies of the struggle – a quite new kind of society.

## TERRORISM

Terrorism is a mode of behaviour that is not of course confined to revolutionary guerrilla wars. As a means of dissuading people from supporting the enemy and to punish those who have supported the enemy it has been found in most traditional guerrilla wars. To give the impression that the guerrillas are more to be feared than the enemy is an old aim in such struggles. There has also in the past been a positive aim on occasion: 'Terrorize the officials, English and Indian, and the collapse of the whole machinery of oppression is not very far off . . . This campaign of separate assassination is the best conceivable method of paralysing the bureaucracy and of arousing the people!' So argued the Indian terrorists early in the twentieth century.[71]

On the other hand, terrorism does not appear to have been a significant feature during the Chinese Communist Party's guerrilla campaigns.[72] Which is not of course to say that violence has not always been an integral aspect, even if varying in intensity, of Communist struggle. Professor Sydney Hook has put it nicely:

71. Quoted in A. R. Desai, *The Social Background of Indian Nationalism*, Calcutta, 1954, p. 301.

72. 'The peasant soldiers who rallied to [Mao's] banner did so from patriotic as well as other motives. Indeed, the needs of patriotism and revolution happily coincided. An important consequence of these favourable circumstances was that Mao had no need, broadly speaking, to resort to coercive terrorism during his years of military struggle' (Brian Crozier, in *Problems of Modern Strategy*, Part Two, Adelphi Papers, No. 55, March 1969, The Institute for Strategic Studies, London). The terror came after victory.

For tactical purposes some national Communist parties have cautiously put forward the non-Leninist idea that they may conquer political power without violence – especially if their opponents are accommodating enough to surrender. I shall not pursue the analysis of the Communist theory and practice of violence and its divagations from Lenin to the present because it is so frankly opportunistic in character that the real intent of Communists can only be construed, not from their words, but from the constellation of forces in which they find themselves at the moment. Simple justice, however, requires the recognition that they too find the ideologists of violence in some countries somewhat of an embarrassment.[73]

Terrorism is a form of violence that has, at any rate until recently, been regarded with peculiar horror by most people. It had normally seemed to be a cowardly form of activity – the murder of an unarmed person or persons by a man (or woman) likely to escape in the confusion – or, where escape was unlikely, the action of someone with a deranged mind. If explosives were used, terrorist acts were likely also to kill innocent bystanders. Even under regulations revised in 1949 in the light of the Second World War resistance movements, terrorists are in no way protected under international law if acting individually and, it would seem probable, even if not acting individually.[74] It was in the face of acts of terrorism that honourable French officers in Algeria came to regard 'special methods' (that is, torture) as being necessary and permissible.[75]

But it has been observed that in conditions of modern guerrilla warfare and its countering by heavy weapons, the matter is less

73. Sydney Hook, *Encounter*, April 1970.

74. H. Oppenheim, *International Law*, Longmans, 7th edition, 1952, p. 257: 'Individuals who are not members of regular forces and who take up arms or commit hostile acts singly and severally are still liable to be treated as war criminals and shot.' See Appendix II.

75. '. . . [the terrorist] must be made to realize that, when he is captured, he cannot be treated as an ordinary criminal, nor like a prisoner taken on the battlefield . . . he is not asked details about himself . . . but rather for precise information about his organization . . . No lawyer is present for such an interrogation. If the prisoner gives the information requested, the examination is quickly terminated; if not, specialists must force his secret from him' (Trinquier, *Modern Warfare*, op. cit., p. 21).

simple than it might appear. 'Punitive artillery barrages on villages suspected of sheltering Communist agents, or the indiscriminate use of artillery and bombings, have played a part in Government operations. The Vietcong's execution of an official is an act of terrorism but it involves only one man and it can be cloaked in the guise of "people's justice". An artillery barrage is indiscriminate . . .'[76]

That it is by no means as simple as that, either, will be shown below. But it is as well to remember in any discussion of terrorism that 'general devastation' under international law is 'only justified by imperative necessity, and by the fact that there is no better and less severe way open to the belligerent'.[77]

For the purpose of this study, terrorism can only be usefully discussed in functional terms. Revolutionary terrorism has recently been divided into its disruptive and its coercive aspects by a distinguished student of the subject.[78] Disruptive terrorism is designed to advertise the movement (for example kidnapping and hijacking), to build up the movement's morale and prestige, and to provoke the authorities into taking 'excessively harsh repressive measures, likely to alienate the population and force a rising spiral of social expenditure in arms, lives and money, resulting in public clamour for the abandonment of counteraction'.

Coercive terrorism, according to this understanding, embraces both an attempt 'to demoralize the civilian population, weaken its confidence in the central authority, and instil fear of the revolutionary movement' and through exemplary acts of torture and/or executions to force obedience to the leadership of the revolutionary movement. Of course, as Crozier points out, though these distinctions are useful for analytical purposes, the disruptive and the coercive aspects may both inhere in actual acts of terrorism. There is a further purpose which should be mentioned: the perpetration of violent acts, very often of a

76. Osborne, op. cit., p. 7.

77. Oppenheim, op. cit., pp. 415–16.

78. Brian Crozier, *The Study of Conflict*, Institute for the Study of Conflict, London, October 1970.

terrorist nature, is an excellent means of irrevocably involving men in the revolutionary movement.[79]

It has been said many times that terrorism is the weapon of the weak, which is true enough so far as it goes. But in terms of revolutionary warfare it does not go far enough: terrorism is also the weapon that small élite groups have used to enable them to render passive the majority of the population. It is therefore necessary to distinguish between terrorism used against an alien enemy and terrorism used as part of a programme for the controlling or cowing of the guerrilla's own folk.

Of course, even in the former case the situation varies according to the nature of the enemy and the degree of popular support enjoyed by the guerrillas. Where the enemy has been a colonial government the terrorists' task has depended a great deal on the make-up of the administration. For example, in India the overwhelming majority of government servants, civil and armed, were Indians. In Palestine and the Suez Canal Zone this impressive involvement of the indigenous with the imperial apparatus was missing. Terrorism in these cases could fairly be called 'a decisive instrument of rebellion'.[80] This is not to say that the majority of Jews in Palestine between 1944 and 1948 consistently approved of acts of terrorism; they did not. But, at worst, the terrorists did not risk betrayal.[81] In the Canal Zone, too, a terrorist campaign was the principal cause of the British withdrawal.

It should be observed that in the Egyptian and Palestinian contexts, as in many others, terrorism meant more than mur-

79. Frantz Fanon, for example, 'The group requires that each individual perform an irrevocable action . . . You could be sure of a new recruit when he could no longer go back into the colonial system. This mechanism, it seems, had existed in Kenya among the Mau Mau, who required that each member of the group should strike a blow at the victim' (*The Wretched of the Earth*, Penguin Books, 1967, p. 67).

80. Crozier, *The Rebels*, op. cit., p. 182.

81. '. . . for nearly half the period [1944–8] the terrorists enjoyed an alliance with the militant mass organization, and therefore the active support of the Jewish population; for the remainder of that time they enjoyed at least a measure of passive support and immunity from betrayal. The terrorists were consequently stronger in Palestine than they were in Vietnam, Malaya, Cyprus, Algeria or Kenya' (ibid., p. 185).

ders; the murders were but *part* of a campaign of sabotage, raids, robberies and general harassment. Such campaigns are very effectively subversive of an occupying power that has not the will to act ruthlessly.

If the 'forces of order' are prepared to act ruthlessly, as General Massu's 10th Parachute Division was prepared to act during the 'Battle of Algiers' early in 1957, in a situation where the target area is confined (as was the case in Algiers), then it is possible to crush a terrorist campaign – if the indigenous population is uncertain in its attitude towards the terrorists. But the 'Battle of Algiers' did not solve the problem of the revolutionary war in general. To crush a terrorist campaign is not necessarily to put paid to a movement.

Urban terrorism should be distinguished from rural terrorism. The role of the former as part of a rural-based revolutionary guerrilla war has been rather nicely stated by Régis Debray:

> Of course, city terrorism cannot assume any decisive role, and it entails certain dangers of a political order. But if it is subordinate to the fundamental struggle, the struggle in the countryside, it has, from the military point of view, a strategic value; it immobilizes thousands of enemy soldiers, it ties up most of the repressive mechanism in unrewarding tasks of protection: factories, bridges, electric generators, public buildings, oil pipe lines – these can keep busy as much as three quarters of the army. The government must, since it is the government, protect everywhere the interests of the property owners; the *guerrilleros* don't have to protect anything anywhere. They have no dead weight. Therefore the relation of forces cannot be measured in purely arithmetical terms.[82]

Here terrorism is being considered solely in its disruptive role while the 'mobilization of the masses' is being carried out in the countryside. Terrorism in the countryside is a different matter even when the main enemy is an alien regime, since the administration in rural areas is necessarily chiefly carried out through the agency of indigenous officials. Terrorism in the countryside serves the purpose of revolutionary guerrilla warfare in both disruptive and coercive ways. But if the two

82. *Revolution in the Revolution?*, op. cit., pp. 75–6.

Indo-China Wars are considered, a difference of terrorist intensity may be observed between the two struggles. 'While the Viet Minh forces generally limited themselves to the intimidation of the local administrators (village chiefs, notables) into a state of positive neutrality, the new terrorists seek out the local police chiefs, security guards, village treasurers and youth leaders and kill them in as spectacular a manner as possible.'[83]

In both cases the revolutionary object is gradually to destroy direct communication between the central government and the rural population, while at the same time establishing the revolutionary 'parallel hierarchies' of the counter-State as the real power in the countryside. For this purpose an enforcement apparatus is necessary. The most deadly component of the enforcement apparatus is the 'Moral Intervention' squad: 'their job is the psychological penetration of the enemy unit or enemy territory through means ranging from friendly persuasion to murder with especially deterrent effects'. Fall believed that it was terrorism, '*the violent act for psychological rather than military reasons*', which was 'the source of the success of the Viet-Minh against the French–Vietnamese forces of the 1940s and 1950s and against the American–Vietnamese forces of the 1960s.[84]

A more recent student of terrorism in South Vietnam, Douglas Pike, has described five objectives sought by Vietcong terrorism: to build internal morale, to advertise the National Liberation Front as a movement, to disorient and isolate Vietnamese who are not believers, to eliminate the opposition apparatus and to provoke the government forces into making reprisals. In Pike's view, which the author accepts, Vietcong terrorism is designed, at its most ambitious, to destroy the traditional village society. As Pike himself has put it:

Terror destroys the structure of authority which normally stands for security. Terror, especially in an isolated village, causes fright, anxiety and despair. It removes the sense of civilization from the village, disorienting the villager by demonstrating to him that he

83. Bernard Fall, quoted in Stephen T. Hosmer, *Viet Cong Repression and Its Implications for the Future*, Rand, California, 1970, p. 8.

84. Bernard Fall, *The Two Vietnams*, op. cit., p. 137.

cannot expect protection from the source he normally depends on, that is the government. When protection vanishes the social world crumbles. Terror isolates. The villager sees himself alone, in anguish and impotent. A terrorized village is a collective condition equal to anxiety neurosis on an individual level. What is perhaps most remarkable is that the villagers do resist. Captured NLF documents are full of reports of individual villagers opposing the NLF machine. One cannot help but wonder about such a person. His is an untold story of the Vietnam war.[85]

The intention to break up the social order by acts of terrorism became clear during the temporary Vietcong occupation of Hue during the 1968 Tet Offensive:

... killing in some instances was done by family unit. In one well-documented case ... a squad with a death order entered the home of a prominent community leader and shot him, his wife, his married son and daughter-in-law, his young unmarried daughter, a male and female servant and their baby. The family cat was strangled; the family dog was clubbed to death, the goldfish scooped out of the fishbowl and tossed on the floor. When the communists left, no life remained in the house. A 'social unit' had been eliminated.[86]

It might seem that such conduct would be politically counter-productive. Doubtless it would be at a certain stage in the struggle, but terrorism is as carefully phased as other aspects of the revolutionary guerrilla war. In the beginning great care is taken either to select unpopular victims for displays of 'people's justice' or to discredit the victims. 'This discrediting can be done in several ways: perhaps by associating him with an unpopular aspect of government policy, or by accusing him of corruption, or, better still, of rape. There is no shortage of keen female party workers who are prepared to engineer a situation which will justify a charge of this nature. It does not have to be proved.'[87]

However, when the struggle reaches its full fury the vital factor affecting men's minds has nothing to do with the popularity of local leaders or the justification for punishments; the only

85. *Politics of the Viet Cong*, op. cit., p. 34.
86. Douglas Pike, *The Viet-Cong Strategy of Terror*, op. cit., pp. 56–7.
87. Thompson, *Defeating Communist Insurgency*, op. cit., pp. 24–5.

serious question becomes, which side is going to win? This is the case with ordinary folk who are the vast majority of the population. Hence the 'certainty-of-victory theme in NLF propaganda ... more attention is paid to it than all other themes combined'.[88]

And yet there are also those who do go on resisting the Communist revolutionary campaign; and in Vietnam their numbers are very large. The Vietcong 'armed reconnaissance cell' is designed to eliminate the more prominent of them – on a quota basis. Hosmer cites a Vietcong directive instructing the reconnaissance cell to kill at least one chief or assistant chief in each of the following: Public Security Service, District National Police Service, Open Arms Service, Information Service and Pacification Teams, as well as a District Chief or Assistant District Chief. There were also quotas for killings on lower levels, down to the village itself.[89]

The Vietcong thus operate against those who support the government of Vietnam precisely as resistance movements operated against collaborators with the Nazi occupation forces.[90] This is a direct consequence of viewing even internal politics as warfare. But in the context of South Vietnam it has been shown that it was also a response to a regime whose leaders understood that the Communists were after total victory – and therefore decided to try to put paid to them in an equally total fashion. The result by today is a struggle waged with the utmost ferocity by both sides, since supporters of the government of Vietnam know perfectly well that if they are in the very least prominent

88. *Politics of the Viet Cong*, op. cit., p. 46.

89. Hosmer, op. cit., p. 15. Hosmer states that assassinations and abductions were running at 400–600 per year in 1958–9; in 1966 over 5,000 assassinations and abductions were reported officially: 'and the figure for 1968 was probably considerably more than twice that for 1967' (pp. 8–9).

90. For example, the conservative *Défense de la France:* 'Kill the German in order to purify our land ... Kill the traitors, kill those who denounce, kill those who have aided the enemy. Kill the policeman who in any way at all has contributed to the arrest of patriots. Kill the *miliciens*, exterminate them ... Destroy them as you would vermin' (quoted in Peter Novick, *The Resistance versus Vichy*, Chatto & Windus, 1968, p. 31).

in their activities, then in the event of defeat they will be liquidated because the Vietminh liquidated all their political rivals in the past.[91]

Leaving aside the peculiarly terrible conditions in South Vietnam, it should be noticed that terrorism is beginning to become a weapon of revolutionary warfare even in societies whose 'repressive apparatus' could not possibly be accused of having provoked or necessitated such behaviour: in Uruguay, for example, and tentatively even in the United States of America. In West Bengal and other parts of India; in and around Israel; in the cities of Latin America; in Northern Ireland; beginning perhaps in London now – the day of the terrorist appears to be dawning again. Though the urban terrorists of recent years have most times spoken the language of revolutionary warfare, they should not for the most part be considered the equivalents of the Vietcong terror squads. The latter are but *part* of a vast apparatus of counter-State repression and aspiration. The former, though they may come to treat the vital revolutionary question of organization wholly seriously, have not done so yet. And so, despite certain exceptions, they oddly recall the élitist youth in Russia a century ago who have been described recently by a scholar in the following manner:

> They preached destruction often enough, but chiefly as a means to an end, the necessary prelude to some dimly conceived, but fervently desired new order. Still, one often seems to discern a powerful death-wish beating behind the high-minded sentiments with which they rationalized such urges.[92]

The chief difference between then and now is that today a combination of gross insouciance and neurotic guilt conspire together in the European mind to create an atmosphere of feeble admiration for these men of violence, these Avengers, to whom

91. Lest the word liquidate be thought to be the author's: 'The liquidating of the reactionaries of the Viet Nam Quoc Dan Dang was crowned with success and we were able to liberate all the areas which had fallen into their hands' (Giap, *People's War, People's Army*, op. cit., p. 18).

92. Ronald Hingley, *Nihilists*, Weidenfeld & Nicolson, 1967, p. 57.

nothing is real except their thirst for vengeance; and their dreams of innocence beyond the days of vengeance, perhaps. Provided their rhetoric is couched in the right progressive phrases, the terrorists should have a promising future. But revolutionary guerrilla warfare is something more again. The men who lead, say, the Vietnamese Communist movement are quite different in so many ways from, say, the English 'Angry Brigade'.

# AFTERWORD

In retrospect, the author has misgivings about an implication that might be drawn from his mode of treating the subject. Treating revolutionary guerrilla warfare primarily *as warfare* might seem to have implied a lack of sympathy for poor men in the Third World who have every reason to seek all available means of liberation from often appallingly wretched conditions.

This is certainly not the attitude of the author. As the descendant of a Scottish farmer of poor circumstances who 'made good' in Australia, he is temperamentally disinclined to discount, let alone to denigrate, the motives that might well move poor farmers of the Third World to join guerrilla units. He is even less inclined to denigrate the human quality of heroism, which he has on occasion observed at fairly close quarters, of poor boys fighting in the ranks of the Vietcong, for example.

It is reasonable to suppose that in many cases there is truth in the assertion by an American 'revisionist' student of revolutionary warfare:

> Partisan leadership does not merely fill a vacuum created by the flight or demise of the landlord-official class ... Rather, at its best, it forges new bonds of unity in which the very definition of leader and led are recast ...[1]

But that is not always the impression even of guerrilla leaders themselves. One of Guevara's band in Bolivia, asked why they had not gained peasant support, replied: 'Because peasants are always with the forces of power and strength. We did not reach the necessary phase of power. A guerrilla movement has three steps. The first is forming a people's army against the government. Next the guerrilla army becomes as powerful as the army.

1. Mark Selden, 'People's War and the Transformation of Peasant Society: China and Vietnam', in *America's Asia: Dissenting Essays on Asian–American Relations*, Vintage Books, New York, 1971, p. 361.

Finally, the guerrillas become the power in the country. That is when the peasants support them.'[2]

That revolutionary warfare is not primarily a matter of popular revolt against oppression is obvious from considering that up to 1940 a mere 11,000 French troops and a militia of 16,000 could control 19 million Vietnamese without difficulty, whereas in 1954 140,000 French and African troops and 280,000 Vietnamese troops could not prevail against the Vietminh 'people's army'.[3]

That the peasant armies are peasant armies only in the sense that peasants make up a large part of the rank-and-file has also been demonstrated. So far as the Vietminh were concerned, according to some findings, 20 per cent of regulars were drawn from Tho tribals and 46 per cent came from 'miscellaneous professions and trades', while not only the leadership but the intermediate and lower echelon leaders were from the lower middle class and all had some degree of Western education.[4] What was crucial was the penetration of the Red River Delta by special armed units from the mountain sanctuaries where the 'people's army' was built up.

The evidence suggests very strongly that interior motivation is not what gets most poor men into guerrilla armies; rather they are involved in the struggle in various ways. One recruiting slogan used at the appropriate time is 'Land to the Tiller'; but at a later period the 'people's army' itself becomes the instrument of agricultural collectivization. The 'partisan' bands are not, as the American 'revisionist' historian put it, leading 'to possibilities of participatory patterns everywhere'.[5] They are the instrument of the Communist Party for the institution of totalitarian rule. In view of the extraordinarily bad results of agricultural collectivization over decades, it cannot be regarded as

2. Quoted in Henry Bienen, *Violence and Social Change*, University of Chicago Press, Chicago, 1968, pp. 61–2.

3. John T. McAlister, Jr, *Vietnam: The Origins of Revolution*, Allen Lane The Penguin Press, 1969, p. 50.

4. Eric R. Wolf, *Peasant Wars of the Twentieth Century*, Faber & Faber, 1971, pp. 184–5.

5. Mark Selden, op. cit., p. 361.

arising out of agricultural needs. Clearly it is a political device for the control of the peasantry, which has always been deeply distrusted by Communists.

It is this that revolutionary guerrilla warfare is 'all about' strategically; not about the fraternal bonds which doubtless are often forged between brave men in guerrilla units.

This fact has become deeply obscured during the Second Indo-China War so far as Western public opinion is concerned; and quite deliberately obscured. As Dennis Duncanson has pointed out,

> A disquieting feature of the acrimony over Vietnam is how little information about the People's Army, or about the regime and the people of North Vietnam, is available to the protestors. There are no secrets about the White House's South Vietnamese protégés, no blemish of Saigon life still waiting to be brought to light. But there is not on the bookshelves a single reliable study of North Vietnam's society; only a few uncritical tracts issued with the *nihil obstat* of the Hanoi Government to set beside the *Pentagon Papers*. Quite elementary things are hard to find out. Are the North Vietnamese soldiers conscripts or volunteers? What sort of lives would they live if they weren't soldiers? What chances of survival do they have if they get wounded in the South but not captured? How many civilian casualties have there been in the North from American bombing, and why doesn't Hanoi publish any figures?[6]

Or as Douglas Pike has put it,

> The true genius of revolutionary guerrilla war is ... that it employs the judo principle and turns the weight of the enemy's philosophic system against itself. It works best, therefore, against a democracy of decent people (and least against barbarians or fanatics). It agrees victory will go to the just, because justice must triumph ... [But] the enemy is the unjust and misled amongst the leadership, perhaps a few selected individuals. The more or less normal wartime polarization is denied. Again and again it asserts to the opposite camp, particularly to the vast civilian population at home, *we are not your enemy*. The enemy is the unjust person who wishes to pursue an unjust war and surely *you* are not among these ... it does not seek to monopolize virtue, but rather will share it ...

6. Dennis J. Duncanson, *Listener*, 20 July 1972.

Thus the ideological struggle becomes a test of virtue. The individual, looking on, is presented, on the one hand, with the communist's own idealized picture of himself (but denied any objective inspection of the communist camp). And on the other hand, he sees or perceives the errors, shortcomings and follies of his own, very human side. Reality seldom stands a chance against image. The further the onlooker is from the scene, or the less factual knowledge he has about Vietnam (and such knowledge in the US is close to non-existent, generally), the more apparently odious becomes the comparison.[7]

The second Indo-China War has come to a close so far as Western military involvement is concerned. What are the prospects for revolutionary guerrilla warfare? Simply to raise such a question is to ask yet again what it is 'all about', since revolutionary wars are normally impossible to predict well in advance. The world learns quite suddenly about Tupamaros in Uruguay, 'Guevarists' in Sri Lanka (Ceylon), Mukhti Bahini in Bangla Desh, Meos in North Thailand, Muslim insurgents in Mindanao. There is no simple relationship between the so-called 'roots of rebellion' and the manner in which a guerrilla warfare campaign, revolutionary or otherwise, will develop. This not least because so much depends upon the means adopted to counter it by the incumbent government, particularly in the early stages.

For obvious reasons, guerrilla campaigns have generally been most successful when waged against clearly alien governments and supported by outside sponsors disposing of modern weaponry for the climactic phase. Such situations are now very few. Moreover, in the cases of South Africa and Rhodesia, particularly the former, armed struggle faces 'a determined enemy which cannot retreat and compromise since its very existence depends on the maintenance of the established discriminatory order ...'[8] The same could basically be said of the two other

7. Douglas Pike, *Guerrilla Warfare in Asia*, 4. *Guerrilla Warfare in Vietnam*, International Documentation and Information Centre (INTERDOC), The Hague, 1971, pp. 54–5.

8. Leslie J. Macfarlane, *Political Disobedience*, Macmillan (Papermac), 1971, p. 48.

governments regarded by guerrilla movements as alien: the governments of Israel and Northern Ireland.

It is perhaps of interest to compare the comparatively small security force at least which held the situation in Northern Ireland in 1971 (13,000 troops, 4,000 members of the Royal Ulster Constabulary, and the Ulster Defence Regiment) with what Winston Churchill believed would have been necessary to hold Ireland in 1921:

> It was evident to Ministers that efforts to restore order in Ireland must be made during the rest of the year upon an extraordinary scale. A hundred thousand new special troops and police must be raised; thousands of motor-cars must be armoured and equipped; the three Southern Provinces of Ireland must be closely laced with cordons of blockhouses and barbed wire, a systematic rummaging and questioning of every individual must be put in force.[9]

This was to be in addition to 50,000 troops and 15,000 police already in the field. However, the outcome was by no means determined only by the guerrillas and it is possible to view the present guerrilla campaign in Northern Ireland from quite a different angle. Despite its not being primarily a nationalist struggle at all, but conceived rather in North Irish terms; despite its commencement at a time when Catholic disabilities appeared to be about to be significantly ameliorated; despite the fact that North Irish Catholics, enjoying higher living standards than those in Eire, as a result of British subsidies, had for nearly fifty years accepted communal disabilities; and despite the fact that the British Army moved in to protect the Catholic population – it was officially estimated in 1971 that '(assuming the best) *it may take over ten years to restore peace in Northern Ireland*'.[10]

It was remarkable how quickly the urban guerrillas of the two IRAs managed to polarize political forces in a manner deeply subversive of constitutional approaches to the problem; to the extent indeed of persuading the opposition in the Northern Irish

9. J. Carty (ed.), *Ireland from the Great Famine to the Treaty, 1851–1921, A Documentary Record*, Fallon, Dublin, 1951, quoted p. 227.

10. Iain Hamilton and Robert Moss, *The Spreading Irish Crisis*, Conflict Studies No. 17, November 1971, p. 21.

Parliament to withdraw from it. The IRA was enabled to exploit the Protestant communal viciousness of 1969, and subsequent outbreaks of violence; it also had available for exploitation the ghetto mentality perpetuated by the Catholic educational system and constantly exacerbated by lower-class Protestant recalcitrance in the social and political fields.

Nevertheless the feat of transforming the image of the British army from one of a rescuing force to that of an army of occupation was the result of now classic guerrilla tactics designed to make the forces of order react so rigorously as to alienate a very large proportion of the Catholic population. The tactics have now become collectively known under the term 'terrorism'. In Bernard Fall's definition of terrorism, 'the violent act for psychological, not military, reasons', the description is fair enough.

The mixture of provocation by snipers, 'tactical crowds' and murder squads, with disorientating bomb and arson attacks, against property more than against persons, spiced with selective terrorism against military and informers alike, dressed with more apparently military-style guerrilla attacks against police stations and communications, was nicely conceived for the purpose of creating a police state in which Catholics were inevitably the chief oppressed.

The British army proceeded in line with its old imperial tradition, in which the massacre at Amritsar in India in 1919 still stands in 'sinister isolation', of employing the minimum force necesary for the attainment of specific objectives in support of the civil power. But as in imperial India when terrorism erupted (and as in almost all independent Asian countries after the Second World War), preventive detention was found necessary if the subversive organization was to be broken up. But the consequent policy of internment proved politically to be even more counter-productive than the armed searches and other 'harassments' of Catholic areas had been.

The middle ground could only be re-created by political means, aided by the increasing organization and violence of Protestant extremists, which was a reminder that, were the British army to withdraw, the far more amply armed and potentially far more desperate Protestants would almost certainly unleash a holocaust against which the IRA and its supporters, even if aided by the Irish army, simply could not prevail.

But this middle ground could not have been re-created without the proroguing of the Northern Irish Parliament at Stormont and the imposition of direct British rule; 'Just as internment was [the IRA's] moment of triumph, so was the end of Stormont their greatest defeat, because it gave civilian political leaders the opportunity to regain Catholic support.'[11] Even if a constitutionalist middle ground has been re-created by the Protestant–Catholic Executive of 1973 and Dublin's recognition of Ulster as part of the United Kingdom in March 1974, which is problematical, the gunmen remain to be disarmed.

It seems doubtful to the author whether the Northern Irish attempt at insurgency is very relevant, except in terms of certain tactics, to the question asked by many people today: Does guerrilla warfare of the urban kind – urban terrorism, if the term is preferred – present a serious threat to Western democracies? Though every guerrilla campaign is different from others in some respects, some seem to be more different than others, if the Orwellism be permitted (the author nearly wrote 'Irishism'). One of the particular features of recent Irish history has been the myth of the gunman as the solver of 'Ireland's English problem'.

This cult of the gun is not generally to be found in Western democracies; nor does it seem to be developing to any significant degree. As Anthony Hartley has recently argued exceedingly cogently, the division – it cannot involve political polarization – in Western societies is between the Organization Man and the Hippie, who share 'non-violence, conformity, and a "social ethos" within their particular circle'.[12] What Hartley calls 'the peasant-guerrilla leader cum international adventurer' remains a hero-figure of peripheral significance.

The beastliness of some terrorist acts by members of the Palestine Liberation Organization and other groups of fanatics,

11. R. D. Scott, 'Northern Ireland: The Politics of Disintegration', *Australian Outlook*, April 1973, Vol. 27, No. 1, p. 47.

12. 'Neither Bureaucrat nor Hippie', *Encounter*, March 1973.

these other groups (the Japanese at Lod Airport, for example) being altogether peripheral to the political societies in which they were formed, has on occasion led to a very unwise overreaction on the part of even very prestigious Western organs of opinion. It was exaggerated, for example, for *The Economist* to editorialize along the line that, 'Terrorism is developing into a form of total war, the kind of war in which there is no distinction between combatants and non-combatants, and passers-by find themselves thrust into the firing-line.'[13] Skyjackings have caused far fewer deaths than mechanical defects and pilots' errors; and the number of passers-by killed in terrorist outrages is minute.

This kind of activity cannot possibly be described as 'total war'; it is peripheral to West European society, or even to Israeli society for that matter. A recent attempt to establish an 'ecology of terrorism' seems to the author to be even more misguided. Arguing that 'Modern outlaws operate with a destructive power often superior to that of the establishment in a "standardized" society, and on any targets of their own selection' – have the writers ever seen the results of aerial bombing or artillery bombardment? – the writers attempt to show that the extremist revolutionaries employing terrorist methods may really be 'sociopaths'. The 'sociopath', it seems, is the opposite of a neurotic: breezy, self-assured, un-bothered by contradictions.[14]

This mode of treating the subject can only lead to misunderstanding. It may well be that amongst the Palestinians there are men like 'the Professor' in Joseph Conrad's *Secret Agent* who move about like 'a disease'. But the explanation for the *organization's* terrorist actions should not be sought in the realm of very dubious psychological typology. Most terrorism – terrorism as the central mode of struggle, unintegrated with political and social policy – is surely, as Eric Hobsbawn has argued, 'really a political version of the familiar phrase "Don't just stand there, do

13. Article syndicated in *The National Times*, Sydney, 20–25 November 1972.

14. D. V. Segre and J. H. Adler, 'The Ecology of Terrorism', *Encounter*, February 1973.

something" '. But in the case of the Palestinians, this is not the whole of it: terrorist acts are designed to provoke reprisals from Israeli aircraft or raids on camps in Arab countries. Such reprisals can be exploited, and have been exploited, most successfully in many Third World countries, at the United Nations, and of course amongst the refugees themselves. To attribute the acts of terrorism to a form of mental disease is both to misrepresent the nature of the problem and to raise the intensity of the democratic response to it in a manner altogether subversive of solving the problem.

It should not be beyond the imagination of Westerners to grasp that, in what appear to intellectuals of the Third World to be desperate situations, violence may seem to some to have a socially therapeutic effect upon those oppressed who take up arms. As the late Frantz Fanon once argued:

> . . . for the colonized people this violence, because it constitutes their only work, invests their characters with positive and creative qualities. The practice of violence binds them together as a whole, since each individual forms a violent link in the great chain, a part of the great organism of violence which has surged upwards in reaction to the settler's violence in the beginning. The groups recognize each other and the future nation is already indivisible. The armed struggle mobilizes the people; that is to say, it throws them in one way and in one direction.[15]

This is, in a sense, the theory behind the Palestinian Liberation Movement, which apart from the PDLF seems to lack much 'social content'[16] and behind the Provisional IRA for that matter, since its occasional Gaelic classes can scarcely be regarded as heightening the 'political consciousness' of Northern Irish Catholics, except in Chesterbellocian terms. But the price of such an approach is very heavy indeed: an acceptance of the atrocity theory of history, which is quite as mischievous and misleading as the conspiracy theory of history. It is not a very long step from arguing, as Al-Fatah does, that the Jewish con-

15. Frantz Fanon, *The Wretched of the Earth*, Penguin Books, 1967, p. 73.
16. See Gérard Chaliand, *The Palestinian Resistance*, Penguin Books, 1972.

quest of Canaan was marked by 'atrocities ... without parallel in history, barring those committed in 1948 on the Arabs of Palestine' to the massacre of Israeli athletes at Munich.

When the atrocity theory of history is married to a theory of destiny – a dying colonialism and a decadent West – then, surely, it is not necessary for its devotees to be 'sociopaths'. If it were as simple as that, the rise to power of the Nazis and of the Stalinists in Russia would be literally inconceivable – unless it be assumed that thousands upon thousands of 'sociopaths' can suddenly coalesce into major political movements. But that would seem somewhat improbable. What is important are the theories, the myths, which have a life of their own (as do modern insurgencies as well): countering a modern insurgency should mean the countering of the myth of the gunman as a prime factor in the solution of political problems. Counter-insurgent methods range across a wide spectrum of activities, from collective punishment and compulsory resettlement to proportional representation and other devices for a sharing of power. If a counter-insurgency ceases to be chiefly political in strategy, though not necessarily at all times in point of tactics, then it has dangerously lost ground to the myth of the gunman.

The dilemma arises when an *armed* political party adopts what Communists call 'legal struggle' while remaining armed, as was the case in Malaya and the Philippines, for example, in the years immediately following the Second World War. The MCP's 'legal struggle', which involved intimidation merging into terrorism at times, was blocked by restrictive trade-union regulations and a turning back of the constitutional clock. The Phillipines Communist Party (PKP), deciding early in 1946 to adopt a policy of 'legal struggle', contested some electorates behind the façade of the Democatic Alliance Party front, only to find that the six seats won in Central Luzon were denied to it on the ground that they had been won through fraud and terrorism. The PKP too was an armed party. The denial of constitutional participation to armed political parties would seem to remain sound today in any society retaining a sense of civilization. The bandit has been around for time out of mind, but out in the wild country; the guerrilla in the modern heartland is in quite a different category.

There is no good reason to believe that he will prosper greatly in the West in future, since his movements will not find acceptance for their claim to represent victims – not even in the USA, short of financial collapse; he is likely to be countered in most Latin American countries by a new kind of military politician – and even today by the tearing of the fabric of the myth when Guevara's band was so easily disposed of; he will continue to advance in Portuguese Africa and in Rhodesia, and possibly in various parts of South East Asia; he is less likely to do so in the Middle East; he has taken heavy punishment in India and Ceylon. But since his opportunity arises out of intrinsically unpredictable concatenations of political circumstances, the task of those who see in guerrilla warfare something subversive of civilization is both to be ever watchful for signs of its development and ever determined to deny the guerrilla the romantic halo he has in recent years been permitted altogether too easily to wear.

## APPENDIX 1

# A NOTE ON T. E. LAWRENCE

Though T. E. Lawrence's character has been held up to mockery since his death, and serious works have sought to cut down the significance of his actual role in the Arab Revolt,[1] he remains important for his theoretical contribution to the art of guerrilla warfare. That this enigmatic darling of the Anglo-Saxon clubland 'Establishment' of yesteryear had ambivalent feelings about his role is certain enough: 'Pray God that men reading the story will not, for love of the glamour of strangeness, go out to prostitute themselves and their talents in serving another race.'[2] 'In my case, the effort for these years to live in the dress of Arabs and to imitate their mental foundation, quitted me of my English self, and let me look at the West and its conventions with new eyes; they destroyed it all for me. At the same time I could not sincerely take on the Arab skin: it was an affectation only. Easily was a man made an infidel, but hardly might he be converted to another faith.'[3]

That there was something ambiguous about his involvement in the Arab cause is also certain. It was not simply that he could write of Palestine in August 1909 to his mother that, 'The sooner the Jews farm it all the better; their colonies are bright spots in the desert.' Nor simply that he was 'proudest of my thirty fights in that I did not have any of our own blood shed' and could write denigratingly that the Arabs were a '... limited, narrow-minded people, whose intellects lay fallow in incurious resignation'. He was a supporter of Zionism for imperial reasons and for the same reasons could speak of a new Arab 'brown Dominion'.

1. In particular, Suleiman Mousa, *T. E. Lawrence: An Arab View*, Oxford University Press, 1966; and Elie Kedouri, *The Chatham House Version*, Weidenfeld & Nicolson, 1970, regarding the occupation of Damascus.

2. T. E. Lawrence, *Seven Pillars of Wisdom*, Cape, 1940, p. 29.

3. ibid., p. 30.

It seems probable also that in one way Lawrence was fitted to 'take on the Arab skin': he was an artist gifted with that mythopoeic faculty which even the most sympathetic observers maintain has by no means died out amongst the Arab peoples.[4] He may have said more than he intended when he wrote shortly before his death, 'The genius raids, but the common people occupy and possess.'[5] On one level, despite his very great gifts, he may have resembled his successor amongst romantic youth, Ernesto Guevara, who, as we have seen, described himself to his parents as 'a little soldier-of-fortune of the twentieth century'.

Against the evidence of his detractors stands the evidence of friends and admirers, including some of those Englishmen who served with him in Arabia, and the military historian, the late Sir Basil Liddell Hart; and the elderly bedouin sheikh who had ridden with him and could say that 'Of all the men I have ever met, *Al Aruns* was the greatest Prince.'[6]

Certainly his words could conjure up very much the same kind of neo-Rousseauan romanticism as is today evoked by M. Régis Debray's pictures of the good clean guerrilla *foco* out in the fine clean air, which has such an appeal (at least in the breast) to urban intellectuals and students: 'We were fond together, because of the sweep of the open places, the taste of wide winds, the sunlight, and the hopes in which we worked. The morning freshness of the world-to-be intoxicated us. We were wrought up with ideas inexpressible and vaporous, but to be fought for.'[7]

But aside from all this, Lawrence's analysis of guerrilla warfare remains a remarkably percipient one. Like Chairman Mao, he understood strategy as 'the synoptic regard which sees everything by the standard of the whole'. He understood, like Mao too, the available gift of space: 'So long as the Arabs had space

4. For example, Bernard Lewis, in *Encounter*, August 1970.

5. Quoted in Robert Payne, *Lawrence of Arabia*, Robert Hale, 1966, p. 250.

6. James Lunt, in *History of the Twentieth Century*, ed. J. M. Roberts, Purnell, Ch. 22, p. 595.

7. T. E. Lawrence, op. cit., p. 22.

to fall back, their delaying power might be equivalent to defensive powers.' Like the Chinese Communists in Manchuria in 1946–7, he knew that 'The virtue of irregulars lay in depth, not in force.' And like them too, he knew there was no point, even if the Arab will had been available, in attacking the cities held by Turkish garrisons. The attacks were to be against communications; and they were to be carried out in such a way that 'Many Turks on our front had no chance all the war to fire a shot at us, and correspondingly, we were never on the defensive, except by a rare accident.'[8]

The mobility of nomads who could endure much and knew their terrain was brought to bear: 'The ratio between number and area determined the character of the war, and by having five times the mobility of the Turks we could be on terms with them with one-fifth their number.'[9] But just as was the case with the Vietminh, for example, the corollary to this was what Lawrence called 'perfect "intelligence" '; like the Vietminh, he believed that for guerrilla operations 'knowledge had to be faultless. 'We took more pains in this service than any other staff I saw.'

Evocative of the French pill-box strategy against the Vietminh in Tongking was his estimation that if the Turks were to 'contain this attack in depth, sedition putting up her head in every unoccupied one of these three hundred thousand square miles', then they would need six times the number of men they had available. Again evocative of that struggle was his echoing of Clausewitz in describing the guerrilla movement as 'an influence (as we might be), an idea, a thing invulnerable, intangible, without front or back, drifting about like gas'. Against this, 'Armies were like plants, immobile as whole, firm rooted, nourished through long stems to the head. We might be a vapour, blowing where we listed. Our kingdoms lay in each man's mind, and as we wanted nothing material to live on, so perhaps we offered nothing to the killing. It seemed a regular soldier might be helpless without a target.'[10]

8. Quoted in B. H. Liddell Hart, '*T. E. Lawrence*' *in Arabia and after*, Cape, 1965, p. 175.

9. ibid., p. 177.

10. ibid., p. 170.

But where Lawrence was most astonishingly ahead of his time was in his appreciation of the importance of what today is called 'motivation' and also of the propaganda component of modern guerrilla warfare in its widest ramifications. Like the commissars of the Chinesse Red Army or the Vietnamese People's Army, Lawrence attached very great importance to what he called 'the psychological ... of which our propaganda is a stained and ignoble part'. But not only did he believe that 'We had to arrange their minds in order to battle, just as carefully as other officers arranged their bodies', he also believed it necessary to 'arrange' the minds of the enemy 'so far as we could reach them'; and also 'the mind of the nation supporting us behind the firing-line, and the mind of the hostile nation awaiting the verdict, and the neutrals looking on'.[11]

It may be argued that the Arab Revolt was something of a strategic side-show, though Liddell Hart has pointed out in his *Strategy of Indirect Approach* that Allenby's army, by destroying the Turkish forces in Palestine 'by a single decisive stroke', thereby aborted the Arab strategy. Moreover, the fact that a force of some 3,000 Arabs tied down 50,000 Turks and compelled their high command to deploy some 150,000 troops 'spread over the rest of the region in a futile effort to stem the tide of the Arab Revolt' bespeaks a very considerable guerrilla success.[12]

Whatever is eventually made of T. E. Lawrence's specific role in this guerrilla campaign and whatever holes are picked in his narrative, a man who could perceive in the context of the First World War that 'The printing press is the greatest weapon in the armoury of the modern commander' deserves a place in any study of revolutionary warfare. So does the man who wrote, 'We had won a province when we had taught the civilians in it to die for our ideal of freedom: the presence or absence of the enemy was a secondary matter.' It is arguable whether Lawrence was read by later practitioners; it is quite certain that he foreshadowed their findings in very important ways.

11. ibid., p. 175.
12. See Major-General James Lunt's article, op. cit.

## APPENDIX 2

# THE GUERRILLA AND INTERNATIONAL LAW

Since revolutionary warfare is waged in part in order to upset the existing international system and in conditions that are not conducive to the observance of legal norms of any kind, the status of guerrillas under international law is perhaps not of pressing importance. However, it is clearly in the interest of those supporting the present international order to observe the provisions of international law wherever and whenever this is possible.

It is not so very long since the British and the Americans were appalled by the German 'Commando' Order of 18 October 1942, which laid it down that henceforth enemies in uniform encountered engaging in 'so-called commando operations, in Europe or in Africa' were 'to be exterminated to the last man ... If such men appear to be about to surrender, no quarter should be given to them on general principle.'[1]

However, the difficulties of giving recognition to guerrillas, and so behaving towards them as though they were regulars, are obviously extremely great. This is made plain by the conditions attaching to such recognition: first, they must be commanded by a person responsible for his subordinates; secondly, the guerrillas must have 'a distinctive sign recognizable at a distance'; thirdly, they must carry arms openly; and lastly, they must conduct military operations with 'the laws and customs of war'.[2]

The difficulties are recognized in Oppenheim, where it is laid down that a trial accompanied by necessary judicial safeguards is 'the absolute minimum' duty of governments towards guerrillas.[3] Governments may still try guerrillas for treason and

1. H. Lauterpacht (ed.), *International Law, A Treatise, by L. Oppenheim*, Longmans, 1952, 7th edn, fn 1, p. 260.

2. ibid., pp. 214–15.

3. ibid., p. 215.

execute them, but only after a proper trial. This, however, applies only to guerrillas fighting 'in bodies, however small. Individuals who are not members of regular forces and who take up arms or commit hostile acts singly and severally are to be treated as war criminals and shot.'[4]

It should be emphasized that these provisions of the 1949 Hague Convention are likely to be implemented only in conditions where the guerrilla force is comparatively small and the administration comparatively well equipped judicially. Though the ordinances relating to guerrillas during the Malayan Emergency were draconic, it was possible to adhere to the absolute minimum of a fair trial because their numbers were small and the administration colonial. Once again, it must be insisted that in terms of civilized behaviour the only really successful counter-insurgency is one that prevents an insurgency developing. Once it has developed, the legal resources of an undeveloped country simply would not permit adherence to this very desirable Hague rule.

But it should also be said that the increasing importance of propaganda and psychological warfare in counter-guerrilla campaigns does to some extent protect guerrillas against being shot out of hand. There is not much point in having an 'Open Arms' programme as a major propaganda instrument and rendering it inoperative by a promiscuous butchery of those who are being induced to desert and defect.

What is most necessary for Western armed forces, acting in support of the government of an undeveloped country, to watch very carefully is the matter of 'general devastation which cuts off supplies of every kind from the guerrilla bands'. General devastation is held to be justified only by 'imperative necessity, and by the fact that there is no better and less severe way open to the belligerent'.[5] The difficulty lies in the nature of modern weaponry and that aspect of revolutionary war that encompasses the deliberate involvement of the people-at-large in the struggle and the deliberate provocation of response by modern weapons. Once again, the only successful counter-insurgency . . .

4. ibid., p. 257.
5. ibid., pp. 416–17.

APPENDIX 3

# THE PALESTINIANS

The Arabs of Palestine were faced between the two world wars with the problem of whether or not to come to terms with a growing Jewish immigration. The British government on 2 November 1917 promised the Jewish Zionists a 'national home for the Jewish people' in Palestine provided that 'nothing shall be done which may prejudice the civil and religious rights of existing non-Jewish communities ...' This vaguely worded promise was not easily reconcilable with promises made to the Hashemite Arab allies of the British against the Turks; the promise was also to prove internally inconsistent.

But though the Palestinian Arabs were later to become involved in the pan-Arab movement, they at first offered resistance in Palestinian terms under the British Mandate which began in 1920. At the same time, they at first lacked any sense of Palestinian national identity or modern political organization: those who thought about such matters probably considered themselves to be southern Syrians, but the contenders for leadership were members of great families rooted in the Palestinian society.

Though there were violent Palestinian Arab 'protest movements' in the 1920s, it seems possible that the twin British aims of facilitating Jewish immigration and protecting the Arab stake in the country could have been carried out if it had not been for the unforeseeable Nazi persecution and the development of political pan-Arabism. Possible but exceedingly unlikely.[1]

Certainly there was a direct relationship between the volume

1. Sir Keith Hancock, *Survey of British Commonwealth Affairs, 1918–36*, Oxford University Press, Vol. I, 1938, p. 440, shows that between 1922 and 1931 the Jewish population increased from 83,794 to 174,610. 'In 1931 it was 17 per cent of the total population of Palestine; four years later it was 27 per cent of the population, which at that date was estimated at 1,308,000 persons.'

of Jewish immigration and the intensity of Arab protest. But despite the extraordinary practice, taken over from the Turks, of considering the Palestinian population in terms of religious confession until the 1930s, it appears clear that there began to grow up a sense of Arabism amongst both Christian and Muslim Palestinians through an increasing awareness of certain disagreeably obvious factors distinguishing them from the Jewish population.

The father of Zionism, Theodore Herzl, had after all written: 'We should form a portion of the rampart of Europe against Asia, an outpost of civilization as opposed to barbarism.' Jews came to form in Palestine, not special occupational groups, but a complete society to which the Arab Palestinians were irrelevant and unnecessary. Whatever may be said in support of the now widespread theory in leftist circles that Israel is the last example of Western imperialism, it cannot be said that Jews sought to use 'a lesser breed without the Law' as menials or even workers. They did their own farming; and did it magnificently.

But this only made the juxtaposition of the two communities all the more blatant; and it was clearly a juxtaposing of unequals – right down to the level of unskilled quarrymen.[2] This overwhelmingly reflected the canons of a juster, more equalitarian society. But it was also the result of the immeasurably superior organizational skills of Europeans, not only in the trade-union field but in co-operatives, housing, finance and agriculture. There was also (as there still is for that matter) a great inequality in access to the powers of the Western world, particularly to the London seat of the Mandatory.[3] (On the other hand, Zionists have argued with force that colonial officials and the British Foreign Office were pro-Arab – the latter remaining so.) There was also, and very importantly, the inequality in regard to land sales that sprang, not from legal or even economic inequality *per se*, but rather from the short-sighted fecklessness of peasants offered seemingly very high prices by much shrewder and more

2. See tables, ibid., p. 448.

3. ibid., p. 462.

far-sighted people from a society that had attained far higher organizational skills.[4]

But the Palestinian Arab mistake, as it came later to be the mistake of the Arab world, was never to take the measure of Zionist colonization and try to *contain it*. Instead, and ultimately fatally, the Palestinian Arab leaders came to believe that their salvation lay in violence. Or was it less simple? Would it all have been different if the British government had not given in to Zionist objections to the development of self-governing institutions before the Jewish population had attained parity with the Arabs?[5]

What is to the point here is that in the face of a very greatly

4. Sir Ronald Storrs, *Orientations*, Ivor Nicholson and Watson, 1939, p. 371, commented: 'Material advantages were admittedly increased for many, though not all, Arabs, especially near the City and the towns. But at what a price! Was it altogether dishonourable for Arabs to sigh for a less advanced, but a traditional, an Arab civilization? The peasant of Siloam would not have been a peasant if he had not profited by being able to sell his cauliflower for sixpence instead of a halfpenny; the improvident landowner would have been more, or less, than human if he refused tenfold the value of his land. Yet both might mutter, in the words of the Palestinian chicken: ... "Feed me up today: wring my neck tomorrow".' Apart from the last sentence, the passage sums up the relationship rather nicely. But what Arabs *believed* happened at this time is also important. The following view is not untypical: 'The bulk of the land sold to the Jews ... was owned by non-Palestinian, absentee landlords who succumbed to the inflated prices offered by the Zionists ... Another group who sold land were the poorer peasants, who were weighed down with debts and a heavy taxation made necessary by the imposition of the National Home and amounting to twice or more what the peasant paid in Syria, Lebanon or Iraq' (*Tension, Terror and Blood in the Holy Land*, Palestine Arab Refugees Institution, Damascus, 1955, p. 7).

5. Storrs, op. cit., p. 389. Cf. Sir Keith Hancock, *Country and Calling*, Faber & Faber, 1954, p. 159: 'In accepting the Mandate, Great Britain had pledged herself to three things: first, to establish a Jewish National Home in Palestine; secondly, to prevent prejudice to the interests and rights of the settled population of that country; thirdly, to establish self-government there. Whereas the Jews laid predominant or exclusive emphasis upon the first pledge, and the Arabs laid it upon the second and third, I believed that all three pledges were binding in law and morality. Of course there were many people who asserted that the first pledge was completely incompatible with the other two ...'

enhanced Jewish immigration after 1932, the Arabs did take to arms, at first against the British, then against the British and the Jews. In memorable language, Storrs referred to 'an explosion of feeling [in 1936] so momentous that the greatest Power in the world, after near twenty years' experiment and experience, required, in full peace time, an Army Corps and all the panoply of war to control the "liberated" civil population; and the Arabs are able to boast that in calling off a guerrilla warfare maintained for six months, they yielded neither to British arms nor to the economic necessity of salving their orange crop, but to the advice of an Arab Dreikaiserbund . . .'[6]

Arab National Committees sprang into existence in all Arab centres; the five Arab political parties, which normally disagreed, formed an 'Arab Higher Committee', including a Greek Orthodox and a Catholic Arab; there was very widespread support expressed by articulate Arabs. The first tactic was a general strike; then there were attacks on isolated Jewish villages, train de-railings and other attacks on communications. The military leader of the revolt was a Syrian military adventurer. Basically it was a widespread terrorist campaign, though bands carried out guerrilla warfare in the hills. It was estimated that over a thousand members of the bands were killed in encounters with the British forces. Hundreds of Jews were done to death.[7]

Sir Keith Hancock recorded in his *Survey*:

> Communalism has its religious aspects, but its most emphatic manifestations are nationalist rather than confessional. The present writer, when he visited Palestine during the disturbed summer of 1936, saw, not a struggle of 'Moslems, Jews, Christians, and Others', but 'two nations warring in the bosom of a single territory'.[8]

The Arab Higher Committee was prepared to obey the appeal of Arab leaders abroad to bring the struggle to an end but the guerrillas fought on. Assassinations and organizational weak-

6. Storrs, op. cit., p. 388.
7. *Palestine and Transjordan*, Geographical Handbook Series, Naval Intelligence Division, December 1943, pp. 126–7, 130.
8. Hancock, op. cit., p. 439.

nesses – foreshadowing the organizational weakness of the 'Liberation' movement in the years after 1967 – resulted in the dissolution of the Committee and the flight of the titular political leader, the Mufti of Jerusalem, who was later to look to the Nazis for support.

However, the drastic curbing of Jewish immigration and safeguards relating to the alienation of land must have given Palestinian Arabs the impression that terrorism and other forms of violence did in fact pay, some of them having come to believe this in the 1920s. Very naturally, the Jews began to think in military terms and commenced building up their defensive resistance movement, the Haganah, with its shock force, the Palmach.

Despite the White Paper drastically curbing immigration at a quite desperate time for the Jewish people, 130,000 Jews were registered for service with Allies by the Jewish Agency, 30,000 of them actually serving. Naturally enough, the Palestinian Arab response was poor, though the Arab Legion (British-officered at that time) of Transjordan fought with distinction.[9]

In 1942 a decision was made by the world Zionist leaders, known as the 'Biltmore Programme', to work for a Jewish State in Palestine. The die was cast. By 1944 two Jewish terrorist organizations, the Stern Group and Irgun Zvai Leumi, were resorting to sabotage and terrorism in Palestine. This was to continue, off and on, until the British had had enough.[10] In 1945 it was very understandably regarded as intolerable by Zionists that restrictions upon immigration of the survivors of the Holocaust should persist. A widespread Jewish Resistance Movement

9. Edgar O'Ballance, *The Arab–Israeli War 1948*, Faber & Faber, 1956, p. 26.

10. 'The activities of Jewish terrorist organizations rendered the British mandate unworkable in less than two years' (Lionel Kochan, in *Israel and the Arabs: The New Eastern Question, History of the Twentieth Century*, ed. J. M. Roberts, Purnell, Vol. 7, Ch. 102, p. 158). The terrorist organizations were normally regarded by Zionist–Israeli officialdom as 'dissident' organizations. But recently this attitude appears to have changed. See *Dir Yassin*, Background Notes on Current Themes No. 6, Ministry for Foreign Affairs, Jerusalem, p. 3, where Irgun is described as 'the second – and smaller – Jewish para-military force'.

came into being, controlled by Haganah – whose own troops appear to have confined themselves to attacks on military installations and communications.

Early in 1947 the British asked the United Nations, in effect, to solve a problem that was costing them too much in blood and money in relation to its new, diminished role in the world. The result was the Partition of Palestine, announced by the UN on 29 November 1947, a decision supported by the USSR and master-minded by the USA. The Palestinian Arabs could not have been expected to accept the partition with any joy: '... while the Zionists' immediate aims were largely met, half-a-million Arabs were to be included in the area of the Jewish state, and by the loss of Jaffa the Arabs were to be left without a port of their own; they were to accept in the interim period an even higher rate of immigration than in the peak years 1934–5 before the Arab Rebellion ...'[11]

Nevertheless it seems clear that what was uppermost in outside Arab minds was not a concern with the particular disabilities inherent in the UN settlement but a determination to destroy the Israeli State. This determination was sometimes stated in frightful terms, as in the utterance of the Arab League Secretary-General, which is endlessly quoted in Israeli propaganda handouts: 'This will be a war of extermination and a momentous massacre which will be spoken of like the Mongolian massacres and the crusades.' Unfortunately, Arab propaganda, in the years after that reference to the attacks by armies of Arab States begun on 15 May 1948, is replete with outpourings that could not but make Israelis believe that they faced annihilation in the event of an Arab victory.

However, fighting by Arab irregulars began very soon after the announcement of partition plans at the end of November 1947. Though parties of Palestinian Arabs may have very occasionally played a part, the irregulars were overwhelmingly invaders organized into the so-called 'Arab Liberation Army', commanded by the Syrian adventurer Kaukji, who had led in

11. George E. Kirk, *A Short History of the Middle East*, Methuen, 1963, p. 220.

1936–9, officered by seconded Syrian regulars, and composed of Arabs from outside Palestine. This was followed by the invasion of Arab regular armies, most importantly the Egyptian and Jordanian armies. Since over half the 600,000 Israelis lived in the three cities of Tel Aviv, Jerusalem and Haifa, and most of the rest in agricultural communities, the Arabs should have been able to accomplish their purpose but for military deficiencies that were to show themselves again and again in future years.

Or, put another way, the Israelis, as soon as they received the necessary equipment, mostly from Czechoslovakia, immediately began to show their clear military superiority in mobile warfare, a superiority that attained great heights in the future also. This is most interestingly discussed in the late Sir Basil Liddell Hart's *The Strategy of Indirect Approach* and elsewhere, but what is relevant to this study is the later adoption of guerrilla warfare as a means of defeating Israel – as a result of the manifest Arab inferiority in mobile warfare shown in 1948, 1956 and 1967.

But the emotional *raison d'être* of the guerrilla-terrorist movement, which assumed a position on the centre of the propaganda stage only after Israel's victories of 1967, was held to lie with the Arab refugees displaced from Israel in 1948 and from what is now Israel-occupied territory on the West bank of the Jordan.

The causes of the Arab exodus in 1947–8 have been debated over and again. They cannot be considered in detail here. The author is persuaded that the Jewish authorities originally took pains to try to get the Arabs to stay; and that the Arab Higher Committee took pains to urge them to leave temporarily and return in the wake of the conquering Arab armies. Whether the Israeli attitudes hardened in general in the circumstances of what they believed with good reason was an attempt to annihilate them is more difficult to decide. The then Prime Minister, Mr Ben Gurion, has been quoted as informing his Cabinet on 16 July 1948: 'War is war, we did not want war, Tel-Aviv did not attack Jaffa. It was Jaffa which attacked Tel-Aviv, and this should not occur again. Jaffa will be a Jewish town ... The repatriation of the Arabs to Jaffa is not justice but folly. Those who have declared war on us have to bear the result after they have been defeated.'[12]

There doubtless were examples of Jewish units urging Arabs to keep moving (or perhaps, get moving); there is also much evidence of panic and the wild stories that grew out of it. As Count Bernadotte, the UN mediator later murdered by Zionist terrorists, put it, 'The exodus of Palestinian Arabs resulted from panic created by fighting in their communities, by rumours concerning real or alleged acts of terrorism or expulsion.' It is quite certain that Jewish leaders were amazed at the evacuation; and there is no evidence encountered by the author of an Israeli government attempt to rid Israeli Palestine of its Arab inhabitants. There was held to be an Israeli atrocity at Dir Yassin and it has been endlessly adverted to by Arab propagandists.[13]

The Arab exodus was very large indeed: nearly 590,000 out of some 740,000 left Israeli territory. Between 1949 and 1958 nearly half a million so-called 'Oriental' Jews moved to Israel from the Old City of Jerusalem and the Arab lands of the Middle East and North Africa, 'as a direct or indirect consequence of the war', in the official Israeli view.[14] Faced by a situation of apparently permanent hostility, indeed war, Israelis came to argue that the refugee problem could not be discussed before the State of Israel was recognized and a proper peace settlement arrived at, though compensation was promised if these objectives were reached. In the meantime the Palestinians of the Exodus were materially left to the mercy of the UN refugee

12. Quoted in Rony E. Gabbay, *A Political Study of the Arab–Jewish Conflict: The Arab Refugee Problem* (*A Case Study*), Librairie E. Droz, Geneva, 1959, p. 109.

13. There is doubt in the author's mind about whether it was an atrocity in the sense of mass murder of civilians *after* the battle, as it is often represented to have been for example by O'Ballance (pp. 57 ff.). The Israeli explanation may be found in *Dir Yassin* (see fn 10, above); *Israel's Struggle for Peace*, Israel Office of Information, New York, 1960; and Menachem Begin, *The Revolt*, W. H. Allen, 1952. The wider causes of the Arab Exodus are argued by both sides in Walter Laqueur (ed.), *The Israeli–Arab Reader: A Documentary History of the Middle East Conflict*, Weidenfeld & Nicolson, 1969.

14. *Israel's Struggle for Peace*, p. 89.

organization (UNWRA) by the Arab powers from whom they had sought refuge. These Arab powers, with the exception of Jordan, were prepared to use the refugee camps solely for their own power-political purposes on the plane of propaganda, though many educated Palestinians found employment in the Arab world. They were pawns in a game designed to end with the complete undoing of the Israeli State; their Palestinian 'national identity' was not for a long time to be a talking point – since there was to be no clearly defined Palestine, Jewish or Arab, in the early calculations of the Arab States.

When the new Palestine Liberation Organization was formed in 1964 with a military branch, the Palestine Liberation Army, it was to all intents and purposes a branch of the Egyptian armed forces. Other guerrilla terrorist organizations, for example the Syrian Sa'Aiqa and the Iraqui Arab Liberation front, seem to have been organized initially as appendages to the Syrian Intelligence Service and the Iraqui Ba'ath Party respectively. But the most famous of them, known as Al-Fatah, with its military wing, Al-Assifa, was founded in 1956 by a small group of Palestinian exiles in the Gaza Strip who observed that Egypt that year had been no match for Israel in mobile warfare. It appears that its leaders determined that Palestinians must win their own freedom through guerrilla warfare. Al-Assifa's military strength was about 4,000 men in 1970. It had made its first raid into Israel in 1964, but it attracted very little notice until after the 1967 war.

Al-Fatah established its operative HQ in Amman, the capital of Jordan, and operative bases in Jordan, Lebanon and to a lesser extent in Syria. Al-Fatah is not in theory socially radical and proclaims as its ultimate objective a democratic Arab State, including the West bank of the Jordan, in which 'de-Zionized' Jews will be permitted to live. It receives part of its funds from reactionary south Arabian sheikhs. In an interview early in 1970 Al-Fatah's leader, Yasir Arafat, stated the chief aims in typically uncompromising fashion:

> The end of Israel is what we are fighting for, and our struggle admits neither compromise nor mediation . . . the points in our pro-

gramme remain the same as fixed when the principles of Al Fatah were announced on its foundation.

First: we can liberate the land of our fathers only by revolutionary violence; second: this violence is aimed at the liquidation of Zionism in all its forms, political, economical and military, and its removal from Palestine for good; third: our revolutionary action must remain independent of control on the part of any party or State; fourth, this action will last a long time.[15]

Though Mr Arafat has claimed that 97 per cent of the guerrilla terrorists belong to Al-Fatah, there are fourteen organizations involved in the Palestine resistance movement, eight of them under the Palestine Armed Struggle Command (PASC), which was formed in 1969 to unify the guerrilla terrorist activities. Politically most of the organizations belong to what is known as the Palestine Liberation Organization (PLO), which claims to represent the Palestinian people and is recognized as such by the states of the Arab League. Yasir Arafat is the elected Chairman; there is a separate military chief of staff of the Palestine Liberation Army.[16]

Apart from Al-Fatah, the best-known guerrilla-terrorist organizations are the Popular Front for the Liberation of Palestine (PFLP), a more-or-less Maoist group under Dr George Habash, now mainly supported by Iraq; and the PFLP splinter-group the Popular (Democratic) Front for the Liberation of Palestine (PDFLP), a Communist organization that enjoys the approval of the Fourth International. The Trotskyite leader, Mr Michel Pablo, who visited the PDFLP, argues that this group does not see the struggle simply in terms of enforcing a military solution upon the Israelis – in part because they estimate that numbers would be against the Palestinians in the ratio of 2.5:2.2 in a Palestinian State – but in terms of a Middle Eastern federation or confederation. The PDFLP apparently sees itself as fighting 'a revolutionary war on two fronts simultaneously against im-

15. Oriana Fallaci, Interview with Yasir Arafat, *The Australian*, Sydney, 11 and 12 April 1970.

16. See Tom Little, *The New Arab Extremists: A View from the Arab World*, Conflict Studies No. 4, London, May 1970.

perialism and its Zionist instrument and against Arab reactionary forces'.[17]

However, if the various groups are considered in terms of revolutionary violence, and not in terms of political ideas and institutions contemplated for the distant future, then the differences between Al-Fatah and the left-wing groups are not very great. It is clear that Al-Fatah, predicating its future on the absurd contention that it is the fact of Israel that lies at the root of the Arab malaise, seeks to eradicate this malaise through a 'mobilization of the masses' by way of violence. Though Mao, Giap and Che Guevara are widely read and the development of the revolution is discussed in terms of moving from one phase to another, there is a deeply neurotic quality about Al-Fatah doctrine.[18]

Anyway, despite the great amount of material put out by Al-Fatah about its 'revolutionary war', 'liberation struggle' and so on, it has in fact operated only as a hit-and-run terrorist organization so far. According to Israeli sources, some 236 Israelis were killed and 870 wounded between the end of the Six-Day War of 1967 and October 1968 at a cost of 900 dead terrorist guerrillas, 800 wounded and 'several thousand more in Israel jails'. Mr Arafat has been quite frank in admitting that the acts of terrorism are altogether indiscriminate; this is deemed proper on the ground that 'civilians are the accomplices of the clique ruling Israel ... if the civilian population doesn't approve the methods of the ruling clique, they have only to say so'.[19] It is not easy to see how the schoolchildren blown up by a mine, for example, could have influenced the 'ruling clique' – if such a term can be applied to a government that has been elected through impeccably democratic processes. (It should be noticed that Arab children have been used at an early age for terrorist

17. Michel Pablo, *Report on the Palestinian Revolution*, September 1969, Revolutionary Socialist Alliance pamphlet, Sydney, 1969.

18. See particularly I. Harkabi, 'Fatah's Doctrine', from *Fedayeen Action and Arab Strategy*, Institute for Strategic Studies, London.

19. *The Australian*, 13 April 1970. The Palestinians lay stress on the number of Israeli military who have been killed and wounded. See Little, op. cit., p. 2.

purposes: for example, throwing hand grenades at Israeli Embassies in Bonn and The Hague in September 1969.)

In theory, the guerrilla-terrorist organizations have the mass base they need. Some 350,000 Arabs live in Israel proper (including Jerusalem); of the twenty-six cities and towns, six are mixed and two Arab, and there are ninety-nine Arab villages. There is also – and more importantly, for guerrilla terrorist purposes – the Arab population of the territories occupied by Israel during the Six-Day War of 1967. Totalling about one million, some 600,000 live in the West Bank area (the administered territories of Judea and Samaria), about 60,000 of them having been living in refugee camps; about 360,000 in the Gaza Strip (175,000 in refugee camps); 33,000 in northern Sinai and 6,400 on the Golan Heights.[20] There would be some 500,000 Palestinians in Jordan and perhaps 175,000 in Lebanon.

However, though analogies have frequently been drawn with the revolutionary wars in Algeria and Vietnam by Arab leaders, there has been little evidence of a 'mobilizing of the masses' in clandestine fashion throughout the occupied territories. This is doubtless in part the penalty paid for the Arab states' persistence in trying conclusions by way of conventional warfare. Otherwise, despite an incapacity so far for modern political organization and modes of activity,[21] it should have been possible for the Arab guerrilla leaders to have established politico-military organizations in what are now the occupied territories.

Of course in the area of largest occupied population, the West Bank, where Al-Fatah tried to get its main operations under way, the Israeli authorities have administered very cleverly. The policy has been to administer as lightly as possible, overwhelmingly through the pre-existing administrative structure. This is believed to permit the Arab police and officials to continue to think of themselves as Jordanians (which they have been only since 1948) and hence refuse to acknowledge that Palestinian 'identity' which very many Israelis see as a myth created by Arab intellectuals. This aim has been enhanced by the 'open bridges'

20. *Facts about Israel*, Ministry for Foreign Affairs, Jerusalem, 1969.
21. See Harkabi, op. cit.

policy, which since early 1968 has permitted visits by inhabitants of Israeli-administered territories to the Arab states, and by inhabitants of Arab states to their relatives in the occupied territories. Some 140,000 visits were made in 1968, 85,000 in 1969.[22] This policy includes permitting commercial passage in and out of the territories, for the Gaza Strip vegetable growers, for example. An enlightened economic development programme and the open terrain add to the problems of the guerrilla terrorists in so far as they are concerned to mobilize the masses.

In fact, it appears that most of the terrorist and sabotage activities have been more in the nature of long-range penetration raids than revolutionary guerrilla warfare. This is not to say that in some places – notably the old resistance centres of the 1930s such as Nablus and Hebron – terrorism has not been carried on with the help of local people. The destruction of housing by the Israeli authorities, known as 'environmental punishment' (presumably in order to distinguish it from the colonial practice of collective punishment), is proof of local participation. But in general the recruitment has been made outside the borders of Israeli-administered territories and the struggle has itself taken the character of commando raids against the military, terrorist acts against civilians. It also appears that more casualties have been inflicted by cross-border firings than by raiding parties. It is very much easier to sneak a mortar into an orange grove on the Arab side of the border for a hit-and-run attack on a kibbutz than to evade the electronic and other devices with which the Israelis protect their borders. (The 'open bridges' policy involves very elaborate searches of those entering Israel.)

The one great danger posed by the Palestinian terrorists – a very present danger at certain times and certain places – was that it might provoke unofficial Israeli violence against the Arabs living in Israel. To provoke such a reaction is of course always an aim of such movements. But such behaviour was almost invariably contained at its source and reprisals of that kind were

22. *Three Years of Military Government, 1967–70* (Data on Civilian Activities in Judea and Samaria, the Gaza Strip and Northern Sinai), Ministry of Defence, Jerusalem, June 1970.

eschewed with exemplary firmness by the Israeli people as a whole. Allegations of torture of terrorists were made, as they invariably are during struggles of this kind, but they have not been proved.

By 1970 it became clear that the Palestinian terrorist guerrilla movement posed a greater threat by far to the governments of Lebanon and Jordan than they did to the Israeli state. This was partly because the guerrilla terrorist movement feared a sell-out by the Arab governments but also, and more importantly, because the movement's leaders believe that the 'Palestinian identity' will be created out of armed guerrilla struggle – and by no other means. It seems fair to say that they believe a new type of Arab will emerge out of the furnace of violence in much the same way as the Chinese Red Army is presumed to have fired a new type of Chinese: a new type of man indeed. (Such was also the belief, in the case of the Jews, of Mr Menachim Begin, leader of the Irgun Zvai Leumi.)[23]

However, the theorists of Palestinian liberation are intellectuals in a difficult predicament, not leaders of a revolutionary war *à la* China or Vietnam. Unable, as events in 1970 and early 1971 proved, to revolutionize the governments of Jordan and Lebanon, their forces are socially peripheral to Arab society – inside and outside the Israeli territories. They are now learning that they cannot use the Arab states for their purposes as the Arab states have used the Palestinian issue for theirs.

The Israelis are just not going to accept – not even the very liberal young – a Palestinian State of the kind proposed by the guerrilla terrorists: a Palestinian Arab State in which 'de-Zionized' Jews are permitted to live.[24] A change of mind about the necessity to 'butcher' Jews or 'throw them into the sea',[25] which is now reflected in Palestinian rhetoric, does not – and

23. '. . . out of blood and fire and tears and ashes a new specimen of human being was born, a specimen completely unknown to the world for over eighteen hundred years, "the FIGHTING JEW"' (*The Revolt*, p. xi).

24. Translated from *El Anwar*, Lebanon, 8 and 15 March 1970: proceedings of a symposium of representatives of seven Palestinian guerrilla terrorist organizations.

25. ibid.

never could – meet Israeli requirements. This for three simple reasons: first, Israel *is* Zion. Secondly, Israelis know that, as a Palestinian liberationist put it, 'natural increase will do the rest'.[26] Thirdly, Israelis have no good grounds for believing the new rhetoric.

If a fourth reason were required, which it certainly is not, it would be this: the general thrust of liberationist argument is to proclaim the Palestinians as a drop in the great Arab ocean of the future. Quite clearly, no constitutional arrangements could ever be devised that could include any kind of 'Israeli (political) entity' in that political vision.

Hence the altogether understandable Israeli insistence upon the recognition of the Israeli State by the Arab powers and a guarantee of its borders before any other problems can be settled. No one who has visited the Golan Heights could expect Israel to settle for a border which includes terrain that permits incessant harassment, by medium machine-guns as well as longer-range weapons, of the agricultural settlements. On the other hand, most Israeli leaders do not wish the admirable Israeli democratic mode of ordering their political affairs to be eroded by the exigencies of military occupation of an alien population. Therefore they may be expected to offer Palestinians living outside militarily secure Israeli borders the opportunity of building themselves a Palestinian State linked in various ways with Jordan.

Having actually fought against the guerrilla terrorist for the existence of their regimes in 1970 – and having shown that in the open spaces guerrillas are no match for regulars – the governments of Jordan and Lebanon may be expected to co-operate in

26. Despite the enormous financial contributions made by Western Jews to Israel (see footnote 27, below), it seems that extremely few of them wish to live there. Net immigration in the famous year of 1967 was 3,737. 'Israel is thus being left largely to its own demographic resources, to a natural increase in population . . . The average Moslem woman in Israel bears 8.2 children; the average Christian Arab 7.2; the average Jewish woman 3.1' (address by Professor Robert Bachi, Israel's leading statistician, *Australian Jewish Times*, 15 May 1969). This fact alone should dissuade Israel from settling for any more territory than is deemed strategically vital.

cutting the ground from under the guerrilla terrorist movement's claim to a Palestinian State embracing Israel. Hijacking and promiscuous use of 'infernal engines' of destruction have been no substitute for mobilizing the masses and building up those parallel hierarchies which have been so effective elsewhere. The Israelis, however plausibly they can be represented as part of the 'imperialistc bloc' in some ways,[27] are not at all comparable with any other extension of European settlement that has occurred in the already settled lands outside Europe.

If it were not for the Soviet Union's strategic policy in the Middle East, and the assistance to the Arab powers that has been a necessary part of this policy, it is reasonable to suppose that the Arab states would already have, at least tacitly, recognized Israel, thus fatally weakening the Palestinian activist movement in its early period of growth. But of course this is only to draw attention once again to the international component in nearly all revolutionary guerrilla movements in the world today. It has been Soviet policy to prevent a settlement of the Arab–Israeli dispute, not to assist the liberation movement to victory, by insisting, as in the Soviet–Egyptian Joint Communiqué of 17 July 1970, upon terms of settlement that could never be acceptable to Israel – in particular, the return to the pre-1967 frontier (which would include abandoning the Golan Heights)

27. This is reflected particularly in the Jewish Agency's budget, which is met by overseas Jewry. For 1971–2, the Budget is $600 millions; two thirds to be collected in the USA. The Budget is devoted not only to settling 50,000 immigrants but to certain educational and social services in Israel. (*Australian Jewish Times*, 18 February 1970). Past figures of immigration, showing a rate of some 50,000 a year, are misleading for the future, since they include 450,000 'Oriental' Jews, who are no longer a significant source of immigration. Clearly, it would in the long run be demographic madness for Israel, with a population of 2.5 millions (immigration being likely to run at less than 35,000 per year), to continue to include a million Arabs, breeding twice as fast, within its borders. (The settlement of Israelis in occupied territory is therefore alarming.) Hence of course the enormous importance attached by both sides to Russian Jewry. As the situation stands, the Central Bureau of Statistics 'cautiously estimates' that the Jewish Israeli population will be 4 millions by 1985 (*Canberra Times*, 23 June 1970). Egypt, Syria, Jordan, Iraq and Lebanon must total some 50 millions at the present time.

and accepting into Israel a great influx of Arab refugees who for years have been submitted to fanatical anti-Israeli propaganda. By insisting upon impossible conditions, the USSR keeps alight the hopes of an otherwise sorely stricken Palestine Liberation Movement. Containment of Israel never having been attempted by the Arab powers, their great protector now argues as though nothing had happened since 1948 – except, of course, 'Israeli aggression' – and that therefore the international community must impose a total withdrawal policy against Israel. It is a measure of the power of propaganda in modern revolutionary warfare that the vital strategic interests of Israel are viewed less and less favourably whereas the rhetoric of the guerrilla terrorist movement appears to be heeded in a more and more sympathetic manner in the West.

This is partly the result of what has come to be regarded even in some Western 'Establishment' circles as a long-term intransigence on Israel's part in regard to the United Nations Security Council Resolution of 22 November 1967, the acceptance of which by Egypt and Jordan implied their *de facto* recognition of Israel and their respect for Israel's integrity. Israel insisted that this could only presage the beginning of a solution negotiated directly between the Israel and the Arab states.[28] The Arab governments saw in the resolution, which did not define which territories taken during the 1967 war Israel would give back, to be the settlement.

On the other hand, the very possibility of a settlement endangered the whole Palestinian Liberation Movement's position and threatened to deprive it of privileged sanctuaries from which to operate in the meantime. What it needed desperately was the emergence of a *fedayin*-based regime; a series of spectacular sky-jackings, culminating in September 1970, was no substitute. That month saw the setting up in the town of Irbid in Jordan of what was described as 'the first revolutionary city-state in the Middle East'. But the Jordanian army crushed the *fedayin*, giving rise to the Black September Movement whose terrorist exploits make the world headlines from time to time.

28. Little, op. cit., pp. 5–6.

But neither the massacre at Lod Airport in May 1972 by hired Japanese revolutionary fanatics nor the murder of Israeli athletes at the Munich Olympic Games in September of that year, to select but the two most spectacular of a series of terrorist acts, advanced the *fedayin* cause. They did, however, provoke, as they were doubtless intended to provoke, Israeli reprisals ranging from aerial bombing of camps in which children were killed to selective commando raids.

The Israeli actions were not, however, simply reprisals; they were designed to force the Government of Lebanon to deny the *fedayin* their new chief privileged sanctuary. Key members of the organization were reported to be moving to other Arab nations, Iraq and Syria particularly towards the end of April 1973.[29] But the *fedayin* remain in Lebanon.

In condemning Israeli raids against Lebanon the United Nations Security Council for the first time condemned terrorism of a 'recent' nature. The USSR and People's Republic of China abstained on the ground that the resolution was insufficiently condemnatory of Israel, the USA on the ground that the resolution fell short of even-handed justice.[30]

The Israeli Ambassador stated that his government 'in accordance with its inalienable rights and its international obligations will continue to protect the people of Israel from Arab murder attacks'. But the situation is a good deal less simple now than those words might suggest. Few people apart from Israeli annexationists would today deny that, however senseless the mode of operation of the *fedayin* may have been in terms of attacking Israel militarily, it has kept the plight of the Palestinians before the eyes of the world – despite the terrorism perhaps, but without it where would the Palestinians be today? Or is it really because of the terrorism? It is difficult not to believe that a combination of wars and terrorism have engendered a deep debate within Israeli society itself about what territory should be retained.

But this debate is not at all really just about territory but

29. *The Australian*, 25 April 1973.
30. *Canberra Times*, 23 April 1973.

about the future nature of Israeli society. If the 'nationalists' or 'maximalists' prevail in their designs to retain a comparatively huge Arab minority within Israel, then Israeli democracy must be placed in grave jeopardy. As a Jewish writer has put it: 'The "liberals" committed to a secular understanding of the Jewish State fear what would happen to civil rights and democratic values in Israel if these rights were withheld from a large Arab minority, and also fear what would happen if they were granted. In the first case Israel could become a South Africa, in the second, a Lebanon.'[31]

The strains within Israel may be expected to intensify; 'world opinion' may be expected to intensify against Israel; the Western guilt about the Holocaust to some extent is now embracing the Palestinians instead; Western concern about the future of oil supplies is likely to be much greater than that about sporadic act of insensate violence in its capitals.

But because of the policies of their various Arab patrons, the Palestine Liberation Movement, considered in terms of revolutionary guerrilla warfare, is still in a weak position. Its 'privileged sanctuaries' have proved to be unreliable and its potential 'popular base' is scattered in settlements from the Gaza Strip to Lebanon. Infiltration into Palestinian areas in Israel has been made very difficult; the establishment of any kind of 'parallel government' will be extraordinarily difficult to sustain if Israeli pacification policy remains as clever as it has been. What the Palestine Liberation Movement has desperately needed has been the announcement of a Provisional Government-in-Exile; that it has not achieved this is a measure of its failure so far, not only against Israel, but *vis-à-vis* the rest of the Arab world.

The fourth Arab-Israeli War in late 1973, combined with the Arab 'oil war' against the West and Japan, however it is settled, cannot materially affect the argument made above: the Palestinian Liberation Movement remains a failure in terms of revolutionary guerrilla warfare. The failure has been of a fundamental nature, illuminating what revolutionary warfare is all about: politico-military mobilization to the stage where the struggle

31. Erwin Frenkel, in the *Australian Jewish Times*, 28 September 1972.

is a competition in government in the heartlands of the contested society. Where the revolutionary guerrillas have been successful, the outcome of the struggle has been the creation of a totalitarian society. But as the author has tried to show, this outcome has not primarily been the result of the exigencies of the struggle itself; rather, the revolutionary guerrilla strategy has been specifically designed in order that the protracted campaign should issue in such a society. And this is why the author, while being quite aware of the disabilities and indeed often the cruel repressions that have driven men of natural nobility to lead such campaigns, is implacably opposed to them. Their success forecloses possibilities more appropriate to true human liberation. In this sense, for all their atrocities, the *fedayin* leaders are human, all too human, compared with the Maos and the Giaps; but of course therein, at least to some extent, lies the source of their failure ... they are the desperate, and so, very often, the atrocious, 'hippies' of revolutionary guerrilla warfare. The future lies with the 'organization men' on both sides: a future which the author finds quite exceedingly disagreeable to contemplate. Not least, indeed quite centrally, because the author has long believed that what informs a true culture – culture conceived in terms of a tradition of behaviour consonant with the deeper realities of life – is the contemplative, rather than the activist.

# INDEX

(Authors cited have been indexed only when they are quoted verbatim)


Abrams, Gen. C. W., 249
Acheson, D., quoted, 118
Adie, W. A. C., quoted, 19
Africa, and Chinese support for guerrillas, 18–19
Ai Ssu-chi, quoted, 290–91
Aidit, D. N., quoted, 126n
Algeria, 205–9; ratio of government to guerrilla forces, 338
Almond, G., quoted, 68n
America, Latin, *see* Latin America
America, United States of, *see* United States
Anti-Fascist People's Freedom League (Burma), 166–7
Ap Bac, 225–6
Arabs, Palestine, 369–72, 375–94
Arafat, Y., quoted, 383–4, 385
army, use in counter-revolution, 307–8
Aron, R., quoted, 35
Asia, development of revolt against West, 78–84; *see also* South-East Asia
Aurobindo Ghose, 74–7; quoted, 74–5, 76
Autumn Harvest Insurrection, 90–91

Ball, G. W., quoted, 260
Bao Dai, 214
Batista, F., 268–74
Ben-Gurion, D., quoted, 381–2
Berlin, Sir I., quoted, 287–8n.
Bernadotte, Count F., quoted, 382
Bodard, L., quoted, 187
Boer War, 55–9
Bolivia, 277–8
bombing, in Vietnam, 245, 248
Boxer Rebellion, 78
Burnham, J., quoted, 284
Brazil, 32–3
Briggs, Lt.-Gen. H. R., 143, 145–6, 149–50
Britain, and Burma, 168; and Indian nationalism, 74–7; and Malaya, 132–65; pacification methods: in India, 46–54; in South Africa, 55–9
Browne, M., quoted, 226
Buddhists, Vietnam, 230–31
Burchett, W. G., quoted, 219–20, 225, 326–7
Burma, 22–3, 54–5, 130, 165–70

Calwell, C. E., 60–62; quoted, 60
Cambodia, capture of embassy (Prague, 1970), 21; Vietnam war, 252, 258
Campbell, A., quoted, 143–4
Carr, R., quoted, 41
Castro, F., 266, 269–75; quoted, 263, 271
'Cedar Falls' (Vietnam), 238
censuses, counter-insurgency, 306
Chapelle, D., quoted, 269
Chapman, F. S., 134
Chassin, L. M., quoted, 116n. 116–17

chemical warfare, Malaya, 150
Chiang Kai-shek, 88–9, 95–6
children, used by partisans, 318, 385–6
Chile, 34
Chin Kee Onn, quoted, 135
China, 85–124; Chinese population in Malaya, 160–63; support for guerrillas, 17–19, 23–5
Chindits, 168n.
Chou En-lai, quoted, 85, 112
Churchill, Sir W. S. quoted, 362
civic action, counter-insurgency, 310
Clausewitz, C. von, views on guerrilla warfare, 42–4; quoted, 39, 42, 44
Clutterbuck, R., quoted, 140–41, 142, 144
Cohen, A. A., quoted, 123n.
Commissariat for Civic Action (Vietnam), 224
committee system: counter-insurgency in Malaya, 149–50
communications, counter-insurgency, 312–23
Communism, and motivation, 294–8; and terrorism, 348–9; attitude to peasantry, 327–35; in Cuba, 268; influence on revolutionary guerrilla warfare, 16–19; revolutionary phases, 335–7; use of propaganda, 284–7, 289, 291–3; *see also* Lenin, V. I., *and under individual countries, e.g.* China, Vietnam
Crosthwaite, Sir C., quoted, 54
Crozier, B., quoted, 270n., 330 341, 348n., 351n.
Cuba, 263-75; land and peasantry, 330–32; ratio of government to guerrilla forces, 338; revolutionary phases, 347–8

Debray, R., 279–80; quoted, 279, 280, 285n., 352
Devillers, P., quoted, 188, 191, 216–17
Diem, Ngo Dinh, regime in S. Vietnam, 213–31
Dien Bien Phu, 196–8
Draper, T., quoted, 265, 271, 332
Ducroux, J., 318
Duncanson, D. J., quoted, 19, 195, 204, 214, 217, 293, 360

Edwardes, H., quoted, 52–3
Eliott-Bateman, M., quoted, 291
Emergency Regulations (1950), Malaya, 146–7
Engels, F., quoted, 46, 49–50n.
Epstein, I., quoted, 106, 110–11
ethics, role in revolution, 72

Fall, B., quoted, 175, 188, 190–91, 191–2, 210, 223n. 353
Falls, C., quoted, 40n., 117n.
Fanon, F., quoted, 289–90n., 351n., 366
al-Fatah, 383–4, 385
Fitzgerald, C. P., quoted, 97, 108n.
FLN (Algeria), 205–8
France, and Algeria, 205–9; and Indo-China, 175–204
Frenkel, E., quoted, 393
FROLINA, 20
Fuller, J. F. C., quoted, 40

Gastil, R. D., quoted, 72n.
Geneva Accords, 211–12
Gerassi, J., quoted, 15
Giap, Vo Nguyen, 194, 196–8, 232, 233; quoted, 189, 197, 198–9, 202, 210, 260, 285, 335–6, 336
Goh Keng Swee, quoted, 318n.
Gold, T., 14

Gott, R., quoted, 33, 34n.
Gourou, P., quoted, 178n.
Greece, 126–7
Green, O. M., quoted, 106
Guatemala, 31–2
Guevara, E. ('Che'), 13, 270, 275–8; quoted, 268, 270, 272–3, 275, 275–6, 276, 276–7

Hague, The, capture of Indonesian Embassy (1970), 20
Halberstam, D., quoted, 226
Halpern, M., quoted, 28n.
Hamlet Evaluation Scheme (Vietnam), 241–3, 251
hamlets, strategic, 323–7
Hancock, Sir K., quoted, 377n., 378
Hartley, A., quoted, 364
helicopters, in Malaya, 158
Herzl, T., quoted, 376
Higgins, M., quoted, 226, 298, 324–5
Hingley, R., quoted, 356
Hitler, A., quoted, 319
Ho Chi Minh, 181, 186; quoted, 181–2, 185–6
Hook, S., quoted, 349
Houn, F. W., quoted, 112, 114n.
Howard, M., quoted, 207n.
Hsu, F. L. K., quoted, 113
Huberman, L., quoted, 331
Hudson, G., quoted, 115n.
Hukbalahap, 170–72, 328
Humphreys, R. A., quoted, 264
Huntington, S. P., quoted, 37, 66, 305–6

identification system, counter-insurgency, 306–7; in Malaya, 148
India, British rule in, 46–54, 74–7, 334–5
Indian Mutiny, 47–50
Indo-China, *see* Cambodia; Laos; Vietnam
Indonesia, 26; capture of embassy (The Hague, 1970), 20
intelligence, counter-insurgency measures, 314–23; in Malaya, 138–9
international law, 373–4
Ireland, *see* Northern Ireland
Irish Rising (1916), 71
Israel, 375–94

Japan, fear of internal rebellion, 21; invasion of China, 95, 97–8, 100–102, 108–11, 114–15; invasion of Indo-China, 179, 182–3, 185; invasion of Malaya, 133–6
Jews, and Palestine, 375–94
Johnson, C. A., quoted, 97, 102, 108n., 114n.
Johnson, L. B., 248; quoted, 210, 235–6
Jomini, H., quoted, 40, 314
Josey, A., quoted, 137
'Junction City' (Vietnam), 238

Kahn, H., quoted, 236
Kaunda, K., quoted, 16–17
Kaye, Sir J., quoted, 48n.
Kennedy, J. F., quoted, 235
Kenya, 338, 339
*Khoi Nghia*, 228–30
Kiangsi Soviet, 94
Kintner, W. R., quoted, 70
Kirk, G. E., quoted, 380
Kissinger, H. A., quoted, 250
Kitson, F., quoted, 8, 165
Koestler, A., quoted, 288n.
Komer Report, 239–40
Kuo, P. C., quoted, 90
Kuomintang, 86–90, 94, 111–17

Lacouture, J., quoted, 185, 193
land reform, 327–35; in Vietnam, 215–16

Laodong Party, 212, 217
Laos, 27–8; and Vietnam war, 252–3, 258
Latin America, 30–34, 283; *see also under individual countries*
Lawrence, T. E., 369–72; quoted, 13, 369, 370, 371, 372
Le Duan, 212; quoted, 259–60
Le Duc Tho, 212
Lee Kuan Yew, quoted, 17, 260
Leites, N., quoted, 19n.
Lenin, V. I., 65–84; quoted, 65, 68–9, 69, 71, 72, 73, 80, 82–3, 83, 84, 129; *see also* Communism
'liberation', use in titles, 289–90
Lien-Viet, 191
Lin Piao, quoted, 123, 124
Lindsay, M., quoted, 122
Linebarger, P.M.A., quoted, 96, 284
Lozovsky, A., quoted, 70n.
Lubis, M. quoted, 260-61
Lukacs, G., quoted, 71n., 81n.

McAleavy, H., quoted, 89–90, 114n.
McCuen, J. J., quoted, 323
McIntyre, D., quoted, 133–4
McNamara, R., quoted, 36
Magsaysay, R., 170–71
Malaya, 130–65, 173, 367; ratio of government to guerrilla forces, 338; strategic hamlets, 323–4
Malaysia, 24–5
Mao Tse-tung, 90–96, 98–100, 118–24; quoted, 67, 85, 90, 92, 92–3n., 93, 99, 100, 107, 110, 119, 335
Marighella, C., 32
Marx-Leninism, *see* Communism
Mau-Mau, 338, 339
'measured response' (Vietnam), 235
Miller, H., quoted, 140, 150
Mitchell, E. J., quoted, 333
Molloy, M., quoted, 27–8
Monnerot, J., quoted, 286
morality, role in revolution, 72
Moss, R., quoted, 283
motivation, 294–302, 372
Murti, B. S. N., quoted, 224n.

Nagas, 29, 303
Napier, Sir C. J., quoted, 53
Napoleonic wars, 39–41
National Revolutionary Civil Servants League (Vietnam), 224
National Revolutionary Movement (Vietnam), 224
nationalism, use in propaganda, 287–9
Navarre, Gen. H. E., 196–7
Naxalites, 29, 79, 334
newspapers, and revolutionary situations, 342–3
Ngo Dinh Diem, regime in S. Vietnam, 213–31
Ngo Dinh Nhu, 214
Nguyen Be, 241n.
Nhu, Ngo Dinh, 214
Nixon, R. M., quoted, 35
NLF (Vietnam), 218–21, 243–4, 254–6
North, R. C., quoted, 111, 114n.
North Vietnam, *see* Vietnam
Northern Ireland, 22, 282n., 362–4
Nu, U, quoted, 166n.

O'Neill, R. J., quoted, 192n., 232, 238, 259, 294–5
Operation Phoenix, 255–6
Oppenheim, H., quoted, 349n., 350
Oppenheimer, M., quoted, 300

organization, importance for Lenin, 65–7; importance in Vietnam, 201–2
Osborne, M. E., quoted, 145n., 308–9n., 332–3, 350

Pablo, M., 384; quoted, 384–5
pacification, of subject peoples, 46, 64; in Vietnam, 239–43, 253–5
Pagniez, Y., quoted, 201
Palestine, 369–72, 375–94
Palestine Liberation Organization, 365–6, 383, 393
'parallel hierarchies', 75, 190–91
Paret, P., quoted, 208
passive resistance, 74–7, 79n.
peasants, 327–35; and Cuban revolution, 264–7, 270, 272–3; Communist attitude to, 82–3; in China, 105, 120–21
Philippines, 26–7, 170–72, 367; land and peasantry, 327–9
Pike, D., quoted, 218, 220, 221, 228, 243–4, 302, 353–4, 354, 360–61
Pindaris, 52
police forces, counter-insurgency, 307
political aims versus military aims, in Vietnam, 202–3
popular support, 302–5; in Malaya, 139–40, 160–63; in Vietnam, 199
Prague, capture of Cambodian Embassy (1970), 21
Pratt, Sir J., quoted, 106–7
press, and revolutionary situations, 342–3
propaganda, 22, 284–93; in Malaya, 149
Purcell, V., quoted, 145
Pye, L., quoted, 154
Race, J., quoted, 223
radio communications, 320–21
Rapoport, A., quoted, 42–3, 66n.
Red Army (China), 91–4, 99–100, 108–11, 113–14
Reitz, D., quoted, 58n., 59n.
Republican Youth (Vietnam), 224
Rigg, R., quoted, 115
Roche, J. P., quoted, 234
Ropp, T., quoted, 39
Roy, M. N., quoted, 81
rural development, in Vietnam, 239–43
Russia, support for guerrillas, 17–18; in China, 114–15; in Israel, 390–91

Sartre, J.-P., quoted, 13
Scalapino, R., quoted, 233–4
Schapiro, L., quoted, 123
Schram, S. R., quoted, 121, 123
Scott, R. D., quoted, 364
Seal, A., quoted, 50–51, 77–8n.
Selden, M., quoted, 358
SEPs (Malaya), 149, 154
Shaplen, R., quoted, 213
Sharkey, L., 130–31
Shore, Sir J., quoted, 46
Short, A., quoted, 138
Sinai, I. R., quoted, 15–16
Singapore, 25
Smedley, A., quoted, 103n.
Smuts, J. C., 55–7; quoted, 56, 57
Snow, E., quoted, 98, 103, 114n.
South Africa, Boer War, 55–9
South-East Asia, 125–6, 128–9, 172–4; *see also under individual countries*
South Vietnam, *see* Vietnam
Spain, Napoleonic wars, 39–41
Stalin, J. V., quoted, 125
Stephen, J. F., quoted, 63

Storrs, Sir R., quoted, 377n., 378
Stracey, P. D., quoted, 303
strategic hamlets, 323–7
Sun Yat-sen, 86–7
Sweezy, P. M., quoted, 331
Szulc, T., quoted, 265

Taber, R., quoted, 271–2, 276n.
Tan Kah-kee, 161–2
Tanham, G. K., quoted, 188–9, 334
Taylor, Gen. M. D., quoted, 235
Tchad, 20
Teichman, Sir E., quoted, 107
Templer, Gen. G., 147n., 151–2
terrorism, 348–57, 363–7; in Malaya, 140, 153; in Vietnam, 219–21; *see also* violence
Tet Offensive, Vietnam (1968), 245–9
Thailand, 23
Than Tun, Thakin, 125n., 167
Thomas, H., quoted, 266
Thompson, Sir R., quoted, 125, 144, 148, 152n., 299, 323, 354
Tilak, Bal Gangadhar, 74-7; quoted, 78–9
torture, 149
tribal poeples, use as guerrillas, 28–9
Trinquier, R., quoted, 338n., 349n.
Trotsky, L., quoted, 88–9
Truong Chinh, 228; quoted, 175, 202–3

USSR, *see* Russia
Ulster, *see* Northern Ireland
United States, and Vietnam, 225–8, 232–62; Communist use of propaganda, 291–3; OSS support for Vietminh, 181; support for Kuomintang, 115; urban guerrilla warfare, 14, 30–33, 265, 275–6, 281–3
Uruguay, 33

Vang Pao, 27-8
Vann, Col. J., 227
Vietnam, *to 1954*, 175–204; *since 1954*, 210–62; Communist use of propaganda, 291–3; land and peasantry, 329–30, 332–4; motivation of Vietcong, 294–5; revolutionary aims, 359–61; revolutionary phases, 340, 344, 346–7; strategic hamlets, 324–7; terrorism, 353–6; war casualties, 14n. 246–7, 256, 258
villages: Hamlet Evaluation Scheme (Vietnam), 241–3, 251; strategic hamlets, 323–7
violence, role in revolution, 36–8, 69–70, 72; *see also* terrorism
Vo Nguyen Giap, *see* Giap, Vo Nguyen

Walsh, M., quoted, 21
Wang Ching-wei, 101
Warner, D., quoted, 214, 219
Wavell, A. P., 1st Earl, quoted, 168n.
Westmoreland, Gen. W. C., 236–7, quoted, 232n., 237, 245
Wint, G., quoted, 98n.
Wolf, C., quoted, 19n.

Yeats, W. B., quoted, 11
Yeh. Gen., quoted, 108-9

*zamindari* system, 334